NEW YORK UNIVERSITY STUDIES IN FRENCH CULTURE AND CIVILIZATION

General Editors: Tom Bishop and Nicholas Wahl

Under the Sign of Ambiguity:
Saint-John Perse/Alexis Leger
by Erika Ostrovsky

The State and the Market Economy:
Industrial Patriotism and Economic Intervention in France
by Jack Hayward

THE TROUBLE WITH FRANCE

Alain Peyrefitte

MEMBER OF THE ACADÉMIE FRANÇAISE

Translated from the French
by William R. Byron

Preface to the first American paperback edition
translated from the French by Dorothea Stillman Halliday

France, whence comes thine ill, now truthfully?
Knowest thou not why thou such sadness bear?
I would explain, for 'tis my duty toward thee.
Hear me then, and thou shalt wisely fare . . .
For, withal, I'd not have thee despair.

—Charles d'Orléans

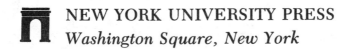

NEW YORK UNIVERSITY PRESS
Washington Square, New York

Grateful acknowledgment is made to the following for permission
to reprint from previously published material:

Editions Gallimard: Excerpt from *La Liberté pour quoi faire?*
by Georges Bernanos. Copyright © 1953 Editions Gallimard.

Editions Gallimard and William Collins, Sons & Company Limited:
Excerpts from *Mystère des saints-innocents* and *Le Porche du mystère de
la deuxième vertu* by Charles Peguy. Copyright © 1929 Editions
Gallimard. Used by permission of Editions Gallimard and
William Collins, Sons & Company Limited.

Librairie Grund: Excerpt from "Le Pelican" from
Chantefables et chantefleurs by Robert Desnos. Used by
permission of the publishers, Librairie Grund.

Library of Congress Cataloging-in-Publication Data

Peyrefitte, Alain, 1925–
The trouble with France.

(New York University studies in French culture and
civilization)
Translation of: Le mal français.
Includes bibliographical references and index.
1. National characteristics, French. 2. France—
Politics and government. I. Title. II. Series.
DC34.P4813   1986   944   85-31075
ISBN 0-8147-6596-3 (pbk.)

Manufactured in the United States of America
First American Paperback Edition
Published in 1986 by NEW YORK UNIVERSITY PRESS,
Washington Square, New York, N.Y. 10003

To Erasmus of Rotterdam
Tireless explorer of the eternal third way
"Guelph to the Ghibellines and Ghibelline to the Guelphs"
On whom five hundred years have imprinted not a wrinkle
Yesterday's teacher for tomorrow.

I am French, which weighs on me.—François Villon (c. 1460)[1]

I know my kingdom's sickness.—Henri IV (1599)[2]

To think oneself a somebody is quite the thing in France.
Here we play men of great weight . . .
Peculiarly a French disease.
Particularly ours is foolish vanity.
The Spanish too are vain, but in another way.
                    —Jean de la Fontaine[3]

The French ailment, *which is the need to perorate, the tendency to make*
everything degenerate into rhetoric, is nurtured by the University's obstinacy
in respecting nothing but style and talent.
                    —Ernest Renan (1859)[4]

I denounce a sickness *that gnaws us in every limb . . . Profligate anarchy or*
reaction, it's all the same, since the sickness comes from the country itself,
which has been incapable of organizing itself under any of the different forms
of government it has successively tried in the past century.
                    —Georges Clemenceau (1913)[5]

It is no service to France to insist without rhyme or reason that the country is
in fine shape, has never been in better shape. Ah! Millions and millions of
men despise our optimism. Our optimism sends chills down their spines.
                    —Georges Bernanos (1936)[6]

The French sickness *is a political sickness. . . . The French have virtually*
abandoned their political function. How can a state subsist when there are no
longer any citizens? What is needed is a structural revolution based on a sud-
den change of public spirit.
                    —Henri, Count of Paris, *Le Mal français* (1954)[7]

The French suffer from a deep-seated sickness. *They will not understand that*
the times demand of them a gigantic effort of adaptation. . . . They cannot do
without the State and yet they detest it, except when there is danger. . . . They
do not behave like adults.
                    —Charles de Gaulle (1966)[8]

Contents

Foreword

When this book was published in France in 1976, it quickly became a best-seller and not just because of the author's personal renown. It represented a well-established mode of anxious self-examination of French identity which had long been popular. But unlike many others of the genre, it was also a skilled synthesis of then-recent social science scholarship on the momentous changes France had undergone in the post-war period. Above all, it was a study of a rapidly evolving France by a well-known practicing politician who had himself helped forge the policies which led to the changes of the sixties and seventies.

This edition of Alain Peyrefitte's famous book is one of the first two works of social analysis to appear in the New York University Press's new "Studies in French Culture and Civilization." (The other is Jack Hayward's *The State and the Market Economy*.) It is also the first translation from the French in a series which aims to bring to American readers important books on contemporary France written by American scholars as well as by distinguished Frenchmen. Peyrefitte brings to his analysis a combination of talents and experiences that place his study on the borders of scholarship, intellectual journalism, and autobiography.

As a graduate of the *Ecole Normale Supérieure*, he was trained to write well and to respect a humanistic approach to understanding society. From his time at the *Ecole Nationale d'Administration*, France's training school for top civil servants, he gained a knowledge of economics, public law, and the massive bureaucratic apparatus of French public life. Finally, almost 20 years of active electoral and ministerial experience gave him an insider's view into the political game under de Gaulle's new rules. Peyrefitte was brought into French politics by the change of Republic in 1958. He was one of the many high civil servants to bring to parliament and to executive posts a level of competence unknown previously. As a moderate Gaullist deputy, he also represented a kind of enlightened, reformist conservatism that had been rare before de Gaulle returned to power.

If the author's introduction to this new edition seems more polemical than the book itself, it is because this edition is published during a French electoral campaign in which Peyrefitte is fully engaged in a thorough critique of the socialist government. Not only is he a parliamentary candidate of the principal opposition party but he is the editorial director of *Le Figaro,* France's most important conservative daily, the flagship of the conservative assault on socialist power. The book, however, was written in more serene times while he was serving in various governments at the end of 23 years of uninterrupted conservative rule. It was also a time when France's remarkable post-war economic growth was leveling off and the "oil shocks" of the early seventies were threatening to cut short the Gaullist drive to make France fully competitive in the world economy.

Unlike most of his colleagues in government, Peyrefitte had followed closely the debate in university and intellectual circles over the reasons for this slowdown and the conditions for further growth. To the conclusions of this debate in applied social science he added his own analyses, some of which were premonitory of the now current free-market school of economic thought and today's new interest in decentralization.

But what makes the book especially valuable is the juxtaposition of the author's personal recollections of politics in the sixties and seventies with his analysis of what is wrong with French society. As a policymaker, he fully accepts responsibility for some of the "trouble with France." As a participant, his observations demonstrate the obstacles to even the moderate reforms he sought while in office. The book is an extended argument for wide-ranging changes in French institutions and social behavior as the necessary conditions for the country's joining the ranks of advanced industrialized societies. The familiar indictment of France's "Latin" and Catholic values as a source of economic retardation is joined to a more modern and sophisticated analysis of the bureaucratic nature of French life and the many costs of the centralizing and *étatiste* heritage of the Ancien Régime, reinforced by recent welfare policies.

The book is also an outstanding example of the French school of "exceptionalist" interpretation, an approach well known to students of American history and society. No other countries have known such a large, home-grown literature on the "uniqueness" of their mission in the world and the "dangers" facing their status among the nations. In the French case, however, Peyrefitte's book may be among the last of these nervously self-regarding studies— what the French call *nombrilisme,* literally a fixation on one's national navel. The constraints of the size, wealth, and influence of France as a medium power—increasingly integrated into the European Communities as well as the world economy—have made the French more restrained in their claims to an "exceptional" identity and hence to a special historical destiny in these closing years of the century. But there is still just enough of the old will to be unique to allow books such as this one to be a source of insight into French habits and problems of the past while offering examples of the themes which mobilize them to adapt to the present.

NICHOLAS WAHL
Petrie Professor of European
    Studies
Director of the Institute of
    French Studies
New York University

Preface

to the first American paperback edition

Translated by Dorothea Stillman Halliday

When I originally wrote this book in 1976, I retained some hope that France would be able to undertake an "intellectual and moral reform" without having to pay the price of a national upheaval. "What," I observed, "if the cure simply consisted in our reflecting on our illness? . . . To know that we were ill and to distinguish ourselves from the sickness, this is the essential part of any therapy . . . All psychotherapy is first and foremost a revelation of reality."

Well, here we are in the midst of our therapy. Under a socialist administration, our "French illness" has gone through a bout of fever, which might have been fatal but from which we might well emerge cured.

Today, the French have the time to hone in on this illness, and to reject its deadliness. This is not someone else's problem. It is ours. France's socialist administration has been showing us quite clearly how harmful all sorts of approaches are—statism, corporatism, fiscal irresponsibility, an ongoing obsession with egalitarianism—all of which have combined for a long time to create that peculiar syndrome that is paralyzing us.

There are a number of very positive aspects to what has happened to France since the election of the socialist President on May 10, 1981, and the effects of these might well prove permanent. Some are directly positive; others are incidentally so.

Democratic Alternation of Parties in Power

To begin with, for the first time in two centuries we French have managed to change regimes without changing constitutions. What is more, the French have managed to carry out a peaceable revolution, without bloodshed, and even without disturbances.

This substitution of one political orientation in the government for another came about without conflict, the type of change which would not have been taken for granted previously. The institutions de Gaulle gave to France had not previously proven their solidity. They are beginning to do so now.

The Anglo-Saxons have not been surprised by this, so natural does the alternation of parties in power seem to them. But what is surprising is precisely that what had never before occurred in France should have apparently become natural there. Two parts of the electoral body, approximately equal in number, are each able successively to win election because each group temporarily gathers in certain voters who are not against crossing the line in the other direction. This is a characteristic of stabilized democracies.

The acceptance of this alternation in power seems proof to me that the French have assimilated, and have earned, democracy.

The Discovery of Reality

Secondly, the Left in power has learned that reality is an obstinate taskmaster. There is no magic. In order to do away with unemployment it does not suffice to "make the rich pay," in order to improve the workers' standard of living it is not enough to declare we will "break away from capitalism," in order to smooth over differences between the various interest groups in France we cannot just call for "solidarity," nor can we obtain the renunciation of some corporatist privileges by simply relying on the good will of the unions.

No, the Left is now beginning to realize that the economy is not so easily malleable, and that the mind-sets of their compatriots are even less so. The failure of the Left in this regard is likely to render it less aggressive, less sure that it is right. Ironically its potential successes (the freezing of salaries, the breaking of the vicious circle of the sliding price scale, an economizing on Social Security) lie in measures which the Left itself would never have tolerated from the previous administration.

For their part, preceding administrations had constantly yielded to the temptation of an unacknowledged socialism. From resignation? From conviction? From electoral necessity? From confusion of "social" and "socialism?" From an insufficient intellectual armor against the pressure of lobbyists? Thanks now to the way the socialist experience has worked out, administrations to come ought to have the political will to break the country free of this unacknowledged, uncertain, insidious form of socialism.

Toward a National Reconciliation?

Thirdly, I believe that the socialists' adherence to principles which they themselves did and do denounce may well prepare the climate for a genuine national reconciliation; it paves the way for an agreement on a certain number of *fundamental* points. This process will be complete if the failure of socialism "à la française" is unquestionable rather than ambiguous.

Thus, French democracy might well emerge from the present experience reinforced. Now that it has proven that power is not reserved for only one part of France, the climate seems favorable for a cooling of political passions. Tomorrow, a change of political orientation in the government might take place without entailing a "revolution" in the opposite direction by the socialists and communists.

There is, it then follows, a serious chance that in the future the French political debate will be less sterile, the polarity less extreme, the rhetoric less partisan. Every general election would then no longer have to mean a risk of upheaval, but simply a changing of the guard—which is just as healthy for the guard being relieved of its duties as for the guard taking them up.

Some will argue that these are not the benefits of socialism but of political change. But what does it matter? Already the country has gained an advantage from the experience: it will come out of it cured of its complex about political change. One might call what the country has lived through a "catharsis of political change."

The Risk of Leaving the Pages of History

These then are the positive aspects of France's experiment. There is a down side too. Should one wonder whether France might still be in danger of succumbing under the dose of socialism with which the victory of François Mitterand has vaccinated it?

By taking the course of "making the rich pay," one will certainly make the rich poorer. A comfort, of course. But one might have hoped too that the poor would become richer. When the poor realized that they too were getting poorer, they found it difficult to believe that this was a necessary prelude to their future wealth—a future growing more and more distant. They asked themselves whether the rich were not the pilot fish of economic prosperity, and whether there was not some truth in the Chinese proverb, "When the fat grow lean, the lean die." Before the persistence of a dreadful foreign trade deficit, an ailing currency, and an invasion of foreign cars when the automobile used to be our biggest export, they have finally come to realize that despite the government-orchestrated chorus of complacency, France—unlike every other western country—has not profited from the lowered prices of oil and raw materials to reestablish itself. The fact of the matter is rather that France is sinking economically, and a nation incapable of holding its head high in economic competition condemns itself to falling behind, and before long falling into oblivion. It abdicates its rank and role in the world.

A similar misadventure occurred in the seventeenth century in the Catholic countries—Spain, Portugal, the states of Italy, and numerous provinces of France. Under the impetus of the Counter-Reformation, the Inquisition or the dragonnades chased out those who did not devoutly bow to official dogma. The Latin countries were thus rendered almost completely sterile by this, whereas the Protestant countries were enriched by the freedom to think, write, print, buy, sell, negotiate, and invent, and by the arrival of free-thinkers who had been put to flight by the Counter-Reformation and who were attracted by these very liberties. The Latin countries, previously the home of a great cultural flowering—the Renaissance, the great discoveries, new inventions, and conquests—wilted like a cut flower. The Protestant countries then took their turn using the dynamic vitality which had emigrated in their direction.

No defence of the "true faith" can be made without an inquisition, no inquisition without oppression, no oppression without regression. France will have tried this bitter experiment, and if in doing so it leaves the leading group of highly industrialized nations, France also risks leaving the pages of history, for a long time to come.

Threat to Freedom

Free communication of thoughts and opinions is one of the rights most precious to man: the Declaration of the Rights of Man and of the Citizen stipulates *every citizen may speak, write, print freely. To print* implies, in the text of 1789, access to all means of intellectual communication that existed at that time. This right to broadcast in print must today be accompanied by a right to broadcast on the air. It is true that the state has, and has had for years, a "monopoly." Should one not, therefore, ensure that the majority in power and the opposition benefit from equal air time—controlled equality substituting for total "liberty?" Yes, yet it is well known that the air time allowed the opposition is, on the average, four or five times less than that enjoyed by those in power.

And in fact the present socialist administration has managed in this way to keep nine out of ten French people ignorant of news the administration could find troublesome. It has known very well how to influence popular opinion by indefatigably airing and re-airing the messages it chooses.

To finesse the opposition into silence and to satisfy public opinion by spectacular acts, all the while chloroforming it with constant propaganda—this is a significant means by which the present majority can hope to remain in power, whatever the rights and wrongs of the situation. Moreover, the audio-visual monopoly, the monopoly of financial aid to the printed news media, the control of fiscal advantages and advertising budgets which are granted to the administration, its being in favor with three-quarters of the journalists were not enough. It also thought it necessary to be able to threaten the independent newspapers, a unique situation in the western world, although commonplace in the socialist world. In the eastern countries, when journalists appear on television in uniform, one knows what one is dealing with. Will our only difference from them soon be that journalists in our country don't wear uniforms?

Freedom of the press has been far from the only freedom threatened. While pretending not to tamper with free education—after François Mitterand's retreat from the Savary law project, which sought to nationalize all private secondary schools—the government tried to make use of finance law to incorporate private schoolteachers in the government: forced certification and constitutional coercive measures. In like manner, first research and then the universities are delivered into the hands of the leftist unions. This is called a law of "orientation" of higher education. The orientation is indeed clear. This is why the law, imposed by the socialist party (which holds a majority in the National Assembly but a minority among the voters), is rejected by the universities on all sides, especially by the men of the Left.

Need for an Opening Outwards

After the disastrous economic downturn of their first year in power, reality dispelled socialist fantasies.

The President of the Republic, himself pessimistic, has now so totally gone back on his triumphal promises of 1981, that he is careful not to promise our compatriots anything other than the continuation of an effort already painful, and to many intolerable, that the nation has been making ever since hard times replaced the good old days. France is weakening, and the ills that socialism "à la française" were to cure by sole virtue of its accession to power are spreading: unemployment not only persists, but has become seriously aggravated, if one is honest about the numbers.

Our inflation has slowed down in absolute value. It has, on the other hand, increased in comparison with that of our principal partners, which is the only criterion that counts. Bankruptcies have broken all records. Industrial production has fallen back. The standard of living has gone down. The weight of indebtedness grows heavier. But as long as we do not reexamine the whole idea of an economy that is controlled by the state, that is unionized, fiscalized, and bureaucratized, nothing is possible.

An Insidious Radicalization

Under pressure from reality, might the Left be in the process of converting? The theory is not to be excluded: human nature is perfectible. But there are limits to the socialists' ability to adapt. Ideological limits.

The measures which tend to suppress freedom, the Left's hold on the state, and the state's hold on society, are remaining proof that the Left has not renounced its objective to create an irreversible situation, and to do so all the more quickly as discontent becomes more pronounced.

Will not a little lightening of fiscal burdens, a few salary increases at the right moment suffice to make people believe the crisis is over and to rally the undecided voters *in extremis?* From that point on the socialization of the country would know no bounds; the deception would turn into resignation.

This course of events is not impossible. But the more conscious of it the French become, the less likely it will be. The people are just like fish at the moment when the net falls on them. Only the more intelligent begin to realize they are going to be imprisoned in a net. If they all noticed it, there would still be time for them to escape. The election results and a growing indignation—both collective and national, show that the opposition has a chance. Deep down, I believe that the French are on the road to recovery from the socialist illness, itself simply a recrudescence of the "French illness." The French have matured from coming in contact with reality. They are ready for new ideas. The opportunity to put these into effect should be seized at the first chance. I believe the French people will not be content now with negative themes. One can no longer make wild promises to them, but rather offer constructive ideas, from which clear choices will have to be made.

Hope is in the air, it seems to me—as misunderstanding was before. And under these conditions, the main force that will be able to bring France out of the crisis will be reborn, and that is the force of self-confidence.

Acknowledgments

I wish to express my gratitude

—for the enriching conversations I have had with them over the years on some of the themes of this book: to Raymond Aron, R. P. Congar, Michel Crozier, Octave Gélinier, Henri Gouhier, Stanley Hoffman, Pierre Moussa, Léon Noël, François Perroux; nor would I forget the late, lamented Gaston Bachelard, René Le Senne, Gabriel Marcel and André Siegfried.

—for having taken the trouble to read my manuscripts and to help me with invaluable advice in their special fields: to Professors Louis Bergeron, Yves-Marie Bercé, Jacques Bompaire, François Bourricaud, Pierre Chaunu, François Crouzet, Jacques Dupaquier, Jean Delumeau, Alphonse Dupront, Jacques Ellul, Jacques Godechot, François Goguel, Alfred Grosser, Pierre Jeannin, Serge Lebovici, Maurice Levy-Leboyer, Herbert Lüthy, Jean-Claude Margolin, Jean Marczewski, Léo Moulin, René Rémond and Marcel Roncayolo.

Needless to say, the author alone is responsible for the views expressed in this book.

THE TROUBLE
WITH FRANCE

Our Natural Children

No nation likes to think of its misfortunes as its legitimate children.
—Paul Valéry[1]

France: sometimes seen in its sons' eyes as the inexhaustible nation, inventor of the world's future; then, at other times, as a tired old country stripped of its grandeur and disgruntled with itself. Why should a nation be thus doomed to neurasthenia unless some grandiose dream lifts it out of itself?

The French: said to be more ungovernable than any other people, holding the world's record for insurrections, for failed regimes, for civil strife—a society's misfortunes. And here they are once again, submitting passively to their bureaucracy and in love (though always disappointed) with authority; rebels against their state, yet incapable of living without this meddlesome tutor.

The Weight of Mentality

So often close observation of our troubles has made me think that they were really psychological or sociological. Or, if you prefer, a matter of mentality, as though the problems the French confronted were not external, but were carried within themselves and projected by them onto external reality.

Why was Great Britain industrialized at an early date? Because it had coal, reply the history and geography books. Why was France's performance so much less brilliant? Because its coal supplies were meager. But how, then, did Japan industrialize so quickly? Other books, or the same ones, explain that the Japanese had to export manufactured goods because they had to pay to import the coal they lacked.[2]

Odd Obstacles to Economics and Democracy

How can we cling today to the nineteenth-century historical materialism that is still distorting our view of the world? Look at a street in Calcutta or Bombay. Can India be expected to prosper as long as its people consent to starve to death beside a sacred cow? How much productivity can be expected of Moslems during Ramadan? How, African leaders wonder, can they direct native workers toward economic expansion who stop working as soon as they earn enough to buy the coveted umbrella or bicycle? And how can Western-style representative democracy function smoothly in societies that are stratified into castes and clans? The habits of centuries obviously weigh heavily here.

But why should they weigh only on the societies we call archaic? Why shouldn't a society's least material features—its religions, prejudices, superstitions, taboos, motivations, attitude toward authority, historical reflexes, individual and group morality and the education and values these distill—affect every people's conduct and every civilization's course, even in its material aspects: investment, production, trade, growth rate? Suppose an economy were not merely a collection of objective data (raw materials, capital, labor) nor a matter of productivity, but depended first of all on an economically inclined mentality. What if democracy were not simply a group of institutions, but also required a public spirit capable of making them work? And suppose the influence of this cultural factor were a cause in France—not the only one, of course, but determinant—of our economic backwardness, our social difficulties and political crises.

Causes and effects are so intertwined that it is futile to hope that a single thread will guide us through the maze. But it seems useful to underline, among the multiple factors of change, the importance of one neglected by our naive materialism: the human mind. Is it unreasonable to think that, after all, this may be the factor that matters most—or at any rate the one over which we have the most direct control?

Tunnel Vision

Every people tends to take itself for the navel of the world. This ethnocentrism can take two contrary forms, however. First, it can pity others for being different, considering the difference irremediable but, eventually, accepting and even—up to a point—respecting it. Like the English, who have often deplored God's failure to grant everyone else from Calais onward the favor of British birth, but who leave these unfortunates to their manners and their manias.

Second, ethnocentrism can be assimilative, like that of the Brazilian Indians with whom the ethnologist Kurt Unkel lived off and on, and who wept bitterly when he returned among them at the thought of how much he must have suffered to be away from their tribe, the only one in which life was worth living.[3] The Latin nations still feel this way: others are not lucky enough to share our culture, of course, but there's still hope. They have only to imitate us and they will become civilized. Other peoples' idiosyncrasies are dismissed by the Latins as negligible and their own even more so, since they are Man incarnate, the standard and measure of all things. "The French," wrote T. E. Lawrence, "though they started with a similar doctrine [to the English] of the Frenchman as the perfection of mankind (dogma amongst them, not secret instinct), went on, contrarily, to encourage their subjects to imitate them; since, even if they could never attain the true level, yet their virtue would be greater as they approached it."[4]

Then how could the French be disposed to recognize in their own failings the reasons for their disappointments? If we do not know ourselves, it is because we refuse to see ourselves, a refusal the more effective for being unconscious. There is an eye ailment ophthalmologists call scotoma, or tunnel vision. Freud showed that the mind can also suffer from scotoma: the unconscious mind refuses to tell the conscious mind what it forbids us to see in ourselves or around us. It censors our vision.

Nothing is more difficult than to judge ourselves. We don't hear our own accents, are not aware of our own language tics. We can't smell ourselves. Because France's weaknesses are profoundly French, they are imperceptible to the French. A people prefers to ignore its own home truths; it would rather blame a passing weakness, an unfortunate combination of circumstances. But a conjuncture that endures becomes a structure; and three centuries of sluggishness—interrupted by occasional flashes of energy—add up to decadence. That French vitality should have flagged in the seventeenth century, just when some of our neighbors were waking up, is a hypothesis we refuse to consider. We also ignore, because we choose to, the real springs of the unfettered society that has so long flourished among our rivals and in which we think we too are living (and even progressing) when we are not really living in it at all.

Back to the Flood

"What do we care," people today like to say, "what happened in past centuries? We're coming to the year 2000. Why go back to the Flood?" The trouble is that, while our intelligence may think it is free, our subconscious does "go back to the Flood." Societies as well as individuals are molded by their childhoods. Social structures, economic activity, political combat reflect and retemper a people's mentality. Nothing evolves so slowly as social attitudes.

Habits often survive long after their causes have vanished. The Japanese drive on the left. Why? Because the Samurai walked on the left in narrow lanes so as to be able to draw their swords with their right hands in case of attack. Why do we use fishknives and forks? Because fish oxidized steel blades, which made the fish taste unpleasant. The eighteenth century invented knives with silver blades as well as handles. Stainless steel long ago made them useless, but fishknives are still on our tables, even if they're not silver. Technique is fluid, but uses and customs are frozen.

"As We Were Saying Yesterday . . ."

Do the French have short memories? They are not alone, and even in their case the allegation is only half true. Every people's *conscious* memory is getting shorter. News is constantly being outdated by the latest report, which is soon routed by the special bulletins. The lifespan of a piece of news, or even of an intellectual fashion, is gradually shrinking. Modern man is bombarded with news; its very abundance keeps him from distinguishing what's important. He is over-informed and under-informed. What is close up is seen; distant perspectives escape notice. The sensational obscures the sensible.

The majority supporting the Fifth Republic (established on the return to power of General Charles de Gaulle in 1958 to succeed the Fourth Republic, which was organized at the end of World War II) convinced themselves that all the troubles of the 1960s stemmed from the Fourth. And those who had been in power during the Fourth swore that the Fifth alone was guilty. No one wanted to admit that France could be ill of its long past. Well, the country did not begin life in 1958, neither in terms of what is good about it, deeply rooted in the distant past, nor unhappily in what is bad about it, which has become its second nature.

In contrast to its conscious memory, a people's unconscious memory is long. Its traumas resound in it as long as those of birth, weaning and rebellion against the father do in the deepest recesses of the individual mind. Cromwell's Roundheads weigh more heavily every day on Ireland. The United States carries the scars of its wars of Independence and Secession, its myths of the winning of the West, of slavery.

Down deep, France has never forgotten its Wars of Religion and the persecution of its Protestants, the magical power conferred by titles and parchments, the Great Revolution, the Terror, Napoleon I's *coup d'état* of 18th Brumaire (Nov. 9, 1798), and Napoleon III's of December 2, 1851, the uprising of 1848 and the Paris Commune; the infallible state, distributor of orders and prohibitions.

Teenagers and revolutionaries convince themselves that today's problems have no precedents, that the lessons their elders teach are pointless. They think the acceleration of history telescopes traditions. Only ignorance of the past can breed this illusion. Without falling into the contrary illusion—that nothing changes—we have to accept that a society is the product of its own past, even in its random impulses to break with that history so as to install a new order. We must gauge the weight of our traditions if we want to spot the changes affecting our habits, our ideas and our people's soul.

To make this journey through a France whose very mutations have something immutable about them, therefore, I have blended past and present. This book has only one subject: Is France or is it not afflicted with a persistent sickness? And if it is, what are its symptoms, its causes? Is it being cured? If not, what are the principles on which a therapy should be based?

I

TRACKING A
HIDDEN SICKNESS

CHAPTER 1

The French Mystery

The pinnace glided over the red waters of the Ogooé between floating sections of bark: tree trunks or crocodiles? The boat drew up to a mangrove-shaded landing stage. Dr. Albert Schweitzer—long Gallic mustache, white trousers, shirt and pith helmet—was waiting on the dock.

"Welcome! And stay a long time. If you spend just a few hours here, like the rare French who do come, you won't understand anything about what I've tried to do."

It was August 1959. During the four days I spent in Lambaréné, I was seldom separated from Schweitzer, sharing in the life of this African village that was called a hospital. Although we were deep in French Equatorial Africa, the personnel—doctors, administrative staff, nurses—as well as the handful of visitors came from a number of Western countries. Except for Schweitzer himself and the woman who served as his supervisor, like him an Alsatian, none were French. People spoke German or English; French was used only with the Africans and even with them, the Fang or Swahili dialects were preferred.

"You Can't Count on the French"

On my last day there, I confessed to Schweitzer my surprise at the absence of the French. "It's no accident," he replied in his deep voice, with its strong Alsatian accent. "When I called on the French, I had almost nothing but trouble. As soon as there's a group of them, they plot. They are not—how do you say it in French?—*vertrauenswürdig* [reliable]."

He searched for the words, but he knew what he wanted to say. "I see them enthusiastic when they arrive, but I know they'll soon be depressed. Most of them are so shocked by our primitive life that they quickly leave. Some stay longer. Then they get the notion of razing my village and replacing it with a European-style hospital. Have you seen what was built in the little town three kilometers from here? Exactly what they wanted to see me do. But it was designed in Paris by people who didn't take the trouble to come here and who do not understand African psychology. A very fine achievement that cost billions and remains almost empty."

I had indeed seen that the modern Lambaréné Hospital was hardly any competition at all for the old straw huts around me. But, in Africa and in Indochina, I had found too many admirable colonial doctors to attribute Dr. Schweitzer's remarks to anything more than prejudice.

"The Negroes," he continued, "feel lost in those white-lacquered rooms alongside patients from rival tribes; many are too distraught to eat and drink and they waste away. I gave them the kind of hospital they could imagine for themselves and they prefer to come to it, often from very far away. They come in every day, on foot through the forest, from Ubangi-Chari, Chad, the Belgian Congo, Tanganyika. Here they find huts like their own."

Prefabricated Ideas

Schweitzer led me into one of the huts, explaining that straw on a bedstead was better than a mattress because the straw kills vermin while a mattress attracts them. "My patients are grouped by tribes," he said. "They are surrounded by their women, who take care of them and do the cooking, by their children, their goats, pigs, chickens. They feel at home. Their will to get well is strengthened. This doesn't prevent the French from being sure they are right. Their ideas are prefabricated. Experience teaches them nothing."

"But my compatriots, *our* compatriots, are changing," I protested. "You're describing the French of yesterday. And only a few of them at that."

"Of yesterday, today and tomorrow. I don't believe they've changed. Individuals change. A people doesn't change so easily. I am not saying that, separately, the French are not gifted. They often are. But together they are like wine in a rotten barrel: even when the grapes are good, it always winds up sour."

We had climbed to the top of a hill from where we could see hundreds of huts seething with life. Beyond them was the jungle, where the hornbills were calling; below, the muddy Ogooé River. "This is the empire I've had for half a century. I've been very stubborn. The French have not helped me much. With doctors and nurses from other countries I never have any trouble. I choose strict Protestants when I can; they are raised to the principle of duty toward themselves and others. I've also noticed that they adapt themselves better to the different circumstances. They understand that when they treat a native they have to love him enough to accept the fact that he is not a European."

Schweitzer was putting his finger on the bad side of Latin colonialism, over-inclined to assimilation but believing in Man, and the good side of Protestant colonization, more concerned to make distinctions—but to the point of creating color bars and apartheid. "They see reality as it is," he went on, "which is the first requirement for overcoming it. Latins, on the other hand, prefer theory. They never form their own opinions. Always theory. But there is no substitute for reality."

A Question of Credibility

Often, too often, disillusionment with the French would later remind me of Dr. Schweitzer's judgment. Like the day in October 1964 when the West German Secretary of State for Information, Günther von Hase, told me he could not go along with a proposal I had been pressing on him for a year. "Why not," I had urged, "cooperate on the German PAL [Phase Alternative Line] color television system and the French Secam [*Sequentiel Couleurs à Mémoire*] system in such a way as to rally all Europe to them, instead of allowing our rivalry to divide it? Both systems have already shown themselves superior to the American technique. A Franco-German system would easily prevail. In combining our efforts, we would prove that we could assure Europe's technological and industrial independence."

"We can only question the manufacturers concerned," he explained, as we traveled together aboard a launch up the Rhine. "We have done that. They are not interested in the prospect of cooperation with French industry. Secam is certainly an excellent system; no one denies that. But . . . it's the figures that decide."

I was being given to understand a naked truth: for the Germans, an equal share in the profits from a Franco-German co-production operation would have been interesting only if they had feared they could not win half the market with a purely German process. Well, they figured to win it all.

"Our manufacturers have already toured all the Western countries that can adopt color television in the next ten or twelve years," Hase said. "They also know their French competitor has not bothered to do this. They are sure the German process will win out. Of course, in prototype, one process is as good as the other. But when it comes to mass production, just about everybody is betting on the success of German industry."

"Your electronics industry is powerful," I interjected, "but David often defeats Goliath."

Over the previous few years, Hase had become my friend. He tactfully allowed his deputy to deliver the coup de grâce. "It's not a question of size, but of credibility," I was told. "If Secam were Dutch or Swedish or Swiss, the reaction would probably be different. Everyone acknowledges French researchers' talent, the quality of their discoveries. But there's not much confidence in the practical accomplishments that might result from them." His implication was clear: the French have the best ideas, but they remain ideas. A nasty strike, a row with the Americans because they refuse to deliver a component, some complication invented by a Paris bureaucrat, a little disorder, and nobody will talk about Secam any more. In short, the French process was not *credible* because French industry, French society were not credible.

The prophecy wounded me. I had heard it frequently enough even in France, in the mouths of industrialists, diplomats, journalists, even cabinet ministers. "Why do you want to drape television in the tricolor?" I was often asked with an amused air.

Accepting the Challenge

Was I to share this polite skepticism? If the government was defeatist toward France, why should the French believe in their country? The Secam was much more than just Secam; like our nuclear force or the Concorde, it was proof that the challenge could be met. Subways in Montreal or Teheran, electrodomestics plants in Singapore, hoisting equipment in Houston—all these challenges converged, were complementary. A few shining examples certainly were needed to counter our rejection of industry, to persuade the French not to value bureaucratic pen-pushing above a career in engineering, our students to stop preferring linguistic flourishes to the stern discipline of technique, of international trade, business, all of which they lumped together in the concept of "capitalism" they had learned to detest.

Hase stood there, sincerely saddened to witness my disillusionment. But that was how things were—it was a matter of national temperament, of *Volkgeist.*

"The French Are the Best"

In incidents years apart, Hase and Dr. Schweitzer had saddened me. A third, more recent conversation both confirmed the first two and soothed their bite by giving me hope for change.

In the North Sea, between the Norwegian fjords and the Scottish lochs, the world's leading oil companies are racing against time. In separate marine districts as large as two French departments, they are licensed to explore, drill, and extract any oil and gas they find there. They are combining ultra-sophisticated technologies under the most difficult conditions: acoustics, hydrogeology, oceanography, data processing. Drilling and piping equipment are stored on barges floating in a perpetually turbulent, fog-bound sea. From them, schools of cables stream toward the sea floor. This is where all the data is centralized, to be transformed at once into curves and figures for immediate interpretation.

August 1975: The French engineer showing me around the installation was confident his company would succeed. "Even a few years ago," he said, "we would never have been able to compete with the American or multinational companies. Our techniques weren't anything like as good as theirs. If we had to, we could do any of the necessary operations separately—prospect, extract, lay piping. But mastering the whole process confronted us with what we saw as insurmountable difficulties. We were forever having to turn to the Americans to ask their help, even on management techniques. We didn't know how to conduct a complex operation from end to end. Around 1967–68 we reached a turning point; we caught up with the others. Now we do as well—better, in fact—than they do."

Yet although the barges were French, the men I met there were of various nationalities. "At first," the engineer told me, "we had only French personnel. That didn't work. They rejected all the constraints competition imposes on us. They stuck their noses in the air and folded their arms. We decided to mix them with Americans, Britons, Scandinavians, Germans, Italians. Pride worked wonders from the start. Emulation stimulates them. No more union jamming. It works! And during the years that we have observed the conduct of all these men, guess who are the best? The French! The toughest, the most resourceful, the most reliable in a crunch. And do you know what they do every month during their two weeks' leave? They have themselves sent back to France, rejoin their families, and almost all of them have second trades—a business, a farm—which their wives run while they're away. It's the French who are the hardest workers."

The foreigners, according to my guide, were not nearly a match for them. "The English? They've grown nonchalant; they never have been able to adjust to the straight two-weeks-at-sea stint. They need their weekend—they can't help it. They love to have tea four times a day. They have no ambition." And he trotted out the other nationalities' defects. Yet the others had to be there for the French to give their best.

A Strange Continuity

A strange continuity ran from the red waters of the Ogooé through the Rhine mists to the steel-gray swell of the North Sea. Seen from Lambaréné, the Lorelei rock or the Shetland Islands, the French seemed hardly different from the Gauls as Caesar described them: capable of gallantry but unruly; enthusiastic but disorganized. Men of dazzling exploits rather than obscure tenacity, of individual prowess instead of collective discipline, capable of amazingly fast recovery, but disappointing in the flightiness with which they jeopardized those recoveries. They were sparkling at one moment, obstinate the next, by turns heroic and panicky, always finding it difficult to live together, sometimes soaring on the powerful breath of an impossible project, at others, prostrated by bitterness and self-denigration. In foreigners they aroused more admiration than confidence—when they were not simply irritating.

A sense of predestination seems to weigh on the French. Why does the people of the Crusades, of the Revolution of Pascal and Voltaire, this lively, generous, gifted people so often show itself divided and impotent? Why, alone among the advanced Western nations, does it combine the most prestigious engineering schools with an industrial establishment that has been backward for so long, and so constantly unfavorable a technological balance? The finest telecommunications engineers and a wretched telephone system? The best bridges and highway engineers and so few expressways? Such excellent researchers and so few innovations, the best of professors and such mediocre universities? The bravest soldiers and the most brilliant officers, and so many defeats? The most carefully chosen administrators, thoroughly capable of acting in any area, and so many failures in the sectors they are supposed to direct, beginning with public administration, urbanism, education, sports, hours and vacation scheduling, the siting of industrial plants, employment, housing? So keen a passion for freedom, and such clumsiness in organization, decentralization and decolonization both inside and outside the country?

At a time when everyone is seeking to define himself, when priests are meeting to discuss the priesthood and soldiers to talk about their armies, when musicians, architects, physicians and writers are interrupting their work to specify its meaning and its place in society, isn't it natural for the French to wonder about France?

CHAPTER 2

Sick to Death

In wartime, people cry treason at the first miscalculation. What they should say is incapacity and weakness of character. Spineless people who, to shirk their responsibilities, make it a rule never "to get involved" and who die covered with rewards and decorations, are the ones who do us the greatest harm by organizing a general collusion for silence when the national interest should be put ahead of individual tranquility.
—Georges Clemenceau (1913)[1]

I decided very early on that France was continually unlucky. The history we were taught proved it. Of the heroes we learned to admire, there was not one who did not end tragically, or, at least, in failure, from Vercingétorix to Joan of Arc, from Henri IV to Clemenceau.

The events of the day sharpened this concern. As far back as I could remember, France had appeared to me to be very sick. *"The Government Has Fallen"; "Financial Scandal"*—often, after my grandmother opened the shutters on my windows in the morning, she would sit on the edge of my bed and, while I got ready for school, she would sum up the news she had just heard on the radio: *"Fusillade on the Place de la Concorde," "Daladier Quits," "Airmail Service Bankrupt."* Or she would read me the newspaper headlines: *"Insurrection Against the Government," "Sanctions Against Italy Fail," "Defeat for French Diplomacy."* And sometimes my grandmother would shake her head and add: "What a mess!"

France's Paralyzed Will

Some evenings, the family gathered around the radio set. A prince of the republic trumpeted: "We will never allow Strasbourg to come under the fire of German guns." In the days that followed, we waited to see what he would do. Nothing. Hitler gave himself permission to do what we would not allow.

More than once between 1949 and 1952, during my years in Germany, I heard Germans blame us for failing to react on March 7, 1936, when Hitler sent his Wehrmacht across the Rhine. Politicians, journalists and historians have all fixed that as the decisive day when the most terrible of wars could have been nipped in the bud—and when, instead, an irreversible step was taken.

The Treaty of Versailles had neutralized German territory west of the Rhine. The Weimar Republic had of its own free will renewed its agreement to the clause in 1925, in the Treaty of Locarno. Clemenceau and Foch considered this demilitarization provision the key to peace. The effectiveness of France's alliance with Poland and Czechoslovakia depended on it: if the Reich ever took it into its head to attack those two countries, France could strike in the Ruhr, Germany's industrial heart. There was not a single German military leader who did not warn Hitler against the wild gamble of putting troops on the left bank of the Rhine. In the cabinet meeting over which Hitler presided on the eve of the German move, Goering, Neurath and Blomberg all spoke against it. This opposition was no secret in Berlin. Our ambassador, André François-Poncet, detailed it in a telegram to Paris; but this was not enough to strengthen the will of men doomed by habit and tradition to inertia.

Ernst-Robert Curtius, the German writer and literary critic who taught at the University of Bonn, knew France thoroughly. I recall hearing him describe, during a conversation in 1950, how impossible it would have been for the Germans to unseat Hitler once he was in power. "The ones who could have barred his way at the first signs of madness were you, the French. All it needed was a little firmness in March 1936 and the tyrant would have toppled. Even he was worried. He sent only three battalions of infantry, not a single tank, behind a barrage of martial music. Paris didn't budge. A dictator whose plans misfire doesn't last long. It was French weakness that made Hitler that day."

"London opposed our moving," I said.

"That's just what I was saying. You need somebody else's blessing. Yesterday it was England, today the United States. When are you going to make up your minds to exist on your own?"

France on Its Knees

In June 1940, after the fall of France, hordes of refugees arrived in Montpellier, where I was a student at the lycée. Their ramshackle vehicles were laden with mattresses, chicken coops and casseroles. They seemed to be stopping there only because the sea barred them from going any farther. Everything was coming apart: abandoned houses were pillaged, French soldiers no longer saluted—I saw one spit on the ground when an officer passed by. In the last class of the year, our literature professor told us: "I am ashamed to be French." He was weeping.

When it was all over, the search for reasons began. From London, a man named de Gaulle blamed the weakness of our armaments; "It is the Germans' tanks, their planes that are driving us back," he said.[2] Vichy, on the other hand, stigmatized our collective bad habits, our institutions, the entire, sinful nation.

De Gaulle's attitude gave us hope. The voice from London sought to restore our faith in ourselves—the defeat was to be laid to circumstances. In other words, it was not courage we lacked, but tanks; soon we would have tanks. This was the language of immediate action. It was not historically accurate, because we did have tanks. Many military experts have since established a truth we still reject out of pride: *with British aid, France had as many tanks and almost as many planes as Germany itself.*[3]

De Gaulle more than anyone was aware of the disaster's psychological and social causes. He simply tried to avoid heightening our humiliation. Today the French have the right and, I think, the duty to acknowledge, however much it contradicts their received ideas, that the debacle was in no way due to a "crushing" superiority in the quantity of German arms.

It was the organization that was wrong, the ideas that were false. The tanks, instead of being concentrated in powerful armored divisions, were scattered through the whole army at the disposal of the infantry, which didn't need them. The planes, instead of being based near the front, were dispersed over a number of fields in the rear—as far away as North Africa. Sometimes there were no pilots for the planes, at others, no planes for the pilots.

How can we avoid comparisons? After Stalingrad and the Allied landing in Italy, the German Army continued to resist step by step for two years against an enemy vastly superior in men and equipment. After Sedan and Dunkerque, the French Army fought a will-o'-the-wisp war. Here and there a colonel, a captain, a lieutenant would rally his unit to hold a bridge or a railroad station; his men would fight like lions. But such spasmodic efforts changed nothing. There were simply a number of acts of heroism—and a disaster. It was less the defeat of an army than the collapse of a society.

The Strange Defeat

Since then, I have often tried to understand this inexplicable shock. I have listened to witnesses, consulted documents. If the "strange defeat" cannot be imputed to numerical superiority of German troops and military materiel, what were the real reasons? A blind military bureaucracy that civil authorities could not rule. Compartmentalization, producing mistakes and intercorps squabbling. Rigid concepts that fought World War II as a continuation of World War I. Ineradicable prejudices. Peremptory reasoning based on fragmentary data. Excessive centralization. Evasion of inextricably intertwined responsibilities. A state that was both interfering and weak, an obsolete economy, a divided nation and a mentality that was not attuned to reality.

A single, little-noticed event sums up the tragedy.[4] The German attack began May 10, 1940. The French Army sent massive reinforcements north to support invaded Belgium. On the evening of May 11, a small Potez reconnaissance plane took off after dark from the base at Montceau-le-Waast, near Laon. It followed the Meuse through the Belgian Ardennes toward Dinant. There the observer, a Captain Andreva, saw armored columns, their headlights piercing the darkness, driving through the region that doctrine declared was impenetrable.

He had hardly landed at Montceau before the group commander, Henri Alias, was on the telephone to division headquarters. He was answered with polite skepticism. Everyone knew—he was told—that the massive Ardennes forest formed a natural Maginot Line and, besides, the Meuse River, from Sedan to Namur, constituted an unbreachable tank trap. Alias's information was not sent up the line. At dawn on May 12, to satisfy his conscience, he sent another observation team in the same direction. The observer, Lieutenant Chéry, was a tank man; his report, Alias supposed, could not be dismissed. The Potez, skimming the ground, flew over advancing columns. Lieutenant Chéry saw motorcyclists, truckloads of infantry, armored cars, light tanks. There was no longer any doubt: at least one armored division, perhaps two.

He returned to base and rushed to the phone, accompanied by Major Alias. He put in a direct call to the duty officer at IX Army staff, the army the unexpected panzers would pulverize on May 15–16. For they were to remain unexpected. The officer, Major H——, a staff college graduate, flatly refused to believe the observer. "Impossible!" he repeated. His theory, the military bureaucracy's theory, was stronger than the facts. Chéry insisted, shouted, staked his word, trotted out figures. The duty officer, ironically, asked this tank lieutenant if he could recognize a tank, and hung up. Information contrary to dogma may be ignored. The Alps can be crossed, because War College instructors described how Hannibal and Napoleon crossed them. But the Ardennes could not be traversed because the same instructors showed that invaders always skirted it.

It was not the armor of the German tanks that won, it was organization and boldness. It was not lack of equipment that lost, it was armor-plated minds. Some generals failed to wage war on the Germans with the same ardor that, in 1914, had succeeded in shaking up an equally obstructionist military bureaucracy. They were thinking first of all of France's war against the French: better Hitler than Thorez and his communists! Defending order took priority over defending the nation.

The Rebel and the Patriot

Not all of 1940, however, is summed up in the crumbling of a nation. Although de Gaulle's voice was the only one raised outside the country, the spirit of resistance was already stirring in many French men and women, even those who did not show it. The resistance seemed to me to be a return of France to its origins. A Frenchman, who is in constant subordination, is naturally insubordinate; after the rout of 1940, he set out almost in the same motion on the route to the underground.

Might it be said that, while the rout was a mass phenomenon, the underground was only a regrouping of isolated individuals? This kind of accounting is deceptive. Four hundred thousand volunteer resistance workers[5] did not even represent one French person in a hundred; but, to survive, to hide, to move around—to act—they needed the complicity of most of the others. In the circumstances created by the German occupation, the resistance could not take the form of a mass uprising. In no other occupied country—with the possible exceptions of Yugoslavia, Poland, and Russia—were the resistance forces larger or more active.

The whole of France is clear in the contrast of 1940: on the one hand, a sudden drop in pressure, a loss of self-confidence that hurled the nation to disaster; on the other, a recovery of that negative instinct which, over the centuries, has given us the Cathares, the Waldenses, the Camisards, refractory priests, Royalist insurrectionists against the French Revolution, the draft-dodgers under Napoleon, and countless provincial resistants who survive only in local history.

What was extraordinary was that the disaster in a way turned our old negative instinct right side up. Now it was the occupier that was victimized by the "no" of the resistants, not the state. And it was probably in 1940 that, from this fact, the first spark of renovation leaped. Yet this forced marriage of the rebel and the patriot did not last long. Not even de Gaulle could mobilize our negative instinct to reconstruct France. The hope born of the resistance crumbled; the straitjacket of our history once more closed around us.

A Series of Massacres

Of all the regimes our people have known, not one has managed to avoid disaster. The absolute monarchy expired in the bloodiest of revolutions. The First Republic in anarchy and a *coup d'état*. The First Empire in two invasions and two abdications. The Restoration, Louis-Philippe's July Monarchy, in a few days of street fighting. The Second Republic in the Caesarism of Napoleon III. The Second Empire in the Battle of Sedan in 1870. And the Third

Republic at Sedan again. The Vichy regime ended at Sigmaringen and the Fourth Republic in the Algiers insurrection.

Such a series of massacres surely indicates a fascination with violence. What kind of children were we who could not grow up without attacking our parents? France, the Roman Catholic Church's eldest daughter, could become adult only by breaking that filiation. Daughter, too, of forty kings, she had to slay her monarchy to be reborn into modern times. Finally, as the daughter of the Revolution, she has been torn since 1789 between those who believed she only then began to live and those for whom she has since then ceased to exist. Unable to build her republic, she has long been misled by regimes without authority, prestige or roots.

But why has there been this long incapacity to found a new legitimacy?

A curse seems to cling to our public life. It is as though, since the moment in the seventeenth century when the monarchy assumed unlimited powers, it has been powerless to overcome the inertia of a stalled society. The sixteen regimes that followed the monarchy from 1789 to 1958 oscillated between lack of power and excess of power in an endless pendular swing.

Are we doomed to absurdity? Plutarch said that a marriage of luck and merit bred a people's destiny. But when the luck is stubbornly bad, more than chance is involved. In the long run, a people has the luck it deserves.

Is there still time for France to unscrew the vise of constraints discouraging initiative and encouraging passiveness? And if this happens, can it avoid releasing centrifugal tendencies, a resurgence of feudal loyalties, an unfurling of special interests, national dislocation? Do the difficulties France experiences in adopting democratic ways and a rational organization exist in other societies as well?

In trying to answer these questions, we open a window on some surprising horizons.

CHAPTER 3

Searching for a Virus

As a student in England soon after the war, I thought I had taken the first step toward an explanation by observing the life of the family with whom I stayed.

Civics at Breakfast

Every morning, at breakfast, the master of the house put on a bizarre performance. Around ten minutes to nine he grew nervous, looked at his watch. At nine sharp he vanished, to return looking relieved. I finally learned what he was up to: using electricity and heating was "not recommended" from 9:00 A.M. to noon and 2:00 to 5:00 P.M. My host was impatient to turn off the meter.

The British were subjected—or rather, they subjected themselves—to harsh privation. The current was not cut off at the generators. There were no checks. An appeal to Britons' civic spirit seemed more productive than administrative measures and a complicated schedule of exceptions. The authorities *trusted* the citizenry. At the same period, French authorities were imposing draconian regulations that everyone racked his brains to elude.

"That's how we were brought up," my host told me. "If a neighbor saw light filtering from under my door . . ."

"He'd denounce you?"

"No, but he'd be shocked."

The power in that common morality! In millions of British homes, this is how children learned, from their parents' attitudes, what no course in civics can ever teach. At the same time, millions of well-meaning French parents were giving their children unforgettable lessons in resourcefulness.

In London, no one crossed a street against the traffic lights even if there were no cars in sight. The public conscience prevented violations. The teaching style used in public- (private) school classes as well as in Oxford seminars was suited to a society of mutual consent. Sectarianism was proscribed. Even young pupils were encouraged to air contradictory ideas and respect the opposite point of view. People were *confident* that the truth would emerge from these exchanges.

A few years earlier this same people, despite the bombs raining down upon it, had been able by its determination and cool-headedness to save Europe's freedom along with its own. This while the French, sometimes out of panic, sometimes even by official order, were taking to the roads as though the better to block their troops' retreat! A certain propensity for disorder in the French, for discipline in the British—these are scarcely within the power of any government to change; yet they can change everything.

As Simple as a Virus

Man is a transformable animal. In the countries where confidence seems to be the basis of social relationships, the French I have met—students, teachers, businessmen—adapted to it easily. But while an individual is quickly acclimated, communities become so only slowly. The British say it takes a hundred years to make a good lawn. I wondered if the same isn't true of the social virtue of tolerance; this fragile flower seems to grow only in slowly accumulated humus.

There was a sort of principle of instability in us. Could it be isolated, reduced to an agent as simple as a virus? Did confidence—alive in some societies, foreign to others—perhaps contain the secret of social organization, the intimate structure, so to speak, of social matter?

It seemed to me that if I studied this mystery deeply enough, I might learn why some countries had outdistanced others in the past few centuries, and why France had suffered and continued to suffer so many disappointments. The French, obviously, had never made a pact of confidence with themselves. Suppose its lack were to blame for our distress. Suppose our inveterate mistrust were the inexhaustible stepmother of our divisiveness.

Delighted by this intuition, I was already imagining two theoretical types of societies. One was the *society of confidence.* In it, the individual, trusted by his society, takes confidence in himself. Persons and groups are free to undertake things, to join together, to reach agreements. Sovereign, the citizen only partially and temporarily delegates his power to his leaders, and then under his control; authority emanates from him by a free and renewable act. Everyone answers for himself and his actions. The individual adapts himself spontaneously, looks for success only through his own efforts, takes the initiatives circumstances authorize, and transforms an innovative idea into a new reality.

Opposed to this is the society in which mistrust—a *lack of confidence*— seems dominant. The individual depends on various hierarchies for all the actions of his life. They command, judge him, indicate what he must do because they know better than he where his happiness lies. Authority is exercised from the top down. The leader's character is sacred. The person higher up in the social pyramid always can do, know, live more than the one below him.

Thus groups, like individuals, are discouraged from taking initiatives. The citizen feels himself surrounded by prohibitions and falls back on routine. He can free himself only through criticism, aggressiveness and sometimes by revolt.

Naturally, no people ever wholly conforms to either of these models; one tendency or the other merely predominates within a given society. Following the advice of one of my professors, I elected to spend a year in close study of one of these forms. The place I chose seemed to be a prototype of a society dominated by a lack of confidence: the village of Corbara, in the Balagne district of Corsica.

A Clan Like a Porcupine

The village, clinging to the slopes of Mount Saint-Ange overlooking the Mediterranean, could not have changed much since the Middle Ages. I saw Corsica through it as a chemically pure body isolated in a scientist's laboratory, instead of the mixture—diluted, adulterated—nature usually offers.

Corsica showed itself to be even more of a society of mistrust than I had suspected. Individuals were enclosed in a web so closely woven that only the most routine activities filtered through it.[1] Man was woman's lord, the father was lord of his children, the patriarch was sovereign over the whole clan. The mayor was lord of the village, the general councillor was lord of the canton and the members of Parliament were lords of the island. And all were chosen by the most powerful clans. From the summit to the base, authority was neither challenged nor delegated. It struck like lightning.

Protected by their insularity, the Corsican village communities had perpetuated a system that had long since disappeared from the mainland. The clan was the perfect model of a hierarchical society in which individuals are both absorbed by and sublimated to the group. It gives them security, dignity, even honor, at the cost of some of their freedom. The French state has imitated this model, so like a Roman legion, since the seventeenth century, but increasingly badly; it is easier to maintain so restrictive a system in a community of a few dozen people than it is in a nation of tens of millions.

Self-Colonized

Some of the islanders asserted that Corsica was colonized by the mainland. I rather thought it had mainly been colonized by itself. It had withdrawn into the clans. The head of the clan was the sole font of power and Corsica's political society was organized along the same line. The voter who wanted a pension renewed or an official family-support payment had first to vote for "his" mayor. The mayor, if he sought a subsidy from the departmental general council, had to demonstrate his allegiance to "his" councillor.

Outside the clans, the Corsicans have the greatest difficulty in forming the associations or groups necessary for democratic life. When they try, the traditional forces soon take over. When a shepherd's union was formed in Balagne, a local clan took control of it and maneuvered it for the clan's benefit. A sub-prefect tried to promote a municipal association to pipe in drinking and irrigation water. The townships soon gave up on the water problem, but they showed themselves efficient in piping in votes and irrigating subsidies.

Democratic voting was not tolerated by the system. More than one old mayor called municipal council meetings in his own home; the councillors placed their ballots in a soup tureen, and when the mayor then withdrew them, the vote was declared unanimous. Voting booths were seldom used; functioning behind a curtain meant an attempt at independence. Authority, obedience and loyalty had to be manifest.

Rival clans attached themselves to rival political parties, national or insular. These were purely formal alliances; it was not unusual to find a communist functioning as a pillar of the Church. The important thing was for the clan to maintain its cohesion. Faced with a state that was also hierarchical and centralized, the clan played a subtle game of complicity and rebellion—complicity when it sought an advantage, rebellion when it felt its privileges were threatened. It always tried, by stratagem or force, to get the better of the bureaucracy, the central authority, even the law.

Whatever some of its inhabitants might think, Corsica was the most French of our provinces. It was no accident that the wartime underground came to us from Corsica; there, resistance to constituted authority—this typically French attribute—existed in a pure state. Yet submission to authority is also a centuries-old habit on the island. It explains both the absolute obedience an individual owes his own clan and his rejection of the others—above all, the *foreign* clan formed by the administration.

The Church sanctified this order. Another hierarchy affirmed its omnipotence over the souls of the faithful: the village priest, the dean, the bishop of Ajaccio. Throughout the year, mass fervor enthusiastically celebrated the cult of the Virgin, the saints and holy images. Yet the Christian cult had not effaced the pastoral and peasant cults that preceded it; Christianity was simply grafted onto them, just as Roman Catholic organization had been grafted onto a network of family and social relationships already well established along the Mediterranean coast. Catholicism bolstered this ancient legacy with its religious dramatization and an immutable order. It had acted as a powerful force for social crystallization.

In this little world, virtually nothing really new was ever possible. This did not, of course, mean that all novelties were banned: electric power lines bordered the roads, a few automobiles churned up the dust, radio sets sat in state in household parlors. Most important, malaria had disappeared, thanks to the Americans; after the island was liberated from the Germans, it occurred to the liberators to free it from mosquitoes as well. But any novelty—which could only come from elsewhere—was long received with suspicion, like a stranger. The future occasioned a vague anxiety when it could not be imagined as identical with the past. For the young, there was no way out but flight to "the continent"; all doors were closed to them in Corsica.

Corsica will never leave me. I had seen that two centuries of attachment to France, of social blending (organized or spontaneous), dispersion, revolutions, wars and schooling had not touched the Corsican mentality. The island seemed an emblem of the resistance to change, the inability to communicate, the economic backwardness, the subordination of etiolated provinces to an apoplectic capital—in short, the very hierarchical and mistrustful society I suspected mainland France to be.

CHAPTER 4

The Two Hemispheres

I carried the question that had sent me to Corsica to the countries where I began my diplomatic career. What secret peculiarities destine one whole society to bounce on springs of confidence and another to be caught in the snares of mistrust? To me, the two Germanies and Poland provided successive answers.

One People, Two Societies

I arrived in Germany at the beginning of the summer of 1949, just after the Berlin crisis and the break between the two zones. For three years I witnessed a rapid evolution: the Americanization of West Germany and the Sovietization of East Germany.

The West was injected with powerful doses of American values. After the collective purification worked by the Nuremberg Trials, the country made itself a replica of the United States. In fact, federalism was a familiar theme in the nation's history. Reaching back beyond the Third Reich, the West Germans renewed their ties with the old Germanic countries' traditional autonomy. Authority vested in the states (the *Länder*) was the rule, authority delegated to the federation (the *Bund*) the exception.[1] Education, from kindergarten to university, was entirely a provincial responsibility. The federal chancellor's power was carefully limited, but solid—the more so for being clearly circumscribed.

What is more, the system pushed market economy principles to their extremes: prices and wages were uncontrolled, foreign trade was free, nationalized industries were returned to private hands, restraints of trade opposed.

At the same time, a leaden mantle was being dropped over East Germany. Everything was patterned on the Soviet model. Centralization was absolute. Pankow decided everything, appointed everyone, dispatched its orders to the smallest hamlet.

Were the German people so malleable that a chance political division could transform those on one side of the line into adepts of the most radical kind of decentralization while those on the other accepted absolutely systematic centralism—unbridled liberalism on the one hand and the strictest planning on the other? If one people, separated into two by the hazard of history, could agree to two opposing systems, wasn't this proof that a given cultural compost could produce utterly different harvests? And that mentalities finally were not so important after all?

Nowhere was the arbitrariness of luck more striking than in that part of Germany called Thuringia. American soldiers had reached there first, in 1945, and had begun to settle in. But, at Yalta, a few strokes of Roosevelt's and Stalin's pens put Thuringia into the Soviet zone. The GIs turned their barracks over to the Red Army, whereupon the Thuringians were suddenly introduced to the system of state-owned enterprises, the single party, political commisars, watchtowers, an omnipresent portrait of Walter Ulbricht flanked by those of Marx, Engels, Lenin and Stalin. Had the mood at Yalta been different, the same Thuringians would have been wooed for their votes by Christian Democrats, Social Democrats and Free Democrats communing in the spirit of free enterprise and limited power for the state.

But when you looked a little closer, the Germans on one side of the line were not adapting to their system as spontaneously as those on the other. Whereas the West German image was one of almost total consensus, the East Germans seemed to show an equally widespread dislike of the system they'd been saddled with. Every time we crossed the demarcation line to go to East Berlin, we were struck by how gray people's faces were, how listless the passers-by, how ill-humored the employees in the state stores in which we shopped on the Alexander Platz. When we returned to the Western sector, the streets seemed gay, the women prettier and more chic, the men livelier. Every day, hundreds of young people left the Soviet sector to seek refuge in the West.[2] In the reception centers set up for them, I sat in on the interrogations and asked some questions of my own. "Why," I insisted, "did you come here for refuge?"

Their eyes opened wide in surprise. The explanation seemed so self-evident to them. The interrogators, wary of infiltration by spies, questioned the newcomers closely, comparing answers, sniffing out contradictions. But with due allowances for anecdotal variations in all those separate lives, the dialogue always went essentially the same way:

"Didn't you have a job? Didn't you have enough to eat?"

Yes, they had work, and they were not starving, but they had no freedom.

"Less than in Hitler's time?"

"Much less. There's no comparison."

Misfortune as a Trampoline

Across the line in West Germany, the dynamism was confounding. The country had been almost destroyed in 1945. German energy made a trampoline of this terrible punishment. Everything had to be rebuilt: the cities, the works

of art, the government, industry—even the families broken by long separation. Surveying the ruins, workers and employers agreed: "We'll never make
it if we quarrel. Let's work together." I listened to moving debates in the
Bundestag (the West German Parliament) on *Mitbestimmungsrecht*—the
right to joint management—in the steel industry. Each company, like the
nation itself, was everybody's creature; workers, executives and managers
were to participate in its direction and its prosperity.

Naziism and the war, each in its own way, had pulverized the old society.
This nation had been homogenized by its ordeal; it wanted to remain
homogenized in peacetime. Between 1945 and 1948, burghers and workers
alike had frequented the soup kitchens. They were still together in the fifties,
in the beerhalls in the evenings, on Sundays around family luncheon tables in
a *Gasthaus* nestling in some romantic ruin.

The uprooting of refugees from the East accelerated this blending process. Everyone was ready to turn his hand to anything. The old hierarchies,
the old habits had gone by the board. This people's energy was unrestrained.
Ludwig Erhard racked his brains to keep from bottling it up again. As the
man responsible for the West German economy for fifteen years, he also
struggled to avoid the Prussian and Hitlerian bureaucracies. He *trusted* the
initiative of provinces and businessmen, *trusted* the banking and monetary
systems to regulate themselves. Within a few years its spirit of enterprise, its
capacity for impromptu organization and its social cohesion had made the
German Federal Republic the West's second-ranking industrial power behind the United States.

In 1944, U.S. Treasury Secretary Henry Morgenthau had recommended
that Germany be made a nation of farmers. Within a very short while, the
notion came to seem as unreal as the myth of the Nibelungen. Firms that
were to figure among the world's mightiest were seen to spring from the
earth like mushrooms after a shower. A man named Grundig, for example,
ran a small radio-repair shop in Furth, in Bavaria. A few years later he
opened a small breach in the record-player field and plunged into it, established himself as a power on the German market, then abroad, and made his
firm an electronics giant.

In 1949, many families in Hamburg, in Düsseldorf, Baden and Munich,
were still living in cellars under the ruins of their cities. By the end of 1952,
the debris had all but disappeared. Six hundred thousand housing units were
put up annually, while France was painfully building 100,000. At the building sites, work went on around the clock, operating at night under the glare
of floodlights.

The Spectacle of Our Disputes

Perhaps the benefit we derive from a long stay outside France lies less in what we learn about other countries than in what we learn about ourselves. Voyages are like windowpanes in which we see both the landscape they give on and our own reflections. We see our own history in perspective, as though it were complete. Foreigners do not know us *better* than we ourselves do, they know us *differently*. But we know ourselves the better for knowing them and their view of us.

After three years abroad I returned to France, eyes and ears still buzzing from the busy German hive. Once more I witnessed the permanent spectacle of our disputes, our crises and, despite everyone's courage and effort, ineffectiveness. I had been breathing other air; ours stifled me. I became convinced that a profound correlation exists between economic growth and the principles of political and administrative organization. There was something scandalous about those people giving us a lesson in liberty. The Germany which had deprived so many people of their freedom was being reborn through freedom. While we who had done so much for liberty knew only a restricted kind of liberty.

The Iron Curtain Reversed?

A year after Stalin's death in March 1954, Etienne Dennery, our ambassador in Warsaw, persuaded me to take the post of consul in Cracow; signs of de-Stalinization were appearing that warranted on-the-spot observation.

In that consular district—the southern part of the country—lived most of the tens of thousands of dual-nationality Franco-Poles. Their fathers had left Poland to work in the French mines. After World War II, they had been persuaded to return to their fathers' homeland "to build socialism"—Poland needed them to work the Silesian mines recovered from the Germans but emptied of their German miners. Many of the returnees were disappointed by what they found. Thousands of them in the mining town of Walbrzych dreamed of going back to France. Their imaginations transformed the dismal mining towns of northern France and the Pas-de-Calais into outposts of paradise. But the police refused them passports. They were caught in a trap. In flocks they came to the French consulate to renew their ties with their adopted country.

I had packed the works of Marx and Lenin in my suitcase, as well as books by such French economists as Charles Bettelheim[3] and Maurice Lauré.* The French have faith in reason, and these experts had explained that, because

---

* A banker, inventor of the value added tax (VAT), and author of *Révolution, dernière chance de la France* (*Revolution, France's Last Chance*).

of rational economic planning, nothing would stop the awesome growth of the "socialist" countries. Soviet production, they predicted, would match America's in 1960, and by 1970 the Soviet standard of living would far surpass the West's. This was the capitalist countries' twilight; they were destined to topple back into a crisis like that of 1929, from which they had emerged thanks only to the factitious business boom caused by the war. Whether the writer rejoiced, as Bettelheim did, or deplored it, as did Lauré, this scheme of things was considered unavoidable. Georges Boris, whose advice was heeded at the highest levels of French government, announced that bread would soon be distributed free in the people's democracies. And one of our leading experts[4] asserted that the Iron Curtain "would soon be reversed": instead of being "crossed from east to west" by those who "chose freedom," it would be "crossed from west to east" by defectors "escaping from penury."

Mess or Miracle?

Such prophecies by serious Frenchmen formed the text for the teachings of many professors at the Institut d'Etudes Politiques and the Ecole Nationale d'Administration after the war. They were believed by a large fraction of the Paris intelligentsia and even at the Quai d'Orsay. Yet one had only to open one's eyes and ears in the offices, the mines, on the building sites, in the stations and workshops in Katowicze, Wroclaw, Lublin or Poznan, to see what a mess the system was in. The miracles of socialist planning trumpeted by the statistics seemed less admirable to the consumers.

I asked a state firm to do some house painting for me. We settled on the quality, the colors, the price. The first room was done perfectly. But, in the days that followed, I noticed that the painters had changed their method. Three coats of good oil paint? Forget it! Now they were using a water-based paint, daubing it on quickly. I protested. The painters referred me to the foreman, who sent me on to the assistant manager, who passed the buck to the manager. He explained that the firm had to satisfy the demands of the Plan. The hours spent on the first room showed that the job would require triple the time the firm could devote to it if the Plan were to be respected. So the oil paint had been abandoned in favor of water-based paint.

I replied that a price had been set for a specific quality; I insisted that the agreed-upon quality be maintained. In the end, the manager gave me to understand that if I consented to a hefty (and undeclared) price supplement, the use of oil paint could be resumed. Things could be squared with the Plan.

The authoritarian organization of labor incurred passive resistance; at best, work was done apathetically, at worst, reluctantly. Efficiency came into its own outside of office hours. Zeal was reserved for moonlighting, resources for the black market. What a contrast between the official production figures on which our economists based their conclusions and the visible evidence of penury! Long lines formed in front of stores. A family drew more than its month's wages from a package sent by cousins in France or America containing a few nylon stockings, lipsticks and a jar of instant coffee. When their tours of duty ended, Western diplomats sold their used cars, absolutely legally, for as much money as their Polish secretaries would earn in ten years.

What Marx blamed capitalism for—sacrificing consumption to investment—exactly characterized the communist economy. It is no paradox to say that the "socialist" countries were the only remaining capitalist countries in the Marxian sense, because they could with impunity place a continuing priority on capital accumulation. And the only truly "socialist" countries were the capitalist states where workers, consumers and citizens organized spontaneous social pressure that made the improvement of everyone's lot the motor of their economy.

Marx had admired the Paris Commune's "direct democracy," its spontaneity. Marxist Poland imposed "democratic centralism," meaning an omnipresent bureaucracy. There was no end to the administrative harassments: the secret police, the mysterious UB or *Urzad Bezpieczentswa Publicznego* (usually shortened to Bezpieka or UB, Public Security) terrorized the Poles. In the train from Cracow to Katowicze, plainclothes police asked the passengers where they were going. If they said Katowicze, they had to pay an immediate fine and were suspected of "counterrevolutionary activities." What they should have said was Stalinograd—Stalin City—the Silesian metropolis's name from 1948 to 1956.

Visitors

Delegations of French economists, university professors, high government officials, journalists, legislators and artists filed through Cracow. Many of these visitors gave me a chance to evaluate how curiously permanent ideologies are. They continued to reject as "capitalist"—and therefore unjust and obsolete—a system like that of West Germany in which capital and means of production were owned less and less by owner-managers and more and more by large numbers of shareholders, among them a growing number of workers; in which nationalized industries distributed 60 percent of their shares to bank account holders who could prove their incomes were low; in which joint management gave labor real responsibilities, and consumer tastes and desires ruled the marketplace. On the contrary, these people came there to admire as "socialist"—and therefore liberal and forward-looking—a system in which all decisions were made, with no public control whatever, by a few men holding a monopoly of power and shielded from all competition; in which labor disdained its work as it disdained political activity; and in which the productivity of the collective farms trailed far behind that on the farmers' private parcels of land. A system of phony democracy and unrelenting surveillance by the political police.

The facts did not seem to trouble our intellectuals much. Their world was still separated into two hemispheres of which the maps had not been revised for a century: the capitalist hemisphere as Marx described it, and the socialist hemisphere as he dreamed of it. Capitalism had evolved; socialism had taken on living form. If there was still a contrast between them, it had been very much turned around. But the French intellectuals were not disposed to admit this, so immutable is dogma even when the reality changes.

Thaws and Freezes

Toward the end of my tour of duty, the ideological thaw was breaking down the dikes. Khrushchev had denounced Stalin's crimes from the tribune at the Soviet Communist Party's Twentieth Congress in March 1956; the Poles, taking him at his word, thought the hour of liberation had struck. In Poznan, workers and students rebelled. They were massacred. The "Police October" raised the people's hopes. After the Hungarian revolt was crushed, Polish emancipation stopped short. Wladislaw Gomulka, conveniently extracted from the prison into which Stalin had had him thrown, was placed with touching fervor at the head of the party and the country. Gradually, however, the bureaucracy relapsed into its old habits and recovered all its power. Everything remained more than ever suspended at the top. And once again, humor helped sustain people's courage. Riddles began to circulate again: "Why is milk short in the cities? Because the first secretary forgot to talk to the cows." "What's the difference between capitalism and socialism? Capitalism is man's exploitation of man. Under socialism it's the other way around."

Fourteen years later, history was to repeat itself word for word. In December 1970, labor riots erupted in Gdansk (formerly Danzig), in Gdynia and in Szezecin (formerly Stettin). Only days earlier, Georges Séguy, secretary-general of the French General Labor Confederation (CGT) and member of the French Communist Party's politburo, had exclaimed on a visit to Poland: "If socialism is established too late in France, then the day will come—and in the near future—when your country will catch up to our living standards and surpass them. The opinion is widespread in France that what is happening now in your country gives a very close picture of what we intend to do in the future in our country. . . ." As they did in East Berlin, in Poznan and in Budapest, the workers dropped by the hundreds under a storm of bullets. Gomulka was run out as he had been brought in—by riots.

The accession to power of his successor, Edvard Gierek, was in turn followed by a period of euphoria. But the new liberalism's limits soon appeared.

A great committee of experts was rounded up to develop a program of administrative, economic and social reforms. A party leader in attendance defined the task in an encouraging tone. "You can attack any problem," he told the members. "You can reverse any taboo. There are only two main planks that must remain untouchable: the party's directorial role—and our links with the Soviet Union."[5] Just those two. Nothing is as hard to escape as a system's logic; even the strikers of 1980 failed to do that.

Cartesians of the World . . .

Why were the French travelers deaf to these implacable lessons? Why did they continue to be so indulgent toward the system's mistakes? And why were they so disdainful of a Germany I had seen come to life?

Naturally, it is not all positive in one case and negative in the other. The "German miracle" was not accomplished without snags: advertising and consumption became obsessive; materialism invaded the society; and American interests in German industry, combined with the American military shield, made West Germany strongly dependent on the United States.

In Poland as in the Soviet Union or China, the communist regime had the virtues of its vices. It could make the vast steel complex and the new city of Nowa Huta spring from fields where nothing had run but rabbits; farmers and "repatriates" who had been given their marching orders peopled these developments according to the Plan, moved by the hope of a better life. For mobilizing workers, changing patterns, restructuring nature, in a word, centralization, has not yet met its match. And what is more, this triumphant materialism provokes an intense spiritual life in reaction to it. "Let us give thanks to this regime," exclaimed the archbishop of Cracow, Cardinal-Prince Sapieha, from his pulpit, with typically Polish humor, "which has succeeded in filling our churches, something all our sermons never managed to do before the war."

But it was not this boomerang effect that seduced the French visitors. It was the very character of the system in which everything was decided in terms of a rational Plan, dominated by a single truth, in which the economy was forced to conform to resolutions devised by the intelligence. Here was something a thousand times more satisfying to their minds than the free enterprise system's gushing, unpredictable multiplicity.

A society in which spontaneity seemed to reject rationality, as in West Germany, bewildered them. They recognized a kind of brotherhood in the communist model: "Cartesians of the world, unite!"

When I returned from Bonn, I had suffered from a feeling that France was bound as though in a straitjacket. On my return from Poland, I breathed again the light air of freedom. France may indeed be nearly as centralized as Poland, decisions almost as high-level and the bureaucracy almost as perva-

sive. But there is no censorship, no single-party rule, no secret police, no arbitrary arrests, no fear.

I really think that the contrary impressions I brought back from my two
forays abroad were equally true. We are free, but we do not know how to use
our freedom. We use it like gold, hoarding it. We do not make it multiply.

CHAPTER 5

The Advent of
the Fifth Republic

Nations rot like fish, beginning at the head.
—Mao Tse-tung

On the afternoon of Tuesday, May 13, 1958, an inauguration ceremony began in the Assembly. Pierre Pflimlin climbed heavily to the rostrum. After four weeks of a cabinet crisis, President René Coty had asked him to form a new government. The public was losing its patience. "He'll make it this time," the experts murmured in the corridors, as though a sadistic jury, weary of turning down candidates, had finally allowed itself to take pity on someone. But interest was already centered on the spot at which, one day, the thrust would enter.

Who would have supposed that the moment of truth would come for this appointed victim from outside, and quickly? No one in the semicircle of the Assembly imagined that, two hours later, riots would rock Algiers and topple the Fourth Republic. Everyone knew the republic was sick, but almost everyone was sure it was a chronic illness that prevented it from acting but could not threaten its survival.

The deputies even felt secure enough to allow themselves the bitter pleasure of lucidity: the "premier-designate" became the officiant in a ritual of mass purification. Once invested with authority, he would be an integral part of the system; before investiture came the fugitive moment in which he could play at censuring it. This was the moment for stern truths. Everyone soothed his conscience through self-criticism. Pflimlin declared: "Once more, a power vacuum is paralyzing the state. Three times in less than a year, ministerial crises have interfered with the national effort. For three of the past twelve months, the republic has remained without direction, without policy, at a time when the rhythm of history is accelerating, in a world that has ceased to await our decisions before making up its mind. . . ."

The hard voice hammering out the words struck down into the thick silence:

"The spectacle of this instability is unworthy of a people whose energies are intact and who remain capable of accepting sacrifices for the country's grandeur. It weakens the attachment of the French to the regime to a dangerous level of disaffection. The degradation of our institutions threatens the republic's existence."

The deputies listened to the indictment without turning a hair.

Dodging the Blame

"A government can be overturned by a momentary combination of mutually opposed minorities [which are] incapable of uniting to constitute a positive majority."

Perhaps we have not registered clearly enough that at the point of the social pyramid, this system gone haywire was simply a specific case of an epidemic that reached—and, as we shall see, still reaches—to its foundations: anybody can do anything without suffering the consequences. When he takes office, no premier knows when or why he is going to fall, but he knows how. In a month, or a year, those who voted for him will vote against him. The existence of a government team is a necessity to which the parties must bow temporarily—and grudgingly. Once they have made their sacrifice to official appearances, they strip it of its reality.

Where does responsibility lie? Nowhere and everywhere. The parties are unfettered, but the governments are on leash; no one special is responsible for anything special, even if everyone is responsible for everything. Scarcely greater solidarity exists among the members of a government than is found between the government and the majority party supporting it. Ministers unfailingly point out that a policy under attack belongs to one of their associates, not them. Deputies do not vote out of conviction, but in terms of what the others do. A shrewd calculator can allow himself to oppose a stern measure he really approves of as long as he knows it doesn't need his vote; he is free to play the demagogue if he thinks no one will go along with him.

Nobody wants to get his feet wet, which means that everybody goes into the water simultaneously—but they all dry out together, too, and quickly. Seeking to ascribe responsibility is not playing the game; if everyone is guilty, no one will be judged.

The laws of parliamentary physics dictate that parties have an interest in bringing to power "combinations" they can later destroy. The enemy is a solid team, capable of hanging on to power. The friend is a weak government to which a successor is already being put together.

Reciprocal Neutralization

"It is becoming clear," Pflimlin went on, "that our liberties will not be protected unless authority, strength and prestige, along with durability, again become attributes of power." The avowal must have been a hard one for a

sincere republican to make. For the justification frequently offered for instability is that it safeguards "freedoms." Most of the people in politics, the majority of members of Parliament, were ruled by this fear of such authoritarian
governments as those the First and Second empires established and the Vichy
regime tried to revive. The nightmare recurred periodically. General de
Gaulle dreamed of such a regime, or so people supposed. But at this point de
Gaulle had been, for twelve years, in retirement at Colombey-les-deux-
Eglises, writing his memoirs.

An Impossible Remedy

Pflimlin was now describing the economic effects of this power deficiency.
"The cause of the trouble is nothing more than the deficit in our trade balance. If lack of foreign currency forced us to make massive reductions in our
imports of raw materials and energy, the result for many families would be
unemployment and poverty. This would also arouse the temptation that despair breeds."

The growth of the French economy, real as it had been since 1954, had
been eclipsed by the "German miracle," the Italian miracle, the Japanese
miracle. And the state's coffers were now empty. Our francs were being refused abroad.

"The government," Pflimlin continued with dramatic deliberateness,
"must therefore envisage measures involving quota systems, rationing and
distribution. If we were to back away from the demands of a policy of austerity today, tomorrow we would have to adopt an infinitely harsher policy of
hardship."

Business was flourishing. The French wanted to produce, work and consume. But the effort was being wasted, the currency was skidding. The Common Market, the wall against which the economy was heading for a crash,
was coming closer.

This united Europe had been awaited with such singular hopes. Well, it
was becoming clear that France was not equal to the obligations or the competition it would face when the borders were opened January 1, 1959. My
own attention to what the premier-designate was going to say was specially
close because since 1956 I had been a member of the delegation charged with
negotiating the Treaty of Rome and putting it into effect. Almost all of us
were convinced that we were contributing to an essential project. The treaty
could change Europe's destiny—beginning with that of France, for it could
wake the nation from the centuries-old torpor into which protectionism had
plunged it.

Our hopes were not solely economic. For some of us, they were above all
political. The Common Market, we thought, coming after the Coal and Steel
Pool, would prepare the way for the United States of Europe. More than one

of my colleagues supported the thesis Alfred Fabre-Luce had so forcefully expressed in *Les lettres européennes:* Since the French had proved to be incurably incapable of governing themselves, the problem would be solved by supranationality. In an integrated Europe, the French could simply pattern themselves on the Germans, who had a sense of organization and discipline.

Early every Thursday morning during those two years, we left for Brussels. The same evening, after long hours in the neo-Gothic Château de Val-Duchesse, we returned to Paris. En route, our conversation revolved around a single question: Would the Common Market ever actually come into being? Our atrophied economy needed European treatment, but wasn't it already too far gone to support the shock? Wouldn't the cure kill the patient? Even if the treaty were signed, would it remain a dead letter? Wouldn't it join the European Army and the European Political Community in the necropolis of aborted projects? During the ratification debate, Pierre Mendès-France defined the situation with cruel clarity: "The very ones who will vote for the Common Market make no secret of their feeling that the first thing we must do when we enter it is to demand that the organization do everything the Common Market forbids doing."[1]

So we waited for Pflimlin. He affirmed that his government would have no more urgent concern than "to arrange the burdens weighing on the economy with a view to preparing France's entry into the Common Market." It was precisely there that the shoe pinched.

The biggest trouble came from outside. The Fourth Republic, like the Third, had managed to survive its political and economic disorders. In these familiar areas, both knew how far was too far. But decolonization caught the system off balance.

A Sick Empire

The vastness of the empire seemed to compensate for the state's weakness; French prestige was no longer reckoned in anything but square kilometers or in numbers of "citizens." In that year of 1958, while visiting the Brussels International Exposition between negotiating sessions, I saw a proud definition inscribed in gold letters on the French pavilion: "France is a country of 80 million inhabitants." (In fact, the population of metropolitan France and its overseas departments in 1958 was approximately 50 million; about 30 million people lived in its colonial empire.) The loss of Indochina had brought the number of French down to 80 million from the 100 million in our schoolbooks, but it had not changed the dogmas. Neither did the Algerian war. The doctrine was proclaimed with the same untroubled certainty it had breathed at the 1941 Colonial Exposition. The republic, one and indivisible, carried the benefits of assimilation and centralization from the Atlantic to the Indian

Ocean. Heiress to the Roman spirit and proud of the principles of the Revolution of 1789, fiercely denying cultural differences, it declared itself a republic of citizens who were not only equal before the law but identical and interchangeable. To doubt this would have been thought racist.

So deeply rooted were these notions that the French felt the decolonization process as an accumulation of defeats.

On that May 13, 1958, as we listened to Pflimlin, it was in Algeria that the drama of decolonization was being played out, closer, more intimate, more racking than it had been in Indochina, Morocco or Tunisia. Algeria was infected with France, France with Algeria. Our atavistic dogmatism was given full play here, pitting those intent on "integrating" the Algerians in the name of human equality against the others who insisted on liberating them in the name of popular freedom. A tangle of high principles, big interests, deep attachments made the opposition between the country's two factions ferocious. How could a National Assembly elected by proportional representation fail to be divided when the national conscience was so torn?

Successive governments avoided proposing solutions because none could rally enough votes to make one stick. A month earlier, Félix Gaillard had fallen because he accepted an Anglo-American offer of good offices. It was considered fitting that the tragedy be kept in the family. Yet almost all those listening to Pflimlin that May 13 thought an internationalization of the conflict was now inevitable. Meanwhile, they were grateful to him for presenting the evidence openly: "The government of France would have no other objective but the reestablishment of peace. Yet there is no way this can be done effortlessly. The government considers that its first duty is to ask that the nation make fresh sacrifices."

Hadn't the republic surmounted the Commune, Boulangism, the Dreyfus Affair, the Great War, *Action française,* Pétain and de Gaulle, the Communists' participation in the government and then their expulsion from it, Dien Bien Phu? I heard many Fourth Republic politicians assert their certainty between 1956 and 1958 that once the Algerian storm blew over, the regime would sail in waters calm enough to allow it to navigate freely. First the storm had to be weathered. Within hours, however, General Jacques Massu would be put at the head of the Algiers Committee of Public Safety; the army itself would take over the colonists' rebellion. Fearing a test of strength, the republic would bow.

A Policy of Fait Accompli

It was not the first time. France was as incapable of prevention as it was of reaction. How many colonies had been brought into the empire during the Third Republic by an endless string of faits accomplis? All that was left, first to the government, then to the Parliament, was to record them. The struggle to keep the colonies was waged the same way. In Indochina, local French officials blocked the way to an understanding with Ho Chi Minh; in Morocco, they deposed the sultan; in Algeria, they kidnapped nationalist leader Mohammed Ben Bella; early in 1958, they bombed a Tunisian town called Sakiet Sidi-Yussef. No government deliberation had ever preceded these historic actions.

In October 1957, I had gone to Algeria with a group of Western diplomats stationed in Paris. We were treated to grim remarks in mess halls from the Tunisian border to the Moroccan frontier: "Fighting is no problem, but being stabbed in the back by a pack of clowns. . . ." The military, constantly fighting on the decolonization front and often let down, nourished with humiliation their traditional contempt for civilians. I could not prevent my foreign companions from learning all this. In the plane on the way back to Paris, an Austrian diplomat commented: "It seems to me that your republic's days are numbered."

In fact, probably never since Napoleon's time had the military felt so justified in seizing power. But where was the power? The shadowy deputies gesticulating in the hemicycle in the Palais-Bourbon gave the illusion of holding it. So, at any rate, it seemed to the politicians in charge—men powerless because they were transitory, pretending to obey irresponsible officials whose power no one any longer controlled.

Sick Diplomacy

Power did not sit exclusively in the offices of cabinet ministers. It was also in a few foreign capitals. Pflimlin bravely acknowledged this: "Hostile forces in the world are coalescing against us, yet we have no assurance of our friends' support."

It was a pathetic summary. Combining a foreign policy of docility to the Americans with a colonial policy the Americans opposed, France generated both irritation in the West and tension with the countries of the Eastern bloc.

The legislators I frequented saw a kind of coherence in a system in which the colonies were subordinated to Paris and Paris to Washington. Why shouldn't France be a protectorate, since it had protectorates? Protector and protégée, it followed orders as naturally as it gave them. Paris knew better than Dakar or Tananarive what was good for the Senegalese and the Malagasians. Washington knew better than Paris what was good for the French.

But in 1958 that feudal balance was upset. The American overlord was encouraging our own vassals to rebel. Confusedly, bitter but already resigned, the French prepared to have to obey again since they could no longer command. What other way out was there? Feudal loyalty to the Soviets? This had its partisans. Only independence had hardly any defenders. Organized factions made a show of their attachment to one of the two superstates. This was the way it had been in the time of the Armagnacs and the Burgundians, the League and the Guises. Thus had Athens and the Venetian Republic expired. Was the changeover near? To the rare visitors who came to his village, a disillusioned de Gaulle predicted that, after Algeria, Alsace-Lorraine would also "get the hell out."

Transient Equals Impotent

How was this evil spell to be broken, these feeble institutions shed? At least one of the drama's leading figures—the government, the Parliament or the people—had to demonstrate both the will and the means.

The government? The sole ambition it could still nourish was to put off briefly the day of its own dismissal. It remained motionless because it did not have time to get under way. "You civil servants are immovable; take full advantage of this to prepare a long-term policy," Pierre-Henri Teitgen told me one day. "Governments can't do this. The best they can do is to adopt a plan already devised by the bureaucracy."

The Parliament? How could the deputies seriously amend the Constitution when a three-fifths majority was needed for revision and they could barely put together a simple majority on less controversial issues?

The people, then? I was able to gauge the people's discouragement in the April 1958 cantonal elections. It was my first contact with the real nation, the voters' France. In the cafés, in the back rooms of stores, I encountered not anger but passivity. "Don't get excited," I was admonished, *"they'll* always be the strongest; no use wearing yourself out over it." "If *they* were all thrown into the Seine, it wouldn't change anything. Because you, if we put you in their place—you'd do the same as they're doing." The voters felt powerless before a blind machine. The Italian writer Curzio Malaparte was right when he wrote: "The French consider themselves a decadent people, if not a people that is finished. . . . They are sick with what I would call a disgust with history."[2] Could the upheaval come from such a resigned public? The past furnished the answer.

As he walked slowly down the steps from the speaker's platform, Pflimlin visibly despaired of bringing France out of that dead-end street.

"De Gaulle Will Never Return"

After the session ended, the storm that had burst over Algiers buffeted the colonnade of the Palais-Bourbon. That evening, in his apartment overlooking the Esplanade des Invalides, Pierre Moussa gave a dinner at which no one could talk of anything but the republic's agony. Robert Buron brought up the rumor that was building up in the Assembly corridors—that only de Gaulle could overcome the crisis.

"Don't kid yourselves," Georges Pompidou, then in private industry but still close to de Gaulle, cut in flatly. "De Gaulle will never return to power. Do you understand? Never! It's not only that he has stopped believing he will. He no longer wants to. He's completing his memoirs. He just wants to remain a man of history. He will refuse to damage his prestige in an enterprise that obviously has no chance of success."

"Nevertheless, some people think that only he can put the military in its place and change the Constitution."

"Maybe, but there's no use in dreaming."

Buron scurried off with the information to the nearby Palais-Bourbon.

In the days that followed, the anxiety deepened. How was the dissidence in Algeria, the army's rebellion, to be overcome? Shaking off his discouragement, despite Pompidou's prediction, de Gaulle made it known on May 15 that he "held himself in readiness to assume the republic's powers." And he added the bizarre comment that "this could also be the start of a kind of resurrection." How could good come from a paroxysm of evil? People only hoped that nothing worse would come of it.

A nightmare in French history recurred: the controls were no longer working. The "full powers" the Assembly had given the government had not prevented the decomposition of authority. A stampede by the police and responsible civil servants was added to the military uprising, dissidence in Corsica to that in Algeria. Could civil war be averted? And what about the Americans' intervention? Their fleet was even then cruising off the Algerian coast. Despite frequent snags, a current was spreading in the Palais-Bourbon for an appeal to de Gaulle. President René Coty, whose sole power was that of designating a premier candidate, was singularly wise enough to reach that decision and, on May 29, to back it up with a solemn objurgation that broke sharply with presidential tradition. On June 1, the general's candidacy was confirmed by a large majority in the Parliament.

Some chronic illnesses suddenly erupt in fatal crises. This is what happened to the republic then. Yet not only did the crisis subside, but the chronic illness seemed abruptly cured. Even with the perspective of time, there is still something strange about the speed of that recovery, which was really unprecedented in our history. De Gaulle was not asked to do that much. He was called in to save the republic from what he called "an enterprise of usurpation forming in Algiers."[3] He wanted most of all to save it from its demons, which he held responsible for the Algerian tragedy, as well as for that of Indochina and several others.

Through the summer and fall, the deputies went from one surprise to another. The installation of the new republic did not go at all as they could have imagined it would. It was not until September that they realized the Chamber would be dissolved and they would have to go for election again. Until November, many deputies, prisoners of the old scheme of things, had no inkling that the general would run for the presidency, a position widely regarded as being wholly symbolic. They were surprised, then, to learn in November that the general would indeed be a candidate in the following month for the chieftaincy of the republic. He had been called in to bring peace back to Algeria and, they supposed, he was quitting the government without doing that, since moving into the Elysée Palace would make him the king post of La Fontaine's fable—a nonentity.

In fact, the Algerian crisis de Gaulle was supposed to solve went on for four more long years; in that time there were even more violent upheavals than that of May 1958. But the cure of what was thought to be the trouble with France, the "French sickness," was virtually instantaneous. France's chronic weakness, its paralysis, its subordination disappeared as though by magic. The fact that the Algerian crisis dragged on only consolidated the cure, because it provided time for absorption of the state's sickness through a continuous affirmation of power unhampered by party pressure.

The state's nature changed. At last it possessed—to an even greater extent than any of our neighbors—those assets I had always thought it so desperately lacked: the certitude of durability, the capacity to take the initiative in any area. In one very special sector, I was a witness as to just how broad and rapid the redressment was.

A Supercharged Atmosphere

Eight hours after the May 13 riot, the Pflimlin government was reduced to postponing indefinitely our entry into the Common Market. The financial and economic situation would not allow us to honor the January 1, 1959, deadline. Our partners heard this dramatic declaration with something like relief; they had been sure for months that France would be brought to this. The hurdle had been too high and the nation had balked.

In the eyes of our partners, de Gaulle's accession to power not only did nothing to reverse the setback, but rendered it irreversible. Still, no official confirmation came from Paris that the treaty was renounced. Patience grew thin, especially Great Britain's. London had refused to come into the Common Market. Our defection would enable the British to destroy it by substituting a simple Free Trade Zone. On December 15, 1958, in the great rococo hall of the Château de la Muette in Paris, the foreign ministers of the Six and Seven* met. The atmosphere was supercharged.

"It's time for action," French Foreign Minister Maurice Couve de Murville told me calmly before the meeting. The evening would be decisive. The Seven, led by Britain, were already joyously burying the Common Market. Our five Treaty of Rome partners, resigned because of us to seeing the Common Market indefinitely postponed, were rallying to the Free Trade Zone. It was better than nothing.

The West German economics minister, Ludwig Erhard, offered a "conciliation proposal," which amounted to accepting the British-style zone while reserving for a hypothetical future the possibility of the Six reviving their organization.

One by one, first the Seven, then the Five approved the project. Couve de Murville indicated that he saw serious drawbacks in the German proposal. Was he going to plead that his country was in no condition to bind itself by a new agreement, not even one that was much less confining than the Treaty of Rome? Not at all. He pointed out that creation of a vast free trade zone would block application of the Treaty of Rome and submerge the Common Market.

Astonishment was etched on some of the faces in that smoke-wreathed Louis XV room. France was talking as though it were not responsible for the impasse—an impasse from which Germany had suggested a way out.

Sir David Eccles, who headed the British delegation, led the attack with a harshness no one present at that session will ever forget. "A single delegation opposes the agreement welcomed by all the others," he asserted. "Yet that delegation represents a country that never keeps its promises." Sir David bitterly denounced the vicious circle in which France seemed caught. The Common Market could theoretically restore our economy's health, but the economy had to be saved in advance if it were to weather the treatment. How did the Paris government propose to break out of this circle? Since it could not do the minimum, how could it carry off the maximum? The British minister said out loud what everyone was thinking: that France was "the class troublemaker." How often we had heard that in the past ten years! We promised—and then we reneged.

Couve de Murville knew that a series of bold measures designed to right

---

* The Six, of course, were the signatories of the Treaty of Rome creating the European Common Market (EEC). The Seven included Britain, Denmark, Norway, Sweden, Switzerland, Austria and Ireland, favorable to a free trade zone in which the Common Market would be diluted. The EEC aimed to create a true community, linked by complex permanent ties. The Free Trade Zone would merely lower tariff barriers in such a way as to allow them to be raised again at any time.

our economy would be made public at the end of the month. The other conferees could not have guessed this; aside from the minister, no one in the French delegation knew about it.

"Tell Them I'm Breaking Off"

Probably never in the past ten years had France been so violently attacked by one of its allies in an international conference. Nor had it ever found itself so isolated. Until then, it had chiefly inspired pity and always gave in at the end. This time it was airily defying its twelve partners. The situation was intolerable.

When Britain's Chancellor of the Exchequer began to threaten France with reprisals, Couve de Murville turned to Olivier Wormser, then the Foreign Ministry's Director of Economic and Financial Affairs. "Go tell the other five delegations that I'm breaking off," he ordered. Wormser went around the table, whispering to each of his counterparts, who in turn whispered to their ministers, who whipped off their earphones. Dismay buzzed around the green baize surface of the conference table. The speaker, realizing no one was listening, finally fell silent. Couve asked for the floor. The murmuring ceased.

"After what has just been said," he declared calmly, "France cannot continue to consider the conciliation proposals presented by its five partners as acceptable. I regret to announce that no agreement can be reached at the present session. I repeat, *no agreement*. Not even on the date of another meeting."

The session was suspended. Erhard offered his good offices in an attempt at conciliation. Sir David expressed his regrets for the acerbity of his remarks; in exchange, France was expected to switch its veto to an abstention. Couve smiled and stubbornly shook his head. Erhard grew purple in the face. Couve's smile broadened. I had seen him demonstrate this suave serenity in more than one international conference during the previous ten years. But in those he represented a France staggering from crisis to crisis, where he could not mask the fragility of his position. Now he radiated a tranquil confidence. He was supported by an impregnable strength: official structures that guaranteed the longevity of his country's executive. He could open or close doors to the British at will. He had been assigned a stance and he would hold it as long as he had to. He had been given an absolute capacity for silent resistance.

When the delegations separated that night, France's five partners never dreamed that the Treaty of Rome had just been rescued from drowning. They were convinced that the small Common Market and the big Free Trade Zone had gone to the bottom together.

This was not the least of that year's paradoxes. The Pflimlin government, solidly behind the policy of European "integration," had been forced to drop the idea: de Gaulle, known for his criticism of supranationality, did everything he could to honor an agreement he would never have signed. He made it a matter of pride not to ask for any changes, any delay. Escape clauses existed in the treaty? Well, there was no question of invoking them. France's plan for economic redress would enable it to live up to its engagements. It could even ask for a speed-up in the schedule.

The Visible Ailment Cured?

In every sector, spectators and actors were amazed by upsets like that in the Château de la Muette. The change was so real and deep that what had seemed to us at the beginning of 1958 as out of reach, almost unthinkable, now appeared self-evident. The rally seemed so strong that the sickness that had made France the butt of the world's derision before 1959 could now be pronounced cured. This was no small achievement if we recall that, before the Fourth Republic, the ill had also sapped the Third, and not just between the wars. In the forty years up to 1914, France had had sixty governments, not counting cabinet reshuffles. A lust for revenge had simply masked instability. So the French were cured of an institutional sickness that had lasted through two republics and had crippled them even in the days of the absolute monarchy.

To succeed where seventeen regimes had failed, to reset the switches of history—after so many derailments—to their original position, the reform of the monarchy that, in failing, had made the Revolution inevitable. In short, to cure a "French sickness" that had persisted for three centuries. I truly believe this was Charles de Gaulle's supreme ambition, even if he never said so. "I have not founded a new republic," he told me one day. "I merely gave the republic foundations, which it had never had before." And, another time: "What I have tried to do is to achieve a synthesis between the monarchy and the republic."

"A monarchical republic?" I asked.

"If you like. More a republican monarchy."

During his first seven-year term as president, de Gaulle's abiding concern was to remake *a state* and *a nation,* the state for the nation and the nation for the state. He wanted to keep the state out of the strivings of parties and special interests by endowing its chief with stability, continuity and independence. He wanted to wrest the nation from foreign domination by giving it the military, diplomatic and financial means consistent with its forgotten sovereignty.

In the long run, he tackled a third dimension: society. With his passion for unity, he had probably always known that he would have to find a way out of the absurd conflict between capital and labor. He thought it unacceptable that the one Frenchman in four or five who votes communist should be an exile within his own country. But he recognized that in this area he would have to feel his way. And, since he disliked groping, he long preferred to avoid this murky path altogether.

Until the end of his first term, he thought that if he increased the state's authority, all the rest would fall into place. Finally, he had to recognize that it would not.

"Two Years"

The first time I talked with him alone was in March 1959. René Brouillet, his chief of staff, had persuaded him to receive one of the young "Gaullist" deputies he still did not know. De Gaulle questioned me about the thinking in my parliamentary group and in my electoral district. All the talk then was about the suppression of veterans' pensions. I told him this. He cut in with sovereign assurance:

"The opinionmakers in France always put the accessory before the essential. In ten years, who will remember this mess except those who make a profession of assailing the state in the name of the groups they represent? It's not the trivia that will be remembered; it is that the state will have ceased to be a prisoner of the feudal obligations that bound it."

There was a brief silence. Then he added: "To establish our institutions solidly, end the war in Algeria, complete decolonization, reestablish our independence—this is my task. Then I can go."

"How long will it take you?" I asked foolishly.

"I don't know. But in two years we ought to be well along."

It was natural, after all, for de Gaulle to be a victim of a mirage mountaineers know well: the summit looks easy to reach, but the closer you get, the further away it seems. When he saw this, he thought the best way to overcome the obstacles before him was by a greater and greater emphasis on presidential preeminence. From April 1962 to December 1965, during Pompidou's first two governments, de Gaulle's primary concern was to accentuate his prerogatives; their only limitation, as he saw it, was the need for a pro-government majority in the Assembly. This would establish the institutional balance France had always lacked. Henceforth, France would be a democracy, because the people would have the first word, in electing both the president and the Assembly, and the last word, by arbitrating any conflict that might arise between the two. At the same time, the state would have the authority it needed.

Jacobin Mysticism

Not once in all this time did de Gaulle give me the impression of believing that the state's power should be balanced by secondary powers. On the contrary, he was annoyed by those that did exist. In his view, any authority not subordinated to his was illegitimate. When he spoke of "participation," he was talking about giving workers a voice in business management, not the citizenry a voice in political management.

This Jacobin severity frightened me sometimes. He would have liked to govern by decree, fiat, ordinance. He was reluctant to draft legislation, mistrusting legislators as potential demagogues. This mystique of the state did not prevent de Gaulle from noticing that too many problems were passed on to Paris, and that settlement on the spot by the people who understood them was the best way to deal with them. "The chief of a squadron in action," he said, "has to make his decisions in the field, without constantly asking divisional staff for instructions." Similarly, civil servants had to be given the habit of deciding things for themselves without looking for cover from the hierarchy. But only the hierarchy had the general interest at heart; local leaders were absorbed in their electioneering and their intrigues. When, around 1963, de Gaulle assessed the need to revive that provincial vitality that had been smothered by Parisian centralism, he never considered transferring bureaucrats' authority to elected officials. His idea was to shift it from Paris bureaucrats to bureaucrats on the scene. He did not question his faith in the state as interpreter and sole agent of the general interest. And the state's sole guarantor in dealing with the nation was himself, the president.

During a press conference on January 30, 1964, he expressed his Roman vision so vigorously that I could hardly believe my ears. "It should be clearly understood," he asserted, "that the indivisible authority of the state is entrusted entirely to the president by the people who elected him, and that no other exists, neither ministerial nor civil nor military nor judicial, which is not conferred and maintained by him."

A Yugoslav Temptation

By October 1965, the eve of what was to be an eye-opening presidential campaign for him, his attitude had already changed considerably. He had sent me to Yugoslavia. On my return, he peppered me with questions about Tito and his system. I described the process of cooperative direction in the plants and the provinces as best I could—or, at least, my notion of it.

"That's what we have to do now," he said, as though he were thinking out loud.

Was he joking? I knew he had reservations about Tito, whom he had never forgiven for having fought and executed General Draja Mikhailovic, the first of Yugoslavia's resistance leaders. But he was indeed quite serious. He was becoming increasingly conscious of the limits of autocracy. I emphasized the drawbacks of the Yugoslav system—the contradictory decisions taken at various levels, with the federal government wanting to buy French locomotives, for example, while the provinces wanted German machines and the railroad workers' rank and file favored Swedish engines; complications and delays in everything; anarchy avoided only by a strongly centralized single party. De Gaulle nodded. He was still fascinated by the blend of authoritarian state and civic responsibility, of centralized planning and a market economy.

De Gaulle dreamed of cooperative management. He had moved from the belief that he was going to settle everything in a few months by exercising the state's authority to a conviction that he was now running into some immense, underlying obstacle that rebelled against the hierarchical order and on which the state had no hold.

Aboard the De Grasse

The shock of the 1965 voting, in which de Gaulle was reelected but by a sharply decreased margin, was probably decisive in bringing him to distinguish between two levels of influence: that of France, for which he spoke and on behalf of which he repeatedly succeeded because of his stability and prestige; and that of the French, for whom concentrated authority was not enough, perhaps not even desirable. Indeed, in wanting everything to depend on him, he found that he was running into obstacles everywhere, that he stalled, that he aroused protest.

Some months later I sat with him on a kind of park bench set up in the stern of the cruiser *De Grasse*. A storm off Mururoa the previous night had prevented a scheduled nuclear test, obliging us to take a forty-eight-hour Pacific cruise. Now the sky was serene again and the general, while staring steadily at the wake's white trench, had been talking to me about the progress made in reestablishing the country's independence. Sadly he added: "The French are suffering from a profound sickness. They will not understand that the times require a gigantic effort of them. They dig in their heels as hard as they can to block the changes the times bring. Look at the past: have they ever shown themselves capable of organizing spontaneously, of investing, producing or exporting on their own? No! They wait passively for the authorities to do everything for them. It's the authorities who have to watch over everything, see to everything, especially to the necessary changes, which the French then refuse because they come from the authorities. They do not act like adults. How can France be governed if the French are ungovernable? I can't do anything for France without the French."

He went on ruminating, half to me, half to himself:

"A totalitarian regime can act as though men were not what they are; but a democracy—that requires us to accommodate ourselves to them. Perhaps, in the long run, the institutions will alter society, the economy and, by degrees, the French. That won't happen without flare-ups, without retreats. And then, it will take time."

"Will we have the time?"

"Me? Surely not. Your generation—maybe. France? Probably. She'll bury us all. She will hold out firmly if the French maintain the taste I've tried to inculcate in them for conceiving ambitions in her name, of being demanding for her. If they couldn't rally around their national pride, around a grand design that is bigger than they are, they would dissolve, they'd wallow in mediocrity, they'd be colonized, they would rush to collaborate with the victors. But for how many years can they keep their independence?"

CHAPTER 6

The Hidden Sickness Appears

Waiting for the Telephone Operator

In 1961, several communities in the Seine Valley complained to me about delays in telephone service—as much as ten or fifteen minutes before reaching an operator. I wrote to the Communications Ministry. I got back a courtesy reply; there followed transmission of the complaint up and down the hierarchy, investigation. Time passed. At last I was informed categorically by letter that the delay was one of seconds, not minutes.

The protests were renewed, however. A year later, subscribers assured me that the delay was then half an hour, sometimes an hour. To alert the fire department, it was faster to drive to the fire station than to phone. Again I passed the complaint to the ministry. This time, to convince me, the administration installed meters in the Provins exchange to measure the time elapsed until an operator replied; it was never more than a minute. The administration zealously admitted this was too long. It hired new operators and reduced the delay—as far as the exchange was concerned—to ten seconds. Yet still the recriminations continued. I investigated on my own and, watch in hand, I found that subscribers were indeed waiting half an hour.

The explanation was finally found. Callers jiggled the bars on their telephones, but no circuits were free, so their signal failed to reach the switchboard. It made no difference how impatient they got, because the telephone operators were unaware of their call. The meters, of course, did not begin to function until a line was free. And it took no less than ten years to restore the service to something like fluidity—even though the administration had stoutly denied it had ever gone wrong in the first place.

How odd that a public service should have to make contact with its customers through a deputy's report to a minister! This slow, cumbersome, politicized channel is a marvelous revelation of serious social malformation.

For the past three centuries the French have been obsessed with the nature of power, the composition of their government. Yet changing governments, even regimes, has by no means given the results they counted on. We have to wonder if this institutional obsession is not in fact a characteristic of the grave illness of French institutions.

The Enlightenment, trying to escape absolutism, convinced itself that we had only to import the Parliament from Britain and its limited monarchy and all would be well. After half a century of tragic national convulsions, the illusion was compulsive; our political regime finally adopted the form the philosophers wished for it. But the basic realities survived the change. The administrative hierarchy established by Richelieu, Mazarin and Colbert lived on as it had before.

For a century thereafter the institutional obsession maintained its grip on our minds; monarchists and Bonapartists, legitimists and Orléanists, conservative republicans and radical republicans, centrists and socialists vied to determine how to label the regime, to decide what colors the flag should be. There was not an election platform without its proposals for constitutional reform—as though deciding this would decide everything.

Hidden Evil Under Visible Evil

By settling the problem of the state—at least for a while—the 1958–62 Constitution relieved us of this obsession. We at once began to perceive the deeper sickness. This was the Fifth Republic's success, but it was not good enough; beneath the peeled-back skin of the visible sickness, which affected our political institutions, appeared the hidden sickness, which affects society.

Very quickly, despite the restoration of the state's authority, street disorders testified that full powers were not powerful enough to establish that authority solidly. We have seen our state, solid, directed and directing, skid and get stuck so many times. Almost never when it spoke for France, but frequently when it spoke to the French—every time it tried to slip into gear with our society, to touch the nationalized industries that make up a society within a society, to interfere with old habits.

Authority will not retreat, but is it really advancing? It holds its head higher, yet it is completely surrounded, as though society instinctively, automatically sought to compensate for any other power by an equal and contrary power of its own. Executive power is countered by a vigilant combination of the parliamentary minority and most of the media or community leaders or the members of the political caste or the unions. A team's dynamism is balanced by its lack of means, as though the supreme rule of the game of politics was that the partners reduce each other to impotence.

The Government Neutralized

This law of reciprocal neutralization applies even to the ministries' authority. In this respect, the Fifth Republic has not changed much. It is all very well for the minister of industry to map out a policy of industrial development; the means at his disposal depend entirely on the Economics Ministry. The minister of labor has no jurisdiction over workers in the nationalized industries, those most inclined toward disputes with management. The minister of research has nothing to say about the work of the National Center for Scientific Research, and so on. And all government functions depend on the Finance Ministry, which is conditioned to forbid everything.

At heart, every Frenchman is ready to stand up to the state. Since 1958, more than ever before, his lack of civic responsibility—disguised as individualism—has grown along with his appetite for deceit and insurrection, his nostalgia for past revolutions or at any rate rebellions, his anarchist mythology, his horror of order (of the cops) and its inseparable companion, an urgent, pitiless insistence on order where everyone else is concerned. In short, he wants a state that is strong but tied down, like Gulliver in Lilliput.

"It's Too Stupid!"

I more than once heard General de Gaulle pound his desk and roar in helpless anger, "It's too stupid!", when some special-interest group stubbornly resisted a measure he considered necessary for the public good; when every organized group in France fought to prevent the popular election of the president; when the French press bombarded him for blocking Britain's entry into the Common Market.

De Gaulle was always running up against the formidable inertia of his country's structures and mentality. Every one of his ventures became snared in the net of acquired rights, of unproductive privilege, of established positions. The 1958 crisis enabled him to repair some of the seized-up machinery. But when he tried to introduce internal reforms to prevent the infection of government instead of merely curing it *in extremis*, he encountered only public indifference, hostility from the establishment and caution in those around him.

He intended to institute employee participation in management, restore order to the nationalized industries, revise the civil service statutes, reorganize the Social Security administration, reform the Senate, and introduce career orientation into secondary-school curricula and a policy of selection for university training. But he was constantly obliged to scheme or to postpone such projects. Can reforms be imposed on a democratic country that does not feel the need for them?

Technological wizardry can tame external nature, but human nature is more rebellious. André Malraux, when he was culture minister, once told me that there were two sides to his function. In its material aspects—cleaning building façades, erecting cultural centers, organizing art shows that brought together in luminous syntheses works of art that had hitherto been dispersed—he succeeded handily. But when it came to expanding people's minds—operating those cultural centers, promoting opera, bringing music courses into the schools—his efforts became bogged in apathy; they stumbled over suspicion.

Every minister has shared Malraux's experience. True, the regime's solid accomplishments—institutional stability, restoration of the state's authority, independence recovered by France and granted to its colonies, the opening out of the nation's economy—remained essential assets the acquisition of which no one would have dared to predict in 1958. But the failures also remain to demonstrate the permanence of our structural and mental rigidity.

The Nation's Basic Personality

In 1959, de Gaulle asked economists Jacques Rueff and Louis Armand to analyze the reasons for France's economic lag and to propose measures to erase it. After a year of work, their report listed an impressive series of defects and prescribed medication. Fifteen years later, public opinion was still unaware of the report and the ills described, and few of the many prescriptions the report contained had even begun to be applied. Withdraw the privileges of taxi drivers, druggists, millers? Out of the question, if many deputies with shaky seats were to be believed. The government did not even dare to publish the economists' enlightening report. This was more than a failure; it was an intellectual and political burial.

The French probably would not have recognized themselves in this description of the ailment afflicting them. We see details, not the whole picture. As the occasion demands, we are obsessed by "unrest among shopkeepers" or "unrest in the unions" or some protest movement. But we take the fever for the illness. We worry more about a few tons of artichokes strewn on the highway in protest than we do about the burden that obsolete farming structures impose on the economy, more about disorders in a few secondary schools than about how poorly our teaching is organized. A toothache makes us groan; tuberculosis eats away at us quietly.

Often, we see things not as they are, but as they are shown to us by pressure groups, which explains some curious climatic inversions. Even when there is no real danger, our ears are so full of the special interests' insistent pitch that we begin to worry. They fall silent when tragedy nears, and then we wax euphoric about our new-found unity, like the soldiers in August 1914 who were sure they would win the war by Christmas.

In the final analysis, the French substratum has remained virtually intact for the past three centuries: it is made up of bureaucratic centralization, dogmatism, a taste for abstraction, Manichaean sectarianism, separation into hostile castes, civic passiveness interrupted by sudden rebellions, incomprehension of growth, demographic and social Malthusianism. A massive inertia dissuades and dissolves efforts at reform. The only changes that slide through easily are those that flatter our individualism.

Repercussion on the State

Worse still, the body's ailment, which remains as acute as ever, can spread to the head, which we had thought was safe. The state feels vulnerable even though it appears strong. It is less loved when it strides firmly than when it staggers. The French do not rebel against power when it is split, as under the Third and Fourth republics, when their antiparliamentarianism never really threatened the regime.

I once questioned de Gaulle about his hesitancy over proportional representation, which he had proposed and later repudiated. "Democracy," he replied, "does not consist of expressing contradictions, but of pointing a direction." We tend to label "democratic" a system that best reflects public opinion—or rather, the various and volatile opinions, obsessions, panics and yearnings for power or destruction that float in a people's soul. But if a democratic regime is merely the mirror of a disordered collective conscience, it can only compound that disorder.

"Point a direction and hold to it," the general added; "that's the state's role, especially that of its chief."

Except that this need of a direction does violence to our taste for diversity. The French no longer recognize themselves in the simplification it imposes.

The Great Vacuum

The paradox of the Fifth Republic appeared with blinding clarity in the double crisis of 1968–69. In May 1968, everyone—beginning with those on the inside during that wild month—was struck by the vacuum that had been hollowed out in the state. Disappointment was scaled to expectations. The state, emptied of its substance, shrank to the size of a government lost in the storm.

This was a French-style psychodrama: a very minor disturbance—a rebellion by sociology students on a suburban Paris university campus—which was sucked upward because no one could settle it at any intermediate level. A thousand unsatisfied claims were whirled into the vacuum. They were uselessly satisfied. The hollow reached all the way, up to the symbolic and real disappearance of the state and its chief. Then the situation was reversed in a matter of hours; the state, pretending to be eclipsed, showed how necessary it was. Everyone wanted to wipe out even the memory of his fright—except de Gaulle who, his analysis confirmed, tried to deflate this hydrocephalus of the state, the gravity of which he had correctly measured. He did so in his own peremptory, dramatic way with the 1969 referendum.

Because he sought to restructure society by initiating regional adminis-tration, decentralization, socio-professional cooperation, because he attacked the root of the ailment instead of treating the symptoms, he was disavowed by the French for the first time. What they wanted was an end of the effects, not the causes.

CHAPTER 7

"Power Is Impotence"

"Power is impotence," General de Gaulle once told me. The paradox shocks me less now than it did then, because I have since had occasion at the head of eight ministries[1] to test its accuracy. I would like to furnish a few glimpses here of a life stamped by unreality, like peaks poking through a sea of clouds.

It was April 15, 1962, and Christian de La Malène, whom I was succeeding as minister of information, showed me a battery of buttons on his desk. "This one is for calling the reception clerk, this for your principal private secretary and that one is for the director of the RTF (the government-operated French radio and television network), the news director, the radio and television program directors. . . ."

Naïvely, I expressed surprise at being able to ring for RTF executives as ladies once rang for their chambermaids. "That's how it is," he said. "Every day around five P.M. you call them in to decide on the main lines of the evening radio and television newscasts. You can also give them instructions at any time via a house phone. Don't leave your office before one-thirty in the afternoon and eight-thirty in the evening. After the television news program, your colleagues will call you to reproach you for what displeased them."

The system dated from before World War II, when the communications ministers ran the government radio. It received its letters patent when playwright Jean Giraudoux was assigned at the beginning of the war to organize the official news reports. It was maintained and perfected, after the liberation of France and, until the start of the Fifth Republic, by thirty-two ministers, among them André Malraux and François Mitterand. The minister, his cabinet, his agencies and the whole RTF general staff were clustered in the same building.

I swore to myself I would never push those buttons. But at precisely 5:00 P.M. the news director was announced. He had come for his briefing. I told him I had no instructions to give him, that I trusted him and the reporters under his authority. If I had any observations to make, I would make them afterward. "Yes, Minister."

The State in the Dining Room

I felt rather than knew what I had learned in those few hours. If the *national* radio and television system lacked credit with the nation, it was because everyone thought he was hearing not so much the Voice of France as that of the government. It was easy to measure popular distrust. Radio stations broadcasting to France from outside its borders—notably those in Monaco and Luxembourg—were enormously successful. A survey showed that in 1962 only 9 percent of the country listened to the national stations, versus 91 percent for the peripheral stations, which were not nearly so well equipped. The peripheral TV stations had the edge in France's border areas; in the rest of the country, where the French stations had no competition, television was largely ignored. There were only 2 million TV sets in France in 1962, compared to 13 million in West Germany and 14 million in Great Britain, although all three countries had inaugurated their television services at about the same time. French TV meant the state in people's dining rooms.

My ambition was to turn RTF into a truly autonomous public enterprise, like the Renault automobile company or the French National Railways Corporation.

Circumstances were hardly favorable. A cease-fire in Algeria had followed the Evian agreement, but the Secret Army Organization (OAS) was doing everything it could to make the truce inoperative both in Algeria and in metropolitan France. Was this the time to relax control over an agency in ferment?

Nevertheless, I tried to promote my conviction that it was absolutely necessary to get the system back in hand, and that to do this it was important that in future the hand not be the minister's. The idea gained ground. Pompidou, then prime minister, understood how harmful the situation was for the government itself, constantly being weakened by an anarchy it could not overcome or compromised by spectacular but ineffectual gestures of authority. At the same time, the wave of OAS violence forced me to do what I had promised myself I would avoid: on more than one afternoon, it was I who shaped the evening news shows.

Five Months Later

Early in September, as I began rounding up agreement of those principally concerned to the idea of a new radio-TV status, I was suddenly drawn away by Prime Minister Pompidou to take charge of a new ministry set up to organize the reception and relocation of refugees from Algeria. Suffice it to say that this interim position taught me much about how incompetent the bureaucracy was in handling emergencies.

Everyone did his best to cope with the challenge; never were so many holes punched in administrative compartments, never did the administrative snail move so speedily. Yet everything seemed to stand still. Thousands of letters, of requests for help we could not provide, came to us daily. In those twelve weeks I became convinced that had France been just a little more bureaucratic than it is, the *pieds-noirs* would still be in their resettlement camps.

In December 1962, I returned to the Information Ministry, and to my former preoccupations. Nowhere was power more important than in the RTF. The organization seemed to sum up all the failings of our public enterprises, exaggerated by the extreme sensitivity of everything touching on information, culture and politics.

Like the state itself, the RTF lived under the Finance Ministry's thumb—more so, in fact, than any other administrative department. Bureaucrats are suspicious of artists. The psychological effects of the *a priori* control stifling the RTF may have been more disturbing than its real consequences; for some, it furnished a convenient alibi for inertia, while discouraging others' enthusiasm. "It's Finance's fault," people would say, rightly or wrongly. Nor did Finance's stringent controls achieve their objective. Waste grew out of prevailing irresponsibility. The RTF was not a corporation but a feudalized bureaucracy—its least qualified people felt they were untouchable. Program producers considered themselves lifetime owners of the screens or the microphones. Advantages earned by the best people were immediately demanded by the worst. Talent opened fewer doors than membership in a clandestine clique. Tight little units dictated program policy and enforced their hermetic control. Every measure disapproved by even the tiniest group provided a pretext for a strike that blacked out some or all of the programs.

These pressure groups were politicized. They never failed to raise echoes outside the agency. Conversely, the RTF had become a sounding board for outside political squabbles. And internal decisions, since they were reached, at least in theory, by government, were presented to the public as politically inspired. There was not a week in which the newspapers failed to report incidents, disorders or conflict within the network. No one was satisfied: not the public, the RTF personnel, the government, the Parliament, the majority or the opposition.

This unhealthy situation was typical of France's ailment. Although the agency was subject to the government's sovereign authority, no authority was wielded over it; the government intervened on matters of detail, but lacked overall control. Then, seeing that things were going badly, the government increasingly tended to intervene in RTF operations. And because the public sensed the system's subservience, it turned away from the RTF. The government reaped precious few advantages and a great many disadvantages from its semblance of power, notably that of appearing both imperious and powerless—in other words, ridiculous.

In short, this public service functioned as though the public did not exist. Stations beyond the French borders treated their listeners as consumers, adults exercising free choice. At the RTF they were administratees whose well-being was provided by an administration that was a better judge of it than they. Hierarchy replaced competition as an organizational principle. There was no way for the public to exert pressure, except by flight.

Interest-Bearing Reforms

To begin with, radio and television had to be separated. But they were stuck together like Siamese twins functioning on a single set of main organs. The radio and television systems' directors were directors in name only, since information and technical means were withheld from them. Journalists and engineers alike feared the disruption of their guilds and dispersion of their power; only at the end did they bow to necessity.

We set out to convert the jumble of radio stations, none of which had its own personality, into the three channels subsisting today: France-Inter, for entertainment and news; France-Culture, specializing in artistic, scientific and cultural programs; and France-Musique, reserved for classical music. Producers moved heaven and earth to block this reform. The first channel, especially, was hotly attacked as the "hippy station"; to "run after" the non-French stations, it was charged, we were "lowering ourselves" to their level. This, critics bawled, was "prostituting public service." But the public soon backed us up.[2]

Standby service during strikes had already proved its value in radio—listeners were never happier than during strikes, when all they were given was recorded music and news bulletins. This, in fact, was the principle on which we organized France-Inter. So why not extend this standby service to television? During a specially unpopular strike one evening, we were able to transmit from a station previously set up under tight secrecy: brief news reports and a film, which was what the public wanted. A flood of letters submerged us: "Do that every night." The dissuasion was so effective that for the five years up to May 1968, strikes (endemic until then) disappeared from TV audiences' daily lives.

Finally, I was able to program fifteen minutes a day of regional news and to set up twenty-three local television stations, not counting our eight overseas stations. The Paris establishment naturally objected to this siphoning off of funds that could have been applied to national programming—that is, to their producers. But the strongest opposition came from provincial newspapers, for the RTF was about to break local monopolies held by a number of dailies.

The prime minister made himself my advocate. He received provincial newspaper publishers and worked at reassuring them. One of them later told me that henceforth they would protest in their readers' names if we dropped local programming—the most popular of all in the provinces.[3]

The Voice of France

On whatever sea or continent you are led by business or pleasure—from Lisbon to Vancouver, from Cairo to Tokyo—try to tune in to a French radio program. Almost everywhere, you will twiddle your radio dial in vain. But you will get the BBC, the Voice of America, Moscow Radio, Peking Radio and even the *Deutsche Wellen,* broadcasting alternately in their native languages and the language of the country you are visiting—or even all in French.

Now, we aspire to cultural influence. Being one of the "big five of radio" would be incomparably easier than being, as we nevertheless are, the number three nation in space, nuclear and aeronautic technology. How is this explained? Very simply. In 1964 I had estimates drawn up calling for an investment of 250 million francs, which would allow us to broadcast on about the same level as Bulgaria. China broadcast nearly one hundred times as much as we did, the Soviet Union one hundred fifty times more, the United States, two hundred times more. There is no way for the potential audience of such a public service to make itself heard, so it becomes par excellence a matter of state sovereignty. But such are the nation's structures that no one cares about it. These programs were financed by the "interested" ministries—the Foreign Ministry, the Cooperation Ministry, and so on. Yet they were not interested in this form of action. The work of diplomacy, they felt, was carried on with governments, not with peoples.

An operation we called "Compass Card" showed that by keeping our small transmitters going all the time we multiplied our audience by ten. The idea appealed to de Gaulle. We decided that after we had finished equipping our regional and overseas television stations, we would build a short-wave transmitter on the southwestern coast and three powerful relay stations[4] around the world capable of uninterrupted broadcasting. Once they were built, funds for operating them would certainly be provided.

None of this ever happened. Since I left Information early in 1966, I have noticed that whenever there was a budget cut to be made it was sought first in foreign broadcasting. If an hour of air time a day attracts few listeners, why spend the money to keep it going? The voice of France has just about gone dead.

The Martian Invasion

Another failure concerned political programs, which were barred almost entirely from television; there had been none before 1958 and hardly any since. Politicians did not have to face the press, party leaders did not duel on television, sensitive subjects were avoided. When three leading newsmen devoted a program in 1959 to the Algerian war, they combed the TV files in vain: no picture of the war had ever been shown. When it came to controversial topics, the state always preferred evasion.

French television had to prove that it reflected French diversity, not the government's will. I asked Jean Farran to produce a monthly program like the American "Meet the Press," which would alternate leaders of the parliamentary majority and the opposition. This was in 1964. Our first presidential election campaign would soon be filling the airwaves. My proposal was so contrary to custom that it aroused lively opposition. Presentation of the program was postponed until after the election.

In mid-November 1965 the French saw the Martians land at dinner time: five talented men who, in leisurely fashion, reeled off their criticisms of the Fifth Republic and its head. Television audiences were astounded. Not a few must have wondered if these sacrilegious men were not going to be arrested as they left the studio. But a pattern was not set; the precedent was a lonely one. There has been little broadcasting of the kind ever since.

Despite these failures, the new office had gotten off to a good start. Authority functioned there. To everyone's surprise, the new directors actually directed. Above all, they were able to restore the RTF's confidence, to make a fresh start. There was no shortage of criticism, of course. Since it could no longer be attacked as a "mare's nest," the RTF's critics spoke of a "gang." And it is true that TV and radio were then being run by men and women whose competence I could measure and who did, I believe, render good service.

For power does not shed its impotence until it gives talented people their chance, choosing individuals worthy of trust, giving them a mission and holding them fully responsible for carrying it out.

CHAPTER 8

The State's Big Brains

The State as Researcher

After the presidential election, in January 1966, I was put in charge of Scientific Research and Atomic and Space Questions, where I stayed for fifteen months, long enough to see that the world of French research was anything but thriving.

Research in France is the government's responsibility. Hence the sector that should be the most inventive, the most flexible and the most efficient, suffers instead from all the state's defects. Like the state, it is centralized, by which I mean Parisianized: two thirds of its equipment, funds, research scientists are concentrated near the capital. Like the state, it is compartmentalized: each ministry has its institutes, its researchers who disdain, or fear, communication with each other. It is bureaucratized: the researchers are usually immovable civil servants and not, as they should be, men of adventure; everyone gets the same "research premiums" whether he finds anything or not, but no one ever gets a "discovery bonus." And it is *budgetized:* it has an annual allotment, subject to the customary bargaining so many other departments are going through in the rush of springtime budgeting.

To this are added the ills of society. Our researchers tend to ignore economics and so to disdain possible applications of their research. They are excited, as they should be, about the secrets of matter, the caprices of nature, the arcana of numbers. But to many of them, exploiting their own discoveries or even allowing them to be exploited by others seems unworthy of science and of themselves.

"I Want the H-Bomb for 1968"

In January 1966, de Gaulle called me in. "Find out why the Atomic Energy Commission cannot manage to make an H-bomb," he told me. "It's endless. I've just been informed it will take many years yet, and I can't wait more than two or three years. I won't finish out my term. I had to run [for the presidency] to make sure things stuck, but I won't go all the way to the end. But before I go, I want the first experiment to have taken place. Do you understand? It is vital. Of the five nuclear powers, are we to be the only one to fail to reach the thermonuclear level? Are we to let the Chinese get ahead of us? If we don't make it while I'm here, we'll never make it. My successors, whichever side they're on, won't dare to stand up to the scolding of the Anglo-Saxons, the communists, the old maids and the priests. And we'll be left standing at the door. But once a first explosion has occurred, my successors won't dare to stop weapons development."

"How much time will you give me?" I asked him.

"1968 at the latest."

I threw up my arms in hopelessness. "Find a way," he concluded.

Armed with this injunction, I relayed it to the heads of the Atomic Energy Commission (AEC). "An impossible assignment," they howled.[1] The program called for shots every two years on our Pacific atolls; much of the fleet was required each time and the ships had to be refitted in the alternate years. So 1968 really meant the next series, since the 1966 program had already been scheduled.

Was this massive show of naval force really necessary? It appeared that the captive balloons under which the devices would be exploded would reduce pollution to almost nothing,[2] so that only a few patrols would be needed to keep other vessels out of the area.[3] We could arrange test firings every summer; this should have meant the intervals could be cut in half.

Then two new objections were raised. The H-bomb required uranium-235 in quantity—we would have to wait until the reactor at Pierrelatte went into full operation. Above all, our calculations could not be properly carried out without the giant computers the Americans refused to deliver. Yet the British had detonated thermonuclear explosions by using simply plutonium instead of U-235, and we were producing plenty of plutonium. And the Americans, the Russians, the British had done without giant computers on their first mononuclear tests.[4] Then I was assured that there was no purpose to speeding up the tests—to test what? We did not have the answers, did not even know in what direction to look for them. I could only imitate de Gaulle. "I don't want to know your problems," I told them. "Find a way."

From time to time, after a cabinet meeting, the general would query me: "Well? And your H-bomb?" I set up an "H Committee," composed of top AEC executives, which met secretly every month. Together we discussed the progress made. I heard a string of embarrassed explanations. Thermonuclear fusion remained a mystery, but we could speed up development of a "doped" A-bomb, an improved nuclear-fission process that would bring us up to 500 kilotons. It wasn't a megaton, but it would double the yield and who would notice the difference? But of course the American planes and Soviet "trawlers" cruising off our atolls would immediately know what we were doing. There could be no lying about dissuasion.

Peering Over the Neighbor's Wall

Figures were lined up on a blackboard that heightened my sense of my own ignorance; obviously I did not know and would never know anything about advanced physics. But I knew a little about the history of science, and I recalled that most discoveries have been made not by experts isolated in their fields of specialization, but by fresh minds capable of peering over their neighbor's wall and of standing off from the prevailing ideas. With the naïveté of a country bumpkin I talked to administrator-general Robert Hirsch, an intelligent and able public servant who tried stubbornly to overcome his teams' inertia: "Since our people are getting nowhere, we ought to bring in fresh talent. Others probably could break through the obstacles that have blocked our research teams for years. Let's find new minds. There's no lack of them either in France or on the AEC."

"But our people aren't to blame," he said. "They're first rate and they're doing everything they can. Taking them off the job would ruin their careers. We haven't the right to do that!"

Hirsch shared my notion of our respective responsibilities: the minister's, to set objectives, see that the means were available, give precise instructions; the administrator-general's, to take full charge in carrying out those instructions—and to be judged by the results. But here, it seemed to me, was where we finally reached the real stumbling block. General de Gaulle had created the AEC twenty-one years earlier, "first of all to manufacture the bomb," as he repeatedly told me. In that time, the commission had amassed an impressive concentration of gray matter and of facilities. But, at the same time, it had become considerably bureaucratized. Like all big organizations, it tended unwittingly to exist a little less for its mission, a little more for its personnel. Its scientists had become civil servants, justifying themselves— like God, according to the ontological argument—by their very existence. The bureaucratic process laid down a paralyzing sediment over their inventive capacities. They had guaranteed careers, private preserves, established positions; it was out of the question to touch a hair on their heads, even if they discovered nothing.

Once more, we dug down into the heart of the "French sickness." The more I examined the workings of this elite collection of many of France's best minds, the more I thought I could guess why it obstinately marked time in the primary mission the government had assigned it: not because of the *individuals'* qualities, but because of the *system's logic*. The caste structure triggered a reject reaction against elements from outside the system. On the one hand were the scientists: they perhaps had the necessary imagination, but most of them were clearly hostile to military research. On the other were the technicians, especially the weapons engineers, who were willing to pick up the challenge but lacked either training in research or the turn of mind needed for success. Their rivalry was made worse by our ideological wars of religion between the political left and right. Within a given team, compartmentalization by specialties paralyzed any attempts at synthesis. Quantitative factors were stubbornly given priority: the size of the computers, the number of ships patrolling the testing grounds, the amount of fissionable matter available. Qualitative factors were relegated to second place: improving communications between specialists, combining disparate elements into new combinations, placing at the heart of the operation a man familiar with all the fields involved.

A Mountain Shepherd

Meanwhile, word was spreading in high places that it was imperative to drop the thermonuclear program and settle for mass production of already authorized atomic weapons. This mountain pressure discouraged the AEC teams, raising the obstacles higher than ever.[5] Somehow the circle had to be broken.

I asked my science advisers to try to unearth the synthesis-minded man we manifestly needed. One morning, one of them announced: "I may have what you need—a young physicist who began his studies late and raced through the stages at lightning speed." I interviewed the man. He had a curious history. The war had carried off his parents, Jews of Russian ancestry who had lived in France since the beginning of the century; his father had died in Auschwitz. Left on his own, the boy had to drop out of school and earn his living as a shepherd for the farm family in the Causses, in south-central France, that had taken him in and raised him. In 1944 he decided, "I'm old enough to take my baccalaureate degree," and he began to study for it on his own while tending his sheep. He won it easily. The following year, he came in first in the entrance examinations for the National Industrial Engineering School. "You were made for the Polytechnic," his professors told him—and a year later, he entered that elite institute.

After graduation at the head of his class, he adopted a French name: Robert Dautray. Since then, he had been doing wonders in another AEC laboratory at the Saclay nuclear research center. He was exactly the kind of man we needed—exceptionally gifted, capable of rapidly assimilating and mastering all the specialties needed for synthesis, able to understand and relate the languages of all the component analyses. I advised Hirsch to make him the mission's scientific director. We would build a reconstituted team around him.

The logjam was quickly broken. Dautray's fresh mind methodically examined all the Military Applications Agency's efforts to find a formula for thermonuclear fusion and other possible techniques. From the panoply of physical phenomena he chose a combination he thought looked promising. Closer examination confirmed its validity. Within a few weeks the synthesis had been worked out, the areas of deeper study defined and the research launched; all work was concentrated on the designated procedure. He didn't need giant computers. Neither enriched uranium nor, therefore, the plant at Pierrelatte were indispensable.[6] In August 1968, de Gaulle experienced one of his last joys when our first two hydrogen devices were exploded.

Thirteen Million Administratees

"You'll Be There for Five Years"

April 1967: A new government was formed, and General de Gaulle and Prime Minister Pompidou gave me the Education Ministry. The general, forgetting what he had said to me fifteen months earlier about his wish to leave before the end of his term, told me: "You'll be there for five years." Then, remembering that the future is wholly in God's hands, he added prudently: "Or at least, work as though you were going to be."

I was concerned about the number of people under my authority. With its 800,000 agents—responsible for a school population of 12.5 million—the French educational establishment was the world's largest enterprise after the Red Army and General Motors. All public schools in France—as well as the colleges and universities—are operated by the central government. But the comparison with the Red Army and GM is valid only in terms of size and by no means in terms of direction. Iron discipline binds the Red Army. General Motors is made up of a great many units, each of them subject to the implacable laws of the market. The entire French university complex could function perfectly if—as its founder Napoleon wished—it were run along paramilitary lines, or if, as in most liberal democracies, it were broken up into autonomous, truly competitive units. But French education is protected against both discipline and competition. Can a complex of this size function when it rests on contradictory organizational principles—monopoly and lack of discipline, uniformity and individualism? Is it reasonable that a public servant should be so sheltered that he can attack with impunity the authority under which he works?

Education's Watchword: How Much?

If we were to believe their spokesmen, the teaching corps suffered from a quantitative delirium—demanding more teachers, higher salaries, fewer pupils per teacher, fewer course hours, more space. In short, with more money, everything would be fine.

I was convinced that money was no longer the problem. Of course we were still short of teachers and of funds, but the growth rate here was satisfactory; not much change could be looked for. To keep children in school for the obligatory period from kindergarten through junior high school, the taxpayer was already paying his head's weight in pure gold. It was quality that had to be dealt with now. For when we assessed what remained to adults ten years after leaving school of the knowledge infused into them by primary, secondary and even university education, all illusions about the value of our teaching faded. We had the personnel for mass education, but our educational organization, teacher training, curricula and teaching methods were still designed to instruct an elite. As a result we educated neither the masses nor an elite. Since 1939, the number of university students had risen from 60,000 to 700,000, while the student population in the junior highs and high schools had soared from 300,000 to nearly 5,000,000. No reform had ever touched the very nature of our teaching. It was time to set about it.

Beginning in May 1967, I quietly formed a working group which, in February 1968, became an official commission for educational renovation under my personal direction. We had set out to define the principles of a profoundly altered schooling system. We would arouse students' spontaneous interest; we systematically favored active teaching methods, ways of stimulating their minds. There would be daily instruction in handicrafts and sports, especially team sports. In alternation with the three or four hours of classes, half the school day, or at least a third, would be given over to physical, artistic and technical activities. Curricula would be lightened; in most courses, formal lectures would be replaced by a documentary film followed by a discussion period. Youngsters would be trained to express themselves—orally, in writing and artistically. Self-discipline and elective democracy would be developed in the classroom. Special training would encourage teachers' imagination and initiative. The plan's sole originality lay in its effort to apply the lessons learned in a century and a half of teaching discoveries. The reception accorded our ideas by the teachers connected with our work indicated that I could count on the cooperation of a large minority of enthusiastic educators.

Making Time an Ally

At the same time, I obtained the funds needed to launch experiments. I thought it impossible to carry through an authoritarian reform in a corporate, politicized system. Sabotaged or merely applied reluctantly, the system would become absurd. Better to enlist volunteers in a series of pilot projects that would encourage others to imitate them.

Beginning with the 1968 fall term, we planned to open one new-model grade school in each ward, a junior high school in each department and a high school per district.* The experiment would be closely watched for a year. The number of such schools would be doubled the following year, and doubled again the third year. At the end of five years—the term of my lease on the ministry—the reform, progressively reviewed and amended, could extend throughout the country.

The Tottering Universities

For the universities I had inherited a reform, and a sweeping one. My predecessor, Christian Fouchet, wanted to reorganize the undergraduate structure. The ministry's bureaus had prepared and issued a set of mandatory rules that imposed a uniform pattern everywhere, beginning in the 1967 school year. Experience showed that it was at once too much and not enough.

It was too much for the poorer faculties, who were unable to institute a reform they neither wanted nor accepted. The liberal arts departments were annoyed at having to submit to a system conceived by and for scientists. Professors withheld the cooperation vital to the plan's success; most of them did not believe in it, or wanted no part of it.

It was also too little to satisfy the students' confused hopes of ending the old system of compartmentalized studies, of lecture halls invaded by anonymous crowds, of courses ill-adapted to their ends, of theses condemned to gather dust—an end to the wreckage of their generation.

To top it all off, the reform, in a first and dramatic attempt at "autonomy," gave the faculties themselves the power to make curricula adjustments for students already in the schools. As soon as problems arose, the deans appealed to the ministry, which told them to handle it themselves. So this hybrid system, neither sufficiently centralized nor sufficiently decentralized, led to loss of time, confusion and the exasperation of both students and teachers.

The issue of selection pushed that exasperation to the point of no return. The need to guide secondary-school graduates ready to enter university seemed obvious to me. But I rejected as brutal and negative the system of "national university competitive examinations"—a kind of super-baccalaureate exam—favored by the Education and Finance ministries staffs. Educationally and morally, it was unjustifiable; politically, it was inapplicable.

Because we knew the subject was explosive, we worked on it secretly at the Elysée Palace, the Hôtel Matignon (the prime minister's official residence), and my ministry on the rue de Grenelle. Because we worked secretly, rumors flew, spreading fear among both faculties and students. Among par-

---

* Because the French and American school systems are only roughly analogous, translations are necessarily approximate. Both *collèges* and *lycées* are forms of secondary schools, but the baccalaureate degree that caps lycée training is far more sophisticated than a U.S. high-school diploma.

ents, too: with their children's schooling already upset by the Fouchet reform, the prospect of possible further disturbance by the process of selection left them worried and hostile.

Again, power was impotence. Power could decree a reform, but proved powerless to enforce it; the state was responsible for the futures of hundreds of thousands of young people, but it soon showed itself to be impotent because no one followed up its initiative.

Small, hostile and determined groups were formed. They functioned as the catalyst of a chemical reaction among potentially explosive elements outside the schools. Because the exasperation was collective, these revolutionaries were untouchable, and they remained so long enough to rock the state on its foundations.

Nanterre: Nursery and Tomb

At the end of March 1968, Pompidou and I decided to close the Nanterre University campus, in suburban Paris, for the summer. Agitation there was exceeding acceptable limits, but any authoritarian measure during the school year could cause an explosion. In the fall we would install a pilot university that would function like a nationalized corporation, under the authority of a president controlled by a board of faculty and nonfaculty trustees with full administrative authority, chosen by the government for their competence. The board would have real autonomy of action and funding. Over the years, this experiment would breed a network of competitive universities that would try to attract the best students and teachers by offering the best of working conditions and direction, the greatest prestige.

There is still no such network. Our work led to a "complementary law to the law on university orientation," allowing for establishment of universities varying from the standard model, and to the creation of the University of Compiègne, the first to be built according to our new pattern. But there are no others like it and, in the long run, a prototype that is not copied stands a slim chance of survival.

In March 1968 I had chosen Nanterre precisely because the centralized, compartmentalized, irresponsible system reigning in French universities was more glaringly evident there than anywhere else. History outraced me. In May, student riots exploded the bomb before I could defuse it.

CHAPTER 9

The Misunderstanding

On September 16, 1969, I heard Prime Minister Jacques Chaban-Delmas deliver a powerful and broad attack on his own state, his own society.

"The state is tentacular," he said, "and, at the same time, ineffectual. By indefinitely extending its responsibilities, it has gradually made the whole of French society its ward. . . . The renewal of France after the liberation consolidated an old Colbertist and Jacobin tradition, making the state a new Providence. . . ."

Probably no one in Parliament since 1958 had passed so keen an analysis of the country's persistent difficulties. Until 1958, governmental instability had supplied a more than adequate explanation. After institutional reform and the end of the Algerian war, the convulsions that continued to shake France seemed increasingly inexplicable. Since the upheavals of May 1968, the question was on everyone's lips: Was the new government going to cure France's fragility, since it could so sternly diagnose its cause? I was deeply impressed by Chaban-Delmas's strictures, yet at the same time I could not but be aware that he was merely a prime minister, at the mercy of a parliamentary majority, fated to serve a team unlikely to permit him the sort of sweeping reforms he spoke of so tellingly.

"These deformations and defects," Chaban went on, "reflect still archaic or over-conservative social—even mental—structures. . . . We will not succeed in instituting reforms except by acting like revolutionaries.

"There are few moments in a people's existence when, except in a dream, it can ask itself: 'What kind of society do I want to live in?' I feel that we have reached such a moment. We can undertake to build a new society, prosperous, young, liberal and liberated."

"Trying to Make the French Dream"

A few days later, Pompidou received me at the Elysée. Warned that I had only a hour, I yielded to the temptation to touch on the basic problem: "I thought Chaban's statement appealing. At least he has a sense of perspective."

The president didn't reply. He asked me about the Gaullist deputies' state of mind, about my work, my election district. I took advantage of a pause in the conversation to raise the subject again. There was a long, heavy silence.

"Chaban thinks the time has come to do something new," Pompidou finally said. "Nothing new is ever done. These are the fantasies of adolescents or romantics. There are never any blank pages. We have to be content to work on a tapestry others have begun, with the weave already established. A new society is impossible. Society is what it is; we have to live with it. There is nothing worse than trying to make the French dream. That's not what they expect of us. Either they won't believe us, they'll think we're demagogues or illusionists, which is the opposite of their image of us. Or they will believe us, then later they'll realize they've been fooled and they won't forgive us for it. Let's keep a sense of reality."

He was very much a son of his native Cantal, as hard as basalt, as vigorous as a chestnut tree. He fell silent again, hesitant to go any further.

"In any case," he went on at last, "Chaban's ambition is disproportionate to his mission. He knows that during my seven-year term he'll have at least one successor, perhaps two—I told him that at the beginning. And here he is opening up twenty- or thirty-year perspectives. Well, what will he do in nineteen-seventy, seventy-one, seventy-two? He'll make people think he's going to change everything and he won't change anything. He'll distribute dreams. He'll sow bitterness. Yet the task is simple. We have an objective that must dominate the others: to make France a great industrial nation. This is within our reach. Let's reach it without dispersing our energies. The rest will come as a bonus."

"But that's just it," I argued. "To make France an advanced industrial country, it isn't enough to build factories. We have to decentralize decision making, knock down compartment walls, appease antagonism—in short, unblock society."

The State in Danger

"And you think we can do everything at once?" the president exclaimed. "In blowing out the compartment walls and the bolts, we could blow up the state and the nation with them, as almost happened in May '68. These are the ideas of irresponsible people who would like to dismantle the state.

"Didn't you notice that in a speech full of talk about society, Chaban *didn't once* talk about the nation, and still less about the authority of the state? You'd think such expressions scald his tongue. Well, France is first of all a nation and only then a society. She was created, she has survived only as a nation. And that nation was saved only by its state. Now once again, with society decomposing before our very eyes without our being able to do much of anything about it, at least let's respect and protect what's still intact and what alone can get us out of trouble: the state and the nation. If we are afraid to use the words that sum up our credo, we are playing the opposition's game, and we'll always be beaten at that. You never win by trying to entice your enemies and disappoint your friends. Cajoling the opposition doesn't soften them, it emboldens them. Chaban has a four-fifths majority in the chamber [of Deputies]. That's unprecedented in any [French] republic. He prefers to set that four fifths against him to seduce the other fifth. No one has ever seen that before, either. When you have a majority, you have to keep it."

"In any case there's something badly blocked in our society," I said, "and that's the reform machinery. When the effective power of the opposition and the unions exceeds the 'blocking third,' as they say in the United Nations, power is blocked; it can do nothing without the opposition's consent. A president elected by a relatively slender margin, which will probably always be the case here, is condemned either to immobility or to governing by consent of the opposition. If we opt for confrontation between two irreconcilable categories of Frenchmen, it means we can't move. For the country to evolve, we first have to reestablish a consensus."

"Perhaps. But in that case, I wonder if immobility isn't preferable to an opposition-dictated policy that our common sense whispers we ought to resist. I'm not afraid of being accused of immobility. Why this mania for movement? When everything around us is moving, what's important is to maintain our balance—avoid the reefs and stay afloat. In the whirlwind of discoveries, of technological innovation, of international exchanges, what matters is, on the contrary, to remain yourself amid changes that are going to happen whether you like it or not. It is to preserve our basic values. Really, we have to have the courage to resist these language tics."

The Anglo-Saxons Idealized

"Here's my prime minister," Pompidou continued, "with his own social plan, only he just forgot to talk to me about it. This leftist nonsense is intolerable. Besides, they talk to the French as though they were Anglo-Saxons. . . . We have idealized Anglo-Saxon society for three centuries, beginning with Montesquieu, who let himself be manipulated by the intelligence service of his day. And that society is one of money—oligarchic, contemptuous of the humble and, with its unchangeable rituals, at least as conservative as ours. It has enormous defects, inhuman, unacceptable. And it is in a state of advanced decrepitude. Now, when it's falling apart, is when people want to take it as a model. Changing society—that means making a total blood change, expelling fifty million French and replacing them by fifty million Anglo-Saxons. The French are what they are, and so they'll remain. Doctors don't tell a patient, 'Sir, you have an excitable temperament. That doesn't suit me. I could treat you more easily if you were the bilious kind.' They take him as he is, without trying to change his temperament, and cure him if they can."

"But don't you think," I hazarded, "that the French are renewing themselves? Naturally, we can't change their temperament just like that, by blowing on it. But we can change their environment, their institutions, their economic situation, their social system, and their mentality will evolve accordingly. In 1959, the new regime and our entry into the Common Market wrought decisive changes. We began to recover from the ailments that had caused our governmental instability and our navel-searching."

"Do you really imagine that the French have changed?" Pompidou replied. "They've changed styles, and maybe their style of living, but not their mentality. In fact, they instinctively understand the dangers of change. They reckon that when you introduce a desired change, it leads to an indefinite series of changes that nobody wanted or even expected. Step by step, the order of things is disarranged. The French are basically conservative. This, I can tell you, is what's called the instinct of preservation. Personally, I consider it a proof of good health. You can't very well tell the French: 'You're no longer the world's leading people because of your mentality and your national culture; we're going to change all that.' Are you trying to preach a Cultural Revolution? We're not in China."

Intellectuals' Toys

Pompidou waved his hand as though to sweep away ghosts. "No," he went on, "if there has been a French decline, it's simply because France has remained an old agricultural country and agriculture has lost its rank in the modern world by comparison with industry. Don't look for things where they don't exist. We were shorter of raw materials than the others. Britain and Germany, which were not gifted in agriculture, developed their industry better. I don't say there's nothing we can do; I say we cannot do everything at once. We can't distribute more than we collect, or buy more than we sell, or use the profits from growth both to increase public spending and raise wages fifteen percent. We have to choose. I've made my choice. What we need to do is to close the industrial gap by creating jobs for just that labor that is being made available by agricultural modernization. There's a very concrete, very real task. But don't talk to the French about their national vices. It won't take. A people has a sense of its own decency. 'Industrialize France,' I tell the French. They understand me. The 'blocked society,' the 'new society,' a 'new social contract,' 'change'—this is valid language for Paris intellectuals who can't tell a cow from a bull. . . . But let's not pretend to govern France with these toys.

"The French are what they are," the president insisted. "And neither

Chaban nor you nor I is going to change them. You can't change one man—and they want to change fifty million. Governing the French means taking them as they are, here and now, and trying to keep them from doing too many stupid things."

I thought of Montesquieu, who had just been accused by Pompidou of Anglomania, but who had wisely recommended that care be taken not to change a nation's general spirit saying: "If there were a nation in the world that was alert, sprightly, sometimes imprudent, often indiscreet and, with that, had courage, generosity, candor and a certain point of honor, one must not seek to disturb its defects with laws, so as not to disturb its virtues."

As I left the Elysée, I reflected that perhaps, in 1969, the team was in the wrong traces. It was the prime minister whose gaze was set on the distant horizon, and the president who was trying to avoid the ruts immediately before us, whereas the spirit of our institutions required a president who took the long view and a prime minister concerned with the short term.

Naturally, the president got his way. He did indeed promote unprecedented industrial growth in France. But, as he said, he maintained things. The "new society" remained a myth, the "blocked society" a reality.

II

THE ROMAN SICKNESS

CHAPTER 10

"The Splendid Century": Dazzling Beginning of Decline

Jonzac, May 1963: De Gaulle was touring the Charente. In his welcome speech, the mayor noted that the young Louis XIV, en route to Saint-Jean-de-Luz to meet his fiancée, had stopped at the château that now serves as Jonzac's town hall. On the table we were shown, he had devoured two partridges.

The general enjoyed such allusions; through them, he felt the history of France flowing up toward him. This was a fine occasion on which to sound him out on the "Great King." After we had eaten, I set about it, with that touch of provocation needed to get him talking. "What a pity," I said, "that Louis XIV didn't remain the young man anxious to do the right thing that he was at his betrothal to the Spanish infanta. Soon he could think of nothing but parading, making war, accentuating his absolutism and centralization to meet the needs of his parading and his warring."

De Gaulle showed neither surprise nor annoyance. For a moment he stirred his coffee silently. Then he said calmly: "You're very harsh. It's the fashion to say that today. It is not how I feel. Louis XIV gave dignity to the royal function. The grandeur of France and of the state was his constant concern." He conceded that persecuting the Jansenists and revoking the Edict of Nantes* had been mistakes, that the king's diplomatic and military adventures had frequently come a cropper; but basically de Gaulle considered Louis XIV's a great reign. He approved the Sun King's accentuation of centralization, his curtailment of provincial, municipal and parliamentary independence. Yet it seemed to me that these policies had bled France white.

* By the Edict of Nantes in 1598, Henri IV partly legalized Protestantism in France.

The Forest Around the Clearing

As far as almost all foreign historians are concerned, Louis XIV's master plan was nothing more than the will to force other princes and nations to bend their knee to him. He devastated Flanders, Holland, the Palatinate, the Rhineland, the Aosta Valley; he bombarded Genoa and Brussels; he forced other states to acknowledge the precedence of France's ambassadors; he humiliated Pope Alexander VII; and he broke treaties, giving his word, only to retract it later. What do we see in the medals struck to the glory of Great Louis accoutered as a Roman emperor, in the equestrian statues, in the frescoes covering the ceilings at Versailles? Sovereigns bowed down before the Sun King. He made France respected only by making it hated.

De Gaulle wanted to make it respected by making it loved. He had formed a wholly different idea of grandeur: the moral grandeur of peaceful influence, of aid in the liberation of men and peoples. Then how could he endorse his opposite?

Of course, he was right when he pleaded extenuating circumstances for Louis XIV. Absolutism was dictated by the spirit of the time. But de Gaulle had been nourished by the images of the "Splendid Century" and the "Great King" that all French historians after Voltaire and until very recently had instilled in the French. These myths are part of our very culture—anyone who tarnishes their glory should be ashamed of himself.

This is largely an optical illusion. The history of France was long a Parisian history. It, too, was centralized. We hear little enough between the ignorant rustics and the busy bourgeois about the provincials' lives. The only accounts or memoirs we have are by the "elite," attracted to the court and the city like moths to a lamp. The culture diffused by the capital perpetuated its own monopoly.

It took the intuition of the great nineteenth-century historian Jules Michelet to see the provinces as "weak and pale" and to guess why: it is "the fate of centralized provinces that are not themselves the center. This powerful attraction seems to have weakened them, attenuated them." But, a centralizer at heart, Michelet quickly reassured himself: "France must not be taken piece by piece, it must be embraced in its entirety. It is precisely because centralization is strong that local life is weak."[1]

Since World War II, a whole army of historians has begun to describe and explain this weakness. Diet, sickness, epidemics, delinquency, prison, madness, death, religious habits, cultural tastes, attitudes and many other sectors of human life and work that had been virtually ignored by the traditional historians now appear in the landscape. As we peer further into the distance, a dark forest springs up around the brilliant clearing of Versailles.

"A Fatal Blindfold"

A few discreet but perspicacious witnesses had glimpsed the tragedy beneath the epic mask. No one listened to their warnings, such as the one raised by physician and writer Gui Patin: "To the poor, waiting for relief is vain; so they are dying everywhere in France, of sickness, of want, of oppression, of poverty and of despair . . . I think the Topinambous are happier in their barbary than the the peasants are in France."[2] Even today, we are unaware of the courageous letter Fénelon wrote to Louix XIV in 1694: "Your people are dying of hunger. Work on the land has been almost abandoned; the cities and the countryside are emptying; all the trades are languishing and do not feed the workers. All commerce is annihilated. You have destroyed half the real forces within your State. . . . All France is no more than a great and desolate hospital."[3] The king, his ministers, his court and his bureaucracy remained unaware of this. "This glory, which hardens your heart," Fénelon wrote, "is dearer to you than justice. You live as though there were a fatal blindfold over your eyes."

A Long Lead Slowly Lost

Nothing exceptional is made of this in what we are taught by today's historians about the kingdom under Louis XIV. Rather, it was Holland, England, Switzerland and Sweden that, at about the same period, were exceptional— in the opposite way. But even this cures us of an illusion that has tended to color all of French history. Louis XIV appeared as the man who had raised France on high, to a level from which it would never again descend except through such historical "accidents" as the defeat of 1870 and the debacle of 1940. Yet if France is a second-class nation today, it is because of a relative decline by comparison with certain other countries. The "Splendid Century" was only the dazzling beginning of this three-century-long decline.

Under Richelieu, France had become, or again became, Christendom's leading power.[4] When Louis XIV chose *Nec pluribus impar*—Superior to all others—as his motto, he was merely underlining the obvious. Three hundred years later, in the middle of the twentieth century, what remains of this superiority? Predominance in Europe? This could have been claimed across the English Channel after 1814, or across the Rhine after 1870. World predominance? That had crossed the Atlantic, or had retreated toward the Urals. Paris merely guided the destinies of a weakened country with a minimal population growth rate* and a handicapped economy, a people ill-used by its perpetually unbalanced political institutions.

---

* This has often been hidden from economic historians by the fact that *per capita* growth was not too bad. Just one more illusion: one cannot blame the economy for France's demographic

This effacement, however, is far from evident. A country can maintain its influence long after the source of its prosperity has run dry, like an extinguished star whose light still reaches the earth. Eighteenth-century Europe bears France's imprint—until the Revolution, no other European nation, not even Russia, was as populous. French supplanted Latin as the international language. France was strong enough to hold its own against all the other European countries together. But this long lead was slowly lost.

Colbert's Exemplary Failure

Let us not try yet to explain why the movement France was riding ran out of breath in the middle of the seventeenth century while others around forged ahead. Let's simply note that this reversal of direction coincided with the definitive establishment of our centralizing and directionist systems, and with a crushing tax burden made necessary by the creation of a tentacular state apparatus and the monarchy's extravagance. It also coincided with the neutralization of our elite classes, the discouragement of initiative, a prejudice in favor of nobility that made it impossible for anyone who was not well-born to rise socially—unless he were ennobled. This was also a time of anti-economic prejudice, which divorced our immobilized elite from all commercial, industrial and financial activity, a time of pensions, sinecures, sales of public office, and of incapacity to renew our methods of doing things. These are the burdens so long hidden by the court's luxury.

Behind Louis XIV was a system. It took a man's name, that of the royal comptroller, Jean-Baptiste Colbert, who attempted (unsuccessfully) to restrain the king's expenditures. "Colbertism" remained long after Colbert disappeared; to a great extent, as we shall see, it still rules us. Beginning in the seventeenth century, this system resulted in a resounding economic failure from which there are lessons for us to learn today.[5]

Colbert was chasing a chimera comparable to that the planned societies are pursuing in the twentieth century: to make the kingdom prosper by making every individual the docile executant of economic decisions reached rationally at the top. As far as docility goes, he succeeded. Prosperity was something else again.

The state was great because it was rich and rich because it was great; since wealth lay in gold and silver and the land produced none, the state had to find ways to obtain the precious metals. France, importing little and exporting much, enriched itself at others' expense.

Nothing was natural about this program. The government could have

---

collapse, of which it was an essential cause (see the following chapter). Three centuries of economic stagnation are clearly apparent when we compare France's overall production over a long period with that of its competitors.

drawn its strength from a strong nation; instead, it gathered all that strength to itself, leaving the nation enfeebled. For when Colbert spoke of "the State," he wasn't thinking of the nation, of the vitality of its trade and industry, its spontaneous and innovative expansion, but of the royal bureaucracy, guiding and controlling all productive activity.

Colbert made decisions on everything. He issued a flood of decrees regulating how timber was to be squared, the size of lengths of cloth, the weight of candles. He intended to create industrial and commercial activity, not to keep pace with it. He founded countless public enterprises—"royal factories," "royal forges," "royal shipyards," "royal companies." Private initiative was suspect *a priori,* tolerated only when it was controlled and bracketed. The economy, laid out with a ruler, trimmed and trimmed again, was "French-style," like our gardens.

State management, conceived so as to render fraud impossible, usually ends up encouraging it. The state stoutly holds one part of the fort, but always forgets about others. Few regimes were as conducive to prevarication as Colbertism. All this discouraged people from taking risks in what the English were already calling "business"—banking, large-scale trading, big industry, which alone can promote true prosperity, as was happening then in northern Europe.

The Paralyzing Hand

Colbert's incessant interference aroused optimism at first. Textile towns revived. But production never regained the level it had reached in the time of Louis XIII. In metal casting, production of sheet iron and high-quality steel, French techniques fell behind to a degree that was to subsist into the twentieth century. We often had to buy cannon abroad, sometimes from the enemy. The royal manufactures tottered as soon as subsidies were withdrawn. And the men who ran these establishments? They were chosen by favor and were favor's clients. How could they fail to spend more time trying to show themselves in the best light than in developing techniques and sales? As for the royal workers, they rarely burned with the sacred fire.

Foreign trade? For it to have succeeded would have meant that the kingdom, girdled with high tariff walls, encountered no such obstacles abroad—a Utopian notion. The British and Dutch hotly retaliated. Our trade was paralyzed. The proud companies created by royal munificence slithered toward bankruptcy.

France, where the state reserved initiative to itself, fell far behind its rivals, whose states allowed private enterprise complete freedom of action. After Colbert's death in 1683, the French state enterprises struggled weakly, or disappeared. Paradoxically, only private business more or less held its own. The Newfoundland cod fisheries and the alum plants in Tolfa, in Italy, earned more for a few Saint-Malo traders than all Colbert's companies[6] ever earned for the king. The royal companies—today we would call them nationalized firms—strangled in the red tape of bureaucratic meddling and rigid regulations. In similar lines of business, private traders who quickly threw together "companies" to send off shiploads of goods pulled off deal after deal, establishing solid links with London or Amsterdam through a thousand private channels. When a customer asked for light, cheap cloth, they did not even try to send him the unusable stuffs made according to the detailed regulations of Colbert's royal edicts.

A Society of Mistrust

France, then, would remain massively rural through inertia—and it would remain inert. Agriculture, which the French think is their strong point, has been their weak point ever since that time because of their technical backwardness. Rural revenues would have had to be higher to stimulate manufacturing; trade would have had to prosper to raise food prices and so encourage agricultural productivity. The English and Dutch instinctively perceived the working of these delicate mechanisms, for freedom of initiative sharpens the instincts. The monarchy at Versailles knew nothing about them because they did not conform to dogma and, since it was absolute, it blocked them.

How could so much effort bring about such sorry results? Because the whole Colbertian system inspired mistrust in proportion as it was inspired by mistrust. Colbert was haunted by a kind of technocratic frenzy; he himself was "the only man he could trust."[7] Traders and manufacturers amply returned the state's suspicion of them. They mistrusted the mistrustful regulations aimed against freedom and private interests, the royal officials who shackled free trade, and the minister's creatures, so skilled in enriching themselves and so inept at enriching France.[8]

It would be as unjust to impute this disaster to Colbert alone[9] as it was naive to give him the credit for an entirely imaginary prosperity. Colbert was rather an exemplary symbol than a decisive figure. The officials of his day shared his prejudices. Caught in the system and eager to win advancement, they could only perfect it—that is, accentuate it. To them, the economy was merely an aspect of the administration, two interchangeable words designating the same facets of a single hierarchical order.

Measuring the Decline

Imagine the advance of nations as trains rolling at different speeds along parallel tracks: one may advance in its own terms, but drop back by comparison with another. France's evolution must be evaluated less in terms of its own growth than of its rivals' growth. The richest country in the West was outdistanced—first in population density, then in total population; in per capita income, then in overall production—by many others that had been far behind it. Only two periods reverse this steady French regression: the reigns of Louis XV and Napoleon III. It is odd and significant that these should also be the two most criticized periods in the three centuries under study.

The Low Countries, Britain, Switzerland, the United States, the British dominions, Germany and Scandinavia all went through the Industrial Revolution and the changes in agriculture at one time or another. Until the mid-twentieth century, France's experience of these movements was only partial and localized. A look at the statistics over the three centuries shows France almost always behind the northern countries.

Let us point the comparison with our most constant rival. Although our population increased much more slowly than Great Britain's, the gap between the two countries' per capita production, already wide in the seventeenth century, widened throughout the eighteenth and nineteenth.[10] In 1800, France's overall production still exceeded Britain's by 70 percent, with a population 300 percent greater than Britain's. But it was already falling behind. In 1810, there were only 200 steam engines in French industry versus some 5,000 in a Britain still three times less populous.[11] British industry, pulled forward by trade, advanced much more rapidly, overtaking ours in 1821. At the beginning of the twentieth century, it was outproducing France by 60 percent.[12]

When we look at Holland, Belgium, Germany, Switzerland and Scandinavia, we find the same trends. France led its northern and eastern neighbors in per capita production and in output per square kilometer. Then, gradually, the situation was reversed. If per capita production seems to have regressed only moderately, it is because the statistics hide the fact that the population of France dwindled in comparison to its neighbors'. This *trompe-l'oeil* masks a frightful decline.

Self-Satisfaction and Masochism

We are only too happy to hide from ourselves the fact of our slow relative decline. The hardest of our false ideas to uproot is the one we have of ourselves. The world bowing to the Sun King, the Revolutionary armies bringing liberty to the world, Napoleon's self-coronation, Empress Eugénie's inauguration of the Suez Canal, Clemenceau leading the world's most formidable army to victory: so many cartoons, shown to French children from grade school on, convincing them that the three centuries since Richelieu have been crammed with French grandeur. The triumphant election of Prince Louis-Napoleon Bonaparte, the future Napoleon III, illustrates this propensity of the French people to transfigure their history into legend and to base their policy on that legend. Waterloo was forgotten; the French voted for Austerlitz.

We oscillate between self-satisfaction and an equally unjustified masochism. Until the middle of the twentieth century, we believed we were still "the great nation." We did not really understand the true situation until our second defeat at Sedan (in 1940). Since then, a feeling of decadence has overwhelmed and discouraged us—precisely when we no longer had reason for discouragement.

Let us compare French economic growth[13] with that of twelve industrialized Western countries—the United States, Canada, Denmark, Sweden, Germany, Belgium, Switzerland, Norway, Holland, Great Britain, Italy and Spain—for the 1871–1913 period (the Third Republic's best years). We see that France, with Italy and Spain, brings up the rear, with an annual rate of production growth nearly three times below that of the leading country, the United States. From 1913 to 1938, our industrial production regressed, despite our recuperation of Alsace and Lorraine.[14] And it was not until 1949 that we matched our 1929 production level.

France was not yet an underdeveloped country in 1939, but it was already backward. In 1945–50 it rose from its ruins; it had fewer ruins than West Germany or Britain, and it rose from them less quickly. After 1958, the indicators show a stubborn slowdown: telephones, expressways, television sets, technological balance, and so on.

The fact is that there was no real French economic take-off before 1945; this take-off became noticeable only after 1954 and was not confirmed until after 1962. In the preceding three centuries, France had endowed itself as best it could with factories, but it failed to develop the mentality that would have enabled them to prosper. It disdained big business; its monetary policy defied economic growth. For a long time it was propelled by so few motors and slowed by so many brakes that it was industrialized without an industrial revolution.[15]

More than one of the French soldiers who entered Alsace in 1918 was astonished to find water mains, sewage mains, electricity, telephones and Social Security offices everywhere. Alsace, annexed to the young Reich from 1870 to 1918, had been transformed in less than half a century. It was as though France had fallen half a century behind that part of itself that had been torn from it. Yet the sky blue French uniforms were cheered. When the liberated Alsatians returned to the motherland, France's soldiers discovered the modern world.

CHAPTER 11

Demographic Doldrums

The relative decline of the French can be measured first of all, very simply, by their number. But the French have never measured it this way. We know that our population level stagnated. We vaguely date this situation from the end of World War I or, if pressed, from around the end of the nineteenth century. Few of us are aware that it developed in the seventeenth century and that it reached disastrous proportions at the end of the Revolution. This is a very recent discovery, but historians have only recently become interested in demography. We are just beginning to suspect that rhythms of births and deaths reveal and ordain a people's history.[1]

A Dizzying Drop

The results of the first serious attempt at a census were published by Sébastien le Prestre de Vauban in 1707.* He advanced a population figure of 19 million—lower, probably, than in the time of Louis XIII or even of Philippe de Valois. Startling declines in population levels occurred throughout the kingdom between 1648 and 1662, between 1693 and 1695, and again from 1709 to 1720. For those eighty years, the number of French remained stable at around forty inhabitants per square kilometer (or about 55 per square mile).

True, the population increased during the reigns of Louis XV and Louis XVI; but this was not the "demographic revolution" it has been called.[2] The population probably reached 24 million around 1740 and grew to 28 million around 1790. During the one hundred fifty years of absolute monarchy, the French population increased by barely 40 percent, which means that it declined sharply in terms of the growth it could and should have achieved.

Beginning with the 1806 census, the figures become more reliable. The

* Based on a sweeping survey made between 1697 and 1700. According to Jacques Dupáquier, the figure (bearing on approximately 0.5 million square kilometers and thus giving a density on the order of 38 per square kilometer) should have been 21 million, which would make the density 42.

roughly 28 million in 1790 became 30 million in 1810, 36 million in 1850. The 40-million mark would not finally be topped until 1946.

This slow rate of population growth, shortly to become no more than marginal, masks a collapse in the birth rate. For the death rate had been appreciably reduced; life expectancy doubled, then tripled. But the number of births fell from 40 to 19 per 1,000, almost equaling the mortality rate. The French nation was subsiding into the grave.[3] In middle-class and in farm families, two children—often only one—became the rule. The number of adults of working age diminished. Immigration alone slowed this aging of the population.

The France–Britain Match

All history is comparative. How, then, did French population levels evolve in comparison with other countries', especially with those who were its competitors in the industrialized world?

From the Middle Ages to the Splendid Century, France enjoyed a crushing demographic superiority, in density and even in total numbers. It was the world's most populous nation except for China. French dominance was intimately related with the "inexhaustible abundance of its men" celebrated by Montchrestien.[4] Yet each of France's competitors was growing increasingly rapidly in population. In comparison with them, France seems to have been paralyzed.

Population growth rates over short periods neither prove nor create anything. Over long periods, they change everything. Under Louis XIII, with French population density in the neighborhood of 40 per square kilometer, Britain's seems to have been around 20.[5] Britain's density reached ours around 1789. During those one hundred fifty years, then, Britain's total population and its density more than doubled, while growth in France lagged far behind it.[6] In the one hundred fifty years that followed,* the gap widened, especially after the turning point of the Revolution.

While population density in France increased from 40 to 75 inhabitants per square kilometer between 1640 and 1940, in Britain it soared from 20 to 220—87 percent in France compared to 1,000 percent in Britain.

Aside from the 1 million *pieds-noirs* (of whom fewer than half were of French origin) and the 6 million French-speaking Canadians, there are practically no French groupings anywhere in the world outside of France. Three centuries after Richelieu's death, the 20 million of French stock had increased to only 45 million, while Cromwell's 4.5 million compatriots had

---

* Britain's population of 10 million (excluding Ireland) in 1800 grew to 20 million in 1850, to 37 million in 1900. Then it passed France, to reach 40 million in 1910. In 1940 it rose to 50 million, while France's population was holding steady.

given birth to Anglo-Saxon communities with a total population of around
275 million. Our demographic expansion has been thirty times below that of
the British.

From the Head of the Line to the End

The comparison can be repeated with other industrialized countries. After
1789, it was clear that our demographic capital was frozen. The Russians had
passed us some years earlier. The states under the Austrian crown were
treading on our heels and so, as a whole, were the German principalities. For
the last time, the military campaigns of the Revolutionary and Imperial
armies demonstrated the French people's numerical superiority over their
neighbors. France was still called "the great nation"; it no longer was. With
our supremacy in human resources abolished, hegemonies in other areas—
political, economic, cultural—vanished one after the other.

Beginning in 1800, the other countries one by one caught up to and
passed France: Austria-Hungary around 1830, Germany around 1860, the
United States in the 1870s, Britain and Japan at the turn of the century, Italy
around 1930.

An Attempt at Explanation

The French have made scarcely any effort to explain this gigantic factor; indeed, they refuse to see it.

Some explanations have nevertheless been advanced. They are fanciful.
In the nineteenth century, some anticlericalists blamed the low birth rate on
the celibacy of priests, monks and nuns. The notion is ridiculous when we
consider that ecclesiastics of both sexes never numbered more than 1 for
every 200 French,[7] which is statistically negligible. And when we consider,
too, that these men and women, relieved on God's account from the duty to
reproduce, did everything they could to persuade others to do so.[8] In the
nineteenth century the regional map of Malthusianism matched that of the
wane of Roman Catholicism. There is also the fact that one of the world's
most clerical societies, French Canada, was incredibly prolific.

The Waxing of New France

The example of Quebec, in fact, serves to refute another hypothesis: that the
French are "naturally" less fecund than other peoples. How can we credit
this when we know that the 6,000 French peasant men and women who emigrated to New France under Richelieu, Mazarin and Colbert numbered
10,000 around 1690, grew to 20,000 in 1713 and 70,000 in 1763? The 60,000
who remained there after the Treaty of Paris—which ceded New France

(Canada) to the British in 1763—left absolutely to themselves, rejecting intermarriage with the British, multiplied until they reached 9 million around 1960, or 1,500 times more than their immigrant ancestors.[9] At this rate, the French of 1640 would have given us a population of 30 billion today.

As far as natural fecundity is concerned, seventeenth-century French families were every bit as productive as their American cousins. The rate of increase was the same: a birth every twenty-four or, at the most, thirty months—the nursing period—over an average of eighteen years.

Natural fecundity . . . but nature, in the Old World, was awesomely capricious. Three differences separated New and old France. First, the number of families shattered by the death of a spouse and so limited to one or two children was greater in European France; in Canada, where the adult mortality rate was far lower, large families were the rule. Second, contraception spread quickly in France, while the French Canadians, sure of subsistence, ignored it. Finally, a third of the children born in Continental France died in their first year and half died before reaching marriageable age; malnutrition and disease slashed life expectancy there to a mere twenty-five years. In New France, however, instead of maintaining the population at a stable level, fecundity tripled the settlers' numbers with each successive generation—decupling them in one hundred years, centupling them in two centuries.

The Food Barrier

The prodigious fertility of New France seems to us to point to the real reasons for old France's sterility. In a subsistence economy, before the advent of modern medicine and the introduction of modern technology, demographic growth was blocked by the subsistence barrier. The numbers of the living increased only if they had enough food for survival. In France, they did not.

Recent research strongly suggests that when average yields of good wheat land and vineyards are balanced against those of poorer soil, a density of roughly 40 persons per square kilometer was the most that western Europe's traditional rural economy could support. France, perhaps because its soil was the easiest to work, the most naturally fertile, had reached that limit long before its neighbors. It was doomed, barring a technical and economic revolution, to stay there. With nine tenths of its population on the land, isolated on smallholdings, a France unable to expand beyond its borders could not feed more than 20 million inhabitants. And a natural disaster might at any time drag the population down below that fateful limit. Only misfortune could regulate shifts in population levels. The natural fertility of the French pushed their numbers violently upward; countervailing violence was needed to bring them back into balance. This was provided by the murderous misery of famine, malnutrition and disease.

A Terrifying Biological Balance

Contemporary evidence abounds for those willing to seek it: complaints by officials and estates of the realm, letters to Vincent de Paul, horrors recounted by Raoul Feuillet during the Fronde. Although, by the late eighteenth century, people no longer died en masse of hunger, food was still atrociously scarce. Listen to the philanthropic baron of Montyon in 1778: "I saw the latest period of misery. I saw hunger transformed into passion; people, in regions where crops had failed, wandering, set adrift by pain and stripped of everything, envying the lot of domestic animals, spreading over the fields to eat grass and share the food of wild animals. . . . There is hardly any city, any province where subsistence has not been compromised."[10] The Ancien Régime would perish in a famine year—the monarchy died because it did not assure people their daily bread.

Plague, famine, war. Throughout the seventeenth and eighteenth centuries, at every mass in each of the four parishes of Provins—and probably in most of the other 40,000 churches in the kingdom—the ardent prayer was repeated: *Libera nos a peste, fame et bello.* Had the third of these scourges, a political accident, and the first, an epidemiological accident, nothing to do with the second, which was an economic accident? In fact, they were probably linked in a terrible chain reaction.

In a study of fundamental importance[11] that nevertheless came to the notice of only a few experts, Jean Meuvret established a relationship between the Ancien Régime's demographic decline and its "subsistence crises." A poor harvest, even just the fear of one, sent prices soaring; in Provins, the price of rye went up 860 percent in the six years from 1688 to 1694. People speculated, cornered markets. These were the times of "dearness." They struck all those who could not pay inflated prices—the majority of the French. Children were dispatched to beg at crossroads. People rushed to buy rotten, fermented, spurred grain at higher prices than good wheat commanded before the shortage. Grass was torn from the roadsides and boiled; green wheat was plucked before it could ripen.

Nonsubsistence in a Subsistence Economy

Famines were merely the critical spasms in an era of chronic malnutrition. A series of bad years was fatal. Two severe winters, three unseasonable summers, and hunger gripped the land with its menacing bands of beggars, its swarms of vermin (including the lice that carried typhus), its invasion of rats bearing the terrible fleas that spread bubonic plague. The weakest in the population were mowed down. It was a permanent massacre of the innocents.[12]

The nobility's wars were disastrous only in an already disaster-prone country. A prosperous population could withstand the requisitioning of food, the taxes, the depredations of the soldiers. A people at the edge of starvation could not support the added imposts, still less the passage of troops and their cortège of marauders.

Rude agricultural methods, low and irregular productivity, the vicious cycles of degradation—ignorance, superstition, dirt, overcrowding in filthy hovels—these were the direct causes of France's hecatombs. But why didn't the expansion of trade and industry, the technical progress, the increase in farm output, the new crops that changed the lives of England and Holland in the seventeenth century fertilize France as well? This is the real question.

A Static Society

Here our hypothesis begins to assume a clearer shape. The plaster corset around the body of France molded by Richelieu and hardened by Colbert rendered French society static at the very period when other societies were swinging into action.

Fénelon thought so in 1694. "The only science of government taught to you by those who brought you up," he wrote to Louis XIV, "was that of mistrust. . . . Your ministers have shaken and toppled all the old maxims of state to raise your authority to the highest point. . . . You have everything in your hands, and no one can now live but on your gifts."[13] Fénelon found the sickness where few were used to seeking it—within the rigorous centralism established by Richelieu as a temporary expedient in a perilous time, which had degenerated, under the name of Colbertism, into a permanent system that did violence to both men and nature. A "French sickness" can already be seen poking through the Ancien Régime.

With an expanding market economy creating jobs in trades and services, France too would have had enough food to feed twice, then four times as many French, and there would surely have been that doubling and quadrupling of France's population. The problem was not in getting people born, but in preventing them from dying. Although the market economy path was nearly closed to the country by the failure of Colbertism, it was the one on which France gingerly—too gingerly—finally stepped out. Under Louis XV and Louis XVI, the population slowly increased.

Mortality regressed slightly in proportion to slight economic advances. A few ports, a few big cities[14] embarked on a trade economy. And these exchanges whipped up other economic activities. The times of "dearness," the epidemics, came less frequently. Prices rose, of course, but moderately and regularly, indicating a growth in earnings that fostered modernization. Markets expanded. But this progressive movement got under way a century later than in England and Holland, and it is still too slow.

Malthusianism, Conscious and Unconscious

During the decades of poverty, the French learned most of all to fear child-birth. There were too many mouths to feed; people lost confidence in their ability to support their families. They were the first and, for a long time, the only people in the West to learn birth control. This alarmed Montyon: "Nature is being deceived," he wrote in 1778, "even in the villages."

We have recently learned that deliberate restraints on childbirth were practiced in France beginning in the second half of the eighteenth century. Experts long believed that the birth control methods—known as the "baleful secrets"—used since remotest antiquity by courtesans and members of the upper classes were not generally adopted by the lower classes until the late nineteenth century. This was true for other countries. But France, a century behind the United Kingdom in its Industrial Revolution, was by a curious symmetry a century ahead of it in contraception.[15]

The Revolution triggered an excess of births: the future was promising. Suddenly, in 1799, the rate swerved again, in a direction it was to maintain until 1940. The old society's family values had collapsed, but they were not replaced by anything but petit bourgeois individualism. Yet the Revolutionary ideology was aggressive, and it favored population growth. It was not really the Revolution that caused these new demographic misfortunes, but its failure.

The Napoleonic Code reinforced the tendency. In rural France, the rule of equal hereditary shares obliged peasants to limit the number of their children according to the father's ability to compensate those children alienated from the land. Everyone was forced into a kind of shabby human bookkeeping in a narrow world bounded not by the frontiers of a whole society, but by the narrow limits of each family.

Prosperity Through Overpopulation

Conversely, Holland and Britain discovered the secret of economic dynamism even before they reached the density limit of 40. They would simply slip past the barrier. In keeping with their changing economy, they would maintain an unrestrained demographic vitality, a joyous confidence in life. They quickly understood that in an expanding society, prosperity and fecundity are sisters. And that all restrictive practices—curbs on free trade, protection against competition in industry and agriculture, birth control—merely shore each other up.

Paradoxically England, where Malthus was born, remained determinedly anti-Malthusian; it was France, where Malthus was never officially accepted, that became the promised land for his doctrine a century before it was established. Malthusianism defined the demographic limits of an agrarian civilization at a time when its country of origin had already repudiated it, but France adopted the Malthusian rejection of life. Because it had fewer children, there were fewer customers for its commerce, fewer workers for its industry, business took shallower roots and French colonies had fewer settlers. Above all, the motivation toward progress was diminished.

An Alarming Outlook

In 1946, France seemed to be moving into a new period. In the following twenty-three years it added 10 million to its population, an increase of 25 percent; it had needed 135 years to add the previous 10 million. This was the first time in three centuries that we can talk of rapid population growth. Had we reached our demographic revolution? Unfortunately not.

The increase was due not only to a higher birth rate but also to the prolongation of life expectancy, which rose in fifteen years from age sixty to seventy-two. There was a real increase in the birth rate, but to think of it as the much-vaunted baby boom is exaggerated: the birth rate between 1946 and 1963 was a merely honorable 18 to 20 per 100. This is a long way from the 60 per 100 achieved by the Canadian French in the eighteenth and nineteenth centuries.

In 1964, after only eighteen years of healthy growth, the birth rate dropped. We had barely replaced the previous generation. After 1972, the downward trend became more accentuated: there were fewer than 730,000 births in 1975, versus 830,000 in 1969 and 870,000 in 1948—not to mention the average of 1.1 million to 1.2 million annually during the three theoretically stagnant reigns preceding the Revolution. France had returned to the social suicide of Malthusianism.

There was nothing accidental about this regression. The accident was the boom, caused by three favorable factors. The first was the series of pro-childbirth measures adopted from 1938 to 1945, such as government-allocated family allowances. Second, a rather novel mystique of expansionism and faith in the future, partly generated by the first of the postwar governments' Five-Year Plans. Finally, there was a widespread and lucid feeling that our poor demographic showing had contributed to the disaster of 1940.

The euphoria was short-lived. Around 1963 the country was flooded with North African repatriates, there was a miners' strike and protest movements by farmers, shopkeepers and others whom the expansion had passed by; the French were experiencing the anguish of change, the irritations of growth, fear of the future. Family allowances failed to keep pace with inflation. Experts thinking in worldwide terms began to spread terror of an overpopulated earth.

Eighteen years of demographic expansion constitutes too recent and too fragile a movement to erase the long tradition of three centuries of stagnation. When growth is confined within such narrow margins, only slight variations are needed to reverse its trends. The elimination of three positive factors was alone sufficient to halt the 1946–63 advance: a failure to continue extending the average lifespan; a decline in immigration; and the persistence of unwanted births.

Life expectancy, continuing to lengthen until 1960, increased to sixty-eight years for men, seventy-five for women, and there it stuck. Enormous progress in medical science will be needed to extend these limits even slightly. Immigrant labor—Polish, Italian, Spanish, Portuguese—had been the chief regenerative factor. The newcomers were easily assimilable Europeans from Catholic societies. Then one by one these springs ran dry.

Finally, it was the unwanted births that, throughout those eighteen years of French demographic redressment, pushed the birth rate over that of deaths. Our society obtained surreptitiously the children it needed for progress—children the parents would have preferred to withhold from it. Now, birth control is increasingly effective in foiling nature's wiles.

A Tragic Failure

While France once more assumed its traditional attitudes of mistrusting life, of reluctance to face risks, the power game expanded beyond its old European boundaries. Now the scale is worldwide. In 1850, there was still 1 French man or woman for every 34 people on earth; in 1977, the ratio was 1 to 83 and, at the current rate, there will be only 1 to 120 by the year 2000. Within two human lifetimes, France will have shrunk proportionally by three fourths.

Of course, the Third World's population explosion, fostered by medical progress, is far more responsible for this relative decline than our own languor. But just suppose that our population density were merely *equal* to that of West Germany, instead of the *double* it was three centuries ago: there would be 135 million of us today. We would be fifth in world ranking, the most populous state in Europe.

With this perspective in mind, the relapse in France since 1964 takes on a truly tragic dimension that neither public opinion nor the country's leaders yet seem to have perceived. It is a fact that most of the nations in which Caucasians predominate have followed the same sinking birth-rate curve since 1964. But in those other countries the decline is unprecedented, and in France it is dropping us back into a centuries-old rut. Densely populated countries can allow themselves a pause; an underpopulated country like France cannot.

What is most disturbing about the French case is that the new collapse occurred just at a time when prosperity might have allowed us to hope for a sharp increase in the numbers of our young people. The nonworking proportion of the population is higher in France than in any other industrialized nation: each 1,000 working French support 1,770 inactive members of the population, versus 1,230, for example, in West Germany. And the proportion can only widen between now and the year 2000. It will be hard to progress when ever greater effort is needed merely to maintain the living standard we already have. France is becoming a unique case, its decadence inscribed in its statistics.

The Barriers Are Mental

Yet the French still fail to recognize the correlation between demographic and economic growth. How can demographic stagnation be blamed for economic stagnation, they ask, when a galloping population boom is ruining expansion in the underdeveloped countries? Deeply imbued with the dogma of human equality, they reject the notion that the effects of population growth vary with a society's level of advancement.

When an underdeveloped country takes its initial steps toward development, the first persons to be protected by medical progress are those who are most vulnerable, children and the elderly. The working population diminishes proportionately, income available for investment is reduced, the rate of development is slowed.[16]

In countries that are already economically airborne, on the other hand, population growth stimulates economic activity. Because the combination of conditions required for development exists, a pronounced excess of births over deaths results in constant renewal of people's needs and tastes. In Europe's two postwar economic miracles, much is owed to excess population: West Germany absorbed 14 million refugees from the East; the Po Valley received 3 million immigrants from the *mezzo-giorno*.

The French subconsciously reject these realities. The certainty remains deeply rooted in their minds that population growth results in unemployment and poverty: "The more mouths there are to feed, the less we have to eat." Now, at the end of the twentieth century, we are still reacting as our ancestors did in the eighteenth. We have not yet accepted the rules of economic development. We retain the mentality of an underdeveloped people, though overpopulated in terms of our resources.[17]

CHAPTER 12

Decadence

We have seen France's natural movement blocked. We have seen this nation seize up just when the other northern nations began to bubble with a zest to live, create, procreate, to open out to the world and to conquer it. Now we must understand that this reversal was not exclusive to France. A whole constellation of countries accompanied us in our misfortune. Why? This is one of history's mysteries—one of those mysteries that are so blinding we refuse to see them.

A Strange Torpor

When the Middle Ages ended and modern times began, it still seemed that the key to the world's destiny would long remain in the hands of that part of Europe that was to remain Catholic after the reformation. The "Latin sisters"—Italy, Spain, Portugal, France—and then Flanders, southern Germany, Austria and Poland, waxed rich. They produced artistic marvels, their businessmen were the world's most gifted, their tradesmen enterprising, their craftsmen able; they sent sailors and adventurers to discover new worlds.

By the beginning of the seventeenth century, that part of Europe had increased its territorial holdings immensely. The Portuguese, the Spanish, the French had conquered empires or established trading posts in Africa, Asia, even China. The whole of America was in fact Latin. Italy, divided into dozens of states, could participate in this expansion only through such isolated pioneers or mercenaries as Columbus, Amerigo Vespucci and Giovanni da Verrazano. But the world's greatest artists and most efficient bankers were Italian, and its dominance in governing the Church gave it enormous influence.

If there was a gap then between northern and southern Europe, it was the north that lagged behind. The United Provinces, Britain, Scandinavia, the Hanseatic League[1] were merely the northern markets for a zone of prosperity controlled by the Latin countries.

Then, shortly after the year 1600, a strange torpor overcame all the Catholic countries, especially the Latin nations. The Dutch and the English took the lead in Western expansionism. In a kind of historical landslip, the

West's epicenter moved from the Mediterranean to the North Sea. There was no sign, really none, by which people then could have foreseen this shift, and historians today still find nothing in the preceding century to explain it.

The Decline of Portugal

In the sixteenth century, Portugal, enriched by countless overseas possessions, glittered with the gleam of its blue ceramic tiles, its cameos, its palaces, with the brilliance of the universities at Coimbra and Oporto, the poems of Luis de Camoëns.

No sooner had the Moslems been driven back to Africa than Portugal's kings, seconded by their nobles and the country's middle class, rushed to conquer ports on the Moroccan coast, then Madeira in 1425, the Azores in 1427, the Río de Oro in 1436, the Cape Verde Islands in 1456, São Jorge da Minha (in what is now Ghana) in 1465; they reached Angola in 1482, Brazil in 1500. None of this would have been possible without the thirst for adventure that drove the conquerors or the prospecting genius of such men as Prince Henry of Portugal (1394–1460), called the Navigator because, although he never sailed anywhere himself, he sent his captains to navigate the Atlantic.

Henry was no romantic dreamer. Realistic, a lover of concrete facts and painstaking detail, this organizer of voyages to the unknown was an amazingly modern manager attentive to every aspect of the ventures he promoted. For example, he was fascinated by scientific research. He encouraged the study of astronomy, meteorology, oceanography and surveying, especially their practical applications. As technician and impresario, he improved navigation instruments, improved his caravelles. His fortress at Sagres, on the continent's westernmost point, became a school of navigation and colonization; Diaz, Magellan, Vasco da Gama and Columbus studied there. Henry called in outside experts, promoting the kind of brain drain and scientific cross-fertilization we think we invented.[2] He organized men into work groups, antedating the Americans' "think tanks" by five hundred years. From his clifftop fortress, he launched each caravelle a few days' journey farther than the last, ordering it back to report its observations—much like the successive Apollo rockets that finally reached the moon.

At the end of the fifteenth century, papal bulls gave Portugal dominion over all the new lands discovered in half the world; mastery of the other half was awarded to Spain.[3]

Yet, one hundred years later, Portugal was immobilized. Since then, it has seemed incapable of adapting itself to a changing world. It let slip its chance for an industrial revolution. Until well past the middle of the twentieth century, it preserved the organization and attitudes of the Middle Ages.

Disconcerting Spain

Spain, too, was expanding triumphantly in the fifteenth and early sixteenth centuries. Even before Cortés landed in Mexico in 1519, the country had carved out an empire in America that included part of the West Indies, the isthmus of Panama, Florida. Within thirty years that empire swelled inordinately; Aztec Mexico, Inca Peru fell to a few men, a few harquebuses, a few horses, but chiefly to the absolute weapons of energy, imagination and faith.

The conquest of Central and South America soon brought gold[4]—the "fabulous metal" which this Eldorado was "ripening" in "its far-off mines"—flowing into Spain. It wasn't hazard that brought this new wealth into the Iberian peninsula, for an economic mentality had burgeoned there in the Middle Ages. In the sixteenth century, Barcelona was heavily industrialized; in Seville, 1,600 looms provided work for 13,000 people;[5] and Toledo and Segovia were crammed with manufactures of silk and textiles.[6]

Yet we next see a Spain enmeshed—even though colonization had begun to earn capital, to mobilize society, to forge fearless men. But values also changed, and radically.[7] Public spirit burned what it had adored: adventure, the spirit of enterprise. Mercantile Europe noted in this hitherto ardent people what it called "Spanish indolence"—a disdain for economic activity. The nation turned away from everything touching on production and trade to concern itself entirely with affairs of the Church, the court, chivalry. "They are infatuated with nobility," wrote one observer.[8]

In every society, the public tends to emulate an elite model. In Spain, Don Quixote replaced the *conquistadores*. Hidalgos—those entitled to wear a sword—monopolized the bureaucracy.[9] In Aragon, no one who had engaged in trade was allowed to sit in the *Cortes* (parliament).[10] People snatched at the chance to claim status as hidalgos and those who could not pretended to it anyway. Everyone longed for conscription into the high bureaucracy of the equestrian order that dominated Spain.

Even before the French, the kings of Spain had expressed this new spirit by creating an administrative monarchy. Just as it drained off its colonies' gold, so it drained the nation's vitality, hoarding it in inactivity or spoiling it in luxury. Even more than in France, this hierarchical, centralized system neutralized every social class: the aristocracy, deprived of real power, was disgusted with land speculation and the notion of economic utility; the middle class turned away from trade and industry and aspired to public office; the clergy became an agent of political power; and the people were kept in awesome poverty. Spain stockpiled its treasure instead of investing it.[11] The country imported the manufactured goods it disdained to produced.[12]

Today, despite rapid progress since World War II, vast sectors of the economy are still archaic in Spain. According to a recent survey,[13] 9 percent of the labor force at the end of Franco's reign had received no schooling. Small farms hold too high a proportion of labor on the land. Modernization of large-scale agriculture is slow because capital is short. Those industries which have been modernized are controlled by foreigners. Spain's trade deficit is impressive; like Portugal's, it is brought into balance only by two factors characteristic of underdevelopment: tourism, and money sent home by Spaniards working abroad. Consumers are imported and producers exported as the country feels its way along the path from dictatorship to democracy.

Latin America: Landed, Hierarchical, Archaic

It is not true then, contrary to the usually accepted explanation, that Portugal and Spain were sterilized by their colonies. The fact is that it was Portugal and Spain that sterilized their part of America, while the northern part, colonized by the Dutch and the English, sailed boldly into the adventure of development.

Latin America's assets, if they were to be properly exploited, are every bit as rich as those of the United States and Canada. But Latin America has shared the destiny of its Iberian mother countries. The descendants of the Spanish and Portuguese colonists have merely carved out fiefs for themselves. Despite countless revolutions, they have often held on to their land, their latifundia, haciendas and fazendas. This hereditary caste, anchored to its traditions, long used its income merely to build palaces for itself.

Such dynamism as exists in Latin American economies comes from abroad, and usually returns there: copper mines in Chile, iron in Brazil, oil in Venezuela. The countries' nationals, no matter how rich they are, make not the slightest effort to buy out foreign owners. The conquerors' heirs prefer not to be involved in trade or industry.

Has the United States pillaged these countries and is it still doing so? In that case, why has the United States's hegemony over the American hemisphere fostered underdevelopment in Latin America and overdevelopment in Canada? An economy, a nation, is colonized only if it is colonizable.

Why, with natural resources as rich in the south as in the north, and despite a considerably earlier start in the south, has so wide a gap opened between the two halves of a single hemisphere?[14] In the 1820s, only half a century after the North American War of Independence, the Latin American colonists did shrug off the yokes of their mother countries. But their imitation of the United States was confined to political independence; it was not extended to include social organization, individual freedom or the northern scale of values.

Italy: From Vitality to Collapse

Renaissance Italy was a place where art blossomed, but it was also a place of prosperity and vitality. The industrial market economy, genuinely capitalistic, really got under way there. It was in Venice, Genoa, Florence, Milan that the *commenda*—ancestor of our joint-stock companies—appeared in the thirteenth century, to be followed soon afterward by the first *compagnie*, progenitors of the modern corporation.

By the fifteenth century the powerful Medici firm, with its group of theoretically independent *compagnie*, was in truth a holding company. In 1455, a Milanese living in Bruges sued the local Medici affiliate for delivering nine defective bales of wool bought from the Medici branch in London. The court advised the plaintiff to bring his suit in London because the two companies were separate. A court today would issue the same decision, notes the American historian R. de Roover, if an American tried to sue Standard Oil of New Jersey for shipment of defective merchandise sold by Standard Oil of New York on the grounds that the Rockefeller family controlled both firms.[15] Like the Rockefellers, the Medicis had learned to spread their risks.

The Italians were not merely bankers and merchants; they were also entrepreneurs, innovators, technical pioneers. When Leonardo da Vinci sought employment at the court of Ludovico il Moro in 1482, he offered his services as an engineer: "I have drawn up plans for very light footbridges. . . . I can re-channel the water in the moats of places under siege. . . . I can vie with any other architect as well in constructing buildings, public or private, as in bringing water from one place to another." And he added, as though incidentally, "in painting and sculpture, I do not fear comparison either."[16]

His was not an isolated case. It reflects a system of values shared by a whole people, one that made it a nation of technicians. Statistical tables have been devised of scientific discoveries and technological inventions by century and by country. They show that between the years 800 and 1600, Italy produced 25 to 40 percent of the West's scientific discoveries and technical innovations.[17] Suddenly, beginning in 1600, this spring started to dry up. And since 1726, Italy's contribution has dropped to a mere 2 to 4 percent. Italy would soon appear in history as no more than a mosaic of poor countries, of dozing cities dreaming of their lost glories.

A Cut Flower

Traditional historians blame this sudden decadence on the "great discoveries." The trade routes, they say, deserted the Mediterranean for the Atlantic. But why were Portugal and Spain, which fronted on the Atlantic, prosperous at the same time as Italy, and why did they decline at the same time it did? Look at a map of the world: Lisbon, La Coruña, Seville and Cadiz are closer to the Americas than London, Rotterdam and Hamburg. Genoa and Naples are nearer to Central and South America, to Africa and Asia, than the big North Sea ports, closer even to North America via the Azores route taken by most sailing ships.

And what if the real causes did lie within the people of the Latin countries? We will not try to pinpoint them here. Let's just give ourselves something to chew on. Lombardy, Venice, Tuscany and Liguria had all been amazingly prosperous when they concentrated on trade, crafts, the textiles and weapons industries. That prosperity dwindled along with their societies' taste for such items. The Italian aristocracy and middle class turned away from production; they squandered their fortunes on Europe's grandest festivals. Art remained, but it was a cut flower: its splendor would dazzle men's eyes for a while yet, but its sap had run dry. The great maritime and trade cities vegetated. In the south, obscurantists fought science and free will as the devil's works. Italy sank into the past.

Industry nevertheless returned to the Po Valley in the nineteenth century. Italy's recent development has raised it again to an honorable rank in the world. But among the nine Common Market states, it brings up the rear, along with Ireland—showing under an average $3,000 in per capita income in 1975, compared to the leaders' average of over $6,000. It has yet to conjugate democracy and efficiency to become a modern society.

Austria and Poland

The Latin nations were not the only ones to suffer.

In the mid-seventeenth century, Austria glowed with the prestige conferred on it by its victories over the Turks, its imperial title, its struggles against the House of France. Yet, as for the Versailles monarchy, an observer can spy the worm in the apple. The yoke of theocratic order burdened the country. Each social class clung to its rights. The state was strictly hierarchical and innovation discouraged; the bureaucracy tightened its hold. The economy and the society remained archaic. The peasantry, representing 90 percent of the population, labored chiefly to maintain aristocratic courtiers in luxury and to supply the state's revenues. The cities were gradually paralyzed by administrative regulation. What ardor remained was concentrated in Vienna.

In 1866, an Austrian army was crushed by the Prussians. While the victory accelerated development in industrialized, free-trading Prussia, it shattered agricultural, ingrown Austria. Its 1918 defeat, which left Germany's basic strength intact, finally sank the Austro-Hungarian Empire.

Poland, too, was amazingly advanced at the end of the fifteenth century. Cracow was the Florence of central Europe; at the Jagellon university, students from all over the Continent heard such illustrious lecturers as Copernicus. A quarter of the male population could read and write. Trade through Gdansk (Danzig) increased steadily.

Then, in the early seventeenth century, decay set in. Poland was the only country where the peasant population increased in proportion to the whole. The cities emptied,[18] and the country was systematically refeudalized. Obscurantism and superstition replaced humanism, curiosity, tolerance. At the Brinicki Palace there were two hundred horses but only seventy books.[19] Poland was ripe for dismemberment and dependence.

A Moving Sidewalk

Austria and Poland share a trait with the Latin countries we have examined. Like them, like France, they remained "Catholic and Roman" after the great schism of Christianity in the sixteenth century. The socio-cultural systems of Reformation and Counter-Reformation countries follow their differences to the logical extremes. Henceforth, the Christian family would have its rich relations and its poor ones.

Before the economic revolution, history was geography. The people— that is, the peasantry—squatted on the land. Their aim was to survive and therefore to encourage as little change as possible. Development converted history into change and, like it or not, countries had to keep pace. They were like a group walking on a diabolical moving sidewalk that raced in reverse: the immobile were quickly swept backward, those walking slowly lost ground slowly, those striding ahead stayed where they were. Only the runners advanced a little.

The countries that felt the full impact of the Counter-Reformation seemed unable to run or even to walk. France could only walk slowly. Why?

CHAPTER 13

The Soaring Protestant Societies

The Protestant nations ran fast on this moving sidewalk. By the middle of the seventeenth century, more than one witness had already noticed the gap separating them from the Catholic countries. In the eighteenth century the breach was wide enough to bring cries of alarm from Fontenelle and Montesquieu, Voltaire and Diderot. Little England's victorious resistance to the great French Empire increased French Anglophilia.

The Netherlands

"Brittany is as big as Holland," a Breton autonomist stubbornly insisted to me. "When Brittany was annexed [by France], it was even more heavily populated. Now it has five times fewer people and it's ten times poorer. That's what France brought us."

His comparison was striking—and accurate. He forgot only one thing: that it could apply to any French province except the Ile-de-France. Save for the core surrounding Paris, the whole country that annexed Brittany fell victim to the same sickness as the provinces it took over.

How then can we avoid amazement at the paradoxical history of Holland, so poorly endowed by nature and yet so important in the past three hundred years to the world's economy? Its climate is harsh: strong winds, hard winters, rain and fog. It is tiny, some 13,000 square miles—the size of four or five French departments. And a good half of that had to be wrested from the sea with great effort, or protected against flooding rivers. There was a time when its coasts offered no safe anchorage. It lacked both raw materials and power sources.

Yet, since the beginning of the seventeenth century, Holland has reinforced its identity as a victorious society, stubbornly intent on enriching itself. As early as 1604, the British were taking Holland as a model; "they are," one contemporary document noted, "the world's best businessmen." Their financiers, traders, navigators took over from the Portuguese, establishing themselves in South Africa, in central India, in the Indian Ocean, the Malay Peninsula, the Spice Islands. They maintained a lively trade with China and Japan. Their hulking transports plied the Mediterranean and the Baltic. The East India Company was founded in 1602, the West India Company in 1621, the year the Dutch founded their first colony in North America. Soon their trading posts and colonies—at the Cape of Good Hope, in Ceylon, Java, Sumatra, Formosa—formed a belt around the world.[1]

Even before England, this small Calvinist nation was in the forefront of the merchant world. The Netherlands adopted a policy of tolerance, becoming a magnet to foreigners. The government it chose was elective and decentralized. By 1614, the United Provinces had more seamen than Spain, France, England and Scotland combined. In 1609, a stock exchange and a bank were opened in Amsterdam, soon to become the world's busiest port.

Stimulated by the country's trade, some industries prospered—shipbuilding, Delft pottery, cloth. A network of cities developed. Capital speculated in agriculture; it had to, to reclaim thousands of miles of land from the sea and to rationalize production. Holland achieved the West's first agricultural rationalization—to this day the most brilliant. In the seventeenth century it specialized in what it produced best: flowers, flax, hops, tobacco, artificial fodder, highly bred cattle that became the world's finest dairy animals. Everything else was imported.

True, it was eclipsed in the eighteenth century, when England and Hamburg forged ahead. But it later resumed its leadership. Today, it acts as a leaven in the Common Market, and Rotterdam is now the world's busiest port. Some of the world's biggest corporations are Dutch, achieving international standing, like the Netherlanders themselves, through a combination of innovation, energy and know-how.

A Nation of Shopkeepers

In the sixteenth century, few English were yet to be found on the world's highroads. The English merchant adventurers went no farther than the Baltic to sell their cloth; they scarcely ventured into the Mediterranean. Despite Shakespeare's genius and the pomp of Elizabeth I, England was still a very small country.

By the beginning of the twentieth century, the United Kingdom led the world. Its small rural population had become true agribusinessmen; the overall population, four fifths of it concentrated in the cities, continued to increase. London was the world's leading port, its principal market. Britain's merchant marine constituted 45 percent of the total world tonnage and, under the provisions of the two-powers standard, its war fleet was bigger than those of its two nearest rivals combined. It was the world's top financier, its biggest investor. The pound sterling was the world's currency of exchange.[2] Britain was Europe's first industrial power.* Its empire embraced a fourth of the globe's population.

"A nation of shopkeepers," Napoleon had contemptuously called it. To which, two centuries in advance, Sir Walter Raleigh had replied: "He who commands trade commands the world's wealth and so the world itself."

It was through trade that the English made their entry on the world's stage. Sheep grazed their pastures. To sell their wool, markets were sought, a fleet built and protected. At the beginning of the seventeenth century, only a few years after the Dutch, Englishmen settled in India and started to colonize that part of the Americas ignored by the Spanish and the Portuguese. Business transformed everything it touched more than a century before Pitt proclaimed that "Britain's policy is Britain's trade."

This first economic breakthrough signalled other changes. In the middle of the seventeenth century, England's rural world changed under the direction of an active and enlightened aristocracy symbolized by "Lord Turnip" (Lord Townsend), who won his nickname by campaigning for crop rotation based on turnips and clover.[3] When rotation replaced the fallow system, it was as if the country's arable land had doubled in extent.

On this followed the irresistible rise of what would henceforth be called industry. Innovations multiplied and cross-fertilized each other. By discovering how to wed coke to iron, by such inventions as John Kay's flying shuttle and Edmund Cartwright's power loom, by harnessing steam, Britain laid the foundations of unprecedented power.

Following in Holland's footsteps, the British—by their ability to trade, innovate, undertake and risk—triggered the process that was to lead them toward a new civilization, technical, industrial and urban. Toward this world, newer than the one Columbus found, other nations, every nation, would try to follow them, more or less successfully.

The Swiss Miracle

Switzerland is so mountainous that half the country's land is useless for cultivation or even grazing. It has some water power, virtually no minerals.

Calvin roughly fashioned Geneva to serve as a Protestant Rome. Switzerland then became a refuge for Protestants driven out of France; they were followed by manufacturers, traders, makers of special steels and food products, pharmaceutical research laboratories. Now the country's banknotes are backed by more than their face value in gold; its banks and insurance companies are prosperous, its financiers operate on an international scale. Swiss

---

* Britain's share of world industrial output in 1850 was 60 percent, and it was still 35 percent in 1890. Then it was passed by the United States; German industry outstripped it just before 1914.

industry uses a minimum of raw materials and a maximum of human ingenuity to produce high-quality, high-precision wares.[4]

What is most striking, perhaps, is the harmony Switzerland has achieved between industry and agriculture, between rural and city life. There is hardly any federal government; the country is still a collection of local administrations. Isn't this what gives it its flexibility in adapting to economic change, its enviable social consensus, so nicely balanced between equilibrium and movement?

"Self-Made Nation"

In two hundred years, the United States has grown from a small rural society of 4 million people to a continental country of over 200 million, the world's most powerful nation. It would be wrong to think of this preeminence as recent; American industry topped Britain's in 1890, and has held the world's lead ever since.

America's demographic thrust both revealed and spurred that economic growth. Between 1790 and 1860, the population doubled every twenty-three years, reaching 32 million in 1860. Its 50 million in 1880 made it the most populous nation in the West. The country is often represented as an empty bin filled up by Europe. In fact, it received only 25 million immigrants from 1820 to 1920; they and their descendants simply went there to share in its natural vitality. America chiefly owes its progress to itself. To create, grow, believe in itself—such is this society's motto. Its first technical innovations came from Britain and Holland, but inventions were soon popping up everywhere in the new country. In 1814, Boston merchant Francis Cabot Lowell, helped by a workman named Paul Moody, built a spinning and weaving plant, the first to combine in a single plant the textile industry's two fundamental operations. Oliver Evans built a high-pressure steam engine. Robert Fulton, rebuffed by Napoleon, developed the work of John Fitch and James Rumsey in building the first steamboats. In 1846, Elias Howe manufactured a sewing machine; it had been invented by Barthélemy Thimonnier of Lyon in 1825, but his invention was ignored and he died in poverty. It was in 1846, too, that Morse developed the magnetic telegraph. By 1851, when Geissenhainer invented a way of decarbonizing steel, people were already talking about the "American system of manufacturing": mass production of standardized, interchangeable parts.

A Complete Case of Civilization

Thus we find two Protestant countries, England and Holland, launching our mercantile and industrial civilization, and other Protestant countries as its leading examples. But let's by-pass the exemplary cases and compare average records. Here again, the contrast is curious.

On the one hand, take the twelve most developed countries among those of a predominantly Protestant culture: Switzerland, Sweden, the United States, Canada, Denmark, Norway, West Germany, the Netherlands, Australia, Finland, New Zealand and the United Kingdom. On the other, the most developed of the predominantly Catholic countries: Belgium, France, Austria, Italy, Spain, Poland, Venezuela, Ireland, Portugal, Argentina, Uruguay and Chile. In 1976, the average national per capita income in the first group exceeded $6,500; in the second, it was below $3,500.[5] And the Protestant countries are far ahead in scientific research.

These countries' development was not only economic, technical and scientific. It also went hand in hand with their political and social progress. It is in the countries marked by Protestantism that low income, inequalities, poor hygiene and censorship tend most strongly to disappear, that the level of democratic consensus is highest and democracy most deeply rooted. These are not merely industrialized nations; they are countries in which a number of constants—social, political, juridical, cultural—united by mysterious correlations, make up a complete case of civilization.

Humanity's Long Procession

Here then is one of history's greatest enigmas. Why this irresistible wave of expansion that swept up only some countries beginning in the early seventeenth century? These few locomotive-nations represent a very small fraction of humanity, and the past three hundred years is a tiny fraction of man's history since his appearance on the earth some 3 or 4 million years ago. Yet this small group of Protestant countries shunted humanity off the track on which, through the ages, it had been alternately pushed forward by its fecundity and dragged backward by the periodic misery to which its very advances condemned it. This handful of countries enabled humanity to escape the tragic equilibrium by which epidemics, famine and war redressed an excessive birth rate.

"The country with the most advanced industry only shows those that follow it the image of their own future," wrote Karl Marx in his preface to *Capital*. This is exactly what the Protestant countries did. They broke away from humanity's long procession to show the others the image of development.

CHAPTER 14

At Different Speeds

After the Counter-Reformation, the nations that remained Catholic dozed. After the Reformation, the Protestant nations awoke. Let's simply say *after;* for the moment, nothing allows us to say *because of.*

The dividing line is not so clear everywhere, however. It cuts some societies in two—a single people, with identical antecedents, yet split into two sometimes extremely unequal communities. Does the disturbing economic inferiority we find in Catholic countries reemerge between the Protestant and Catholic communities within a single country? If so, the religious factor clearly must be given decisive weight; the national factor would cease to coincide with it, might perhaps even confuse it.

There is no lack of examples to supply this supporting evidence. Let's look at four: those of Germany, Ireland, France and Canada.[1]

Germany: Catholic and Protestant

Although it was born in Germany, the Reformation did not conquer all the Germans. It shattered their religious unity. Since then, Germany has been a marquetry pattern of Protestants and Catholics.

Its Protestant areas did not enter the industrial age as quickly as Holland, England, Switzerland or even the United States. Before we seize on this as an exception to the rule, it should be noted that Reformed Germany is Lutheran, not Calvinist. It launched the Reformation, but it clung to its early Protestantism. Lutheranism remains a Church, anti-Roman of course, but still a Church, hierarchical and dogmatic. Psychologists and sociologists place it somewhere between Catholicism and Calvinism. This must have some connection with the fact that the Calvinist countries began their development in the seventeenth century, the Lutheran countries only in the nineteenth, while the Catholic countries waited until the twentieth.

It can also be noted that Prussia's image is very similar to that of the Catholic countries: a strong central authority bolstered by a powerful military establishment, a hierarchical, extremely disciplined society. A warrior state more than a Protestant society. Like the Lutheran Church, the Prussian state remained impregnated with Romanism.

Yet when Germany began to modernize its agriculture and industry in the nineteenth century, it was the Protestants who dragged the rest of the country with them. In the pluri-religious principalities—and in Germany's overall equilibrium—it was the Protestants (or the Jews) who usually controlled big business, big finance, big industry. Protestant Prussia had a well-developed railway network in 1840, before France. Germany's Catholics stuck chiefly to small businesses and household crafts.

In 1900, Max Weber took as the point of departure for his thesis on *The Protestant Ethic and the Spirit of Capitalism* a study by his disciple Martin Offenbacher on the situations of Catholics and Protestants in the state of Baden.[2] Offenbacher showed that the Catholics, less urbanized, less cultivated, were shopkeepers, artisans, office workers, farmers. The Protestants had moved in force into the ranks of industrialists, technicians, bankers, traders. Subsistence farming remained largely the rule on the smallholdings in the rural, Catholic west and south; the Protestants in the north and east quickly adopted modern agricultural methods.

This conflict of influence came to a test of strength in the nineteenth century. In a Germany broken up into a cluster of small states, the clash of vitality and immobility was polarized around the Protestant north, led by Prussia, and the Catholic south, centered in Bavaria and supported by Austria. Vitality won. Germany, united in January 1871 under the Hohenzollern crown, opted for industrialization and expansionism.

The French habitually see the half century (1866–1913) following the Battle of Sadowa,* when Germany's power and potential were really established, in the guise of "Prussian militarism." They too easily forget that the German empire was not centralized "*à la française.*" It was merely a federation of constitutional monarchies, each of which maintained its own dynasty, its parliament, legislation, budget, sometimes even its army and diplomatic corps. Germany remained a complex, heterogeneous, multifarious world—polycentric—in which the Catholic states fully played their part. Change came through flexibility. This too-often misunderstood fact may go far toward explaining Germany's vitality.

At the heart of this diversity there was, nevertheless, a unitary dynamism. In 1906, the Swiss historian Paul Seippel wrote: "Germany today seems to me to be at the beginning of a change that could lead it to the point the most Romanized nations have reached. The administrative spirit is flourishing magnificently."[3] A quarter of a century before the event, Seippel guessed that one day "an illustrious personage would incarnate, not without brilliance, the principle of infallible spiritual power extended to every sector."[4] The personage came from the south—the most Romanized part of the Ger-

---

* The decisive battle of the Seven Weeks' War that confirmed Prussia's hegemony in Germany was fought at Sadowa, in Bohemia, on July 3, 1866.

manic Holy Roman Empire. It was in Bavaria that the Austrian-born Hitler enjoyed his strongest popular support. And most of the conspirators in the July 1944 plot against Hitler were Protestants, mainly Calvinists.

After 1945, as we have seen, under British and American influence, the tendency toward decentralization prevailed in West Germany, forging a link with a centuries-old tradition. And its federative structure seems strong enough to have routed the demons that, behind the shield of centralization, had plagued the German people.

Modern Ireland and Backward Ireland

Here the basic facts are simple, but odd. Eire, the homogeneously Catholic part of Ireland, won its independence in 1921. Ulster, six times smaller than Eire, remained attached to the United Kingdom; its population, half that of its neighbor, is 65 percent Protestant and 35 percent Catholic.

Economically, Eire resembles an underdeveloped country. Agriculture is its leading industry, holding half the country's population on the land and providing the raw materials for three fourths of Eire's manufactured exports, chiefly whisky, beer and sweaters. In any case, exports cover only 70 percent of its imports; tourism alone enables it to balance its payments. Three out of four farms are still primitive, operating at subsistence level.

All this is reflected in Southern Ireland's standard of living, its gross national product is inferior to that of smaller Ulster, for the six counties around Belfast have long been industrialized; it was in the nineteenth century that they began processing flax and building ships.

Can this disparity be traced to a difference in natural resources between Ulster and Eire? Not at all. Indeed, Catholic economic inferiority is just as strong inside Ulster.

Whether we compare wholly Catholic Eire with mainly Protestant Ulster, or the Catholic segment of Ulster with its Protestant population, the correlations are the same. The Protestants have "created" (according to them) or "taken over" (according to the Catholics) the wealth-producing jobs in industry, technology, shipping, big business, banking, insurance. The Catholics are locked into the traditional chores of a subsistence economy— farming, digging peat, fishing, small business, the crafts.

Is this simply a matter of colonial domination? Of course, no Irish Catholic has forgotten the massacre at Drogheda in 1649, when the town's inhabitants—those "miserable savages," as Cromwell called them—were ruthlessly exterminated and English exploitation of Ireland reached its stride. But have the English prevented Irish Catholics since the nineteenth century from modernizing their agriculture, from engaging in trade or developing industry? No, neither in united Ireland until 1921, nor in bi-religious Ulster since 1921, nor, of course, in independent Eire.

The Irish Catholics, like the French, the Spanish, the Portuguese, ran stubbornly up against the population density wall of 40 people per square kilometer. When the wall was breached, there was no relief for them but mass emigration. Throughout the nineteenth century this hemorrhage drained Ireland, mostly to the benefit of the United States. Even if we were to opt for colonial exploitation by Britain as the single explanation for Irish backwardness—and the historical facts in support of this are irrefutable—we would again have to reply with the painful question: Why are the Catholics colonizable where the Protestants are not?

It is no mere theological quarrel that has bred the hatred which for centuries has divided Catholics and Protestants in Ulster. The rivalry there has the ferocity of a holy war, aggravated by racial conflict and a class struggle between an advanced commercial society and a backward agrarian culture.

France's Busy Minority

In the light of the Irish situation, France offers another kind of evidence to support our hypothesis. Here it is the Catholics who are the "oppressors"; the St. Bartholomew's Day massacre (in 1572) was France's Drogheda. But the "oppressed" in France have not reacted as the Irish have. The country's Protestant minority is very small, yet its vitality in proportion to its size exceeds that of the Catholic majority.

When Louis XIV revoked the Edict of Nantes in 1685, Protestants made up barely a tenth of France's population, but they were among its best educated, most enterprising, most progressive citizens. In the century surrounding the revocation, at least a fourth, perhaps as many as half of the country's roughly 2 million Protestants, fled abroad to escape persecution.* The emigrants were often those who, having already succeeded brilliantly in life, felt themselves best equipped to succeed elsewhere. And so they did. Rapidly assimilated in Switzerland, Holland, England, Prussia, and even as far away as Sweden and Finland, many rose to prominence. Deposits in the Bank of Amsterdam doubled almost overnight after 1685. Along with their capital, the French Protestants brought their technical knowledge, their trade secrets and their spirit of adventure.

Meanwhile, the Protestants who remained in France continued to display more economic dynamism than the rest of the population.[5] They excelled in finance, which was the monarchy's weak point. The crown called on their services even after the revocation—the state's well-being took priority over any edict. Barthélemy Herwarth, a commissary to the army of Bernard of Saxony, also acted as agent for Richelieu, Mazarin and Colbert. As Superin-

* The most recent estimate, by Pastor Samuel Mours, places the number who left France *after* the revocation at 250,000. But the period of persecution and flight extended over more than a century.

tendent of Finance in 1650, he used his vast personal fortune to further the king's enterprises. Samuel Bernard took over from him. Louis XIV was careful to ignore their Protestantism. Nor could his successors decently act more sectarian than he toward French or foreign Protestant bankers; Protestantism could erase frontiers.[6]

During and after the Revolution of 1789, it was the Protestants, many of whom returned to France from Switzerland, who along with the Jews, became the powers (virtually the only powers) in French high finance. From then until now, there has not been a single private bank of any importance in France that was not founded by Protestants or Jews.

Browse through the *Yearbook* of the Institut d'Etudes Politiques (established by Protestants in 1870), through the lists of tax officials, the diplomatic corps, business consultants, the Court of Accounts, of big-business managers and industrialists. You will find that the prominence of the Huguenots' descendants in the key sectors of French economic life is out of all proportion to their numbers.

Canadian Codicil to the Revocation

"Ah! If Richelieu and Louis XIV had let the French Protestants migrate to the New World," Daniel Johnson told me when he was Quebec's prime minister, "the first men on the moon would have spoken French, not English."

"Iffy" history is always a little ridiculous. Yet, when we think about it, how can France today fail to regret that its half-million Protestant emigrants did not go to New France? That would have been a very different thing, in numbers and in knowledge, from the 6,000 poor peasants from western France who made up our entire American colonizing force. They would have been three times more numerous than the population in the English colonies. Unlike Britain and Holland, where emigration overseas was made easy for dissenters, France refused to allow its banished and dispersed "religionaries" to try their luck there. Absolutism gave no quarter; it was intolerant even to its exiles.

An Inferiorized Majority

Today, even in Quebec, where 80 percent of the people are French-speaking, English remains the language of power, French the language of the poor. Like Ireland, Quebec poses the problem not of an oppressed minority but of an inferiorized majority. It is not the minority that needs the protection of the law, but the majority. New immigrants there—Italians, Greeks, Germans—perceive this; nine out of ten try to be assimilated into the small group of English speakers, determined to melt into the dominant minority, not the dominated majority.[7]

English-speaking Canadians in Quebec control three of the province's six universities, half its radio and television stations, almost all its industry, its trade and its major financial institutions. The French-speaking population unquestionably holds political power in Quebec, both provincial and municipal, which is essential in a decentralized federal system. But their troubles stem less from law or politics than from attitudes. Out of shame, Quebecois pretend that their tragedy is "linguistic." But English is merely the exterior sign of a dynamic mentality, a dynamic society, French that of a mentality and a society on the defensive.

From the time Champlain arrived in Quebec until the Treaty of Paris in 1763, the French in New France were under the remote control of the home country. The central administration in Paris ruled on "quarrels concerning a cow that strayed into a garden, a row at the church door, even a lady's virtue."[8] Left to its own devices after the Treaty of Paris, this primitive, timorous, inhibited society resisted change. The French in Canada retreated into hierarchical communities under the clergy's authority. Afraid to coexist, they chose isolation.

Is change still possible? The French-Canadian community today feels that it is not catching up to the Anglophones. So prolific until around 1960, it has since registered the sharpest drop in birth rates recorded in any modern society. It is as though the French Canadians had given up an impossible adventure—barring a sudden reversal, of which a few signs are visible.

Germany, Ireland, France, Quebec: a cultural tour that confirms the early lessons learned along our route. Within a given society, some people are liberated by their mentality while others are fettered by theirs. Everywhere, with almost irritating regularity, the same distinction is found: the seal of liberation is on the Protestants, of repression on the Catholics.

CHAPTER 15

The Exception
That Proves the Rule:
Britain's Loss of Will

Our cultural geography has confirmed case by case the Protestant communities' greater aptitude for development. Yet isn't the United Kingdom, long the leading model of a merchant and industrial civilization, in the process of showing that it too is mortal? And isn't this therefore a whopping exception to the rule we were beginning to reach?

Britain today is one of Europe's poor relations. As long ago as the eve of World War I, it had rivals for leadership. Between the wars it showed some signs of exhaustion. But the real upset occurred in the 1950s. Britain's per capita income growth slowed down; West Germany and France, moving faster, caught up to it around 1960. Now it is dragging along—with Italy dogging its footsteps—in the rear of the EEC. In 1979, the most recent year for which figures are available, it ranked seventeenth among the twenty-four members of the Organization for Economic Cooperation and Development in per capita gross domestic product.[1]

The British do not seem aware of the danger, unless they are exercising their sense of humor and refusing to dramatize a painful reality.

A Retired Nation

That they are failing to react to their decline may in fact explain their failure to overcome it. But how did the decline come about? Through the loss of the greatest colonial empire any nation ever conquered? It is true that the British Empire is no longer anything but an alumni association. But Holland, France and Belgium also lost colonial empires that, each in its own way, mattered as much to them as its empire did to Britain. Indeed, decolonization spurred their development. And Britain did successfully manage political decolonization without sacrificing its trade relationships with former colonies.

More serious was Britain's abandonment of its worldwide financial possessions. Despite the drain on its capital in World War I, London in 1938 was still, with New York, the world's creditor. It became a debtor to pay its way through World War II, borrowing a total of £3.6 billion; but until then it had been the income from capital invested abroad that had made up for Britain's trade deficit, and the loss of that income was reflected in the country's balance of payments. Worse still, the City has not lost the habit of exporting capital that would probably be more useful to the nation if invested at home.

To modernize British industry, for example. Britain's success had rested on its technological lead. Yet the British neglected to rejuvenate their industrial plant, and so their products ceased to be competitive; they were unable to carve out their share of the vast expansion of the 1960s.

Here we come up against the real question: Why did the French, the West Germans, the Belgians, the Dutch set about modernizing their equipment after the war and why did Britain go slack, even though the aid it received from the United States was proportionately greater than that given to its rivals—including, despite the legend, West Germany?

For three centuries the British spent their energies lavishly. Through discipline, boldness, self-sacrifice, they succeeded magnificently. World War II demanded a greater effort of them than ever before merely to survive. They accepted the challenge, not without suffering. For a while, major labor disputes hobbled the war effort; Churchill ended them only by promising a welfare state.

When the ordeal was over, the British were eager to reap its rewards—to live it up, go home early in the afternoon. They took to insisting that they were more concerned with gross national happiness than they were with the gross national product. They convinced themselves that the other industrial nations would eventually follow their example.

But aren't they insulting the future when they act like a pensioner legitimately anxious to enjoy his retirement because he knows he is going to die? A people does not die. Yet the world's most energetic and adventurous society gave itself up to the joys and the poisons of the welfare state: everyone for himself and the state for all.

Decompression Sickness

Churchill, the man of war who was beaten in the peacetime election, made way for the Labor Party, which unstintingly distributed what he had been forced to concede: guaranteed well-being, regulated and bureaucratized. Britain turned its back on its traditions. Nationalization of certain industries dealt a stunning blow to free enterprise and a market economy.[2] The new social policy collectivized a people hitherto conditioned to competitive individualism.

History has never granted a country the advantages of increased government intervention in private affairs without the inconveniences attached to bureaucracy. But when you resign yourself to living in a retirement home, you have to put up with its little annoyances. Better take it good-humoredly.

The welfare state was probably too contrary to the principles on which British grandeur had been built: a willingness to take risks, initiative, a spirit of enterprise, voluntary austerity, ruthless competition. The reversal of values brought with it a reversal of the national destiny.

Deep-sea divers grow accustomed to high undersea pressures. But resurfacing too quickly causes decompression sickness: at best, a loss of will; at worst, death. The British social body must have decompressed too fast. Sweden took forty years to cover the same ground Britain tried to cover in less than a decade; its nationalization policy was far more cautious than Britain's. Even so, the prudent progressiveness of Sweden's socialist leaders has not prevented it from reaching the limit of what is tolerable—and beyond it to the intolerable.

Hypertrophied Union Power

Government bureaucracy is not the only kind. Trade-union bureaucracy is just as pervasive. The British unions are often cited as models in France—"If only our union leaders were as reasonable," people say. But the cliché lost its meaning long ago. Until 1969, Britain was the world's second biggest exporter of automobiles. This comfortable position was ruined in a single year by massive strikes.[3]

Big labor, big business, big government: the balance used to be fruitful. Yet, confronted by an etiolated capitalism and a weak government, the trade unions grew stronger. In the nineteenth century they became the first unions to be legalized in Europe; by 1914 they had 4 million members, then the world's largest force of organized labor. Now they are too strong. The Labor Party is the unions' party. The Conservatives have been unable to curb this new kind of feudalism.

An unexpected shift has occurred in the traditional balance between unionism and business: the establishment has allowed the trade unions to expand their power on condition that the City's role as a world brokerage center for capital and raw materials be preserved. By this objective complicity, Britain's financiers have directly imposed a heavy sacrifice on the country in the interests of an already obsolete prestige; indirectly, they have aggravated union corporativism. The middle class is being ground between these two millstones.

Because union members naturally prefer not to change either their jobs or their place of work, the unions block any impulse toward revision. What good is it to an employer to increase productivity through the use of new machinery if he can never reduce staff? The British aeronautic and automobile industries employ twice as many workers as their French counterparts. Fierce competition, mobility of firms and personnel, constantly renewed techniques—Britain's economic dynamism was rooted in all these stimulants of unrestrained capitalism. Now it has given way to unrestrained unionism. But the result is not social dynamism, it is economic stagnation and therefore, in the long run, social disorder. It is true, however, that the democratic alternation of political power could redress these imbalances and alert unheeding Britons to the dangers facing them.[4]

Exhaustion or Eclipse?

When an individual ages, his whole organism ages. A society ages piecemeal. The parts that do not age are ill at ease. And Britain's aging can be measured by the siphoning off of its youth. Since 1950, many of those who might have injected new vigor into British society—researchers, scientists, technicians, engineers—have left the country.[5] To replace this elite has come a wave of poor immigrants who pull the country backward and teach it racism.

Was Britain merely the first stage of a rocket designed to put the United States into orbit? To judge a device's validity, we have to consider the whole rocket, not just the fallen first stage. It would be highly imprudent to write Britain off. We have noted Holland's eclipse in the eighteenth century after its streak through the seventeenth; why shouldn't Britain be going through a temporary eclipse now?

Its entry into the Common Market after much hesitation showed that the Commonwealth dream is fading, that Britain's isolation was worrisome. Alignment with Europe forced it to think realistically. There is an abundance of oil and natural gas in the North Sea.[6] Britain still has plenty of assets: an extremely high scientific standing (thirty-five living Nobel prizewinners in 1976), advanced technology, the City of London, an incomparable network of trade and financial relations throughout the world.

But a recovery will be possible only on condition that its social organization ceases its insidious perversion of the British soul by discouraging effort and initiative while delivering the country over to demagoguery. Until Britain rediscovers the values—individual and collective responsibility—that made it strong, until it rebels against bureaucracy and indolence, there is small chance of its recovery.

CHAPTER 16

Explanations That Explain Nothing

Is there a natural explanation for the Catholic nations' stagnation and the Protestant nations' expansion? Is there a southern inertia, a heat-induced poverty?

Climate? In the seventeenth century, Nicolas Boileau spoke of it as a commonplace: "Climate often makes for divers humors." One scientist has even calculated "optimal climatic energy."[1] Yet it was humanity's vital energy, not climate, that veered from south to north. Rameses II's Egypt, Assurbanipal's Assyria, the Greece of Pericles did not wait for air conditioning before becoming fertile. When man wants to work, he works just about anywhere, in Alaska and the Negev, in Siberia or Tahiti. It's as hot in California as in Sicily, as cold in Sweden as in Tierra del Fuego.

What is true of climatic explanations is also true of those based on terrain—whether its configuration or the resources it holds. Topography and geology deal the cards; it's up to us to play them. Maritime trade requires ports and safe harbors. A jagged coastline or islands can polarize growth. Yet Greece has lost its power although its geography hasn't changed since the age of Pericles. The Norman port of Saint-Malo prospered and declined with no change in its profile. What geographer, what engineer could have imagined that Venice la Serenissima would have risen from a scattering of sandbanks in the Adriatic?

Fundamental differences between nations cannot be explained by the distribution of resources. There is as much natural wealth in Siberia as in all of Europe together, in Brazil as in the United States, in Pakistan as in Japan. Yet compare the results. When a people has an aptitude for industry, it is not stopped by lack of natural resources. Switzerland, the world's leading producer and exporter of chocolate and powdered coffee, grows neither cacao nor coffee. Never mind; it buys what it needs. Does Japan lack coal?* It sells manufactured goods to pay for the coal with which it manufactures them.

---

* Some coal is mined in Japan, but not enough for the country's needs. And Japanese coal is not suited to making coke for steel production.

.   .   .

Well then, if nothing is explained by a country's natural physiognomy, how about its people?

How can we avoid noting that all the advanced nations except Japan are peopled by the white race? Or that the predominantly British, Scandinavian and German countries are especially favored? Is the white race, and particularly some of its ethnic components, more gifted than other races in creating an industrial civilization?

This theory is not often written, but it is murmured. Yet the sole differences science has so far found among the races are anatomical: pigmentation, eye color, nose and cranial formation, hair color, size. No one has ever successfully associated character traits with these physical attributes.[2] The language of popular racism, on the other hand, is expressive. The defects it lays to nonwhites resemble those ascribed to Europe's proletariat a century ago. Weren't poor whites then considered thieving, lazy, improvident, lying—all the vices of man gelded of his responsibility and his dignity?

It is situation that molds character. Even stripped of their cloak of insults, the nonwhites' defects exist; they are connected with economic and social underdevelopment, and in turn prolong it. But we see them disappear among black workers whose living standards rise, as they disappeared among white workers.

Still, we have not disposed of our initial observation. There is no denying the inequality of aptitudes among peoples for furthering an industrial civilization. But neither can we reduce a complex psychological reality to a simple matter of biological differences among races. A nation's character, its culture—these are what make for such striking and lasting differences. It is from these that its customs grow—its conventions, prejudices, basic values and principles of social organization.

The Religious Factor

Climate, resources, race; physical properties of the air, the earth or the species. All these explanations lead us back to man's psychology. The rudimentary geography of development we traced in earlier chapters thus seems to give rise to a rudimentary supposition: Is the merchant and technical civilization the daughter (or sister) of Protestantism?

The question seems almost scandalous. What has religion to do with economic growth? Yet it is an inevitable one. "Behind Alexander the Great there is always Aristotle," said Charles de Gaulle. Behind the conquests of the "nation of shopkeepers" so despised by Napoleon, that Latin genius, why shouldn't we find the doctrine of Puritanism?

Unless it's the other way around and the shopkeepers were behind the Puritans. Karl Marx would then have been right. Economic facts, according to him, could only have economic causes; spiritual, religious and moral manifestations would have been superstructures on the economic foundation.

Marx, Engels and many Marxist historians[3] had also remarked the disparity in rates of progress between the Protestant and Catholic countries. But they had no doubt about the reason: the capitalist, industrialized countries became Protestant in order to adapt their religious ethic to the needs of their economic system. To them, the reformation was capitalism's daughter. The most recent historical research corrects this explanation.[4]

The Reformation was a spiritual earthquake. For Marx to have been right, an economic revolution of comparable magnitude would have been required beforehand to engender this religious revolution. Yet there is no sign of any such upheaval. The great discoveries, the great Renaissance voyages of exploration, may have opened men's minds, but they caused no economic change. And Luther nailed his ninety-five points to the door of the church in Wittenberg two years before Cortés landed in Mexico.

Had Marx been right, the Reformation should have appeared and spread in the richest and most dynamic countries of the age, these in which capitalism had advanced the farthest—Italy, Spain, Portugal, Flanders, Brabant. But none of these countries went Protestant. Sixteenth-century Europe's leading businessmen, the Genoese, Florentine and Barcelonan merchants and financiers who were to control European economic life until the early seventeenth century, remained faithful to Rome. The Fugger dynasty, the Rothschilds or Rockefellers of the time, lent money for indulgences. And Pope Leo X, the son of a Medici banker, excommunicated Luther, who called down anathema on bankers.

In fact, it was in the economically backward countries, such as Switzerland, in some of the poorest of the German states, the depressed, mistshrouded regions of northern Europe, that the Reformation found its most fertile ground.

Another Theory

If Marx was wrong, was Max Weber right? For it was this illustrious German sociologist who most subtly linked *The Protestant Ethic and the Spirit of Capitalism,* as he called the book he published in 1904. The book and the idea were hotly debated in the Protestant countries;[5] they have had hardly any effect on Latin countries like France.[6]

Weber did not claim to have discovered that the Protestant peoples were more gifted than the Catholics for economic progress; this had been widely acknowledged in the preceding three centuries. What Weber did was to try to show the affinities between the capitalist spirit and Protestant morality. The Calvinists, he explained, believed in predestination. They could do nothing to change the choice of heaven or hell God had made for them. But they thought that in worldly prosperity they could perceive a hint of divine providence. The more successful their business affairs were, the more certain they felt of being among the elect.

Moreover, this prosperity, sought as a sign and not for itself, was purified by asceticism. God condemned luxury, so they lived frugal lives.[7] Idleness was abhorrent to Protestant asceticism, which incited to toil and rational activity. The old inhibitions against acquisitiveness were uprooted, but the ascetic spirit castigated excessive enjoyment of wealth;[8] it encouraged production, but restrained consumption.[9] Caught between their need to enrich themselves and their insistence on living simply, the Calvinists turned spontaneously toward savings and investment.

Weber knew his time too well to pretend that Puritan asceticism still called the tune. But he insisted that between the sixteenth and eighteenth centuries—the "take-off" period—it was that ethic which gave the Protestant countries a lead in the formation of capital from which they continued to profit even after the original motivations were diluted.

No Single Cause, No Single Effect

As careful as he was with qualitative factors, Weber, like Marx, succumbed to the nineteenth century's quantitative tendency. His reasoning remained materialistic—it sought the elements in Protestantism that produced a capital surplus. Weber reduced industrial development to capitalism and capitalism to capital. He introduced the religious factor into industrial development chiefly as the lever for savings and the systematization of profit. Was he looking through the wrong end of the telescope?

In the decades that followed the Reformation, the enormous phenomena of Protestantism and the economic revolution developed together. Weber reduced the first to a cause, asceticism, and the second to an effect of that cause, the accumulation of capital. Shouldn't we rather establish a cause-effect relationship between the complex of Protestant attitudes and the complex of industrial civilization?

The Economy Is More Than the Economy

Marx saw only two factors at work, capital and labor. Weber saw a third, cultural factor. But he didn't dare follow his discovery to its conclusion; he made the cultural factor a subfactor of the first—capital. Now, it seems to me that this third factor is more decisive than the other two, that it dominates them both. In the Reformed countries we see a release from stewardship by divine right, confidence bestowed on individuals and groups, an appetite for scientific and technical research, a boost for initiative: an *economic mentality*. In the Counter-Reformation countries, on the other hand, what we see is submission to hierarchical authority, mistrust of individuals and groups, an organization hostile to autonomy and innovation: an *anti-economic prejudice.*

St. Thomas Aquinas believed that wealth could be morally good if it is used toward legitimate ends.[10] Conversely, Calvin, although he authorized lending money at interest, did impose restrictions on it. To be legitimate, a loan designed to stimulate production, the vital motor of capitalism, had to bring the borrower as much profit as it produced for the lender, or more. Professional lenders—bankers—were still condemned. None of these ideas were precisely in harmony with capitalist thinking.

Calvin very cautiously opened a door a crack. Many clerics and humanists before him had been bolder.[11] It was the whole Western world that opened the intellectual and moral roads to capitalism in the sixteenth century. Protestantism's religious rigor at first blocked some of them. Most of the original Calvinist communities—in Geneva, Holland, Scotland and the Palatinate—regulated economic activity conservatively.[12] Hardened by religious struggle, they were prey to fanaticism. Only under the "deviant" Calvinism of the disciples of Arminius and Socinius could economic expansion truly get under way, in the "Arminian" cities of Amsterdam and Leyden,[13] in a Geneva relieved of orthodoxy in the late eighteenth century.[14]

The Origins of Dynamism

Perhaps, at this stage, we can hazard an explanation of why the Latin nations grew poorer beginning in the early seventeenth century while the northern countries seemed to grow richer. There were contradictory elements in Christianity before the Reformation and the Counter-Reformation. As a religion of personal destiny, it released forces of emancipation, of vitality through a dialogue between effort and grace. At the same time, it taught detachment from worldly concerns and submission, fostering a spirit of resignation, of fatalism, of acceptance of the hierarchical principle. This conflict explains the ambiguity of Christendom's whole career up to the sixteenth century.

Few ancient civilizations prized work very highly. As soon as they could, they assigned it to slaves.[15] It was the Judeo-Christian civilization that conferred dignity on labor, making it a duty the religious man lovingly embraces. The servant who failed to make his master's money multiply was consigned to the shadows by Jesus.[16] St. Paul proscribed idleness; he that worked not, Paul declared, was unworthy of his bread.[17]

Christ's appeal was above all personal. For the first time, religion was no longer a means of appeasing external demons through ritual and sacrifice. Misfortune was interiorized. By placing the battle between good and evil in every heart, this new faith created an unprecedented upheaval. It unbalanced man and, in so doing, it got him going, launching him toward adventure, but with God's help. It was a religion of confidence, capable of founding a society of confidence, of exalting the instinct to excel.

But these dynamic principles in Christianity were largely annulled by the principles of rigidity on which Church organization rested from the fourth century onward. The message of emancipation was taken over by a hierarchical, dogmatic system inherited from the Roman Caesars. Relieved of persecution, the Church fell into the trap opened by the conversion of the emperor Constantine: it slipped into the mold of a declining Roman Empire. When the empire disintegrated in the panic surrounding the barbarian invasions, the Church was the sole structure to resist, probably because it was not merely a structure. But it was *also* a structure and it carved powers for itself out of the institutional desert.

Vitality and Fertility

By the twelfth century, the spirit of enterprise and innovation was nevertheless at work. This was the period of the rise of the cities. Christendom, led by the Latin countries, swelled with a prodigious intellectual, artistic and economic exuberance to which market halls, belltowers and cathedrals still bear witness. In Venice, Bruges, Rouen, Nuremberg, people manufactured things, they traded, they traveled. Not only did a modern economy appear in these cities, but the cities also succeeded in escaping the enveloping net of military and ecclesiastical feudalism. The spirit of innovation and freedom flourished in new trades, in exchanges and franchises. The towns won the right to govern themselves. In this gestating new world, political and economic freedom awoke together, were interdependent. And from them rose a new figure, the middle-class entrepreneur.

Benedetto Zaccaria was such a figure.[18] Born in Genoa in 1248, he left for the Orient at the age of eleven. He exploited the alum mines in Phocea, and built a personal fleet that brought to Genoa wheat from the Ukraine and Bulgaria, hides and fish from Russia. It carried goods to the Levant: cloth from Champagne, Italian weapons, salt from Corsica. Zaccaria traded as far away as Armenia. He lent his fleet to sovereigns. At the age of fifty-eight he returned to Genoa to die in his palace on the sea.

Such men were animated by the spirit of responsibility present in the Christian mentality. Their freedom developed at the margin of the Roman-style hierarchic order—at the margin, but not in opposition to it. Renaissance humanism tried to widen that margin, and at first it succeeded.

Until the beginning of the sixteenth century people who asked questions, even in areas we would consider minor, risked excommunication for heresy. Only unitary thought was allowed. But, led by Erasmus,[19] humanists in the late fifteenth and early sixteenth centuries reacted strongly against such dogmatism. Erasmus insisted that real unity must come from diversity, not uniformity; that tolerance is the condition of peace.[20] Only differing viewpoints can produce truth, as the spokes of a wheel converge on its hub.

Erasmus had disciples throughout Europe. He could proudly write that they included "the Emperor [Charles V], the kings of England, of France and of Denmark, Prince Ferdinand of Germany, the Archbishop of Canterbury and many others, princes, bishops and scholars." In 1522, his friend and fellow countryman Hadrian VI became pope; progressive emancipation was within Christians' reach.

Yet it was aborted. Or rather, it exploded in the Reformation and smothered in the Counter-Reformation. The movement that should have carried all Christendom forward split and, in the process, divided Christianity for centuries to come.

The Reformation: A Cultural Revolution

Almost all the Reformation's lasting contributions are already to be found in the works of Erasmus, even though Luther, who called him an "eel," thought otherwise: respect for individual freedom, the affirmation of personal responsibility ("true theology is in every man"),[21] the need to translate the Bible into vernacular languages to bring religion closer to the people. While these ideas were slowly taking root, Luther's activism intervened to create conflict. Erasmus' method lay in debating ideas, in stubborn, widespread infiltration. Luther's technique was assault.

Luther refused to submit to Rome. He pushed Erasmus' theory of a universal priesthood to its extreme, insisting that everyone is his own priest.[22] This was too much; it forced a break. Erasmus had been a reformer. The Reformation was a revolution and, like all revolutions, it spawned a counter-revolution, the Counter-Reformation. On both sides, the battle became a war to the death. A holy war is not the best climate for the growth of intellectual and economic freedom.

At first, then, Lutheranism and Calvinism replaced one theocracy with another. Yet—and this was to be of essential importance for the future—they built it on unstable foundations. When Calvin, as a disciple of Erasmus, exhorted his co-religionaries to be responsible for themselves, he set in motion a process he could not foresee and which would not be easily channeled. It was finally to break down the hierarchical structures of the Middle Ages and replace them with democratic structures.

Faith and Works

For Calvin even more than for Luther, man was intrinsically perverse, forever corrupted by original sin. Only the free miracle of divine grace could save him. How is it that among the Calvinists, who rejected salvation through good works and believed in salvation through faith alone, we see faith so often wither while works were exalted; whereas the Catholics, who glorified the notion of salvation through works, so often lived lives rich in faith and ignored good works?

The problem here is dialectical. To the Catholics, good works, being in the divine interest, were subject to the hierarchy's glowering supervision and so sterilized by the spirit of orthodoxy. Protestants, on the other hand, shed their illusions of reaching God; since they were too corrupt, they thought, to reach heaven, their business was on earth. God was indifferent to good works. The Church remained aloof from them, freeing men to deal with them as they could. Catholics satisfied their instinct to excel mainly by sinking themselves in prayer; Protestants excelled by throwing themselves heart and soul into the most mundane occupations. What peace of mind there is in working out a doctrine for man's spiritual needs that allows him to prosper materially as well!

Does this liberation from dogmatic taboos in itself explain the difference in growth between the Catholic and Protestant countries? Not entirely. The Protestant countries' development beginning in the seventeenth century merely followed the road all Europe had been taking since the thirteenth. What made the break visible was the underdevelopment of the countries that remained Catholic. It is this downward Catholic curve that challenges us. To understand it, we must measure the extent of the rupture in Christian history inflicted by the Counter-Reformation.

A Cultural Counter-Revolution

In the eighteen years—from 1545 to 1563—of the Council of Trent, the Church cleansed itself of a host of impurities; it once again aroused fervor. But, under Protestant attack, it formed a defensive square, protecting itself with all the weapons of its authority, reinforced and militarized.

The Reformation multiplied, divided and subdivided into a throng of sects. Often these were fanatic, of course, but the power to choose one's fanaticism is the beginning of freedom. The Counter-Reformation took the opposite tack, pushing the spirit of Roman systematization and unitarism to its extreme. Its shadow fell over that part of Europe that remained faithful to Rome. The inhibiting climate it created stifled the technical, mercantile and industrial progress that had been taking such promising shape in those very areas. And, at the same time, it stimulated rigid centralization of governments. It was a reactionary and totalitarian movement in the exact sense of those terms.[23]

We should not succumb to the temptation to put the Counter-Reformation on trial. Its task was to preserve Christian order. When the house is on fire and swarming with looters, can quarter be given? The Church was, after all, Roman, and it had always tried to solve its crises by juridical rigidity, by over-regulation. The "Roman sickness" was constantly intensified.

Religion was the first area to be affected: a single catechism; a single translation of the Bible, the Vulgate; a single truth, that of Trent. Human intelligence was summoned to sleep. The Church fired on anything that moved. There was no limit to the Roman panic. Erasmus, who a year before his death had been offered a cardinal's hat, was soon considered a heretic. A monk in Cologne devised the saying that "Erasmus laid the eggs that Luther hatched. May God grant that we crush the eggs and kill the pullets." Even during his lifetime, Erasmus' books were condemned in Paris; his translator perished at the stake. In 1559, all his works appeared on the Church's Index of Forbidden Books.

Free thought was persecuted just as science was beginning to develop. Of what use was science, since Revelation rendered it useless and therefore unwholesome? Through the Jesuits and the friars of the Christian schools, the Church itself supervised the modeling of men's intelligence. For centuries, it put Christian minds on a merry-go-round of rhetorical exercises and an unreal cult of ancient Rome.

The Brain Drain

In Flanders, France, Spain, Portugal and Italy, trade had brought power and respect in the Middle Ages. Rich merchants gave gifts to the Church, assigned members of their families to it, but they invested the bulk of their wealth in business or craft. In the seventeenth century, however, society withdrew its recognition from them. Its values had changed to suit those at the top of the new hierarchical pyramids. Where once, to protect his fortune, a merchant tried to increase it, now he needed outside guarantees. Instead of investing in the "great adventure" of maritime trade, he bought posts for his children in the bureaucracies of Church and state.[24]

For the Church imposed its pattern on politics as well as on economics. The governments of countries affected by the Counter-Reformation in turn became hierarchies, complex bureaucracies tightly controlled by a central authority. The Counter-Reformation created or protected hierarchies, discouraged novelty and instituted a society of mistrust.

Many of those persecuted in the Catholic countries as heretics—deviants—went abroad to seek their fortunes or simply to find refuge. They were welcomed in the Protestant countries as brothers in persecution, but also as brave and enterprising men who brought with them the knowledge and capital of southern Europe, then so rich and so advanced.

It is difficult for us to imagine the collective effect of these individual migrations. The British historian H. R. Trevor Roper[25] studied the great "capitalist" entrepreneurs of the seventeenth century. He found that all of them were emigrants or sons of emigrants—Jews from Lisbon or Seville, Erasmians from Portugal and Spain, Flemings persecuted by the duke of Alba, Walloons to whom Alexander Farnese gave the choice of submission to Rome or exile,[26] Italians fleeing persecution for their religious convictions (generally less Calvinist than Erasmian). The first artisans of Swiss prosperity were Italians who emigrated to Switzerland in the first half of the seventeenth century, followed by French Huguenots in the second half.

Development Commandos

We have seen in our own century the fertilizing effect talented emigrants can have. The many German and Austrian Jews who abandoned the old Continent after 1933 to settle in the United States revived America's development, especially in the laboratories and universities that were wise enough to welcome them.[27]

The advance guard of the seventeenth century's mercantile economy was small and fragile. The departure or arrival of a few hundred, sometimes only a few dozen, of its members meant stagnation and decline in the place they left behind them, stimulation and prosperity where they went. The process was cumulative: when a few members of a persecuted community fled, the anxious feeling of besiegement settled more heavily on those who stayed behind; as soon as the emigrants made places for themselves in their new countries, they sent for their families and friends. Why did Amsterdam expand so rapidly in the early seventeenth century while Antwerp withered? Because a handful of enterprising Antwerp citizens traveled the few leagues separating them from freedom. Development was a commando operation.

The First Society of Confidence

In the process of crystallization, the form a crystal finally takes is determined by the initial molecule around which the rest of the solution condenses. The hitherto backward countries that went Protestant crystallized in large measure around these immigrant colonies. The newcomers imposed their values on their new neighbors: a willingness to take risks, a sense of responsibility, of personal achievement.

An emigrant escaping from the social cocoon had to break the taboos surrounding him. This was especially true in the United States for the educated and wealthy Protestants who went there from strife-torn Europe in the seventeenth century; the Irish and Italian Catholics who joined them in the nineteenth century would settle into a society that had already made its rules and meant to keep to them. Men became pioneers just to survive.

Marked by those first immigrants, a whole part of the West became adventurous, individualistic, eager to excel. There, society ceased to be a fact imposed on everyone and became, at least in the beginning, a collective undertaking in which each person took part with equal fervor and equal rights.

In America, this responsible and contractual society developed rapidly. In Europe, it gradually disengaged itself from the old society, but only in those countries where the genius of innovation could take hold. The nations dominated by intolerance were emptied of their adventurers—and, worse still, of their spirit of adventure.

CHAPTER 17

Caesar's Granddaughter

[John] Law said to me: "Sir, I would never have believed what I have seen while administering [the state's] finances. I would have you know that the kingdom of France is governed by thirty intendants. You have neither parliament nor committees, nor states, nor governors—I would almost add, neither king nor ministers; it is on the thirty masters of requests that depend the happiness or misfortune of these provinces, their abundance or their sterility."

—Marquis d'Argenson[1]

And what of France? It remained a special case within the group of Catholic countries, becoming monocentric—in its fashion.

Protestantism penetrated there, developing rapidly and powerfully. It could not conquer the country, but it survived its defeats. The Wars of Religion ended in a stalemate with the ascent to the Catholic throne of the Huguenots' leader, Henri IV, converted to Catholicism for reasons of state. And the king had the last word. The result was that France never, properly speaking, experienced the Counter-Reformation. Its ruler did not trouble to ratify the Council of Trent's decrees, even though the clergy hastened to apply them. The Inquisition was not established there, and intellectual life largely escaped clerical domination.

France at the Junction

It was later, after Richelieu came to power, that France knew its own kind of Counter-Reformation of absolute centralization by divine right, a barely secularized form of theocracy and, under it, persecution of the Protestants. But, a century later, it also received the Reformation in the Enlightenment that came from England, Holland and Switzerland via Anglomania, Freemasonry and Rousseauism.

Thus France stood at the junction of the Reformation and the Counter-Reformation and so at the confluence of development and underdevelopment. It was not pulled brutally short, as Portugal, Spain, Italy, Austria and Poland were. But neither could it plunge briskly into a trade economy in the manner of the Netherlands, England and Switzerland. It lagged behind, though with scattered islands of active modernity. Free thought in France asserted itself against the Church and the state, whereas in the Protestant countries it asserted itself within the Church and the state or, in any case, alongside them.

The struggle between the Reformation and the Counter-Reformation did therefore influence the history of the French. It thrust them on the path of slow decline, but in the French style. In the other Latin countries, the Church was dominant. In France, the state took over—because it was there. Over the centuries it had woven a unique fabric of regulations, institutions and allegiances. When panic forced a need for greater discipline, the crown had only to tighten the weave.

An Anointed King

From the very birth of France, power was essentially religious. For France was the child of the marriage of the Church and state. Its whole history stems from the baptism of King Clovis in 496. With the active support of the bishops, the Gallo-Roman people's only natural authority, this obscure chieftain of a Frankish tribe rid himself of his rivals and carved out a kingdom that remained the mold for France. Political authority immediately took on a quasi-divine character. In the chaos of the West in the fifth century, the hand of God seemed to safeguard this island of orderly authority.

Five centuries later, when the Carolingian Empire dissolved under the violence of Viking raids, France again became a kind of Far West without a sheriff. Authority disintegrated. Counts and barons gathered up the debris for themselves. Royalty, transplanted into the Capet family in 987, was at first no more than a symbolic, moral authority. But it used that very nub of holiness to extend its power. Amid the violence of feudal chaos, people looked for guidance to him in whose person religion and politics were joined.

The phenomenon has no real equivalent in the West. Joan of Arc arranging the anointing of a feeble king could only have been a French saint. Once anointed, the monarchs of France, from Hugues Capet to Charles X, accomplished miracles, healed the king's evil: "The King touches you, God cures you." Everywhere else, power was human, too human. Machiavelli's cynical policy of "take and hold" exaggeratedly expresses this desacralization of power. France alone deified its monarchy and, through it, its state.

The Long March from Rome to Paris

It was because of Roman bureaucrats that Jesus was born in a stable: "And it came to pass in those days, that there went out a decree from Caesar Augustus, that all the world should be taxed. . . . And all went to be taxed, every one into his own city."[2] Not just in Judea, but from Brittany to the confines of Persia, tax officials and taxpayers set out on the same day—a fabulous machine, extraordinarily effective and extraordinarily vulnerable too. For four centuries the Empire resisted every onslaught, unified its world, brought the organization of government to a peak of perfection.

Rome not only conquered the world; it numbered it, sectioned it off, inscribed it on tablets. This was the system's good side. But there was a less admirable side: it burdened the world with a proliferating bureaucracy. "Rome's principle of government," said one historian, "was to destroy the individual for the state's benefit, to destroy the provinces for Rome's benefit, to destroy everything for the emperor's benefit."[3]

Strength versus weakness—this vast organization would collapse in whole sections. Which strongly suggests the hypothesis that by concentrating all its resources at the top and so exposing the entire edifice to shock, Rome caused its own defeat.

In less than a century and a half, from 1180 to 1314, three great kings transformed France from a feudal kingdom into a national state. Philip Augustus unified the kingdom; Louis IX—St. Louis—reconciled power and justice; and Philip the Fair rallied the French around a centralized administration.

Philip the Fair's ideas were inspired by his "legists," who had taken them from what survived of Roman law (in fact, the law of the "second Rome"—Constantinople—as codified by Justinian in the sixth century), piously preserved by the Church. Southerners who had attended Italian universities, these jurists imported the principles of the late Roman Empire. To the French, they were a kind of rediscovery. Hadn't Rome, in five long centuries of impregnation, taught the unruly and capricious Gauls the preeminence of a capital, of surveying, of numbered roads, sales taxes, tax officials, a hierarchy—in a word, of order?

Later, when the Reformation arrived to test France, the state, solidified by centuries of patience, was firm enough to withstand it. The shock's failure to crack it would leave it even firmer. And when Louis XIV appeared, it was to rule a French people who had been misled by fifty years of Italian administration, by twenty years of Spanish invasions, by years of saturnalias on the part of German, English and Scottish troops and by the convulsions of the Fronde. They idealized the absolute power of the throne as the symbol of their unity. They adored themselves in the person of their king.

Caesar's Granddaughter

It was then that France truly became the eldest daughter of the Church and the privileged granddaughter of the Roman Empire, of which the Roman Church itself was the daughter. These structures are amazingly long-lived. In the fourth century, the Roman Church had modeled its organization on that of the late Empire; in the early seventeenth century the Catholic states, especially France, in turn fashioned their organization on that of the Church. Priests received their power from the bishops, who received theirs from the pope; similarly, the state's subdelegate, deep in the provinces, received his powers from the intendant, who received his from the minister by authorization of the king. The humblest of functionaries shared in the crown's secular sovereignty just as the simplest village vicar shared, in the eyes of the faithful, in the spiritual sovereignty of the Holy See. Thus was born the bureaucratic centralization that survives so hardily in France's institutions because it is still alive in the French spirit.

The Administrative Monarchy

The history of France is that of a long climb toward centralization. An administrative monarchy gradually took form, increasingly centered in the sovereign and his ministers, or rather in their bureaucracy, which coolly acted in their name. The duc de Sully, Henri IV's great minister, gathered together the instruments; Richelieu formed the orchestra; and Louis XIV conducted, *fortissimo*, a symphony that is still deafening us.

This logical progression reflects not so much the conscious will of France's governors as the longing of the collective French conscience, from Philip the Fair to the Fifth Republic. Sully gave temporary assignments as intendants to state councillors or masters of requests; Richelieu converted them into permanent civil servants. This was a decisive move: scattered throughout France, they channeled all matters to themselves and thence to the bureaus in Versailles. Henceforth the state, patterned on the Roman example, would supersede the medieval tradition of local autonomy—which, in the Protestant countries, was the basis for local democratic structures.

The marquis d'Argenson noted that in 1672 the French system was fully developed: "Our government is entirely arranged on a new system, which is the absolute will of the ministers in each department; everything that shared that authority has been abrogated. Thus, the court resembles all that the heart is in the human body; everything passes and re-passes through it several times before circulating to the body's extremities."[4]

The intermediate bodies through which the French administered their own affairs dwindled and vanished. Louis XIV had instructed his ministers to refer to him "for everything, even if only the issuance of a passport." His intendants had administrative authority over municipalities and alms houses, they checked on communities' debts, sat in person in city assemblies. Raising taxes, running the finance bureaus, food supplies, military measures, public works—everything fell to them. Through these thirty powerful officials, the sovereign was present everywhere. Nothing was shaded from the royal sun. And France grew used to leaving the taking of initiatives to the state.

The revocation of the Edict of Nantes was simply the final step in this process. The government at last nibbled away the powers of all the kingdom's little "republics"—the Protestant cities. The rallying cries incorporated by persecuted Protestants into their insurrectional manifestos were the same ones used by rebels against government interference.[5]

A Hierarchical Counterpoint

Aside from the administrative hierarchy, the king also held the aristocratic and ecclesiastical hierarchies in his hand. He played each against the others. In fact, the aristocratic hierarchy was reduced to a shadow of its former self. Louis XIV distilled titles for those who served him. To appear at court, to attract the king's glance, to be honored by a word from him—these were what transfigured an aristocrat's life. Versailles became a closed world in which a disabled caste gyrated.

With the aristocracy neutralized by ritual and a stream of new titles, and the commonalty neutralized by the administration, there remained only the Church to neutralize. The vehicle successfully used was Gallicanism—the traditional semi-independence of the French Church from Rome—through which was achieved a kind of fusion between the throne and the Church, welded together like the two faces of national pride.

If centralization then did not yet create the steamroller effect it has since assumed, it was only because practical obstacles still blocked the machinery. Slow communications maintained a certain level of local initiative. Instructions often had to be general and their application left to the judgment of the king's delegate. Technical progress would later enable the central administration to intervene in even the most minor local affairs. The postchaise of Louis XIV's day gave his intendants more independence than the telegraph—or worse still, the telephone—allows modern prefects.

And yet, the king's "despotism" finally horrified people who should really have incriminated the crown's centralization—excessive because what seemed its unfailing arbitrariness crystallized public resentment, yet inadequate because the king was not strong enough to sweep away the (bureaucratic) privileges that paralyzed his good will. The country experienced the system's inconveniences but not the advantages that might have justified it. It is probably in this paradox that we should seek the essential cause of the French Revolution.

The Revolutionary Circle

The Revolution truly deserves its name. It lived up to its etymological origin as a return to its point of departure: the all-powerful bureaucracy. The upheaval it provoked in order to end centralized absolutism only succeeded in accentuating it.

The Constituent Assembly could have imposed reforms reinforcing the local democracy of those institutions that remained to balance excessive central power: city administrations, guilds, aristocratic traditions, ecclesiastical independence, parliaments, hereditary offices and those sold by the state. It could have replaced hereditary and mercenary officials with elected officials; clerical power could have led to separation of Church and state, magisterial power to the separation of political and judicial authority. Instead, the Revolution brushed aside these last obstacles to absolutism. It made France an institutional desert, then covered it over with a flimsy democratic veil that was blown away by the first difficulties the republic faced.

In the immense disorder it created, the Revolution had no recourse but to return to the system it had set out to abolish. And it began by using the old system's men. Relying on the underlings whose chiefs had just been guillotined seemed convenient. Bureaucrats who often had occupied obscure posts under the old regime took advantage of the talent vacuum left by the elimination of the former directorial class to grab positions of power. And they had little trouble persuading an inexperienced government to exaggerate the centralization on which their influence rested.

Napoleon's Roots

The Revolution propped itself up as best it could on camouflaged centralization. Bonaparte brought France out of the Revolution with centralization triumphant.

Later governments, from the Restoration to the Second Empire, would have too much trouble establishing and maintaining themselves not to view a centralized authority as providential. The Third and Fourth republics aggravated the situation: their governments were so ephemeral that they had little choice but to leave the problems they faced in the hands of the bureaucracy.

That France has been mined by an administrative cancer for the past three and a half centuries is the truth the French know least about. On this point, they are doggedly illogical. Who has not heard some harsh critic of the government's "quill-pushers" announce proudly that he has just landed a government job for his son or daughter?

The most glaring French inconsistency is the belief that the state's power should be limited at the summit by the instability of its executive, instead of at the base, through the extension of power to legitimate groups—on township, cantonal, departmental or provincial levels—to manage their own affairs. The French know too well what they owe the state to resist its logic. It has given them their *grandeurs;* they can't refuse it its weaknesses. So, under a strange illusion, the French have slowly declined while thinking that they were ascending.

CHAPTER 18

An Attempt to Interpret History

Invent and you will die persecuted like a criminal, copy and you will live happy as an ass. —Balzac[1]

We are used to thinking of development as a normal process and underdevelopment as scandalous. We forget that what we term "underdevelopment" today has been humanity's natural condition from the start. Misery and violence have always been man's companions. Let favorable circumstances help him to take hold, to multiply even for a few decades, and we speak of it as a golden age. Ordinarily, though, what do we have? Families mutilated by the deaths of young children and women in childbirth, the monotonous, constantly renewed cycle of famine and epidemic.

How long ago did *"la douce France"* spin out of this cycle? Much later than we think. Underdevelopment was with us until the heart of the nineteenth century. When the Revolution exploded in the summer of 1789, France was gripped by a thoroughly archaic famine and a fear in people's hearts that recalled the panic of the year 1000, when many believed that the world would end. In 1832, cholera ravaged Paris; rabies stalked the land until the end of the century. Even today, adults are careful not to waste food. The misery of the past survives in France's collective memory.

A century or two of development compared to three or four thousand years of underdevelopment corresponds to twenty minutes at most in a twenty-four-hour day. Is it any wonder that almost the whole of human history has been determined by underdevelopment and that four fifths of the world's people are still underdeveloped?[2] It would be more logical to reverse the question and ask: Why did a form of civilization appear some three centuries ago that today enables one fifth of the world's people to escape this tragic destiny?

The Need for Achievement

In Erie, Pennsylvania, the closing of a factory put 450 employees out of work. Most of them stayed home for a while afterward, waiting for another job offer. A few, on the very day they were laid off, began looking for work. They haunted the employment agencies, placed and answered classified ads, investigated occupational training programs with an eye to learning a new trade, even inquired about work in other cities. All 450 workers faced common problems; they all needed food, money, a steady job. Yet only a few actively went after these goals.

Hundreds of similar cases show that people fall into two categories: "those to whom every situation represents a challenge and who strive to meet it, and those who don't worry so much about it."[3] D. C. McClelland calls the force that motivates the active minority "the need for achievement"—a "desire to do well not in order to acquire prestige or social position, but to reach an inner sense of personal achievement."[4] Motivational psychology tells us that our most powerful motives are not a hunger for gain but a sporting zest for winning, the joy of creation, a desire to give form to new ideas.[5]

"The Instinct to Excel"

This eagerness to succeed, which I prefer to call "the instinct to excel," is what chiefly distinguishes men from beasts. An animal is governed by an instinct of repetition. Since ants and beavers and deer first appeared on earth, each individual creature has behaved as its species does, and each species as it always has. Conversely, man—the fallen god who remembers heaven—heeds an instinctive call to excel, to outdo himself and others, to overcome what seems to be the human condition. Albert Camus while working on *The Rebel*, André Malraux preparing his *Memoirs*, Darius Milhaud composing music in his paralytic's cart, all told me very much the same thing: "I don't think anyone has ever done what I'm doing." This is not the language of pride, but of the enthusiasm—the god within the soul—that drives people to go ever further, that makes them hunger to know, to imagine, to create something new, to achieve. Could there be a finer prayer than the plea to "give us this day our daily hunger"?

A Mile a Year

A potential in everyone, this instinct to excel is in fact developed only in a minority of people.[6] An innovative society is one in which such a minority is relatively large and free to act. In a static society, it remains small and paralyzed.

Anyone who studies the innovative process down through history is struck by how few people contributed to it and how large the herd of those who accepted change only tardily. In England's Norfolk County in the early eighteenth century, three men and six horses were needed to plow a plot of land. Thomas Coke—Coke of Norfolk—developed a plow that enabled one man and two horses to do the same job and increased the yield of wheat land by 50 percent. The local peasants waited twenty years to adopt his plow; "my improvements," Coke said wryly, "are progressing at the speed of one mile a year."[7]

And for every innovator, there are so many imitators. A few dozen pioneers—builders, businessmen, promoters—how small this group is, and how careful we must be to avoid hampering it. For the instinct to excel can be repressed or stimulated by social and mental attitudes. It is vexed by a monocentric society, with its private preserves, its established privileges, an economy protected from competition.[8] Polycentric societies' free market economies incite individuals and groups to outdo each other.

"People always tend to think others' motives are contemptible," Pompidou remarked to me in January 1974, "the most contemptible being to make a lot of money. It's as though you said that Solzhenitsyn put on a persecution act to increase his sales."

Why shouldn't an economy obey more pressing motives than pecuniary gain? A businessman who continues to risk his profits after he has made his fortune, a craftsman who likes to fiddle with his work, an executive intent on making his way, are moved by dreams more secret and compelling than money hunger. Profit is the basic law of economics in both capitalist and collectivized societies; to reject this is to reject reality. But it is not the only nor even the principal spring of economic initiative. It is simply a post facto way to measure achievement—that is, the effectiveness of action on reality.[9]

Challenges

Usually, we act in order to react, we outdo so as not to be outdone. Arnold Toynbee called such situations "challenges." The expression has been debased, but it in fact is what they are.

Until December 1941, the Americans refused to enter the war against the Axis powers. The surprise attack on Pearl Harbor forced them into war and their reaction was in keeping with their vitality: they were not content merely to produce war materiel and mobilize their armed forces. They also cultivated a rich crop of inventions. War is the supreme challenge.

The call is not generally so dramatic. The great technological inventions that ushered in the Industrial Revolution in England were the offshoots of a duel between spinners and weavers. The spinning mills were five times less productive and the gap widened even more after John Kay invented the flying shuttle. They could not supply enough fiber to keep the looms going. Needled by necessity, James Hargreaves and Sir Richard Arkwright devised a spinning jenny. This reversed the situation—now the cotton mills could no longer keep up with the spinners' output. Then Cartwright invented the power loom. Thus, from challenge to challenge, inventions mushroomed, beginning in the cotton industry, then spreading to textiles in general and finally to other industries.

An "Immaterial Third Factor"

What we are dealing with here is the play of mental forces, what I propose to call the "immaterial third factor," a qualitative and invisible sign with which to multiply or divide the first two factors, capital and labor, which are material, visible, quantitative.

Regardless of Marx's belief, the ownership of capital appears today to be of secondary importance. Are basic economic conditions changed if capital is held by private owners, by cooperatives or the public? Not at all, as long as competition survives and market mechanisms are not blocked by administrative interference. In whatever political and social system, capital and labor are both indispensable. And if capital changes hands, the shift has little effect on the laborer's condition, assuming there is no change in technical standards. Nationalized Renault and privately owned Peugeot both make automobiles; how do their employees' lives differ?

Labor is also a secondary factor, as harsh as this may seem. Workers can always be found, even if they have to be imported. They can usually be trained, improved—or made redundant by automation.

But what does change everything, what traditional economists have neglected, from Adam Smith through Marx to Keynes, is this third factor which is so difficult to pin down. Among individuals, it often takes the form of talent; it is always to be found in the great captains of industry. "Leave me naked as a worm in the middle of the Sahara without a sou but near a caravan route," I was told by entrepreneur-industrialist Sylvain Floirat, "and within a few months I'll be a billionaire again." This wasn't just a manner of speaking. As a cartwright's son who quit school at eleven, he had been virtually naked. He didn't miss the caravan.

In societies, the third factor is a bundle of mental attitudes. A cultural environment is the soil in which some plants can grow while others wither. Look at an English lawn, so different from a French lawn; it can only be achieved by constant repetition of the same process—mow, roll, water, mow, roll, water. It's simple, but the French almost always forget one of these three steps (rolling) or their proper order, or they neglect to do them regularly. So they grow weeds instead of grass. On the other hand, the British are avid cookbook-readers whereas the French can cook. It's a matter of culture.

We rebel against this third factor. We don't want to admit that our way of thinking or our collective conduct can have material consequences. We prefer to explain matter by matter rather than manner. We resist the admission that if Britain became industrialized before France, it was really not because it had coal, as many other countries did, but because it had more pioneers capable of using that coal.[10]

Routine Through Hierarchy

The vitality of a society and an economy is surely measured by how much they encourage innovation. Doesn't this help to explain the difference between hierarchical societies, enclosed in a shell of routine, and innovative free societies? Of course, the members of a hierarchical society tend to think routinely: they are part of an order in which the head does the thinking, and they are expected to submit undeviatingly to its impulses. This makes life simple, as long as the routine is maintained. But the slightest variation throws everything out of kilter. Should a crisis arise, there is only one satisfactory solution—the *status quo ante*.

Many people are prepared to pay the price for this system of collective security. The Roman Empire, the French monarchy at its apogee, Napoleon's empire, Stalinist Russia, the Church between the Councils of Trent and Vatican II, all left behind them a long wake of regret. Nostalgia dies hard in those who have experienced this imperious form of order in which the individual is subordinate to the community, but also shares in its grandeur.

Authoritarian economies always have trouble progressing. In France before the Revolution, members of each guild were bound by punctilious norms governing the production and sale of what they made. In most cases, innovation failed to survive its passage through the regulations. Luckily, there were a few holes in the regulations in which it could flourish. In the Alsatian city of Mulhouse, Protestants using Swiss techniques founded a mill to produce printed cottons; the operation was unhampered by regulations because it did not happen to fall within the jurisdiction of any guild, and so it prospered. Craftsmen by the dozens, feeling stifled in the regulated trades, flocked there and launched the city on its way to wealth.

For centuries, the very term "innovator" had a pejorative meaning. "Madwomen, schismatics, innovators," Racine tells us, were the insults hurled at the Jansenist nuns of Port-Royal.[11] And Diderot remarked that the word "innovator" is "almost always taken as offensive, so attached are men to the established things."[12] Are we so different now?

Pity the Poor Potato

As an example, take the potato, that most useful innovation in an undernourished Western world. The English quickly understood what a dietary boon this American curiosity could be. Shakespeare and Francis Bacon praised its virtues. In 1619 it was already among the foods authorized for the royal table.

In 1664, John Forester wrote a treatise proclaiming *England's Prosperity Increased by Cultivation of the Potato.*

But France stubbornly rejected the tuber that could have spared it so many famines, so many deaths. As late as 1787, the Royal Agricultural Society of Paris considered potatoes "fit for cows"—and for the English. Yet Antoine Parmentier, the agronomist and pharmacist who popularized the potato in France, had almost won his battle by then, for he had understood that the problem was not to adapt the potato to French soil, but to break down a mental block. So Parmentier went right to the top: he persuaded Louis XVI to decorate his buttonhole with a flower from the new plant, and the potato immediately became fashionable at court and in the cities. To win the peasants over as well, he had soldiers stationed day and night around a field where he had planted this strange vegetable. When the guard was withdrawn, the neighbors rushed to steal growths so precious that they merited a military guard.[13]

In a hierarchical organization, all the elements must march in step like an army. Change is rejected if it cannot be adopted en bloc, which means that it is almost always rejected, except in case of a crisis. A swell of unrest in the French Army in 1975 illustrated the point. "We registered the unrest," one colonel told me. "I did propose some changes that would probably have eased the tension. But I was warned by the higher-ups: 'Don't you play that game. Yours isn't the only regiment. Don't forget that any change in the regulations has to apply to all units at the same time.' "

Innovation and Self-Reliance

In contrast to the monocentric societies, which see any change as aggression, polycentric societies welcome and encourage innovation. It is surely not by chance that a map of the world's highest living standards exactly matches the map of those countries where democratic pluralism and a competitive economy operate conjointly*

Researchers are like wild ducks—tame them, and they lose their sense of direction. How can we program the unforeseeable? Joseph Black discovered carbon dioxide while looking for a salt to relieve indigestion.[14] It was Pasteur, not a physician but a chemist, who developed an anti-rabies vaccine. The scientific and inventive spirits have only really been able to develop in the modern Christian world. Lewis Mumford calculated the number of scientific dis-

---

* See Appendix I, which lists countries according to per capita gross national product for 1976. The first eighteen are pluralistic democracies; of these, fifteen are organized on the Protestant model, three are sociologically Catholic (Belgium, no. 8; France, no. 9; Austria, no. 16). Note that this ranking has changed relatively slightly in the fifty years since it was first established.

coveries and technical inventions from the fifteenth through the nineteenth centuries: 127 in the fifteenth, 429 in the sixteenth, 691 in the seventeenth, 1,574 in the eighteenth and 8,527 in the nineteenth.[15] The more of them there were, the more they were concentrated in the polycentric societies. The rate has increased in the twentieth century, and so has the concentration in pluralist democracies, despite the effort devoted to research in the totalitarian countries. Since 1917, scores of innovations have changed men's lives—jet planes, radar, the electric locomotive, television, laser beams, rockets, antibiotics; not one originated in any of the countries bearing the monocentric stamp of the October Revolution.

The Nobel Index

An ingenious sociologist has established a "Nobel Index"* for the experimental sciences (physics, chemistry, medicine and biology).[16] Relating the number of Nobel prizes a country has won to its population gives a reasonably good contemporary indication of the country's capacity for scientific innovation. The findings are impressive: Switzerland leads the list, followed by Denmark, Austria, Holland, Sweden, Great Britain, Germany and the United States. France is ninth.

The study shows:

—an overwhelming predominance of Protestant over Catholic countries (four fifths of the total) and, in the Catholic countries, of Protestant or Jewish scientists over Catholics;

—a high percentage of Jewish prizewinners (Austria owes its third place in the list to a generation of Jewish scientists who worked in Vienna until 1933 and then fled from Naziism);

—a preeminence of small over big countries. Each of the first five countries on the list has a population of under 10 million. In scientific research, as in economics, numbers are not a necessary precondition for success. A mass economy is an asset, but the proliferation of small, autonomous units is a far greater one.

The Pioneer Spirit

For the scientific spirit to be truly fertile requires more than just unfettered curiosity. There must be a ravenous appetite for transforming a hypothesis into a discovery, a discovery into an invention, and an invention into an innovation. A people must be able to make an enterprise of research. This is the essence of what I would call the pioneer spirit. A man moved by the pioneer spirit is a winner. Without him, it is impossible to move from an idea for change to a reality changed by an idea.

* See Appendix II.

Take Willem Beukels, for example. It occurred to this fifteenth-century Hollander that herrings could be kept from rotting by discarding their innards and preventing air from getting to the fish. He devised the process of gutting them, cutting out their gills and laying the herrings down in tight rows. This easily preserved food at once became so sought after that the Low Countries used its herrings as an exchange currency. The discovery changed the nation's fate.

Replying to a challenge is by no means the rule in human history. A million Israelis, then 2 million, 3 million accepted the desert's challenge. The tens of millions of people who until then had inhabited similar terrain had made no effort to change it; they had simply bowed to their fate.

CHAPTER 19

The Development Hormones

For thousands of years, men thought they had only to eat their fill in order to grow and become strong. It was a question of quantity. We all know today that an organism's development is governed by qualitative elements, catalysts that function merely by their presence, without even seeming to operate. These are the enzymes and hormones. Should they be deficient or unbalanced, the organism's metabolism is upset, appetite wanes, spirits droop and growth is stunted. The same is equally true of economic growth, but in this case the catalysts are cultural—what I have called the third factor.

Underdeveloped countries may very well have an abundance of raw materials, the foreign currencies earned by their export, an adequate labor supply. But if they do not cultivate an economic mentality, their growth will be limited, outgrowth rather than real development.

It was not so much Protestantism and Catholicism in themselves that guided the Western countries' careers as their organizational principles— polycentrism on the one hand and monocentrism on the other. These principles went far beyond religion as such, so much that they continued to animate Western societies long after religious passions were appeased. They have even survived the nineteenth century's secularizing movement and the twentieth century's dechristianization.

It is as though the hierarchical societies had neutralized the development catalysts they contained before retrenchment set in. The liberal societies on the other hand secreted these catalysts abundantly.

Thomas Cook versus Don Quixote

Responsible self-reliance, as we have seen, is the principal development hormone because it governs all the others. The responsibilities with which you are invested, the risks you are free to take, spur you to act. Economic dynamism is rooted in the gamble of financial credit, which in turn depends on moral credit because the lender assumes that the borrower is trustworthy. Credit is confidence deserved and granted. Your energies are mobilized by that confidence, but you also have to show that you deserve it; rational conduct, regular effort, punctiliousness, order and method, discipline and a respect for agreements are all mandatory crossing points to economic development.

In 1845, Thomas Cook, a Scottish Baptist preacher and temperance leader, organized a group voyage for his co-religionaries that provided reduced fares and low prices in clean hotels that served no alcohol. People liked the formula and he organized more excursions. They inspired confidence; they were cheaper; everything was laid on in advance, the hotels carefully chosen. In 1851, bolstered by his initial success, he organized Cook's travel agency. Soon he was offering round-the-world tours.

Cutting costs through mass sales, moderate prices, sobriety, tenacity, a spirit of adventure, a need for practical achievement—this minister-businessman was the very incarnation of the Puritan mentality and the development society. Don Quixote traveled nowhere but around his dreams. True, it's Don Quixote we would rather know. But if we are going somewhere, it's Thomas Cook we consult.

Money Buys Independence

From the chain reaction's beginnings in the seventeenth century, clear minds perceived the characteristics that economists and sociologists today associate with development. Thus, money as a sign of and means to independence has been rehabilitated. A free man is judged capable of putting money to good use and of restraining himself from abusing it. "We must exhort Christians to earn what they can and to save all they can—that is, in fact, to become rich," said John Wesley, the founder of Methodism.

Good management assures that the value of goods produced is higher than that of goods consumed. Contrary to a widespread belief in the countries with anti-economic attitudes, the surplus is not taken from anyone's pocket. Rather, it is the result of a stubborn struggle against routine, penury, imperfection and waste. Profit is the objective, under the less provocative term of "viability," in any industrialized economy, even the communists'.

The Spirit of Investment

The spirit of saving and investment is another essential development hormone. It goes along with the individual's effort to outdo himself, with the self-control that sacrifices short-term benefits to long-term goals, the rejection of ostentation and a kind of abstinence. The Jesuit explorer priest François-Xavier Charlevoix, visiting North America in the eighteenth century, was struck by the abstinence shown by the English settlers in contrast to the ostentation of the French: "In New England and in the provinces subject to the British Empire there reigns an opulence from which the people seem not to know how to profit, and in New France, poverty hidden by an air of ease. The English colonist amasses wealth and spends nothing; the Frenchman spends what he has and makes a show of what he does not have."[1] There is a kind of natural inflation in the French spirit.

In the Latin countries, the rich tended to spend gladly for show, for novelty—celebrations, fireworks, great hunts, palaces, richly decorated churches. In the Protestant countries, many of the wealthy preferred to invest in mass production, which forced them to expand their businesses to amortize the cost of the assembly lines, increase their clientele and create a body of solvent consumers.

The Struggle for Competition

Independence also encourages competition, another development hormone. The biological struggle for life, the struggle for power in politics, the military's armed struggle, all are natural. Economic competition, however, is highly artificial. It does not exist in primitive societies, nor in the feudal or corporative systems that long prevailed in the West and that still exist in barely renovated forms. It represents a decisive step forward in social organization.

Competition is the school of responsibility. Whoever creates an enterprise in a competitive situation does so at his own risk, with the promise of profit if it succeeds and the threat of bankruptcy if it fails.

Anyone holding a monopoly is tempted to abuse it. An employee who cannot be fired lets things drift; what's the use of straining? The head of a firm with a cornered market feels free to raise his prices; why increase his productivity? In the seventeenth century, Holland's Jean de Witt explained the advantages of competition among free enterprises:

> The country can profit best from those who work most, to which monopolistic companies do not contribute much because they have no fear that their trade might be disturbed. The monopolistic Greenland Company made little profit from fishing, as much because of its great expenditures on equipment as because the oil, fat and whalebone were not very well kept and because they were stored in warehouses and not distributed soon enough. Private shipowners, on the other hand, were more sparing in their equipment, they were wholly diligent in fishing as promptly as possible and making everything pay, deriving profit from everything, seeking new places to sell [their wares] at higher margins.[2]

How very modern it all sounds!

The rules of the game force the players to live dangerously, which is not to everyone's taste. This explains the commercial understandings, frauds and hidden protectionism that the state must constantly combat. The moment of truth comes when a firm is threatened. If a government gives in to the temptation to help a declining industry beyond a reasonable point, then the economy will be encumbered with a living corpse. It is a common idea that economic liberalism implies an absence of government intervention. In fact, the opposite is true. According to the logic of a market economy, a government must be strong enough to impose competition on business. The greatest weakness of a planned economy allied to a liberal political system is that it perverts competition. Pressure groups—businessmen, labor, politicians—can successfully blackmail the state into becoming the instrument by which the laws of the marketplace are evaded.

Competition in international trade is essential. The security an economy draws from protectionism is illusory and temporary; protected products sold on an internal market at higher prices than the same goods manufactured abroad only impoverish a national economy. A modern economy is a permanent improvisation. It is created by fighters, and it cannot progress nor even survive except through struggle.

It is surely symptomatic that the most backward sectors of the French economy, such as the building industry, agriculture, distribution—or, in another sphere, education—are those that are least competitive. France has almost never known a truly competitive system. From Sully to the Treaty of Rome, it has virtually always protected itself by customs barriers from its principal competitors. And it still dreams of reinforcing its corporativism and returning to protectionism, even though since 1958 its official policy has been to favor competition.

The Machinery of Freedom

To defenders of a planned economy, the workings of a market economy are chaotic. Let us try nevertheless to see how a competitive system works.

Every day, millions of consumers choose whether to spend or save, to consume meat or fish, wine or beer, to go on doing what they are doing or to make a change, to live in the city or the suburbs. Through this chain of decisions, the consumer exercises sovereign power over the direction an economy will take; the way he uses his income constitutes a far more concrete and continuous vote than the one he drops into the ballot box. In economics, the workings of the market are direct democracy; they might even be called the most democratic of all institutions. To keep in step with these tens of millions of autonomous centers of decision, firms must adapt their output, revise their plans, rethink their investments.

Are many of these decisions irrational? It might even be said that they all are and should be. This is the great, ordered play of millions of freely determined choices upon billions of competitive proposals—a vast movement of individual and collective adaptation to the fluid diversity of life.

Advertising, it is objected, manipulates buyers who cannot resist the mirages it projects. But why should they be asked to resist the mirages of dema-goguery? It is consistent for a totalitarian regime which denies its citizens the right to vote also to deny its consumers the right to choose what they consume. Not so a politically free system. Nothing prevents another producer or a consumers' association from warning against misleading advertising. Let's not pretend that a market economy is perfect; let us simply acknowledge that it is the most effective lever of economic progress.

Japan and the Naval Challenge

The correlations we have established between Protestantism and the progress of an industrial market civilization, and between Catholicism and its persistent sluggishness in adopting this civilization, should not discourage the French. Luther and Calvin in particular involuntarily accelerated a process that had existed before their time, just as, equally involuntarily, the Counter-Reformation braked that process. Acceleration or braking have long been remarked outside of a religious context. Japan is the best example of this; there religion had nothing to do with the energies it brought into play.

In 1853, Commodore Perry's American war fleet forced open the ports of a feudal, agricultural country to international trade. A few years earlier other Western gunships had done the same for China. Like its big neighbor, Japan was on its way to becoming an Anglo-American economic satellite. But China retreated into the pride of its civilization; by refusing to cede in its attitudes, it instead ceded its wealth and power to the West. Japan grew rich and powerful by radically changing its way of thinking.

A century later, the world realized to its astonishment that Japan had become its third great power.[3] The country had accepted Perry's challenge and prepared its revenge by studying in its masters' school. It sent its young people to American and European universities; it excelled in the art of exploiting Western patents and processes, adapting to its own uses Britain's parliamentary system, American budgeting, Prussian police and educational systems, Swedish ball bearings, Norwegian trawlers, German optics and commercial law and American-style campuses.[4]

Japan's success was a resounding one, achieved with very few assets to begin with: only two thirds as large as France (but with, today, double the population), 80 percent of its territory is uninhabitable and a mere 16 to 18 percent is arable. Typhoons, tidal waves, earthquakes are part of its normal life, sometimes a staggering part—like the 1923 earthquake that leveled Tokyo and Yokohama and left 100,000 dead.[5] Its many islands and forbidding terrain make communications difficult. It is poor in natural resources, with coal scarce and of low quality, oil and natural gas almost nonexistent and scanty minerals.

Yet in less than a century Japan became a laboratory of growth. It produces three fourths of the food consumed by its 100 million-plus population. In 1976 its industrial output equalled that of France and West Germany combined—or that of all the other countries of Asia, including China and Soviet Siberia. It is the world's leading builder of merchant shipping, its most prolific producer of motorcycles, sewing machines, cameras, microscopes, transistor radios. Of the two hundred biggest companies in the world outside the United States, forty-five are Japanese.[6]

Economic Taboos

France's anti-economic attitudes were initially formed and maintained by an elitist influence. Under the monarchy, the elite class was the nobility and, especially with the advent of Louis XIV to the throne, the French nobility was obsessed by the idea of special privilege. Because they paid their tax in blood in wartime, they were exonerated from paying taxes in money; they lived only to serve God or the king. They lost their gentility if they "cheapened themselves"—by practicing a mechanical art (manual labor) or engaging in trade.[7] The marquis de Jouffroy d'Abbans was spurned by his family (in the same year in which the United States proclaimed its independence) because he had built with his own hands a steamboat capable of navigating the Doubs River.

Even Montesquieu, modern as he was, adhered to his class prejudices: "It is against the spirit of trade for the nobility to practice it in the monarchy. It is against the spirit of the monarchy for its nobles to engage in trade." There were a few exceptions to the taboos: nobles could retain their standing if they patronized mining, glassmaking, shipbuilding. On the eve of the Revolution, 1,000 noble families were thus involved in industry—1,000 out of 80,000.[8] In fact, the taboo permeated the entire society.[9]

And so it continued to do until well after the Revolution. Just as "people of quality knew everything without having learned anything," they were rich without having earned anything. Honor was for those who consumed what they did not produce—the nobility, officialdom. Pardon was granted to those who burned up a hard-won fortune in the cavalier spirit of someone lighting a cigar with a banknote. In the Protestant countries, meanwhile, the values were reversed.

The Bourgeois Betrayal

France's anti-economic prejudice would not have been so serious if the nobility's values had not also infected the middle class, with no counter-effect from the bourgeoisie. The middle class, which *was* subject to taxation, had to earn money. The nobility saw in this the mark of bourgeois inferiority. And so did the bourgeoisie. How could it have tackled enthusiastically something it despised itself for doing? The very people who could have engineered France's economic development were so persuaded of the nobility's values that they thought only of terminating their fortune-hunting as soon as their fortunes were made. At least until the Belle Epoque, many wealthy commoners, or their sons, renounced all commercial activity for government jobs and a life of ostentatious luxury in order at last to acquire social status, to take their places in the privileged procession of persons drawing their prestige from the state.[10]

However it might surprise an anticlerical intellectual, hostility to profit must be recognized as having clerical origins. The medieval scholastics, inspired by Aristotle, lent it the majesty of a theological interdiction. They gave short shrift to production and trade. Montesquieu was right to stress that "we owe to the scholastics' speculations all the misfortunes that have accompanied the destruction of commerce, which was linked to lack of faith." The "progressive" pattern that began to take shape at the end of the Middle Ages was stopped dead by the Counter-Reformation's flat condemnation of profit; it was not only lending money at interest that was now sinful, but economics in general.

Consumerism Condemned

Against this background—as solidly implanted in our souls as our childhood memories—how many past Utopias, how many modern ideologies have perished! In 1534, an unsuccessful tradesman named Jan van Leyden seized power in Münster, Westphalia, and proclaimed himself "king of the new Zion." As master of Münster for a few months, he abolished private capital, "selfish" private property, buying and selling, interest and usury as "sins against love." He failed again, but not as completely as we might think: his spirit lives on in all the builders of earthly paradises. A poster in Paris in May 1968 condemned the consumers' society: "We reject a world where the certainty of not dying of hunger must be paid for by the risk of dying of boredom."

In England and Scotland, the greatest names are allied with the greatest fortunes. In Germany, I was surprised to see how important the *Almanach de Gotha* (the social register published in both French and German from 1763 to 1944) was in business. A prince of Salm represented a soft-drink firm, Prince Henry of Prussia promoted a brand of lipstick. These grandsons of reigning princes were proud to rebuild fortunes that enabled them to restore their ancestral châteaux.

It is easy to understand why collectivist regimes, which prohibit elections, also ban a market economy: their leaders know better than the consumer what he ought to consume, and better than the citizen who ought to lead him. But rejection of a market economy in democratic societies seems explicable only by the persistence of age-old taboos. In primitive societies, commercial transactions were rare and profit was often linked with theft. Theology gave these taboos intellectual justification. Nowadays, Marxism imbues them with a tang of rational modernity. Hence the fascination that Soviet-style planning long held for the French intelligentsia.

Rejection of a market economy simply engenders a black market. A corseted economy must find some way to bend, and so a parallel economy springs up. A tourist in the Soviet Union learns that beef is not to be found at the official price in the state stores. It can be bought at any time on the kolkhozian market, but an average Soviet worker would have to spend a fifth of his monthly wage for a pound of it. And the yields on Soviet farmers' tiny patches of private land are eight to ten times higher than those on the state farms.

Economic Planning

The technocrat's dream is to fix the future on paper by coolly deciding what suits the public. It is exciting to line up all those figures in close ranks, like an army on parade, all those factors and objectives. But this lust for "rationalism" eliminates good sense.

For thirteen years, from 1963 to 1976, the French Finance Ministry stubbornly opposed raising the prices of paperback reprints because, unlike regular editions, these books were included in the cost-of-living index. Controlled sale prices no longer covered production costs, which were not controlled. If the publishers of pocket books had not found a way around the ban, these publications would have disappeared. Books that until then had appeared as singles were rebaptized doubles and so-called double volumes were rechristened triples or quadruples. Price control officials were not fooled, but what mattered to them was untouched: the regulations were respected and the index was unchanged. The trick was played successfully.

We French fall easily into the notion that official intervention in private affairs is inevitable today; it is probably because we believe this that we submit to it without rebelling. We should wake up to the fact that it has been a French characteristic for centuries and has played a basic role in France's backwardness. Perhaps, if we do, we will realize just how old-fashioned it is.

In Brittany, early in the eighteenth century, the royal bureaus maintained close control over the application of regulations prohibiting the import of foreign fabrics, governing the production of domestic cloth, supervising cottage industries, and so on. Soon they were working to reduce the number and size of shellfish beds and fisheries; on the strength of an inspector's report, the naval secretary decreed that "the excess of fisheries in Brittany is harmful to the community."[11] At the time, France was beset by famine.

Legitimate and Illegitimate Profit

Yet a little common sense, rather than advanced degrees in economics, is all we need to distinguish *illegitimate profit*, which is derived from privilege or speculation in public misery or dishonesty at the community's expense, from *legitimate profit*, which is earned as a reward for an innovator's risk in creating something new, that is, in being enterprising, in investing his energy, his time and his strength in pursuit of a fugitive goal, of something that would not have existed but for him.[12] By amalgamating legitimate and illegitimate profit, the antiprofit mentality has created havoc in the Latin countries; profit from innovation there is still penalized.

Rejection of an economic mentality is the major aspect of the rejection of liberalism in all the countries stamped with the Counter-Reformation's reinforced dogmatism. What is called the "condemnation of capitalism" is largely a rejection of the modern world. Indeed, Rome has repeatedly affirmed this publicly, notably in the *Syllabus* issued by Pope Pius IX in 1864, unequivocally condemning "progress, liberalism and modern civilization." The decree objected particularly to economic liberalism, which it accused of converting labor into merchandise and wages into prices and of concentrating too much power in too few hands.

With Roman purism and Marxist purism, state purism completes the triptych. Through most of the nineteenth century, the French Council of State insisted that government authorization was required for the creation of any corporation, as it was for the opening of a bawdy house. Article 71, Section V, of the French commercial code stipulates that "the Stock Exchange is the gathering *under the government's authority* of traders, ship captains, exchange agents and brokers." The great eighteenth-century jurist Locré ruled that "it is forbidden to assemble anywhere but in the Stock Exchange to propose or carry on negotiations." No business dealings, then, except with government authorization.

Learning to Swim

Economic motives play a role in community life comparable to that of the libido in an individual's life. Our hierarchical societies have repressed them for centuries by inhibitions tangled in a web of complexes. But we will never make up our backwardness and become an adult society unless we free ourselves of these taboos.

Sometimes a chance event can uncover and liberate a repressed personality. For France, the creation of the Common Market may have been such an event. France does as its partners do, observing and imitating economic gestures with which it is not really familiar, flailing bravely in the water. One wonders how long will it remain afloat. It would really do better if it learned to swim, and to enjoy the water.

CHAPTER 20

Martha and Mary

Mary's Advantages

When the West split in the sixteenth century, it gave up any hope of moving in every dimension simultaneously. Part of Christendom settled under the sign of Martha, the other under the sign of Mary, the two sisters of Lazarus. One, Martha, was "cumbered about much serving" and was "careful and troubled about many things." Mary simply "sat at Jesus' feet."[1] Every people makes its choice between busy Martha and contemplative Mary. But let's not forget that, for Christ, it was Mary who "hath chosen that good part."

France, under the sign of Mary, has maintained a more intense spiritual and intellectual vitality than the Protestant countries. Religion there has not been reduced to a vague deism; it continues to produce mystics and saints and rebels. Catholicism has made each soul the stage for a personal drama; what better way to create persons?

The blossoming forth of art in Mary's countries is related to Catholicism's persistent vitality. Inventiveness, banished from technique and from the active pursuits, is fulfilled in art and literature; barred from reality, it bursts forth in the realm of the imaginary. It was in the countries touched by the Counter-Reformation that baroque art triumphed. Economies froze, societies hardened, but art was exuberant, prodigal, liberated. Daily life became opera, theater, the novel, poetry; a social cult grew up around writers and artists.

In their fashion, the lives of the humble have shared in this spirit, which long preserved a quality that was startlingly degraded in Martha's countries by industrial concentration—the systematic uprooting of ancient peasant communities, the "massification" of public life. Society in the Catholic nations is still a community where men like to parade themselves, where they know how to cultivate life. Social advancement may be slow, but it does not rob the underprivileged of their true, human, wealth; their talents and their genius are preserved. The village storyteller might have been a university professor, but would the village have been the happier for it?

Moreover, hierarchical organizations are formidably durable—witness the centralized state in France and the Roman Church throughout the world.

This durability is in itself a virtue. After all, anarchy is the gravest danger facing human society. The ability to maintain order, to rein in the headlong rush of power and violence, to enforce the community's laws and ideals—all this deserves respect.

Stifling and inert though it may be, the state has kept the French together. It has expanded the national territory to its present borders, has survived military disasters, the Revolution, political instability, its divorce from the Church, social upheaval. And the Church, stifling and inert though it may be, has preserved the spirit of charity; it has made the word of God heard above sound and fury, standing as a continuing witness to man's spiritual unity.

Martha's Advantages

There remains the superiority of Martha's countries in everything touching upon practical effectiveness in the areas of both economics and political organization, and in defining a national consensus.

For each group of countries has its own coherence. The Christian fission in the sixteenth century set off two independent, contrary chain reactions. In recapitulating the preceding chapters, let us try to see a pattern in these two movements, even if this forces us to simplify them a bit and even if we risk making what were probably only lines of coherence and convergence appear to be cause-and-effect relationships.

Most of the "Catholic" and "Protestant" countries are neither exclusively Catholic nor exclusively Protestant; most are largely dechristianized. But, in each, it is either the Catholics or the Protestants who set the tone of the country's public spirit, its institutions, its scale of values. These countries can be said to be sociologically Catholic or Protestant, even if unbelievers are in the majority in all of them.

In Protestant-style societies, Christians' relationship to God is direct. Their own consciences are their sole judges. They read the scriptures for themselves; they form equally independent religious communities. The fragmentation of the universal Church into various sects fosters independent thinking. Refugees are eagerly welcomed. Religious and civil power are quickly separated in fact without really opposing each other.

Further, common law tends to prevail over written law. Guiding principles carry more weight than detailed regulations. The judiciary constantly brings the regulations into phase with reality. Individual liberty is soon affirmed.

Reading the Bible is a condition of personal achievement. Primary and secondary education develop rapidly.[2] The primary mission of instruction is to prepare students to live in their society. Schools are either autonomous or under local authority, and this diversity encourages constant renovation of educational methods. Teaching is based on confidence, which in turn fortifies the spirit of initiative, energy, endurance and self-discipline; to betray that confidence is the gravest of faults.

Instruction is as concrete as possible. Subjects with a practical application are favored. Sports are as important as any other subject, being thought of as a training in ethics. The team sports played throughout the world originated in the Protestant countries. Girls are admitted into the schools very early on. Women's rights, both civic and civil, are quickly won (except in Switzerland, where women were not given the the vote until 1971).

Innovation and Exchange

Such societies are highly innovative. Their technological aptitude is readily apparent, and their economic circuits are extended chiefly through technical renovation.

A well-regarded entrepreneurial class soon appears, creating new techniques, new sources of capital, energy and raw materials, new outlets, a new clientele. The rules of an industrial market economy are proclaimed and accepted: the law of supply and demand, private initiative, the search for a return on investment and competitive profit, freedom of contractual agreement. Making money becomes a sign of professional achievement.

A decentralized social structure, municipal power and the rapid spread of technical knowledge all accelerate the movement of exchanges both of ideas and goods. Even agriculture, the sector most resistant to change, moves rapidly away from subsistence level to become agribusiness. Mechanized farming releases most of the people working on the land for jobs in industry.

These are mercantile societies, where business is a highly honorable calling. Diplomacy and colonization are aimed at developing trade. Credit fosters the growth of banking, insurance and savings. They are also industrial societies, respecting and rewarding firms that try to sell their products to the widest possible public at the lowest possible price. This engenders mass production, automation, rational management.

Democratic Societies

Executive power is very quickly subjected to the control of elected assemblies. Powers are balanced. Constitutional stability does not prevent gradual adaptation of the laws to new conditions, but local democracy completes and balances the national democracy. The local authorities are given broad powers. The national bureaucracy by contrast is relatively small, which allows the citizenry to place responsibility where it belongs. The public accepts its political institutions along with its economic and social system. The system's defects are considered remediable. Rival parties succeed each other in power, or share in it, without difficulty.

Finally, civic spirit is at a high pitch. Social pressure incites respect for official policy—social cohesion is tight. Labor unions, an early feature of Protestant-style societies, form the habit of compromising; tensions are high, but they are eased by negotiation. Class cooperation is preferred to class struggle. Opposition does not weaken this consensus; it operates within narrow limits and favors continuous change. Communism puts down no roots.

A Torpid Mary

In the hierarchical societies, it is the clergy who command the faithful and who act as God's interpreters. The notion of the Church blends with that of the clergy. In the religious hierarchy, national Churches submit to the Holy See's supranational authority. Believers who do not understand Latin are long accustomed to viewing religious ritual as a body of magic spells. For centuries the clergy clings to its wealth, maintaining its monopoly of education, its privileged relationship with the state. Those who do not share the dominant ideology are rejected. "Deviants"—Protestants, Jansenists, Jews, and so on—are long persecuted, even expelled.

Civil society rests on written law based on Roman law. Regulation, precise and proliferous, impedes change. Individual liberties develop late.

Dogmatic Societies

Education tends to pattern itself on the hierarchical model. Primary and secondary instruction develop slowly. Almost all the schools are dependent on a hierarchical authority, that of the government or the Church; virtually all private schools are Catholic. The public-school system tries to erect a clerical-style monopoly of education adapted to its own purposes. Government education ministries become tentacular bureaucracies, regulating school life and teaching methods down to the smallest detail. Such centralized organization and uniform methods hamper teaching experiments. Lack of confidence becomes the rule in instruction: a class is a show given by a teacher who knows things to students who do not. Opposition tends to stiffen the centralized authority's resistance—or to cause its total collapse.

Instruction is deliberately abstract, and any intensification of the abstract is considered progress in education. Pure speculation is preferred to any practical application—more prestige is attached to theoretical mathematics than to the experimental sciences. Sports are considered unimportant. Such rare national sports as do develop are those demonstrating individual prowess (bullfighting, fencing, bicycle racing), or team sports where individual skill is paramount (soccer).

Women's rights are long withheld. Organized schooling is extended much later to girls than to boys, and legal equality for women is won only through struggle.

Repetitive Societies

The metamorphosis of scientific discoveries into technical inventions is slow in these societies, and their transformation into industrial innovations even slower. Growth is expected to come solely from increased consumption rather than from the constant search for new techniques, products and sciences.

Entrepreneurs face hostility. Discouraged from taking risks, they seek safe profits protected by privilege rather than attempting to change their methods, products or markets. There is little respect for economic activity as contrasted with religious, governmental or intellectual work. The rules of an industrial market economy are often rejected. Wealth that is not inherited is suspect.

Exchanges of all kinds are difficult in such societies; social compartmentalization, individuals' isolation from the hierarchies to which they are responsible, the slow spread of technical information, all brake the progress of modern communications. Agriculture long resists change. The farm population remains relatively large and forms a separate society. Commerce, too, remains archaic; the upper social classes may not participate in it without losing caste. Its basic objective is to impose its merchandise on the market.

With lending at interest long banned, credit mechanisms are not easily acclimatized in these societies. Banks remain in the control of ethnic or religious minorities (Protestants, Jews). The state, suspicious of them, tends to absorb them. Industry is more concerned with quantity than quality, less interested in lowering prices to attract customers than in protecting itself through monopoly. Manufacturing long remains at the artisanal stage.

Convulsive Societies

The representative system is difficult to establish in the Catholic countries, where authoritative regimes alternate with government by legislature. There is a high mortality rate among overly rigid constitutions—local democracy is even harder to establish than national democracy.

The citizen has practically no part in reaching the decisions imposed on him, even in matters that touch him most closely. The decisionmakers are anonymous and elusive. Consensus is rare. A considerable portion of the population rejects not only its political, economic and social systems, but also any reform of those systems.

Only officials elected by large majorities are thought to have an incontestable right to their offices. Protest is attracted to the extremes; the strongest labor unions are those that forward the most radical claims. Much prestige is attached to the idea of class struggle. Civic spirit is low. Resourcefulness, hustling, making shift are encouraged and honored.

The Communist Party takes root as a substitute—and as an inverse image—of the Catholic Church, offering a supranational, dogmatic, disciplined organization. Armies succumb to the temptation to intervene in politics.

New Factors

Today, these summaries no longer provide explanation enough, because new factors have been added to the situation in the Catholic countries, especially France. Catholicism had its own reformation in the Vatican II Council, which in effect shed its armor of Romanism. This was a crucial event. In the short run, the faith has paid dearly for this *aggiornamento*. In France, for example, two out of three Catholics stopped attending church between 1962 and 1977. But, among the confusion of changes, the remaining third is finding new vitality in its Church.

Vatican II's immense achievement was to associate the faithful with the hierarchy. In societies fashioned by Catholicism, even those that have been largely dechristianized, Christianity has lost its apparatus of intellectual constraint to resume its exemplary function. With it vanished a primary reason for the Latin societies' blockage.

Some economic bolts were blown at the same time. Since 1945, and especially, because of its entry into the Common Market, since 1959, France has been in a new orbit. By throwing itself resolutely into Europe, it has learned to enjoy the bracing air of struggle.

The other Latin countries, despite their difficulty in reconciling authority and liberty, can overcome their backwardness. Southern Europe has already gained ground and can go still further. The very fact of having remained archaic until so recently means that it has reserves now lacking in countries with a long industrial tradition. After centuries of decline, the four Latin sisters may be undergoing a kind of resurrection. This change, then, reduces the contrast between the two social models we have isolated.

Now, in the late twentieth century, every country in the world is confronting the same crisis, that of too-rapid change. And all the Western countries, those which have imposed these changes on the others, are going through a crisis of capitalism.

A third crisis faces the French, one proper to a social and administrative structure saturated in Romanism. The shock of the future is sending spasms through our centralized social structures and our dogmatic mental structures that could heighten efforts to impose order on them. At the same time, the air the hierarchy is breathing is increasingly libertarian. The level of social consensus in France is at its lowest point. Imposed discipline is becoming intolerable, but there is no long habit of self-discipline to replace it. France is too liberal for its hierarchical side, too authoritarian for its democratic tendencies. In this disintegrating structure, authority acts as a counter-irritant and democracy as a dissolvent; it is as though both had lost their positive principles. Will France bring off its own Vatican II? And at what cost? It could be extremely high, for the nation's burden of liabilities is still heavy.

Residual Magnetism

France has made great progress, thanks to its institutional stability and its opening out to the world. But it has by no means overcome the consequences of the ills that have assailed it for the past four centuries.

When a piece of iron is magnetized, the magnetism survives long after the attractive force is withdrawn. France's social physics is full of these residual effects. For example, religious fervor has dwindled, yet French minds are still marked by the attitudes religion imparted. The government no longer hangs rebellious farmers from trees, but extreme antagonism persists between the dominators and the dominated. The most modern of the political parties loudly proclaim their strategies of breaking with the system. There is a crack running through society that could widen at any time.

To this political and social fragility, the consequence of France's cultural fractures, must be added the economic fragility resulting from our cumulative backwardness. We are living in two economies; one is modern, busy, expanding, the other is backward, in recession, doomed. The inertia of the second is a heavy handicap to the first's development. It is not by chance that the French own a fourth of all the world's privately held gold. This means that much of their capital is dormant. Another portion of the nation's capital is administered by the state, but constant government intervention hampers the proper use of still a third portion, the active capital in private hands that must pay the costs from which the first two are exonerated. There is a mass of dead wood, and our economic habits are not helping to clear it away.

This excursion into the history of the "French sickness" suggests that there is no social progress without economic progress and no economic progress without an economic mentality. The French, it indicates, must love their business, their industry, their techniques and, therefore, their exporters, manufacturers and technicians. They must concede that the laws of the market are nothing less than the laws of democracy applied to economics.

The persistent handicaps with which history has saddled us can only be overcome, after so many useless political convulsions, by a mental revolution.

III

SICK SOCIAL STRUCTURES

CHAPTER 21

Irresponsibility

Deep in the labyrinth lurks a little-known system of authority. To understand its sources and its effects is to understand the "French sickness." I do not propose a scientific analysis of this system here. But as a guide offers a traveler a choice of excursions, I would like to organize a few exploratory tours of our command apparatus.

The first will acquaint us with the landscape's basic feature: irresponsibility.

No rung is ever skipped in the hierarchical ladder. Even if a minor functionary wants leave, he must request it through "channels." The decision comes back down to him via the same route. The thickness of a file relates not to its purpose but to the organization handling it.

Energy is squandered in climbing and descending discouraging steps— often it is exhausted before the top or bottom are reached. Momentum from the top does not always reach the bottom and the bottom cannot always alert the top. Those who know do not decide; those who decide do not know.

While official communication is atrophied, clandestine communication functions smoothly. A teacher is informed by his union of a transfer or promotion weeks before official notice reaches him. Union newsletters familiarize him with their version of ministerial policy, translating the illegible *Official Bulletin* into comprehensible if not always comprehensive language.

The hierarchy covers the decision-making process with a protective veil: no one knows who made a decision, if indeed someone did. For sometimes no one decides, yet a decision is carried through by momentum without ever having been made. The hierarchy endures, however slight its output may be; it has become the *raison d'être* of those who compose it. What authority would a middle-level official have if he could be by-passed? Unwittingly, he opposes faster communications that might short-circuit him and the decentralization that would evict him.

Little Caesars

When the flow of energy is blocked, it stagnates; at the hierarchy's middle level, it crystallizes around the minor section heads. They are far enough from the top to escape surveillance, and protected from it by their status.

They are also sufficiently detached from the bottom to remain unmoved by the reactions their decisions arouse, knowing perfectly well that the administratee has virtually no recourse against it. This is the ideal situation for bureaucratic authority. Bureaucrats are tempted to run things as they please, with impunity. Theirs is the most implacable authority, not conferred by election and so subject to control by the voters and competition from other candidates, nor entrusted to them by direct and revokable delegation, but conferred by the delegation of power and practically never recalled.

These functionaries do not consider themselves technicians at the disposition of elected officials, whom the elected officials would be free to place in competition with others, to push aside or reject. Rather, they think of themselves as the true repositories of the *imperium,* masked by puppets occupying the front of the stage.

These little Caesars are not necessarily employees of the national government. The administrative sickness, buried within the civil service statute, has invaded the municipal bureaucracies as well. I knew one town clerk whose cantankerous ineptitude was experienced by a succession of mayors who were never able to get rid of him. A painstaking investigation by an administrative inspector-general amassed so thick a bundle of complaints that one braver—or bolder—mayor began disciplinary proceedings against him. Nothing more than a reproach came of it. And even that was considered too much: the "victim" waged a series of lawsuits against the city, which the municipal clerks' union, acting in his name, always won. A union official, playing the benevolent prince, went to see the mayor one day. "The way the courts are," he advised, "you will always lose. But the person in question is unimportant. We don't like winning all the time. I'll make a deal with you." And a deal was made, to the detriment of union discipline, but to that honest gentleman's honor.

On the eve of the Revolution, Arthur Young, an English agronomist traveling in France, encountered a functionary who refused to give him a permit to reside in Besançon. The man had that ill-tempered air *"véritablement d'un commis de bureau,"* camped amid his regulations and his habits, who never went back on a decision because he was intent on showing where authority lay.[1] Unless, that is, a few <u>gold louis</u> . . .

Impersonal Power

The more arbitrarily a civil servant uses his power, the more he tries to impersonalize it. That way, it is the power that is arbitrary, not he. The system is the opposite of what was originally the feudal system, which we ignorantly identify with it, but which was in fact a web of personal obligations, mutually accepted by the vassal and his overlord. The hierarchical system that replaced feudalism is and sees itself as impersonal. It is not Monsieur Dupont or

Monsieur Durand who makes a decision, but Dupont's office, Durand's agency. Bureaucrats are interchangeable and should remain anonymous, so they shelter behind this collective anonymity. Even a civil servant's efficiency rating, designed to distinguish him, is submerged in the equalization process that effaces the best people's skills and diminishes the failings of the worst, bringing everyone into the same fuzzy line.

Posting a functionary's name on his window or on his desk, a frequent habit abroad, goes against the French tradition. If the public were to encounter a human being, it might be moved to threaten him. Yet how can we fail to see that the more elusive an administrator is, the more detested the administration?

An instance is the assignment of teachers to the lycées. The schools' principals have absolutely no say in the choice, any more than the teachers themselves may choose the school to which they're sent. Few teachers know their students' parents. The spirit of responsibility requires that a personal contract be reached, binding the head of a school to the person responsible for a class and to the head of each family. But the system excludes personalization and imposes irresponsibility. And such blindness is progressing: henceforth, teacher assignments are to be made by computer. This is logic gone mad.

People wonder why there is constant unrest in the public schools and not in private schools that fulfill the same mission and pay the same salaries. Depersonalized administrative relationships become sources of frustration. The links between men are broken, not to be welded except in the heated play of counter-forces and clandestine cliques. Encouragement, warning, blame and praise provided a social code for the individuals they mobilized. Anonymity abolishes that code. But the individual is none the happier for it.

The 1958 Constitution was attacked chiefly because it introduced personal power. Yet surely this is its newest contribution, and its best. In place of the impersonal power, the anonymous irresponsibility of a parliamentary regime, it substituted an authority to which the man exercising it must personally reply. This is a healthy system, in which decisions are forged in the solitude of a man's mind and heart and then carried out by a united team under general scrutiny.

The Reign of Mistrust

"Don't lose your money!" "Don't loiter after school!"—a mother's worried imagination races ahead of the child's misdeed, submerging him in a world of prohibitions. Modern psychology has shown how these negative orders can paralyze a nervous temperament.

By bridling freedom, protecting against trial and error, the hierarchical system inhibits the sense of responsibility, replacing it with a system of previous authorizations. The great administrative family is likewise dominated by the mother's style of suspicious authority. A *priori* control is not an adventitious complication—it lies at the heart of a society of mistrust. The man who spends money must not be the one who authorizes the expenditure; a subordinate manager, although theoretically responsible for the funds budgeted to him, is not trusted to spend any of them. There is not a mayor, not an agency director or minister who is not treated like a young prodigal placed in ward by a family council. It's an astonishing system that boomerangs against the spirit of economy which inspires it.

Competition would place civil servants in the position of having to answer for their actions; this is excluded, even while it is affirmed in statements of principle. Look at what happened to the universities. The 1968 orientation act established their "autonomy." Autonomous universities are supposed to mean freedom of initiative, careers open to imagination, emulation—in a word, competition.

What actually happened? Not much. The universities' autonomy is false. Their competitiveness, therefore, is also false. Not that the faculties really insisted on true competition; perhaps they feared for their job security. The act authorized a university to reduce the staffs of sections with no students in order to expand those with too many and to close unproductive research centers in favor of new teams working in new directions. This would allow the universities to arbitrate constantly between the interests of science and the needs of society. Really free, competitive universities, like those in Britain and the United States, excel in this kind of compromise. Those that are paralyzed by centralization, the inevitable attendant of noncompetitiveness, do not.

Emasculating Power

A dynamic section chief proposes a measure, an enterprising nationalized company works it up into a project. The technical adviser who briefs the minister on matters in this sector, although he never takes responsibility for it, appears to endorse the project. The next time it comes up, however, he offers objections—he would look bad if he acquiesced immediately in every project submitted to him. To exist in his job he has to delay, limit, or halt at least one out of two of them. The hierarchical scaffolding thus becomes a prohibitory structure.

Men of action tend to avoid this hierarchical structure and its emasculating power. Jean Monnet liked to say that if he had had to work through the ministries to plan France's reconstruction, he would have gotten nowhere. He organized the Planning Commissariat to by-pass them. But, with time, the bureaucracy succeeded in absorbing the Economic Plan the way urban sprawl converts highway by-passes into city streets.

In becoming a bureaucratic machine, the Plan grew deaf and blind to the real problems of the French. Mistakes in forecasts, purely theoretical and thus easily pardonable, were infinitely multiplied by the machine's centralization. Had planners been able to rely on society's self-regulation, they would have recognized the need for expressways, telephones, domestic airlines, hospitals and hospital staffs. They would have steered away from today's monstrous urban concentrations, would have built fewer tower-and-wall housing developments (which public housing authorities cannot fill) and more single-family homes (which renters cannot find). They would have felt and translated into policy the French people's rejection of gigantism, their stubborn dream of villages, of private homes and scattered factories.

Not even the Parliament manages to collect enough information to control the bureaucracy. Ministers' answers to questions in Parliament are as vague as courtesy to the nation's representatives allows. In practice, the legislature has no investigative rights, no access to official records, no chance to summon appropriate functionaries as witnesses. It is the minister who is "auditioned." To the opposition, he is an adversary and he is evasive; to the majority, he is a friend for whom they hesitate to make trouble.

The State's Church

At the ground level, 4,000 general councillors, 36,000 mayors, 450,000 municipal councillors also have responsibilities. But despite their numbers, they cannot build a network of local responsibility; their power is atomized. And their impotence leads them to shirk their responsibilities.

Just outside Paroy, in the Seine-et-Marne, a little Gothic church perched on a hillock, defying the heavens and inviting the lightning to strike it. It had been ravaged by fire several times since the thirteenth century. "You ought to put up a lightning rod on it," I remarked to the mayor. "You could be in for an unpleasant surprise."

"It's not my church!" he exclaimed. "It belongs to the Beaux-Arts. I can't touch it. If we so much as moved a nail, we'd get our knuckles rapped."

It is a fact that the church was classified as a historical monument, which took it out of the mayor's hands. He wasn't complaining. Requesting a lightning rod would have meant days of paperwork, and putting one up would have entailed a row with the bureaucracy. But with the conscientious wisdom of almost all rural mayors, the mayor of Paroy took a step only he was authorized to take: he insured the church. It was not a moment too soon. A few weeks later, the building was struck full on by lightning and burned before firemen could reach it.

Civil servants are full-time professionals; mayors and general councillors are amateurs, who work only a few hours a day receiving no salaries. Mayors and general councillors alike daydream of being truly responsible. But as soon as reality sets in, they understand that they are merely spokesmen for local interests in dealing with all the bureaucratic machines and that, to succeed, they have to court those machines. If a mayor is a realist, he will settle for this role, acting by turns as defense attorney, prosecutor and mediator. He will capitalize on his own ambiguity.

His life is one long wait. He exhausts himself in approaches to one machine or another. He doesn't "handle" a matter, he "follows" it—an admirable expression—from bureau to bureau. France's extraordinary administrative complexity seems to be maintained to discourage him. How can the country's 36,000 mayors keep up with all the prohibitions, the obligations, with what is possible and what is recommended? They are deluged with circulars they have neither the time nor the appetite to read. Too much information results in a lack of information.

The departmental director of a technical service once explained to me his theory of the inequality of responsibility. "We are really obliged to make the decisions. The local authorities don't know anything about the subject. They can't discuss a project with us, we don't talk the same language. Liaison is a very pretty idea, but the reality is something else again. So we command; yet we manage to give the local authorities the impression that it's they who are giving the orders. You have to put on an act." The local officials aren't fooled. Neither is the public.

Often a local official will seek safety in immobility. He is tempted by the sole power available to him, the power of inertia, which he uses, and sometimes abuses. Here again it is the system that has disseminated irresponsibility. Occasionally, though, the reverse is true. A mayor gets an unusual idea, but it is rebuffed by the bureaucrats as being "unclassifiable" or "outside the norms." If he persists, alarm spreads. Prohibitions are awkward, so the bureaus stall. Suppose the mayor tries to organize skiing classes for youngsters with fees scaled to the parents' incomes. The man in charge of dealing out subsidies dares neither allow it nor ban it, but he is inventive: the township is asked to pass a resolution in which the names of eligible families and their incomes are cited. That will put things off for a good two months—and the snow will have melted by then.

A Vague Terror

If the local power network is no more responsible than the government apparatus, much of the fault lies in the fact that it is atomized by the excessive number of French municipalities. Over 30,000 of them have fewer than 1,000 residents each. Two serious consequences flow from this. The first is that rural areas are given too much weight in national structures, in general councils as in the Senate. What the rural areas thought to have gained by this in influence these bodies have lost in authority; they have become, for all practical purposes, purely consultative.

Second, there are no real urban decision centers. Fifty residents or 50,000, the institutions and areas of authority are the same, in keeping with the principle of equality. In 1880, the cities' powers were aligned with the villages' capacities. Are 36,000 mayors to be made corporate presidents, with full responsibility for their ideas and achievements? Impossible! Have them work in groups? They don't want to. And the bureaus are no keener to face collective groupings capable of giving them orders—or of by-passing them.

As soon as a mayor asks a government technical agency to undertake a public project, he becomes its prisoner. The agency's technicians will draw up plans for a lavish project. Why should it try to hold down costs, since it quite legally collects a handsome percentage—from 2 to 4 percent according to the project's size—on all the public works it carries out on behalf of a local authority?

If, by any chance, the mayor rejects the agency's estimates, quiet pressure is applied. Most mayors are filled with a vague terror. They dare not think they can compel a public service to serve the public.

In Saint-Ayoul, a lovely Provins church where Peter Abelard used to preach, the organ's bellows needed changing and its pipes retuning. An organmaker submitted an estimate of 50,000 francs. Since the church is a classified monument, the Cultural Affairs Ministry was informed. The appropriate commission intervened. "The organ is much too beautiful simply to be restored like any other," it decided. "It's a museum piece." The Beaux-Arts granted a subsidy. The trouble was, only one French craftsman was capable of satisfying the experts' requirements, and he asked for four years to do the job plus four times as much money as the original estimate called for. The tumbledown organ will remain silent.

Occasionally a crisis erupts. A mayor or a town council will lose their tempers: "If we don't get satisfaction, we'll resign." The prefect is inclined to accept with alacrity, and he sees to it that the word gets back, indirectly, to the interested parties. But it does not serve his purpose to make waves so a tacit compromise is reached. The local authorities are determined to show their voters that everything bad that occurs happens in spite of them, everything good because of them. The administration lends itself to the game and does what it wants to do.

It is the case of the mother who so suffocates her child with love that she prevents it from growing up—Freud's "castrating mother," Otto Rank's "spider-mother lurking at the heart of her web," François Mauriac's "Genitrix"—and the French have met this too-powerful mother through the centuries at every stage in their collective life. They are still encountering her today.

Genitrix prevents her son from becoming a man, then reproaches him for not being one. She uses the pretext of the immaturity in which she has kept him to refuse him the right to outgrow it. The aging adolescent recoils before the harsh apprenticeship of freedom. Sterilizing mother and sterilized child are accomplices, plunging down the same dead-end street.

CHAPTER 22

Substitution

As They Should Be

Michel Debré, the prime minister, stopped short on the tree-lined path. "No!" he exclaimed. "The bureaucracy is not a power. Its role is limited to preparing the groundwork for decisions and then carrying them out. It does not make them. Political authority alone is responsible. And political authority can be wielded now, under the Fifth Republic. It should be. If there are lapses, they are personal."

It seems to me that Debré was painting politicians and civil servants as they should be, not as they are. Power is in fact usually wielded by those who do not have to answer for it. This is what I call "substitution."

Sign, and We'll Do the Rest

Under the monarchy, a *secrétaire de la main* imitated the king's signature. Most of the "autographs" of Louis XIV, Louis XV and Louis XVI sold to collectors today were written by obscure functionaries. Even today, many ministers have no choice but to let aides counterfeit their signatures.

When I arrived at the Education Ministry, clerks brought me several wicker baskets stuffed with hundreds of appointments and transfers: secondary-school principals, prep-school headmasters awaited my signature to learn where they were being assigned. Every evening after that, the "signature wheelbarrow" was pushed into my office. What sense was there to those flourishes of the pen? How could I check on whether a teacher about whom I knew absolutely nothing would make a good secondary-school principal in the Meurthe-et-Moselle Department? Responsibility devolved on a blind man, while those really responsible for the decision sheltered in the folds of the system. Although I had no real grip on this enormous machine, my ridiculous but decisive flourish nevertheless imprinted on decisions the seal of the state's authority. I was magically linking the top to the bottom.

This is the paradox of substitution.

There are two kinds of men: those who prepare decisions with great deliberation and carry them out at leisure, and those who assume the responsibility for those decisions by the lightning-quick virtue of a signature. The former, if only out of concern for efficiency, propose dossiers that almost never offer alternatives. Take it or leave it—"If you don't sign, you block everything." The latter, then, are obliged to take it. Hence politicians assume the responsibility for actions in ignorance, often, of their details and effects. In the bureaucracy's view, it is the politicians' duty to make *its* speeches, to authenticate *its* actions. Civil servants, however sincere they may be with their ministers, form a network with their colleagues over which the ministers have scarcely any hold.

Members of the government sometimes resent the existence of such networks. A minister newly come to public life prepares his first debate in the National Assembly. He consults the prime minister for his opinion and instructions. "I've gone over your speech," the prime minister tells him. "It seems all right to me." His visitor is surprised: "What speech? I haven't started on it yet. I was waiting to see you before tackling it." The prime minister laughs. "Oh, I see," he says. "They've pulled the same trick on me several times." The minister's chief of staff had sent the prime minister a draft he had written on his own authorization, neglecting only to show it to his own minister. The cabinet officer dismisses his aide, who was guilty only of doing what is often done.

The Ignorance of the Knowing

In the days of the Fourth Republic, I had frequent occasion to gauge the domineering attitude of my associates in the administration toward the men in political office. We represented solidity, they instability; we were immovable, they were subject to their constituents' whims. We served only the nation's highest interests, they lived by demagogy. We were tireless workers; the same could not always be said for them. We thought we had the competence of genuine experts as opposed to the incompetence of false men-of-all-trades. In 1957, in Brussels, I heard one of my colleagues, representing the Office of the Budget, *forbid* Maurice Faure, a minister and chairman of the French delegation, to announce to our five partners in the Common Market that France was ready to contribute amply to a European development fund for the Third World. "No," the Budget man said, "you can't do that." "And why can't I do it?" "Because I'm against it." This was said with all the assurance of a monarch asserting that "it is legal because I will it so." Faure, rendered speechless for a moment, then swore he would complain to Premier Guy Mollet. But the young inspector of finance got his way; Faure had to give in.

That decisions by-pass the politician to rest with the functionary may slight democracy, but at least, one might think, it promotes efficiency. The power of decision is transferred from the man anxious for votes to one who is objective because he is neutral, from a man in ignorance to one who is knowing. But is this really so?

The opposition between technocrats and politicians goes back for centuries. Henri IV reproached the magistrates in the Parliament of Paris with ignoring reality in France. "You do not know the bad in my kingdom any more than the good. I know all the sicknesses that are in it because the places in which I have found myself taught them to me. I could not have known them so well without the experience I have had of them."[1] Antoine Pinay once made a similar remark to me: "The young people who come out of the Ecole Nationale d'Administration think they know everything because they have done a lot of bookwork. They don't really know anything because they haven't lived. They don't know the French. Because he meets the voters, an elected official knows the people. They don't. They can render service to us, the politicians. But they must obey us."

This is really the heart of the matter. But a politician can put his ideas *directly* across to a few hundred people, not to hundreds of thousands. The gigantism of today's bureaucratic organizations can only bring about the effacement of individual politicians and the emergence of technocrats functioning collectively.

The Subsidiary Level

Yet it is surely natural for civil servants to relieve political leaders of the need to deal with minor matters, thus freeing them to act on the major issues. Unfortunately, most often, things happen the other way around. When a minister goes to the Parliament, he returns with his pockets stuffed with notes he has scribbled as he encountered people: "You haven't answered the letter I sent you last month . . . the subsidy for my festival . . . construction of a laboratory . . . exemption from the television tax. . . ." Legislators submerge members of the government in minor details. What remains of the parliamentary system in the present regime forbids a minister to slough off these details because the legislators will judge his effectiveness by them and will reach an implicit accord with him. I have seen six prime ministers face up with courage and good humor to the avalanche of requests falling on them. But to allow them to play this part serenely, their aides, lacking even the time to discuss things, had to make the essential decisions for them.

When Prime Minister Pierre Messmer gave his speech before the 1973 elections, I was surprised to hear him say that in the next legislature, "civil servants' salaries will be brought into line with those in the private sector." Not even the government employees' unions had ever dared put forth such a demand, sensing that the constant risk in private industry of dismissal or company failure should be compensated by higher salaries than those paid to functionaries who cannot be ousted until they retire. It was one of the prime minister's aides who, at the last minute, had added this excellent idea to the speech. And there was the majority committed by an anonymous but strategically placed bureaucrat!

It should not be supposed, then, that bureaucratic power, content with authority over details, will stand aside on major questions. At the High Council for Atomic Energy, the wits borrowed a leaf from Parkinson's book and framed a law for this inversion: "The time spent in deliberating on a question is inversely proportional to the cube of its budgetary importance." The council would approve a multi-billion-dollar atomic program without demur, but a proposal to build a bicycle garage sets off a lively debate.

In a general council, bureaucratic policy on the right-of-way for a turbo-train or the location of a new town receives only summary consideration, if it comes up at all. But an hour is devoted to discussion about replacing the chandeliers in a criminal courtroom. In the National Assembly, the big budgetary items are hardly ever challenged; the palaver is about how much the television tax should be.

This paradox is explicable. The major options require thorough study, but politicians scarcely have the time to do this themselves, nor the means to conduct a study outside of the established agencies. So the bureaucracy's monopoly over such examinations often produces <u>Hobson's choice</u>. Details, on the other hand, lend themselves to facile discussion. The bureaucracy goes along with this; the king, after all, must be amused.

Waltz of the Portfolios

Bureaucratic substitution did not cease along with the fragility of the Third and Fourth republics, for several reasons. The first is ministerial instability, which did not disappear in 1958. True, the position of the head of state is stable; that of the prime minister is less so, but enough to allow for action because he holds the office for two or three years on the average. But the fuses have to blow. Bureaucratic centralization rules out localized fuses. Since no departmental or regional executive can serve the purpose, it is up to the ministers to do so.

Only ministerial stability can enable political authority to dominate bureaucratic power, for action is only possible with durability—this is the raw material of power. The names of the great ministers float on the surface even of the inconstant Third Republic, and they are always attached to durability records. The Third and Fourth republics compensated for the waltz of the premiers by the constant reappointment of certain ministers. The Fifth Republic compensates for the prime ministers' stability by a quadrille of ministers. The expiatory rite has switched victims.

The ministries most deeply rooted in society are those in which ministers strike the shallowest roots. For example, between June 1958 and June 1974, the Agriculture portfolio passed through the hands of eleven ministers, the Information through sixteen and Education through sixteen. The ministers who accomplished something durable were the ones who held on: Couve de Murville stayed ten years at the Quai d'Orsay, Valéry Giscard d'Estaing nine at Finance, Malraux eleven at Cultural Affairs, Messmer eight at the Army Ministry.

A New Symbiosis: Government by Technicians

The bureaucratic system's second ruse has been, since 1958, to create a new symbiosis between technicians and ministers. It stems in part from the first ruse. Getting to know a ministerial department, familiarizing himself with its complicated regulations, evaluating its top personnel, devising a policy to put talents to best use, ripening reform projects, drafting legislation—all that takes at least a year for a minister who doesn't belong "to the house" if he wants to avoid irremediable mistakes. Yet ministerial longevity is, on the average, less than twelve months. To shorten the apprenticeship time, the temptation is great to give the ministries to functionaries who know them perfectly.

The present regime's spirit encourages this temptation. In the vision of service to the state that inspired the Fifth Republic, top civil servants recognized familiar language. Their rise toward the command posts was speeded up. Some of the principal ministries were given to the most distinguished of their permanent staff members. But the bureaucrat who becomes a minister runs the risk of being merely the highest ranking of his bureaucrats. Political ministers quickly grasped that, since their strength no longer came for the most part from the importance of a parliamentary group, they had to base themselves on the administration they headed. This led them to defend their ministries against the Parliament, rather than the other way around.

The two milieux came closer together. While the elected officials became more "technicalized," the technicians got themselves elected.

"Be Red and expert," Mao urged. In its way, the Fifth Republic also asks that political commitment be married to administrative competence. Two ways of being, two styles of action are combined in a typical French state system. Bureaucracy and politics meet at the top. The president, the prime minister, most of the ministers, belong simultaneously to both worlds.[2] The bureaucracy loses nothing by this. But does politics gain?

Dual Loyalties

The bureaucracy is so compact, so strong and so well organized that escaping it is difficult. Not that the politicians wouldn't like to. But when they do try, their spurt of independence almost always kicks back on them.

Christian Pineau, foreign minister in 1956, wanted to mount his Suez expedition alone, without his bureaucracy, even without Louis Joxe, the secretary-general at the Quai d'Orsay. Pineau thus stripped himself of the means for any diplomatic preparation. His staff's mute resistance to an operation they were left out of probably helps explain not only the violently hostile reactions to the French venture, but its pitiful failure as well.

More commonly, and more adroitly, ministers try to shield themselves from their bureaucracies by their cabinets; but this remedy, too, is not without its side effects. Made up almost exclusively of men from the civil service, a minister's cabinet remains bound to it by subtle ties. A dual allegiance is required of this ambiguous corps: personal to the minister, collective to "the house." Often, the cabinet's mediation serves only to make his subordination to his bureaus more tolerable to the minister; the cabinet gives him the illusion of command even when he is hemmed in.

Can "substitution" be avoided? Never entirely. An efficient minister is one who cuts his losses and concentrates his energy on a few matters. Surrounded, he cannot fight on every front without going down to total defeat. He can score one or two breakthroughs, hardly more, in a year or two. His problem, then, is to avoid choosing a futile goal.

How can he repay the citizenry's touching patience? They know he is as much a prisoner as they, yet they look to him for their deliverance: "*They* don't tell you everything. They hide things from you. You're not really informed on what is happening. We know, you don't." The deputy, the minister are absolved. Causes, responsibilities lie with "those who form the screen." Before combatting the pope, Luther appealed "from the ill-informed pope to the well-informed pope." The citizenry is less interested in putting a legislator on trial than in preserving his function, in restituting his authority. The elected official, the minister, is a man caught in the middle of a system. The French have an inkling of the system's irrepressible strength; their appeal is addressed constantly to the man.

The same cry informed the lists of griefs in May 1789: "Ah, if the king only knew!" The consequences were bitter.

CHAPTER 23

Encroachment

We are obsessed by the spirit of regulation and our masters of requests will not understand that there is an infinity of things in a great state with which the government should never interfere.
—Baron de Grimm (around 1760)[1]

The bureaucracy is not satisfied with substituting itself for the political power over it. It also tends to substitute itself for the administratees below it.

It provides unlimited areas in which to exercise the intolerant passion for the common good that moves the best of its members. The traditional compliment of "zealous civil servant" is often justified; the paradox is that it can be cause for complaint.

The technocratic temperament is immutable. Saint-Simon, describing Louis XIV's intendant Daniel-François Voysin, said: "Authority was his law and his prophets, his code, his custom, his right. Diligent, hardworking, scrupulous of details, doing everything himself; a man who was barely visible, shutting people's mouths by something in him that was dry, decisive and imperious." He might have been talking about some director, inspector of finance or prefect today.

Neither its disavowal by history nor the public's impatience breaches the feeling of infallibility that permeates the bureaucracy, that intoxicating conviction that only those at the top of the hierarchy know what's good for the lower ranks. In the traditional Church, it was the priests—bachelors by vocation—who initiated betrothed couples into the mysteries of married life; in our society, it's the civil servants who know what industrialists and exporters, farmers and artists should do.

The Unreason of State

The state assumes functions that far exceed its national mission. Step by step, it substitutes itself for local authorities, groups, families; through a multitude of measures, it intervenes in agriculture, industry, commerce, social welfare, the environment; it appropriates to itself the police, highway and health services. As the philosopher-statesman Pierre-Paul Royer-Collard said: "It is the sovereign's delegate who lights the streetlamps." There is no branch of activity into which the functionaries of the old and new regimes have not tried to extend their influence through regulation, prohibition, subsidy or favor. Today more than in past centuries, "reasons of state finally lead to madness of state."[2]

Centralized power is never discouraged from centralizing, even when there is everything to lose by it.

By appointing itself as film censor, for example, the government has often made itself odious or ridiculous with no other result than to publicize the banned films. It has almost abandoned this prerogative now, but without delegating it to any other authority. Yet decentralizing such decisions would be more effective. It would leave the mayors of the roughly 4,000 communities that have movie theaters free to forbid the showing of a film classified as violent or pornographic if it threatened to disturb public order in their towns. In fact, this is the only justification for banning a work. The system cannot be applied on a national level, however. The public spirit is different in Lourdes and in Saint-Tropez; what is considered provocative in one place is received indifferently in another. But the bureaucratic mind does not allow for such differences.

For 10 Meters . . .

The obsessional control has steadily spread—in 1970, the Ministry of Agriculture published a decree in the *Official Journal* regulating the mating of goats!

Failure to appreciate local situations is a corollary of directionalism. Facts do not exist if they do not confirm the information the administration thinks it has. In Neufmoutiers, a small village in the Brie, only one store remained open: a combined café–general store. One fine day the administration ordered it closed. The problem was the school, which was, by careful count, 190 meters from the place where alcoholic drinks were sold. The regulations insist on 200 meters. Despite the missing 10 meters, school and café had ignored each other until then.

I thought this would be an easy one to settle. Ten meters more or less. . . . But the administration stood fast: who could say that this unfortunate precedent might not reduce the limit of student morality everywhere to 190 meters? Ten meters, then 10 more—how far might it go? We compromised. One door to the café would be walled up; customers would have to enter by the back door, and this would add 8 or 9 meters to the distance from the school. We would make believe the full count had been observed; Neufmoutiers and the administration would be safe. But it took a year to reach this settlement. Meanwhile the café owner, discouraged, moved away. The store is still shuttered.

Impotent Omnipotence

Every service tends to justify its existence; it feels that its duty is to prohibit whenever possible. The administration prefers that nothing be done if it cannot be the *best*—the best, that is, according to its norms, its notions. Better no day nurseries at all than economy-style nurseries; too bad if mothers don't know where to leave their children. Better no swimming pools than pools that aren't Olympic or semi-Olympic in size, with staffs that only big cities can support.

Small, tree-bordered rivers cut through the Brie plain. Sometimes a dead tree trunk or a heavy branch snapped off by the wind falls into one of these and forms a dam. When heavy rains swell the creek, it floods. A mechanical shovel could clear it. Consulted in the matter of one particular stream, the bureaucracy launched a grandiose project that was several years in the planning. The creek became a broad canal. In the process, the curtain of trees that bordered it disappeared. Under these conditions, the widening wasn't needed at all; a chain saw would have done the job.

When perfectionism is allied to ignorance, the result is the Tampon sanatorium on Réunion Island, in the Indian Ocean. The prefect told me the story as he guided me around the place.

"We had sent the project, absolutely complete, to the Ministry of Health," he said. "All it lacked was the stamp of approval. After a year it was sent back to us, unstamped. Why? Because all sanatoriums have to face south for maximum sunlight and we had planned ours facing north. The bureau that had taken a year to come up with this answer forgot just one thing: Réunion is in the Southern Hemisphere and at noon the sun is in the north!"

How can the state be expected to discipline itself? Even in countries like the United States and Switzerland, centralization is advancing every day. But at least there are counterweights to the tendency there: it is the local authorities who apply federal measures, not the central power's agents.

The only way the bureaucracy can think of to relieve its congestion is to employ more people. The French did not wait for Parkinson to formulate the law that subordinates have subalterns standing in for them who, since they are also too esteemed to work, have their work done by other clerks below them.[3] That happened under Louis XV.

What a loss of substance, this mass of functionaries busy stamping, checking, filling out forms and having them filled out, continually peering into the cracked mirror of statistics! And what a shame to attract so many excellent minds to administrative tasks when France has such need of enterprising men to renew itself at home, to seize its opportunities abroad.

But we are so used to administrative hypertrophy that we have a hard time imagining we would do better to use fewer people. The city of Provins provides a free public bus service—because charging fares would have required so large a bureaucracy that it would have absorbed half the system's income. A city can defy a taboo. The state cannot.

The Finance Ministry's Dictatorship

There are two stages to administrative omnipotence. The first is that exercised by the administration over everything outside itself. The second is the Finance Ministry's power over all the rest of the administration. The bureaus tremble as much before the functionaries in Finance as everyone else does.

Between <u>Finance</u> and the rest of the ministries and their dependencies a war of attrition rages that exhausts all the belligerents. An order for pharmaceutical supplies for the infirmary was sent back to the director of a leading women's graduate school without the required stamp of approval. She finally got the comptroller on the phone and asked him why the request was refused.

"The list includes a lemon balm that I don't think is necessary."

"Students who feel ill sometimes are helped by it," the director protested. "At least you could have explained your reasons."

"If I had to explain my refusals, I would never again refuse anything."

You might suppose that the prime minister sets major budget policy and that each minister is then responsible for allocating the funds allotted to him. Not at all. A minister has to justify each measure in every chapter of his budget sou by sou, not to the prime minister, nor to the minister of finance, but to the functionary from the Office of the Budget who quibbles over the smallest details of every program the minister wants to implement. Expenditures are often vetoed. The issue must then be sent to the prime minister for arbitration. It's a risky procedure: the arbitrator cannot really find for the spender against the economist more than half the time. And Finance often shows wily bad grace in applying a decision in which it has been overruled. Wisdom dictates that a minister come to terms with Finance, which means recognizing its sovereignty and begging its good will.

Finance's overall power promotes irresponsibility. Ministers who are free to approve requests should also be free to refuse them. On their own heads be it. But some don't always resist the temptation to tell their petitioners or the unions or the pressure groups that "I would like very much to do it, but Finance is opposed."

The state compromises its authority by intervening in too many areas. Observers from the liberal democracies are surprised that the French government owns and operates the country's museums, that it presides over the destinies of dancers and governs theaters, and that <u>the most famous of its theaters, the Comédie Française</u>, functions under a decree signed by Napoleon in Moscow.

In such a system, a government that does not perform miracles seems, in the long run, unequal to its task. It bores and disappoints people. The French have formed the habit of expecting almost magical powers of their political leaders that keeps their spectators in suspense like Neapolitans waiting for St. Januarius' blood to liquefy. Unfortunately, the tricks of these heroes so plentiful in our political history always end in failure, often in disaster.

The Focus of Resentment

Because the state has gathered all authority to itself, the French hold it responsible for everything. Citizens, local officials, functionaries throw all blame on the central power whose subjects they are. Very little has changed since the early nineteenth century, when the poet René Vivien declared that "the government takes so large a part in everything that the malcontents consider its destruction as the first of all remedies."

The French sickness is to be found at the root of this paradox: responsible for everything, the government is censured for everything. Because it takes a direct hand in the most concrete chores, it is pursued by the most abstract of claims.

When the Odéon Theater was occupied during the demonstrations of May 1968, actress-manager Madeleine Renaud suggested that the invaders would do better to occupy the Folies-Bergère. But the students wanted nothing to do with a private institution, however representative it might be of the consumer society they said they were fighting. They had it in first and foremost for the state, symbolized by a subsidized theater.

Are the French insubordinate? Well, they don't criticize the state when it makes decisions in the sectors in which it alone can make them—basic economic balance, public security, diplomacy and defense, war and peace. Currency devaluations have seldom been protested. The state's power of life and death over the people it governs is not contested. But it is snarled at for getting lost in apparently futile areas. People are instinctively irritated at it for wasting its time and energy so fecklessly. The president was not elected nor the government confirmed by the Assembly merely to govern France in detail.

This is all the more irritating in that it is precisely these details that most directly touch the citizenry and which they are most capable of managing on their own. That a home owner cannot widen a window without petitioning for a building permit or a township improve its sewage system to protect it against flooding in a rainstorm without the joint approval of the equipment and interior ministers is what the citizen finds most intolerable.

The Struggle for Power

Since everything flows from the central power, local elections are interesting chiefly for the springboard they provide to conquest of that central power.

Political struggle has no other meaning but to conquer the state. This concentrated public life ineluctably tautens the nation in the attitudes of a bloodless civil war.

In the countries where true local democracy functions—the United States, Britain, West Germany, Switzerland—central governments and local authorities of rival political persuasions always manage to live together. This coexistence forces cooperation. Thus each party serves its apprenticeship in maintaining civil peace. Tensions can arise in the relations between local and national governments, but they do not lead to confrontation. Changes in electoral fortunes are like the defeat of one soccer team by its traditional rival.

Daily Crisis

Centralization offers great advantages to a nation at war or in a state of alert, when order is not challenged. But it provokes grave dangers in normal times, and even when preparing for extraordinary periods. Excessive governmental responsibility encourages lack of responsibility in the citizen. From this excess and this absence, in fact, have arisen the revolutions and rebellions with which France's history is so replete. Centralization perpetuates the crises it was created to dispel.

Allied with absolute power—its natural element—centralization inspires despotism, which leads inevitably to adventurism, war or revolution. When it is grafted onto free institutions, it perverts them; at the same time, they become the stakes in so passionate a political game that their long-term stability is curtailed.

True, things have evolved somewhat since the end of the 1960s. The bureaucracy is becoming more accessible to those who need it. People are received more humanely. Forms are being simplified. But the reasons for their complexity have not changed. The cleavage persists: the bureaucracy continues to think of the citizen as the personification of incompetence and fraud; the citizen still views the bureaucracy as a malevolent institution.

CHAPTER 24

Confusion

Political centralization is as necessary as bureaucratic centralization is hateful.

—Louis Blanc[1]

The huge truck labored up and down the Algerian dunes, plummeting nose first, slipping on one side, hauling itself up on the other. The oil-drilling engineers at Hassi-Messaoud who were showing us this hundred-tonner were delighted. "When we wanted to bring in drilling equipment," they explained, "our trucks got bogged down in the sand. Since the wheels were interlocked, they were all powered by the same motor. When one wheel got stuck, it blocked all the others. The solution is separate drive. The six wheels are independent, linked to different motors and so powerfully sprung that they hold the ground however rough the terrain. If one gets stuck, the others keep going."

The tricolors floating above the oil derricks were soon to be hauled down. The trucks would remain as a modern form of French presence; we would leave an advanced technique in the Sahara, adapted to new needs. What if we were to draw our inspiration from this achievement for our own country? Independent wheels, powerful springs—these were what we sorely lacked. We have never been able to understand, in France, that the country's overall strength might derive from individuals' freedom of action.

The partisans of centralization have always pretended to believe that their adversaries sought to tear the country apart. They do not see that instead of contributing to national unity, bureaucratic rigidity threatens that most precious of freedoms—freedom of initiative. And, by extension, unity itself.

The reason for this is simple: long confusion prevents us from distinguishing between the political and administrative spheres. Political power is a prisoner of bureaucratic power. The truck gets stuck, but it is the driver who is blamed.

Baubles and Lollipops

Under the Second Empire, tax collectors were accused of granting or denying taxpayers extensions of payment deadlines according to how they planned to vote. Prefects were long the chief organizers of election campaigns for the party in power. Those days are over, of course. But the temptation is still strong to profit by bureaucratic influence to keep a political group in office. This is a direct consequence of political-bureaucratic confusion. And even when the politicians resist the temptation, an atmosphere of suspicion persists.

All those subsidies granted, strings pulled, decorations awarded, are seen as a measure of a deputy's effectiveness, but they also diminish him: he becomes a politician who does favors. This is what he gains by becoming a sort of parasite on the bureaucracy. The voter reproaches himself for playing this game, and he projects his guilty conscience on the government.

Do election districts prosper more if they vote for or against the government? It is virtually impossible to calculate. But the people are left with an uneasy feeling, a vague sense of being governed by means of baubles and lollipops.

Confusion as a Pretext

So a minister, to win his bureaucracy's approval, covers for it even to the point of justifying its mistakes. But in the corridors of Parliament, in the press section, he invokes the bureaucracy's omnipotence as an alibi for the failure of his plans, the fruitlessness of his good intentions. A deputy gets himself elected by inveighing against the bureaucracy and reelected by soliciting its favor. This is the rule of a double game.

In this system, no one is satisfied because no one is in his proper place, and uneasiness grows because, on the evidence, confusion produces poor decisions. When a disagreement arises between two ministers, it is the prime minister who decides. And since such disagreements are continual in a compartmentalized administration, the prime minister, or the president, has to arbitrate them—in a few moments, the way a magistrate hands down assembly-line sentences for petty thievery and indecent exposure. As a way of doing things, it is like bad Impressionism, all fuzziness but no light. Thus the regime, however democratic it may be, rejoins the monarchical tradition, doomed to it by a system in which no one in the final analysis knows who really decided what.

In such countries as Switzerland, Holland, West Germany and the United States, polycentrism is effective because the central government limits itself to issuing general guidelines. Gradually, in apparently anarchic confusion, the local authorities move in the direction pointed by the federal government. It is a halting process, led by the velvet glove of pluralism rather than the iron fist of centralization. But in the long run, it is more likely to follow the road of reality.

Many people believe that its unitary regime gives France a great advantage. Three decades of observation have convinced me that, on the contrary, the polycentric societies are more flexible, more at ease with themselves. The bureaucratic center's identification with the political center is dangerous to the state and to its citizens.

More Jobs, Less Power

Confusion among levels of public authority also does another kind of damage: it perpetuates the confusion of political attributes.

An American, a Briton or a West German is always surprised to learn that a French cabinet minister or deputy can be a mayor and a general councillor at the same time. In their countries, such duplication of attributes is banned. Each election has its own character: general elections deal with national problems, local votes with local issues.

In Great Britain, for example, a municipal official cannot be a Member of Parliament at the same time. No law spells this out, but it is honored in practice: MPs must be physically present for the many votes that punctuate the 1,500 annual session hours of the House of Commons. A white paper published in 1975 notes that duplication of office in the British and the new Scottish and Welsh Parliaments will be effectively impossible, but it considers it preferable that there be no legislation on the question.

Since passage of the Succession to the Crown Act in 1705, a British functionary seeking to run for a seat in the Commons must first resign his bureaucratic job. The Parliament Act of 1918 and the 1927 Servants of the Crown Order reinforced measures designed to maintain the bureaucracy's neutrality. A hereditary peer who is also a functionary can sit in the House of Lords, but he may neither speak nor vote. And a functionary who resigns is not readmitted to the civil service.

In France, the Parliament, the general councils and municipalities are invaded by bureaucrats who preserve all their career advantages and who later regain their former rank—or a higher one—in the civil service. They politicize their agencies before, during, and after their political service.

It is a local official's dream, moreover, to become simultaneously a deputy, mayor, district chairman, departmental general councillor and regional councillor. Some add a refinement by getting themselves elected to one of the European assemblies, others become chairmen of departmental or regional councils. Still others are also cabinet ministers who continue to function effectively as members of Parliament even though, as the Constitution fortunately requires, they cede their seats in Parliament to a surrogate.

In fact, since the key to local problems is in Paris, it is desirable for the voters to have the same man represent them as mayor, general councillor, deputy and even minister. By failing to decentralize the running of the country, we have brought national political debate down into the cantonal seats;

the resultant confusion muddies local administration as well as national options. Municipal and cantonal elections become trial runs for the legislative contests, scrutinized for early signs of changes in the national line-up.

Such a system can subsist only because there is so little substance to elective office. And its effect is to perpetuate that lack of substance. Accumulating offices may seem to strengthen an elected official, but in reality, it weakens representative power *vis-à-vis* bureaucratic power. Overwhelmed by requests for favors, the official with many hats turns to the bureaucracy, which he finds is always ready to assume the burden. If, to top it all off, he practices a trade or profession, he may very well be unable to perform properly in *any* of the offices he holds. He is tempted to resign effective responsibility to the bureaus. The bureaucracy confiscates his power and reimburses him in prestige.

Another consequence is that local democracy, concentrated in too few hands, has grown anemic. Cumulative attributes thus become one of the chief obstacles to a real diffusion of responsibility. Offices are monopolized by a small political caste that is almost impossible to uproot.

Finally, multiple mandates accentuate centralization. The officeholder always prefers to operate at the highest level, the one his highest office allows him to reach. A mayor-deputy wrestling with some departmental agency will appeal to the minister. And the mininster will take the matter "up" to Paris, even if the problem falls under local jurisdiction. The topper is that he will have done so at the request of a local official.

Such practices, when they are not forbidden, become obligatory. Since most candidates in Assembly or Senate elections are also mayors and general councillors, those who cannot benefit from these assets are handicapped. In practice, therefore, they have to fall in line.

It will take a long process of disintoxication for the French in general and especially, perhaps, for the country's ruling caste to understand that when the general interest is not truly at issue, individuals should come before the state, not after it, and that local authority should precede, not follow, the central authority. Three and a half centuries of veneration for centralized power have concealed from them the quite simple idea that bureaucratic centralism is incompatible with a free, responsible society, but that such a society can coincide perfectly with centralized political authority. Legislative and governmental centralization constitute a country's strength, bureaucratic centralization its weakness.

CHAPTER 25

The Gray Faces

Everything about them was gray: their calloused hands, their once blue boiler suits, even their faces, as though the colors had faded in the underground tunnels in which they worked.

I met them during my first election campaign, in the canton of Bray-sur-Seine, in 1958. They sat in twos and threes at tables in the cafés in which I held my rallies. They remained mute, their gaze unwavering, before glasses of white wine. They didn't even play cards. The intruder who disturbed their immobility drew suspicious looks. "Don't pay any attention to them," a waitress said. "They're clay miners."

Labor doctors told me that these clay miners wore out fast. The slate dust that coated their skins and their clothes filtered into their lungs. Many suffered from silicosis; after the age of fifty, breathing was difficult. Dampness in the mines gave them chronic rheumatism. Most important, they lived without hope—of better pay, of other jobs in the community. Moving to another region took too much energy. Only retirement could deliver them, but they could not expect this until they were sixty-five.

Down in the Mine

I had no sooner been elected a deputy than, in December 1958, I was stuffed into coveralls, boots and a white helmet with a miner's lamp on it to visit the clay mines. Seven hundred men worked for ten companies in digging out and processing the clay used in making fire clay and ceramics. Primitive cages, which were also used to bring the clay carts to the surface, carried the men down the shafts dozens of meters into the earth. To reach the minefaces, they had to walk bent over through kilometers of timber-shored tunnels, jumping over props and patches of mud and water. Because of the time needed to get to their posts, the men work straight eight-hour shifts, stopping only briefly for lunch. The clumps of clay are ripped out by a pneumatic shovel held at arm's length. Bodies drip sweat in the damp air; the deafening noise of the shovels resounds through the tunnels.

Accidents are not uncommon: a train of loaded carts derails and rackets down a sloping tunnel into the men below; men are asphyxiated by leaking methane gas; there are sudden gallery cave-ins. Sometimes a pocket of water collapses, sending a tide rushing through the tunnels.

Visits to mines in the north and in Lorraine awoke me to the fact that, of all France's miners, the clay miners were the only ones whose lives still fitted the descriptions in *Germinal*. Since Zola's time, conditions in the coal and iron mines had been eased: tunnels were widened, steel shoring had replaced the timbering, cutting was completely automated. But in the clay mines conditions had hardly changed at all.

To top it all off, clay miners have none of the privileges enjoyed by coal miners since 1945, including that of retirement at fifty. The miners' code was generously extended to cover the coal mines' office staffs; junior executives and manicured secretaries enjoyed the "black faces" advantages. The "gray faces" did not.

Deadened by their living conditions, few clay miners even thought of protesting; they were crushed by a feeling of hopelessness. What could seven hundred do? Their 80,000 comrades working for the nationalized Coal Board could rock the government on its foundations. But they were powerless.

Their union, an affiliate of the coal miners' union, limited itself to demanding reduction of the gray faces' retirement age to sixty. It was a ritual demand, made with an air of discouragement. Every year their delegates came to see me, led by the secretary of the union local, Mertille Hennebert, who had spent nearly fifty years in the mines. They wrote to the appropriate cabinet ministers, suggesting they go down into the mines and see for themselves. "We are convinced," their letters said, "that such a visit would persuade you of the justice of our demand to advance the retirement age from 65 to 60."[1]

Nothing happened. The next year new petitions, new letters went into the files along with the yellowed pleas from previous years.

A Problem of Definition

In 1958, I was surprised to learn that management had never met with the workers' delegates to discuss the problem. Getting them around a common table was the first move, and it was done easily. Over the years, new executives, more concerned with social problems than their elders, had come to power. Besides, they were finding it increasingly difficult to recruit new miners. If the clay miners were allowed earlier retirement, recruiting would be easier. They declared themselves ready to increase the companies' contributions to old-age pension funds if I could arrange things.

For twelve years, from 1959 through 1970, armed with the workers' complaints and the mine owners' agreement, I tried repeatedly to win, if not full coverage under the miners' code, at least the most important concession, the miners' retirement system. I besieged the ministers in charge of Social Security as well as five successive ministers of industry, and had no trouble convincing them. Both mine owners and physicians agreed that a clay miner is hardly able to work underground after he is fifty or fifty-five, and that after sixty most are useless even on the surface. The ministers found the gray faces' claim legitimate and promised to get to work on it at once. The months went by. Nothing happened, except that I received a strained letter, always the same one.

No, my request could not be granted. Clay works are not classified as mines, but as quarries. Working conditions had nothing to do with the question. My miners were not miners. The High Council for Mines classifies workings according to what is extracted from them. If the material is economically important—coal, oil, natural gas, for example—it is declared *concessible.* The right of exploitation no longer belongs to the land's owner but is *conceded* to a company by the government, and the mine is considered a mine. But if the material's economic value does not justify extraordinary protection—as is the case for clay, limestone, cement, gypsum—the owner retains control of his land and you have a quarry. So bauxite, extracted from open pits, is mined; clay, dug out underground, is a quarry. "That's the way it is. Nothing can be changed."

The bureaucracy scratched its itching conscience by suggesting that it deal with individual cases. It could not better the lot of all clay miners, but it could help an individual miner by granting him early retirement, between the ages of sixty and sixty-five. He would simply need a medical certificate declaring him unfit to work. The proposal fell flat with the miners. Medical pensioners could not take other jobs, and the miners, while admitting they could no longer work in the mines, felt themselves up to working as gardeners or watchmen. Since other miners who retire at fifty, along with teachers, railway workers and electricians who retire at fifty-five (not to mention the military), could work while collecting their pensions, why couldn't the clay miners?

Besides, they looked on a declaration of unfitness as insulting, especially if one of them was so declared by an individual judgment while his mates continued to work. They wanted early retirement for all of them, on the same conditions, or nothing at all.

A Mania for Secrecy

To try to break the deadlock, I suggested that a Social Security inspector-general make an on-the-spot investigation. The ministry opposed this on the grounds that such a visit would arouse untoward hopes. I finally got an inspection, on condition that it remain a secret. So it did, even to me. A Social Security inspector-general appeared on the spot several times between 1965 and 1968. Although I was a member of the government, I was never able to see his report. It was more than a state secret, it was a bureaucratic secret to which the government had no access.

Another tack was suggested to me, but it turned out to be another dead end. The Social Security Code calls for special consideration for persons having held "particularly wearing" jobs for at least twenty years that could cause "premature wearing" of the worker's constitution.[2] A commission was to "draw up the list of hardship trades."[3] After several years of work, it had proposed a list of eight such trades, including "underground miners."[4] But the Finance Ministry flatly opposed acceptance, seeing in it a dangerous precedent that might lead to lowering everyone's retirement age.[5] The commission never met again; the Social Security provision remained a dead letter. Yet the definition of hardship trades would have ended a number of crying injustices.

A Powerless Prime Minister

Perhaps the prime minister could stop the ministerial merry-go-round? I took advantage of a relaxed conversation with Pompidou to cite the problem as a typical case of a French bureaucratic bottleneck. His response came with his usual speed and precision: "When Finance opposes a reform, its chances for adoption are slim. When both Finance and the technical service involved block it, it has absolutely no chance unless the situation is so important politically that the prime minister or the president can intervene. That, unfortunately, is not true in this case. I'm sorry, but there's nothing I can do about it."

Michel Bokanowski, then minister for industry, whom I had also badgered, confirmed the diagnosis. "Your only chance of bringing this off," he told me, "is to personally convince the official responsible, make him your ally. Try to change his mind."

The Polytechnician to whom I appealed had piercing eyes, a precise way of talking and a compacted dialectical sense. "Come and visit the clay mines," I urged. "You'll certainly feel how unjust this situation is."

"A civil service officer should avoid feelings," he replied politely but firmly. "If we stick our fingers into the machinery, all the rest of the privileges will follow, which would inevitably bankrupt their employers. In the workers' own interests, we must oppose this."

"The clay miners' union is ready to sign an agreement with management in your presence promising not to claim any other advantage in the code."

"That," he retorted, "would not prevent workers in similar trades from immediately making the same demand. There are sixty thousand people working in quarries of nonconcessible materials." He referred to his dossier. "As long ago as 1946, the minister for industrial production asked us to do what you are asking now. Nothing came of it. The communists in the National Assembly introduced a draft resolution in 1947 toward the same end,[6] and they have repeatedly renewed the attempt since then. Your own efforts since 1959 have brought similar results." And he added with a smile: "You see, we don't discriminate."

All or Nothing

Since the miners' code was adopted after the war, communist deputies had proposed its extension in full to the clay miners—not just retirement but all the other privileges: all or nothing. It was a shrewd maneuver. If the issue remained unresolved, the party would have a field day denouncing the government, management and the majority party; if a partial solution were found, it could claim the credit and press for further concessions.

My civil servant didn't seem to appreciate the difference between the communists' claim and mine. "We can't reopen the miners' code," he said. "The High Council for Mines has always ruled against revision."

Here, I thought, was the real motive. The High Council is to mining officials what the Roman Curia is to the Catholic Church. To agree to a reform it had been refusing for a quarter of a century would amount to tearing up a statute as untouchable as Justinian's or Napoleon's code of laws. It would mean reversing the unwritten law of hierarchical infallibility. This high official showed his respect for the state by imposing intransigent respect for his agency's policies.

"He Can Do Anything"

The clay miners then thought of going to the top. Mertille Hennebert and his friends asked me to arrange a meeting for them with General de Gaulle, who was to make an official visit to Provins. I tried to dissuade them, but they were moved by a magical confidence: "Oh, if he wants to, he can do anything."

June 17, 1965: I had invited a miners' delegation to the city hall for the great day. The general listened closely to them, asked precise questions, promised to look into the matter.

More months passed. Hennebert came to tell me of the miners' disappointment. "He couldn't possibly have dropped us," he said. "I've always trusted de Gaulle, since 1940." I advised him to write to the general to remind him of the case while I renewed my siege of his staff.

In Paris, the old machinery had started up. De Gaulle, preoccupied with major problems, had to turn the matter over to his staff. The Elysée had queried the ministers, the ministers queried their bureaus. Slowly but surely the refusal wound its way back toward the presidential palace: impossible. The miners' disappointment was scaled to the hope they had placed in the chief of state's supernatural powers.

Only in Case of a Crisis . . .

When I was elected to the National Assembly again in 1968, I introduced a bill to correct the injustice. It was unanimously approved by the Assembly's Social Welfare Committee: a pious gesture—introducing legislation is the prerogative of the executive branch. Bringing the motion to the floor would have required the executive's complicity and that, in this case, I obviously did not have. I was back where I started. I began to wonder if a crisis wasn't needed to get the case unstuck. But how was so local a problem to be made urgent? By luck, however, my position as chairman of the Social Welfare Committee was to provide me with an unhoped-for opportunity.

In November 1970, Education Minister Olivier Guichard asked me to push for approval of a bill validating a national competitive school examination which the Council of State* had disqualified on a technicality. I warned Michel Jobert, then secretary-general at the Elysée, that I would expect a favor in return. Then I alerted Jacques Delors, an adviser to Prime Minister Chaban-Delmas on welfare problems. "We're squarely in a 'blocked society,' " I told him. "If you don't want [Chaban's] memorable speech of September 16, 1969, to remain a dead letter, you must settle this question."

After several phone calls, accusations and promises, we reached an agreement. Without daring to tell them what I knew, I at once invited Hennebert and his miners and Robert Chevalier and his mine owners to be present in the visitors' gallery at the debate that was to seal the miners' fate.

Chirac Disapproves

December 9, 1970: A night session. In the Assembly's Hall of the Four Columns, Jacques Chirac, then Secretary of State for the Budget, bore down on me. "I'm accepting your bill because the prime minister ordered me to," he said. "But I must say that your conduct is radically contrary to my idea of government."

Chirac was not the only one. In the weeks that followed, the echo came back to me from any number of top-rank bureaucrats whose respect for hierarchy was shocked by my attitude. Chirac nevertheless played the game gracefully. He introduced the bill as the government's and requested supplementary legislation authorizing financing of the proposal, as only the administration is empowered to do. I thanked him briefly from the committee's bench and, equally briefly, he praised the social concern shown by both me and the government.

The bill was adopted unanimously, on a show of hands. It was 1:00 A.M.

---

* The Council of State's powers are in some ways analogous to those of the U.S. Supreme Court.

The process had taken less than two minutes to complete. I went up to the visitors' gallery to see the only people who had followed the debates: the clay miners and their employers. I took them to the bar. Hennebert was choked with emotion. "Twenty-five years I've fought for that and it's arranged in the twinkling of an eye," he said. "And nobody opposed it!" He and his friends had asked for retirement at age sixty; it was granted at fifty. They had never dared even to dream of this.

In the weeks that followed, joy overflowed in Provins. The clay diggers, now legally miners, organized a celebration. The basin's oldest miner—he had begun in the mines when he was eleven—was chosen to present me with the miners' symbol, a Davy lamp. He stayed close to Hennebert, huddled, timid, not knowing what to do. Together they represented a century of hardship. They blotted their tears with their thumbs.

The Party Regains Control . . .

Hennebert insisted on writing me a letter of thanks to which he obtained the signatures of five hundred of his mates. He mailed it at the local post office. It never reached me. An investigation was made. It was learned that at the post-office counter, before several witnesses, Hennebert had recounted what was in the letter. No trace of it was found after that. Hennebert came under violent attack; he was accused of scabbing.

The mining union took things in hand. A national official arrived in Provins and forced Hennebert to resign as local secretary; he was replaced by a more disciplined comrade. Despite his distress at this settling of accounts, he remained radiant with victory. Since he had nothing more to lose to the union, I arranged for him to receive the Order of Merit. That was too much! His mates boycotted the ceremony. He was quarantined. The new union leadership saw to it that its orders were followed.

. . . And So Does the Bureaucracy

I may have been armed with the law, but the bureaucracy had its arsenal of decrees, orders, official circulars, which it wielded with consummate skill. When, six months after the act was voted, I noticed that the decree of application had not even begun to be written, I pestered the bureaus about it. I was courteously asked to help write it, but the decree remained buried. After a year of this, I went to see Chaban-Delmas. "A year's delay on a pay increase isn't too serious; it can be made up," I pointed out. "But a year's delay in lowering the retirement age can never be made up."

Chaban exploded with rage. His anger brought results: forty days later the act was promulgated by publication in the *Official Journal*. But six more months elapsed before the order of application appeared in the *Journal*, and without it, the decree of application was inapplicable. "Consider yourself lucky," Health Minister Robert Boulin told me. "Eighteen months is a record. Sometimes it takes four or five years."

Next came the battle of the circulars. The bureaus had come up with new demands that reopened the whole issue to discussion. Once more I had to go to the prime minister—now Pierre Messmer held the post—and he decided in the miners' favor.

By this time, however, over two years had passed since the law's enactment. Enthusiasm among the miners had turned to rancor. Most of them believed that the same people—"they"—were trying to take back with one hand what they had pretended to give with the other. The "thank-you" letters became letters of reproach and no invisible hand filched these. The committee charged with reviewing the miners' files was not even created on paper until June 1973; the first application dossiers were not processed until 1974. The law's retirement machinery did not start to function regularly until 1976, thirty years after the first claim was made, eighteen years after I had begun working on the problem, six after the law was passed.

Meanwhile, the mine union had adopted a posture of radical opposition. "Full application of the code, a fundamental claim, is still to be achieved," it asserted. "It would bring all the mines' employees, diggers as well as surface and office personnel, other benefits besides retirement: free housing and heating, unlimited sick leave, longer vacations."[7] The new union leadership reneged on its predecessors' agreement not to ask for any of the code's provisions except retirement. Bad faith and bureaucratic delay had transformed an occupational claim into a full-scale labor conflict.

A Sad Story

After the elections in March 1973, there was mockery in the laughter of a Provins mine owner when he said: "I warned you. The clay miners didn't vote for you. All the trouble you went to was thoroughly useless."

We must not have much democracy in our souls if we suppose, as he did, that all acts by public officials are motivated by their vote-getting power. Was it "useless" to bring a little relief to a few hundred men?

Throughout this long process, owners, workers, legislators, civil servants, ministers, heads of government and of state, everyone had played his part, sketched in his situation. Everyone, from the base to the summit, had been caught in the system as in a trap. It was almost impossible for me, a majority deputy and a member of the government, to push through what had really been a very simple reform.

No one was guilty. It was just that no one was in the right position to work the key in the lock. They were either too low to reach up to it or so high they hadn't time to reach down to it. So much wasted energy; so much accumulated bitterness!

CHAPTER 26

Compartmentalization

"They're All Directors!"

On each step of the stairway in the old colonial residence that served as a prefecture in Cayenne, a couple waited. General de Gaulle was at the top of the stairs, shaking hands with his guests. The clerk acting as majordomo announced them:

"Monsieur the Director of Registration and Madame . . .

"Monsieur the Director of Health Services and Madame . . .

"Monsieur the Director of Agriculture and Madame . . .

"Monsieur the Director of the Archives and Madame . . ."

Between two handshakes, the general leaned toward me. *"They're all directors!"* he marveled. There were only 35,000 people living in French Guiana, but they were administered by exactly the same offices and subdivisions as any metropolitan department—an administrative microcosm reconstituted and intact among the palm trees like a medieval castle rebuilt stone by stone in California.

When the procession of directors ended, I questioned some of them on what changes were taking place in this far-away chunk of France. I didn't learn much about the changes, but I learned a lot about the directors. None of them seemed interested in anything but their own sectors. Each was familiar only with the bureaucratic branch whose bridgehead he held in Guiana. They lived in hermetically sealed compartments.

A Mosaic of Tribes and Classes

Seen from the outside, all these functionaries belonged to the same caste, closed in on itself. But seen from the inside, they displayed amazing diversity. The civil service dissolves into a mosaic of tribes dominated by tenuous hierarchies and divided by ancient rivalries.

Subcastes have formed within the castes. Each exists in a closed circuit, with its own rites, its own folklore. Rivalries are not rivalries of emulation; they are more like guerrilla conflicts across caste frontiers, with each trying to expand its territory: Bridges and Highways engineers versus Agricultural engineers, administrators versus engineers, Finance versus the Quai d'Orsay.

Political authority has given up trying to destroy these fiefs. It simply plays them off against each other, dividing in order to rule. The Prefect of Paris is not supposed to know anything about maintaining order, nor the prefect of police anything about administration. The DST and the SDECE* are strangers. The gendarmerie is attached to the Ministry of Defense, the police to the Interior Ministry. When they have to take part in the same manhunt, their coordination is acrobatic: even their radios do not operate on the same frequency. I have seen a police inspector looking frantically for a telephone slug to call a gendarmerie captain a few hundred meters away who was participating with him in a combined operation. In May 1940, unit commanders who were neighbors at the front but belonged to different service arms phoned each other at the post office in the nearest village.

One can learn to live with the impossible. The bureaucracy has found the way to avoid inter-agency quarrels: civil servants avoid each other. When they are thrust so close together that they can't ignore each other, the struggle can be ferocious. The most common result is reciprocal neutralization— immobility. What resulted from the separation and rivalries between the French National Railways Corporation (SNCF) and the General Secretariat for Civil Aviation, the Highway Authority and the Navigable Waterways Authority, but a long delay in the development of France's communications system? The idea for a high-speed aerotrain was killed before it could solve its early propulsion problems because it had not originated from the SNCF, which feared the train might threaten its monopoly. In the north, widening of canals was not undertaken until declining coal output made the railroad less eager to defend its monopoly—in other words, when wider canals in the north had become practically pointless.

Before World War II, France thought it could combine a wholly offensive diplomatic policy with a wholly defensive military strategy. Hitler soon spotted the contradiction, but the experience hasn't cured us.

Shattered Urbanism

When it comes to city planning, the Fourth and Fifth Republics are as alike as two sisters. Their policy was and is the result of compartmentalized centralism. A city is an ensemble or it is a monster. Each element in the delicate mosaic must harmonize with all the others. How can harmony be created in a system in which everyone goes off into his own little corner to make his own decisions? It's like an organ with no master hand at the console and every pipe playing as it pleases. A mayor who wants to build a new quarter must beg the support of as many government offices as there are types of equip-

---

* The Direction du Surveillance du Territoire handles internal security, while the Service de Documentation Extérieure et de Contre-Espionnage operates abroad. The jurisdictional lines have been known to blur.

ment: the Equipment Ministry for the streets, the State Secretariat for Housing for the public housing units, the Ministry of Health for dispensaries, the Education Ministry for the schools, the Interior Ministry for the police station, the Post and Telecommunications Ministry for the post office, the Youth and Sports Ministry for a gymnasium. The mayor is quite incapable of persuading these services to work together. If the operation grows, the only way he can see it through is to create a "concerted development zone," which means turning it over to the national administration. His choice is limited to incoherence or dispossession.

To build a secondary school, a mayor needs twenty-four different operations and authorizations involving fourteen different agencies. And this is only in the simplest cases. If the school is to be located less than 500 meters from a historical monument, things gets complicated. We wanted to build a dormitory for boarding students and a gymnasium near the Provins lycée. The dormitory came under the jurisdiction of the Education Ministry, the gym under that of Youth and Sports and the ensemble, because Provins is a medieval city, under Cultural Affairs, which found the gym offensive to its aesthetic sense. The project labored from commission to commission for ten years before any decision was reached; ten more years would have been needed for a satisfactory one. The gymnasium was finally built a full kilometer away from the school.

The ENA: A Dream of Unity

In 1945, my eye lit on an item in a newspaper that was lying around the reading room of the Ecole Normale. It announced the foundation of a school that would monopolize access to the major government services and the top civil service posts. I had dreamed of entering the Foreign Office. I jumped on my bicycle and raced to the information office. In an old mansion in the aristocratic Faubourg Saint-Germain quarter of Paris, I found an attendant idly moving a few chairs. "We're not installed yet," he told me, "but there's someone on duty." A young man received me—I later learned he was Michel Debré, who had conceived the idea of an inter-service academy, and who was himself destined to be prime minister one day. He stood behind an Empire desk on which there was not a single sheet of paper, and answered my questions enthusiastically.

"This new school will put all the country's elite in competition with each other," he said. "It's going to abolish those absurd frontiers. It will train all our high civil servants in the same principles, the same passion: service to the state in its service to the nation."

What has become today of this laudable ambition? The castes opened to each other; from one ministry to another, alumni of the Ecole Nationale d'Administration (ENA) address each other by the familiar *tu*, they phone each other. Their friendships have thrown footbridges across the moats separating the various bureaucratic bastions. Yet the moats are still there, and they are deep.

In some small degree, the ENA did become a crucible of unity. But it is also the center for apprenticeship in bureaucratic rivalries and hierarchies. Student competition is fierce. Whose names will appear in the "boot"—the fifteen top places whose occupants can aspire to jobs in the most prestigious services? Whose will at least be in the next twenty, giving them some choice among the leading ministries? Everything rides on a student's rank in his graduating class. Once he is slotted into a specific service, he has practically no chance of leaving it.

Even if he wants to, a civil servant who belongs to one caste is not free to give way to another; each seems like a state in itself, defending its sovereignty. To make a concession is to risk disavowal, and it is the business of a hierarchical system to eliminate risks. The services prefer to refuse agreement, not to cede on any point. A service conceals information from anyone outside it, keeps its own hierarchy abreast of things and awaits instructions.

Within any guild, new compartments, vertical or horizontal, are built. In a barracks you can find a higher officers' mess, a lower officers' mess, a noncommissioned officers' mess. It is a universal organizational principle that the line of cleavage runs, as among magistrates and lawyers, between the old and the young.

Our whole society is compartmentalized. Where are the natural communities where everyone once rubbed elbows with people of different characters, different interests and ages, and was enriched by these differences? Today it is everyone to his own kind: workers in their shop, executives with other executives; the young in aggressive gangs, the old in their solitude. Bars are the only places where communication is maintained.

Self-Perpetuation

"You only enter the [Ecole] Normale once, but you graduate from it all your life," wrote one historian.[1] The statement is equally true of the Polytechnic Institute, the ENA and the engineers' Ecole Centrale. In the big elite schools, what most students chiefly learn is that passing through the hallowed door at the age of twenty destines them for a place at the top of the social pyramid.

Of 1,000 young French, 250 take baccalaureate degrees, 150 go on to universities and only 1 makes it to the elite schools—the *"grandes écoles."* From that moment, most of that tiny elite's place in society is fixed—as is that of all the others. Yet between the lowest man to be admitted to the Polytechnic and his *hundredth* nearest competitor the average difference is less than 2.5 percent; between the last man admitted and his closest rival the difference is measured in hundredths of points. A wondrous exactitude separates the elect from the rejected and determines the course of a lifetime.

With the possible exception of Japan, there is probably no other country in the world where diplomas are more highly respected or their validity is as permanent. In the United States, a university degree merely launches a young man. After a few years, it is the man who is judged—what he can do that counts, not where he went to school. In France, a diploma is a long-range rocket which, barring accidents, can propel you all the way to retirement.

The republic itself long remained a mandarins' preserve. The oligarchy of the "political class" in its parliamentary quintessence chose a leader from among its own. The new system of elections (beginning in 1958) made the French Republic a popular republic. But the French people love their mandarins. In 1969, and again in 1974, the winning presidential candidate bore the stamp of the Normale in one case, of the ENA in the other.

One becomes a mandarin at twenty, but many receive their mandarin's button in the cradle. The language one must speak, the intellectual mechanisms one must acquire, the contacts that must be brought into play if one is to enter the right networks are all obstacles difficult to hurdle for one not schooled to it from childhood. Created to assure greater equality, or greater equity, meritocracy soon creates other inequalities.

Elitism

After 1958, the public—from the most obscure village schoolteacher to the highest men in government—fell prey to a strange illusion. They imagined that the student population "explosion" resulted from a "demographic wave." Yet the number of young people of school and university age increased by only 25 to 30 percent. Had the problem simply been to expand teaching facilities by 30 percent, it would have been easy to solve. It was the school population that increased between 1,000 and 1,500 percent. (The overall number of secondary-school students rose from 300,000 in 1939 to over 4.5 million in 1968; in the universities, enrollment in the same period increased from 60,000 to 700,000.) The "demographic wave" was really no more than a ripple compared with the *democratic* tidal wave that made secondary-school education mandatory for all and higher education accessible to all.

This mistake about the cause of the increase was deeply meaningful. By blaming the expansion on the birth rate, the French excused themselves from having to change the quality of the education provided. The school system had been conceived to fit a few tens of thousands of high-school and college students, most of them middle-class youngsters bathed in the culture of a privileged social milieu; there were also a few gifted scholarship students. It was not adapted to handling millions of teenagers whose adaptation in turn would suffer because they came from an entirely different social environment; using the same teaching methods with them condemned them to failure. The schools to which these youngsters were called in droves became traps. The policy of upward social mobility through education boomeranged. Despite appearances, privileges of birth remained important.

Most of the ideas developed by the students in May 1968 were aimed in fact at toppling elitism. For a moment, it looked as though they might do it. Within a few months, however, virtually nothing was left of the movement. The mandarin system had regained the upper hand with hardly a concession.

How can we surmount the system's tendency to reproduce itself eternally? Nothing is as difficult to establish—beyond equality before the law, which is inadequate—as equality of opportunity. Those in the places of privilege use a thousand stratagems to keep such places for themselves and the people close to them. Reform is mired in their resistance, unless revolution replaces this institutional injustice by insurrectional injustice, which in turn becomes institutional.

Hollowing the Steer's Horn

The supreme caste—the intellectual caste—is also fragmented.

To express "erudition," the Chinese draw an ideogram that combines the symbols for a gimlet, a horn and a steer. Erudition consists of hollowing out a steer's horn—the deeper the gimlet goes, the smaller the hole becomes. The deeper learning goes, the narrower it becomes until, soon, no one can keep up with the specialist, who remains alone with the infinitely small product of his research.

A young archeologist got the idea of devoting his thesis to the weapons used by Homeric warriors. Then, overwhelmed by the mass of documentation, he decided to limit his study to their helmet. It was still too vast a field. Finally he settled on the plume. "No one will ever again be able to talk about the plume on a Homeric warrior's helmet without referring to my thesis," he said wryly. Yet a plume of glory floated over him.

The intellectual mandarins, by erecting hermetic walls between disciplines, have bred a swarm of analyses and a shortage of theses. Of course experts must devote themselves to specific subjects. But if our culture is to remain alive, it is important that it not be cut off from other research or from the intellectual and moral lives of the majority of people. The flame of invention must be allowed to leap from the friction of different disciplines.

Twentieth-Century Diafoirus

Montaigne, Calvin and Rabelais wrote good French. All cultivated men easily understood them. The same was true for Descartes and Pascal, for d'Alembert and Diderot, for Claude Bernard and Henri Bergson. But in our century, and especially in France, jargon and castes have grown together. From the Napoleonic Code (which Stendhal took for a model of style) to today's ministerial circulars, from Marx to the Marxist exegetes, from Freud to his imitators, the same degradation is to be seen as from the Evangels to a school catechism. Clear ideas limpidly expressed have given way to opaque dogmas, abstruse glosses that are out of the common reach. In the character of Diafoirus, Molière immortalized the man who says in complicated language what can be expressed simply. Diafoirus lives among us today.

A conference was organized at Royaumont, near Paris, around a fine theme: Happiness. Some of the great intellectuals of our time spoke, not always worrying about being understood. The more they discoursed, the more I felt I was in Babel. After one address of which I could not grasp a single, miserable word, I questioned the speaker, a psychoanalyst. "Can I ask you two questions?" I inquired. "Are you happy? Do you make those who confide in you happy?" He launched into a long answer that to me was just as unintelligible as his speech. No doubt he was teaching me that happiness is not within reach of simple minds and that clarity is vulgar. The man was Jacques Lacan, then little known but already obscure.

A theoretical justification has been found for this behavior. The principle is advanced that exploring reality requires the invention of an esoteric language. It is not certain that the explorers have gone very far, but before you can know that you have to take the infinite trouble of deciphering their travel journals. Racine and Molière preached that "the supreme rule is to please." Compartmentalization leads to the contrasting rule: "What is incomprehensible is profound, what is comprehensible is flat. The true scholar knows himself by the fact that the public cannot follow him."

CHAPTER 27

Congestion

There is only one department in France, the Seine, and only one city, Paris. At the base of our society there is a principle of continuous enfeeblement, a death principle.[1]

—Louis Blanc[1]

In France, one out of every two telephone calls is made to or from Paris and its suburbs. The more calls there are, the higher the Paris agglomeration's priority must be in the allocation of telephone equipment. A vicious cycle appears: Paris attracts subscribers, the subscribers saturate Paris, Paris absorbs telephone investments, which aggravates Paris's saturation in proportion as it is eliminated. The blood flows to the head.

It's an old story. "France used to be a beautiful woman, well proportioned to her size. Little by little she has come to resemble a spider: big head and long, thin arms."[2] The comparison dates from the early eighteenth century. Since then, the head has remained swollen, unbalancing the social body. And modernity has accelerated the movement.

Before the telephone, it was the railroads. Before them, the royal roads and the network of diligences and mail coaches. There were traffic jams in Paris even in the carriage days. The center of a giant communications spider web, Paris enjoys a decisive economic advantage. An 1842 law made Paris the head of all the major rail lines. There are smooth routes in France, those that go via Paris, and rough ones, those that do not.° It is cheaper to go via the capital if you want to get from Strasbourg to Lyon or from Bordeaux to Brest. Physically and psychologically, the nation gave itself up to its capital. And while Paris may not be the world's biggest city, it is the most densely populated in the West, with 300 inhabitants per hectare versus 132 in London, 254 in New York.

Today, like the trunk of an old tree that is going hollow, the center of Paris is emptying. And it is becoming more middle-class. Office and factory workers are leaving for the suburbs. Business and professional people are

---

° In the mid-nineteenth century, passenger trains between Paris and the provinces rolled at 40 kilometers an hour and freight cost 0.12 francs a ton per kilometer. From one provincial city to another, the speed fell to 8 kilometers an hour and the freight charge rose to 0.20 francs a ton.

concentrated in the city. Paris is losing what was best about it: the function of a city where people communicate, where all the social groups learn to live together.

Paris's economy is no less hypertrophied than its demography. Nearly a fourth of all the nation's jobs are concentrated in Greater Paris;[3] its average per capita income is approximately double the national average. More and more people live in the suburbs and work in the city center. With displacements within the region averaging 13 million a day, the capital is merely the heart of a gigantic circulatory system.

In an amusing sociological study,[4] André Siegfried located the residence of inspectors of France, councillors of state, French ambassadors, academicians and Suez Canal Co. administrators over a one-century period. They all lived in the fine quarters of the capital. Between the heydays of Louis XVIII and Raymond Poincaré, they emigrated from the Marais and Faubourg Saint-Germain districts to the Monceau plain and then to Passy, Auteuil and Neuilly. In 1968, the National Development Commission registered the home addresses of whole classes of former Polytechnic and Administration School students. The conclusions were the same. All real power in France resides within a few hectares.

Did the ENA succeed in weakening the Paris bourgeoisie's monopoly? It took a few steps in the right direction, but only a few. The so-called civil service competitive examination, designed to funnel half of all administrative posts to provincials or Parisians of more modest means, partly missed its aim. The circles from which leaders in the business, newspaper, publishing, banking, medical and university worlds are recruited retain a majority hold on the most prestigious openings, even if their monopoly is not as exclusive as it was before 1945. And this establishment is still largely Parisian.

Nine out of ten French people are born outside Paris, but the tenth who is born in the capital has a far greater chance of acceding to the posts in which the big decisions are made.

Parisianism

The Parisian oligarchy will assimilate outsiders, provided they identify with it. In the seventeenth century, a few grumblers voiced surprise that the whims of three hundred people prevailed over those of 20 million.[5] Today, a few thousand hold sway over 50 million. Change has been minimal.

Since all decisions are made at the summit, nothing has greater influence on them than the microclimate surrounding that summit. It is composed of a social milieu—the most powerful of pressure groups because it is the most discreet. A kind of osmosis associates those who belong to the same world, who speak the same language, use the same symbols, affect the same vocal inflections and implicitly understand one another.

If French culture has been Parisianized, the responsibility lies largely with the state. Colbert took over the arts and letters as he did industry. Kings recruited architects, painters, sculptors and writers to celebrate the royal image. De Gaulle inducted Malraux into the administration to establish a Ministry of Cultural Affairs, and Pompidou's dearest ambition was the Beaubourg Center of Arts and Culture.

The Vulnerable State

Because power is concentrated in a few hectares, it is vulnerable to the concentrated pressure of organized forces. Paris is like a playing field on which the struggles for influence rage before grandstands crammed with privileged spectators.

France draws enormous prestige from its capital, but there is another side to the coin: the concentration of most of the top jobs in a single city creates an electric atmosphere that hampers profound reflection. What writer can exert an influence from anywhere but Paris; what writer can work properly if Paris snaps him up?

Provincial anemia is first of all demographic. For the past three centuries, the birth rate in the provinces has been higher than that of Paris, but the exodus from the provinces more than makes up for the difference. The capital absorbs the nation's youth and regurgitates its pensioners.

True, things have changed here and there in the provinces, especially since the mid-1960s. A tremble of life is being felt: orchestras have been formed, theatrical companies appear, art shows are seen, cultural centers irrigate the desert. But—and this is Parisian imperialism's supreme trick—these efforts long went unnoticed. The capital pays scarcely any attention to them, as though it alone existed and the image of a provincial cultural vacuum had to prevail.

This death principle could reach the entire nation tomorrow. When Corsicans, Bretons or Basques talk to us of intolerable oppression, we tend to smile at the exaggeration. Instead, we should recognize that oppression is not limited to them, that it affects more or less all the provincials. Demands for autonomy are just the local language to express anger.

The people in these dying provinces become more and more aware of their feeling of alienation and neglect. When history, language and a sense of their difference give them wild reasons to hope, is it any wonder that they cling to those reasons? Let there be no mistake: in Brittany as in Bastia, what stirs disorder is a sort of spasm of the dying who seek stubbornly to live. Mainlanders often tell Corsicans jokingly: "You accuse us of colonizing you. In fact it's you who have colonized the 'continent.' " But the Corsicans did not go to the mainland as conquerors; they went into forced exile. Now they claim the freedom to live normally on their island, in the society of their own people. It's a mad kind of order in which men must threaten, even fight, to preserve their native land from disintegration at the risk of furthering that disintegration.

Was it necessary to sterilize the provinces for France to exist as a nation one and indivisible? The question is fundamental, and it confronts us with a choice: to think of unity either as a product of the central power's will or as a result of mutual recognition among its various components. The French did not want the system they chose; centralization imposed it, in a way, on their fascinated will. Not everything is reparable. Some parts of the French national body have suffered irremediably. Another option is still open, however: a real distribution of responsibilities.

But the autonomists' impulsiveness threatens to wreck the chances for this. They act like drowning swimmers who fight their rescuers in panic. The moment they appear to threaten national unity, they justify what they claim to be combatting: the central power's omnipotence. Those who sincerely wish their province to be autonomous within the framework of national unity would do well to understand that panic leads to the opposite of what they seek.

For there does seem to be some chance, after all. The state itself has begun to react. Regional development, become an official concern, aims at redistribution of the nation's economic arms among its national partners. Statistics are already beginning to show that thousands are leaving the capital annually for the provinces. Some are even thinking of making their careers away from Paris. Since the early 1970s, scientists have stopped thinking of a transfer to Paris as a promotion. The country's leading mathematicians are now to be found in Grenoble and Strasbourg. Growing public awareness could amplify these early trends and accentuate the slow change in our scale of values. These glimmerings could become a dawn.

CHAPTER 28

Disintegration

*There is a radical incompatibility between the unitary system of govern-
ment we have made for ourselves and the exercise of the rights the Revolution guaranteed us.*

—Pierre-Joseph Proudhon[1]

Counter-powers Instead of Counterweights

In exalting the resistance of the "citizen against authority," the man in the
street has a word we have already encountered to express his hostility:
"they." "*They* do everything they can to annoy us." "What have *they*
dreamed up now?" "They," by turns or simultaneously, are the government,
the administration, the Parliament, the majority and the opposition—but especially the bureaucracy. "They" are the ones who make the decisions.

"They" are responsible for the high price of bread and the low price of
wheat; for the cost of living climbing too fast and the failure of wages to rise
fast enough; for the taxes, too heavy, and the subsidies, too small; for the
slump in wine sales and restrictions on wine production; for inadequate Social Security coverage and the excessive Social Security deficit.

The State at War with the People

In the people's eyes, the authorities are vaguely malevolent. A new automobile attracts no attention if it belongs to a private individual, but if it transports anyone who holds any part of public authority, it seems to have been
stolen from the populace. Turgot called attention to this in the eighteenth
century: "They look upon the exercise of authority as the law of the mightiest, to which there is no reason for bowing except their lack of power to resist and which one may elude when a way can be found. It might be said that
Your Majesty is at war with his people."[2]

That war is continuing under the republic. The president and the deputies are indeed elected. But do the people choose their functionaries, their
state? They are there, and that's that. Between bureaucrat and private individual there is an ambiguous relationship consisting of routine, sometimes

arrogance on the one hand, and a mixture of awed fear and sullen irritation on the other. The man in the street, taught by ancestral experience, usually obeys—and grumbles.

A wine dealer sold his business before retiring. Since his successor did not want his stock of vermouth, he planned to store the bottles in his home. In that case, however, the government insisted on collecting 5 francs in tax on each bottle. Unable either to pay the tax or to find a buyer, he finally emptied the bottles into the river—780 liters of vermouth that had aged twenty-seven years in the wood. How can such procedures fail to arouse more deep-seated resentment than mere political disagreement could produce?

In Britain, Holland, Switzerland and the United States, guarantees of individual rights are as inexpugnably binding as a private contract. They are supported by the force of tradition. They were not wrested from the state, but the state is their guarantor. In our French hierarchical system, rights are either unilaterally bestowed and thus revocable, or else they are wrested violently from the state or the privileged and so threatened by counter-violence.

All or Nothing

The bureaucratic state has never stopped trying to be as untouchable as the royal bureaucracy it replaced. Whether divine right devolves on the king or the people, the state remains theocratic in nature. Its power to intervene everywhere invites global contestation. On each side, the principle is that of all or nothing. Political and labor counter-power does not reject specific decisions but the system itself; it opposes not the government but the regime and the constitution. The unions reject a free enterprise market economy—in other words, the Western world.

In a debate between the secretary-general of the French Democratic Workers' Confederation (CFDT) and the president of the West German Labor Federation, the Deutsche Gewerkschaft Bund (DGB), the Frenchman attacked workers' participation in management as practiced in Germany. "We do not believe it is possible to democratize business," he said, "if ownership of the major means of production is not changed." His opponent declared that a firm can be democratically organized even if it is owned by capitalists, while a nationalized firm might not be democratic although it belongs to the state. The French union leader refused to admit this because it was contrary to dogma.

Hunger for a monopoly of power is answered by hunger for a monopoly of counter-power. The unions detest seeing an employer address his employees without going through the union hierarchy. This is why they were so afraid of the creation of *comités d'entreprise* (labor-management committees)—now required by law in any firm employing more than fifty people—

to which the workers' representatives are directly elected by the personnel. The unions' fear was ill-founded, since they usually manage to get control of the labor delegation.

The bitter rivalry between France's three major union federations—the left-wing, socialist CFDT, the moderate socialist Force Ouvrière, and the communist-dominated CGT—disappears as though by magic when it comes to opposing the creation of other union groups and the exercise of another freedom, the freedom any company employee, unionized or not, should have to run in any company election (labor-management committees, shop stewards, etc.). No such freedom exists even though three fourths of French wage earners are not unionized. To be a candidate, a worker must be sponsored by one of the labor federations authorized in 1944. It is exactly as though only candidates sponsored by the political parties extant at the liberation of France (in 1944–45) could run today for municipal office or the national legislature.

The New Roman Party

Why is the Communist Party strong in France and virtually all the Latin countries, in many of which it was prevented from coming to power only by military dictatorships? Why has it managed to attract so many intellectuals despite their lively critical sense, while, like the fascist movements, it has been reduced in the Protestant democracies to mere folklore?

Among all the industrial societies, those that provided the most fertile soil for the growth of the revolutionary ideal have been those under the yoke of a heavy political and spiritual hierarchy. The ideal went dry in societies where decentralized structures, freedom of initiative and a pronounced capacity for adapting to change appeared early. Communism is a counter-society. It cannot even be imagined in a fluid society, where personal and collective action are intertwined.

The Roman model lives in communism in a negative form. It takes the exterior forms of a church, being based on sacred writings, insisting on their correct interpretation, cultivating the values of collective discipline and submission. To its faithful it offers public ritual, a compact dogma and inner security. It can reprimand, but it can also aid and look after people.

The Roman spirit still breathes strongly in France and the other Latin countries. The strongest unions, the most deeply rooted parties obey the same organizational principles as the Church that was for so many centuries society's great educator. The communists are inverted Catholics, but pre-Vatican II Catholics.

A polycentric society deals with discontent as it arises. A monocentric society drives dissatisfaction back toward revolt. And the communist parties harvest this dissatisfaction. They prudently store the stocks of political and social dynamite they accumulate. Leftists affirm that unused dynamite becomes unusable and that the communists prefer to store their explosives than to use them. Possibly, but can one ever be certain? Here again, a violent shudder runs through France.

Too weak to face a monolithic and centralized counter-power, the state too often abandons to their sometimes pitiable fate those who in turn are too weak to constitute such a counter-power: old people, for example, the poor, and many who are on the margin of society. Nor has any opposition party or union federation forced the state to deal seriously with certain of the community's vital needs. Staggering vacation schedules, combatting urban sprawl, encouraging urban diffusion, repeopling rural areas, promoting a higher birth rate, struggling against society's rejection of the life principle—all these could constitute great national causes.

So long as the self-obsessed centralized power creates counter-powers that cannot balance it but can shackle it, so long as we fail to lighten the responsibility weighing on the central power, the art of governing will consist of an adroit disposition of lightning rods to prevent its principal personage, the president, from being struck too soon.

The State Versus the State

To this paralysis by the counter-powers is added a process of self-destruction. Worse than the people versus authority, worse than a state within a state, is the state versus the state.

The Handshake Withheld

One evening in February 1959, de Gaulle went to the Ecole Normale. By tradition, the president of France in his first winter in office presides at the school's annual ball. De Gaulle headed for the ballroom escorted by a small group of officials. Then something happened that left us all dumbfounded.

A group of students in dinner jackets formed a sort of circle around the general, separating him from the other people present. As he habitually did, he advanced toward these young people with his hand outstretched. No hand gripped his. The students crossed their arms behind their backs and pressed closely against each other, protected by their chain from the temptation to shake the hand offered to them.

We looked at each other in consternation. De Gaulle didn't persist. As impassive as ever, he strode rapidly around the ballroom, then left as though nothing had happened. During the evening we questioned the young pioneers of protest. Why had they affronted the republic's first magistrate in this way?

"We don't shake the hand of a dictator," came the reply. "He's a man of

the past. We have nothing to do with these fossils. . . . He's a *bonvoust*.* . . .
After all, we can't tolerate cops in the School" (pointing to the ceremonial
line of Republican Guards in their dress uniforms). One of the students added
with a fine toss of his chin: "The School resisted Napoleon I, Napoleon III
and Pétain. It will resist the general-president."

"Are you a communist?"

"That has nothing to do with it," replied some, who probably were. "Not
a chance," others said. "We don't give a damn about Moscow. We're Marxists, naturally, but Stalinists? Never."

Did they know that their predecessors had courteously received Presidents Vincent Auriol and René Coty? "Sure. You couldn't blame those two;
they were figureheads."

"The general was the School's guest. The laws of hospitality are obeyed in
all periods and in every country."

"*We* didn't invite him. He may be the director's guest. An employee has
to invite his boss. He follows orders; he's alienated."

"You are functionaries, too. You are boycotting the chief of the state you
have promised to serve, to which you owe your privileges—you are comfort-
ably housed and fed like fighting cocks. In return, the state asks only that you
consent to pursue your studies as you see fit."

They retorted that their salary (twice the minimum wage) was too low,
that they were being exploited by the rule that they should devote ten years
of their lives to the service of the state. A state they hated because it was the
state.

The incident, about which the newspapers were curiously discreet, illustrated a number of traits of French society: the tradition of resistance to authority, allergy to the police, intellectual antimilitarism, embryonic civil war,
romanticism in the spirit of 1848, abstract and static ideas, the process of
amalgamation, the desire to build the future by sweeping away the past
combined with an inability to escape the patterns bequeathed by history; and
finally, the rebellion of privileged youngsters against the state they serve—
spoiled children who detest their compliant benefactor.

The general never mentioned that evening to me afterward. But it was
because of that incident that, while always making a point of visiting universities on his trips abroad, he never again set foot in a French one.

Civil Servants of Irresponsibility

The brain, the center of sensitivity, is itself insensitive; an encephalic tumor
can be operated on without anaesthetic and the patient will feel no pain. The

---

* The term for a soldier in Normale jargon, from the name of Captain Bonvoust, who commanded the school battalion in the 1880s.

state, center of national sensitivity, escapes the constraints weighing upon the rest of the nation.

Functionaries in rebellion against the state have nothing to fear because they *are* the state. Whether they do good or evil, the result will be the same for them. If they are zealous, they will be accused of being eager beavers; there is no worse insult in the bureaucracy. But if their work drags along in routine fashion, the hierarchy is virtually powerless to punish them. "Productivity premiums" exist in the bureaucracy. Under union pressure, they are uniformly distributed between industrious functionaries and lazy ones.

Thus grows "the affliction of functionarism," the effects of which on public character were already noted by Jules Simon in the nineteenth century: "Public spirit, so necessary to liberty, cannot be established in a country where in every twelve citizens there is one functionary, a functionary's son and three or four aspirant functionaries."[3] Since those days the affliction has worsened considerably. Today, Simon would say one state employee in every six persons in the labor force. There are now 4 million people on the state payroll.

The State Sector's Opposition to the State

Why does union behavior differ in the public and private sectors when the union federations involved are the same, obeying the same orders? In private industry, disputes, however knotty, are usually quickly settled. A firm cannot sell more than it produces, borrow more than it can repay or distribute more in profits than it earns. The law of supply and demand forces employers and unions to be humbly realistic.

In the public sector, everyone knows the company won't shut down, whatever its deficit. The national budget is there to soak it up. Employees will be neither laid off nor locked out; the state often forgets to dock their pay for the days they are out on strike, thus converting the time into paid vacations. Managers of nationalized firms are not risking their futures, being practically certain of not leaving their posts except for another of at least equal rank. The administrative economy substitutes its comforting rules for the inexorable rules of a market economy. The former protects its personnel, even to the customer's detriment, while the latter puts the customer's interests before those of the personnel. In the state sector, especially when the element of competition is absent, nothing checks labor's claims.

This gives rise to a new paradox. In the labor code, the state is by definition disinterested and private employers by definition "profiteers." Yet it is the state rather than the "capitalists" that labor fights most bitterly. The big strikes are always against the nationalized companies. This is the area in which the counter-power finds the least resistance and the greatest number of temptations.

And authority is nowhere so weak as where it should be strongest. When the CGT attacks the SNCF or the Coal Board, the blow against the government is much more effective than a motion of censure by communist deputies in the National Assembly. The state's monolithic character makes contagion easy. A long strike at, say, the French Joint Co. does not even spread to other plants operated by the parent company. Bureaucracy and nationalized firms, on the other hand, together comprise a single savannah—a fire anywhere spreads across the entire plain.

Between Two Stools

France thus is at grips with two opposing systems, the bureaucratic and the liberal. Because of the bureaucratic system, the liberal system functions poorly; and the liberal element hampers the bureaucratic system.

The anarchists are right: there is no society that does not pressure and repress the individual citizen. But what is extraordinary in France is that the state imposes no constraints on its own servants.

There are corollaries to nationalization in the socialist countries: strikes are forbidden, unions are subject to single-party control, workers falling below the norms are punished and zealous workers glorified, psychological conditioning is permanent, information is controlled and the secret police is omnipresent. It is a logical system. The liberal system is no less so. Respect for consumer preferences is imposed by the pitiless law of supply and demand, restrictive practices are banned, competition is waged on equal terms and success and failure are implacably recognized.

In France, however, social organization rests on contradictory principles: theoretical authoritarianism and the absence of real authority; hierarchical command neutralized by corporativism; freedoms without responsibilities; rights without obligations; absolute security of career and retirement without obligation or sanction. Shouldn't we someday choose between a system in which the pressure comes from the top and one in which it is generated by the facts?

The Council of State has constantly reinforced the bureaucracy's autonomy from political authority. But is so much freedom, independence and security for the state's agents compatible with elementary discipline? By reinforcing civil service security, aren't we in fact diminishing its effectiveness? A public service employee has nothing to fear from joining the chorus of protest of the pressure group formed by his agency, but everything to fear from opposing it. The hidden terrorism waged by the counter-power is far more fearful than official discipline. What is surprising is that only a small minority of functionaries abuses this situation and that the vast majority remains conscientious and upright.

More Freedom or Less?

The defects of bureaucratic remote control are too serious to be eliminated by changes in details. When the state—which subjects everything to its duty to maintain order—tolerates lack of submission in its own vitals and becomes a source of disorder, the hour of choice is not far off.

We may decide to establish a politically authoritarian regime and an openly state-run economy in harmony with the prevailing administrative centralization. In this case we would doubtless have to accept the consequences we have seen ensue elsewhere: elimination of all nongovernment trade unions, suspension of individual rights, an energetic policy of repression and the growth of a political police force.

"The trouble is at the heart of the public sector," General de Gaulle told me in June 1968. "We were wrong to grant it the right to strike. It's illogical. In the private sector, strikes are indispensable for giving the workers sufficient weight to face up to employers. Labor has no other way to defend itself against capital. There has to be equilibrium between them. But in the public sector, the state's employees must be controlled by the state. The workers who occupy a private company are on their own ground; state employees occupying public buildings are not. It is probably too late to withdraw the right to strike from those who have it. But ways must be devised to get out of this absurd situation in which those who should serve the state are the ones who most gravely threaten it."

And in which, we should add, those who least gravely threaten it (and who are still in the majority) are most subjugated by it.

If France wants to emerge from its incoherence without stumbling into the coherence of dictatorship, only one way remains to it: the coherence of freedom. Its people, beginning with those in the directorial class, must concede that there is no freedom without responsibility, no law without obligation, no confidence without trustworthiness.

CHAPTER 29

Imbalance

If the French society's structure is lopsided, are its political institutions, at least, seated on solid foundations? Since 1958 we seem to have escaped the alternation of dictatorship and impotence. How long can this continue?

General de Gaulle once took me to task for my admiration of the Anglo-Saxon democracies. "We have the best institutions in the West," he declared. "Neither in England nor in the United States or West Germany do the governments have the prospects we have of continuity of action. This is an enormous advantage. Our stability is comparable to that of the totalitarian countries. And yet the people vote more often than they have ever voted."

The Sixth Republic

In 1971, I heard similar ideas expressed by André Malraux, but they were mixed with considerable fear for the durability of this institutional miracle. "We have as much stability as the dictatorships," he said, "with democracy in addition. This was the luck Athens had with Pericles. Splendor came to us from the moment a strong man was wedded to democracy, when it supported him without submerging him, when he maintained it without manipulating it. When the Athenians were headed by demagogues, that was the end, and Sparta took it over. Our Pericles is dead too. . . ."

Such pessimism was widespread. When Pompidou acceded to the presidency, and again when Valéry Giscard d'Estaing replaced him, the newspapers announced that "The Sixth Republic Is Beginning." But no profound change either in the laws or in practice justified this. The referendum of October 1962 had made the presidential palace the center of French institutional gravity. The style of the regime's leadership has changed with each new president; the regime itself has not. The Sixth has not begun. But the Fifth is tending toward deformation.

The Presidential Temptation

Couve de Murville was driving me back to Paris from a visit to General de Gaulle's grave in Colombey-les-Deux-Eglises. "In the general's time," he told me, "hardly any questions were asked about how our institutions functioned.

He dominated everything. But after him we should have rebalanced the powers, distinguished jurisdictions, reinforced the prerogatives of the prime minister and the government and therefore of Parliament. His successors did not do this. On the contrary, they have slid irresistibly toward concentrating everything in their hands. They have acted more like heads of government and thus less like presidents. Well, a president who tries to decide everything from day to day is not compatible with the behavior of the French in France."

A presidential regime is a temptation. Many dream of it without seeing that the American situation is different from ours. There, the President and the Congress, independent of each other, can very well be on opposite sides; this does not trigger any real crisis because the national temperament inclines toward compromise and because no one dreams of challenging either the Constitution or the bases of society. In France, our tradition of religious warfare, of the refusal by part of the opposition to play the constitutional game and to accept the social structure, would push situations to extremes; the resulting conflicts could quickly put the regime itself in jeopardy.

Moreover—and this is especially important—the United States is a federation. The fifty states constitute a counterpoise to the central authority. The American President's freedom of action is confined within the limits of federal sovereignty. If we were to try to "presidentialize" France in the American fashion, unitary France would first have to be transformed into a federation of autonomous provinces. Presidential regimes uncircumscribed by a federal system do exist—in Latin America. In both political and university structures, we think of ourselves as examples to the Americans, but it's the South Americans who copy us.

The President

Universal suffrage has replaced the holy oil at Rheims that was once used to anoint kings. It is the spirit of our institutions that the president take charge of the country's higher interests. He embodies, not symbolically but really, the nation's independence, its unity, its permanence. Chief of the armies, he alone controls the supreme weapon of dissuasion on which the lives of his constituents may depend. And he wields a power that is never spoken of, but which is of capital importance and which can be called the "interstitial" power that weaves public authority into a continuous fabric:

In time: The president is there, for example, to guarantee the legitimacy of governments censured in the National Assembly in the absence of elections that would enable him to appoint a new prime minister. Thus the plague of a power vacuum can be avoided. He assures the continuity of policy from one government to another, when the temptation is so strong for a new prime minister to distance himself from his predecessors, even to reverse their policy: "My predecessor, that incompetent; my successor, that intriguer . . ."

In space: The president is there to fill the gaps in power. In this rapidly changing world, a new need might appear to call for a new authority. Compartmentalization must be overcome, communications reestablished. It is up to the president to see to this.

Most important, the president can and should assume the heaviest of responsibilities when circumstances require him to do so. It is toward him that all eyes turn in moments of doubt and anxiety. His election does not reflect merely a fraction of public opinion; he should represent something wholly different from the political movement from which he issued: the will of his countrymen to live together as a nation.

No one was more convinced than de Gaulle himself that a president should be essentially a recourse. A recourse in national quarrels, provided he can keep the people's secret trust by remaining, as often as possible, above the mêlée. A recourse in times of great danger. "History," de Gaulle told me aboard the cruiser *De Grasse,* "recommends that we safeguard this function. Our people run the risk of adopting an 'every man for himself' attitude. In adversity the French, led by the bourgeois, have only one worry: each wants to haul his chestnuts out of the fire. They don't trust each other. September 1870, August 1914, June 1940, it was the same story. They reel at the first shock, after having announced that they would make a mouthful of the adversary. They are cowardly braggarts except when they are well flanked. But they do not always have a Joffre to regroup them on the Marne. . . . Well, God willing, there will be someone at their head to do that from now on. This is probably the principal gift I'll have given them. The president of the republic they elect will be the Joffre destined for them."

From Bipolar France to Two Frances

Any election creates a majority and a minority, a victor and a vanquished. This is the law of democracy. There is nothing disquieting about it unless we shut ourselves into this division—if, after the election, the minority does not feel it has been rejected by the community, but instead accepts the victor as the representative of the whole electorate. But in France a confusion of levels contaminates the entire system. The cleavage that emerges in a presidential election is reproduced in all the other elections, legislative, cantonal, municipal, even in the trade unions. The process deepens the cleavage and its pitiless logic spreads into every institution, every group. It multiplies party rivalry by class warfare and produces our national nightmare: the confrontation of two irreducible blocs of almost equal strength, each struggling to become monolithic. Two sectarian forces ostracizing each other: a domestic cold war.

I do not believe we can end this as long as we insist on talking about a "presidential majority," on making the president the chief of that majority, and on maintaining majority dominance on every electoral level. Should a poll or an election contest show a shift in public preference, the presidential majority suddenly becomes a presidential minority. The state, through its head, is suddenly made illegitimate. From the day of his election, the president should be everyone's recourse. On the day after the election, there should no longer be a presidential majority. Since ours is a parliamentary regime, we should have a parliamentary majority, the members of which support the government or at least abstain from censuring it. The natural head of this parliamentary majority is the prime minister.

When the president behaves as the head of the majority and of the government, there is nothing left for the prime minister to do but to become the chief of one of the parties in the majority coalition. Each has lost stature. The chief of state divides the nation if he persists in expressing a national division. How can he be a judge if he is also a party to the case?

Pompidou felt that the president cannot bear all the weight of the national executive for a full seven-year term; he proposed shortening the term to two years. There is another way: to diminish the weight of the president's responsibilities, not their duration, which is the gauge of our political stability.

But the opposition needs to relegate the president of France to the rank of chief of the majority in order to deconsecrate his function and attack his policy and person the moment he lends himself to this. And, given the opposition's determination, the president must mobilize his own troops. Embryonic civil war feeds on itself.

With rare exceptions, General de Gaulle sought throughout his ten years in office to restrict himself exclusively to the major issues vital to the country's future. When we tried to talk to him about projects we were devising in our ministries, he listened attentively, but usually declined to take a stand on them. In this he was respecting others' responsibilities, not refusing to assume his own. On the contrary, he insisted on taking full responsibility for the most troublesome problems. But he unloaded everything else on his ministers. "We need a president of the republic," he repeatedly said. "We also need a prime minister."

When I ventured the opinion to Pompidou one day in October 1972 that he was intervening in too many details, he replied hotly: "But a president who distances himself from daily political life loses touch. He is cut off from the facts. He is no longer the boss. I will not be a do-nothing king passing power back to the governor of the palace. Remember Lebrun in 1940 during the debacle, remember Coty in May 1958, when he exhorted the army to obey: they didn't count. If the president wants to be heard when events come to a boil, he must have formed the habit of listening for it."

I am not sure he was right. The president is the sole Frenchman elected by all the French. He does not derive his power from his direction of day-to-day affairs but from his ability to stand above the mêlée and answer for the nation's destiny.

Threatened by Its Own Strength

There are a thousand good reasons why the president should intervene in more and more day-to-day problems. He was elected because he was judged the most competent of the candidates. From his position, he can see further than anyone else and he has more authority; the decision he makes, therefore, is likely to be the best and, in any case, to be better implemented than anyone else's. Prime minister, cabinet ministers, high civil servants are all anxious that their actions should be approved by the man whose political longevity is assured, and so they form the habit of referring to him for everything. Moreover, de Gaulle could limit himself to historic matters because he was a man of history. His successors do not have that attribute. Besides, in his time de Gaulle had to perform the labors of Hercules: build a new republic, win its independence and bestow independence on France's colonies, end the war in Algeria. Since then, the president's lot has been more modest. Finally, a presidential election might also appear to designate the losing candidate as chief of the opposition—too powerful an adversary, it would seem, for the prime minister to face without presidential support, given what's at stake in the face-off.

I think these good reasons are false reasons. Perhaps the man at the top of the hierarchy will commit fewer errors, but their consequences will be heavier and they will be harder to reverse. It is better to give lower levels the right to make mistakes than to expose the man at the highest level to the danger of taking a stand when what is needed is his impartiality. It is risky to show himself to be fallible when infallibility is what is hoped of him. And to place the chief of the opposition on a level with the president is to build a formidable counter-power.

Naturally, there is a danger that the gulf separating a president from a prime minister could become a cleavage. De Gaulle was very conscious of this. "This Constitution has a weak point," he told me in October 1965. "If the prime minister breaks with the president of the republic on a subject that disquiets public opinion, and the majority of the Assembly supports him, the president is paralyzed. This is the chink in the armor."

He had thought of a precaution against this. In April 1967, Prime Minister Pompidou told me confidentially, a little sadly, "I don't know how long

I'll last. The general is so suspicious. He asked me for an undated letter of resignation!" Neither Pompidou in his first two terms (in April and December 1962), nor Michel Debré before him or Couve de Murville after him was asked to do this.

Some people find such practices unpleasant and feel that the Constitution should be amended to avoid them. Others judge it more prudent that the supreme law of the land retain a certain ambiguity.

Balancing at the Base

Choosing a president by popular election has, for a while, given the state coherence and strength. The benefit will not last unless the state profits from its attributes to diffuse responsibility, to organize democracy at the base as it has been organized at the summit.

If the state refuses or fails to do this, popular election itself will annul the president's power because it will focus national exasperation on him. If he does not deflect protests and demands to secondary but legitimate and responsible levels of power, he is sure to be brought down eventually by a coalition of dissatisfactions and frustrations. Like an oak on a mountaintop, he will draw the lightning. His constitutional function will fall with him, and France will be reintegrated into its unhappy history.

It is up to us in this waning century to find a new equilibrium between the people and public authority. It is an immense task in which progress in one area facilitates advances elsewhere, but where failure on one front has dangerous consequences on the others. If we can restrict the central power's attributes and limit its direct action by enlarging and strengthening individual and group initiatives, we will consolidate the foundations of the public edifice. Then, but only then, will the architecture of society resist the storms' buffeting.

IV

SICK MENTAL STRUCTURES

Good imposed from outside is ultimately the supreme evil, which, for a nation, is lethargy, vulgar materialism, lack of opinion, official nullity under whose empire no one knows anything or loves anything. . . . Bureaucracy destroys the soul's motivation.

—Ernest Renan[1]

CHAPTER 30

The Hall of Mirrors

Le pélican de Jonathan
Au matin pond un oeuf tout blanc
Et il en sort un pélican
Lui ressemblant étonnamment.

Et ce deuxième pélican
Pond, à son tour, un oeuf tout blanc
D'où sort, inévitablement,
Un autre qui en fait autant.

Cela peut durer pendant très longtemps
Si l'on ne fait pas d'omelette avant.[1]*

In a few lines of verse, Robert Desnos traces the closed social circle: every-thing imitates itself, reproduces itself. The Symbolists had divined the uni-versal harmonies—"scents, colors and sounds respond to each other."[2] They probably did not know that their obsession could extend beyond physical na-ture to the nature of society, correspondences between "visible things" and "invisible things." Society is also built like a game of mirrors, in infinite repe-tition. Like Louis XIV, the social order leads its cortège through a hall of mirrors that multiplies its effect.

A Genetic Chain of Mistrust

Society strives for homogeneity. Its various cells reproduce themselves, as though they obeyed a code analogous to the genetic code modern biology is deciphering in individuals. In the family, a child discovers the world through the models offered him. Family, religion, school, army, business and political institutions infinitely reflect the same image. Everything seems to proceed

---

* Jonathan's pelican laid a white egg one morning, and from it came a pelican that resembled it amazingly. And this second pelican in turn laid a white egg from which, inevitably, came another that was every bit as much like the first. This can go on for a long time, unless an omelet is made of them first.

from the way societies react to gentle Jean-Jacques Rousseau's explosive little phrase, "Man is born good." Two reactions, two models: societies of confidence, which are open; and societies of mistrust, which are closed.

To suppose that man is naturally good is equivalent to saying that he can find his way unaided. Authority, hierarchy, order are merely the framework in which freedoms live. Individual fates are the individuals' business, not the group's.

To suppose, on the other hand, that man is naturally evil is to judge him unable to discern for himself what is good or harmful for him. Order must be imposed on this social invalid from the outside.

The French have never been Rousseauists. For centuries they have reproduced a society in which everything by and large diffuses, reinforces and legitimizes remote higher authority. In Paris, the British historian Edmund Burke said early in the early nineteenth century, everything is governed according to the supposition that no man understands anything about his own interests or is able to take care of himself. One hundred fifty years before Burke, as one hundred fifty after him, supervision in France created the incapacity it supposed existed. The Roman dream has been fulfilled. The meticulous exercise of power leaves virtually nothing untouched: school, workshop, hospital, prison. Your daily life, your rank and role are conferred on you by the authorities, whose jurisdiction is constantly expanding.

In the Beginning Is the Family

The family is the mother cell. In it, the child of a remote-control society learns authority—at first protective, later defied, but always tolerated. Until the 1960s, the family remained the primary mold of authority in France. The authority of the chief, on whom everyone learned to depend. That of the male, the best able to defend the group against danger, to take up arms. This is the macho—the superpowerful and reassuring virility principle in Latin societies; the authority of age. "Why is France governed by seventy-five-year-old men?" went the refrain during the Third Republic. "Because the eighty-year-olds are dead." The repeated willingness of the French people to grant authority to old men well shows how prized age remains here.

Less rigid than in the past, eagerly affectionate, authority justifies itself by its concern for protecting the child. In Anglo-Saxon families, education aims at making him independent at an early age. We, on the other hand, put off as long as possible the moment when a child flies with his wings, as though we were doomed to a premature death should the family cell burst.

In the 1960s, a tornado from the Anglo-Saxon countries shook these traditional characteristics of French society. The head of the family, the male, the elder was downgraded and the "base" (women, the young) was exalted. Authority and family were harshly attacked. The traumatic effect was deep: time moved faster because it stood still.

Women Less Equal Than Men

The family continued to dictate a certain image of women; in the Latin countries, this was still that of a subordinate.

With a gesture of fury, Isabelita Perón threw a page of her speech at her confidant, José Lopez Rega. In front of Argentine television cameras, the president had exploded in rage against her trade unions. Twenty-four million viewers held their breaths: was this woman trying to play the macho? On the following day, a general strike paralyzed the country. In a Catholic land, a woman may do many things. She may even be taken as a graceful symbol of national unity—provided that she respects male authority.

Woman is weak and therefore inferior, incapable, since Eve, of resisting temptation and therefore dangerous. She is herself a temptress. She has only an inferior place in a society in which the army and the Church were long the archetypes. To the warrior she is negligible except as a diversion, since she cannot fight effectively. To the priest she is, as Tertullian put it, "the devil's gateway."

Yet by exalting chastity and maternity through the cult of the Virgin Mary, Christianity promoted respect for women as men's equals, if not in society, at least in the love of God. How did it happen, then, that these egalitarian potentialities in Christianity developed much faster in the Protestant countries where the cult of the Virgin was repudiated? Probably because the central element of Protestantism is a personal call, whereas Roman Catholicism is dominated by a hierarchical Church. Under Protestantism, vocation visits human beings whatever their sex. But the Catholic clergy does not put men and women on the same footing. For centuries, the Church followed the Decree of Gratian subjecting women to men "in all things." It was not until 1957 that a pope, Pius XII, declared that men and women are "persons equal in dignity, and one may not maintain that woman is inferior." The priestly hierarchy nevertheless remains exclusively masculine.

In the Latin societies, attitudes inside and outside the Church are very much the same. True, the law has finally granted women absolute equality with men: equal pay for equal work, common voting rights for common citizenship.[3] But there are a thousand ways to get around the law, and they are used.

As always, a blocked situation promotes a mushrooming of Utopian frauds. By insisting on equality, women risk abolishing the difference between the sexes so essential for their mutual enrichment. What if femininity were an element no society could do without?

Jesuits of Church and State

"And for heaven's sake, do something about . . . " Until recently, how many schoolteachers heard such pleas in the mouths of exasperated parents delivering up their unruly children. Schools were there to serve as a back-up to the family and to consolidate children's education in the principles of hierarchy and authority.

Our schools have assumed the Jesuit heritage. The Society's teaching methods were organized under the impetus of the Counter-Reformation. They left their mark on it—and what a mark! "One must let oneself be governed by one's hierarchical superiors," proclaimed St. Ignatius, "as though one were a cadaver which they could place in any position and deal with as they chose." This is the watchword of Roman education.

At the turn of the century, Emile Durkheim showed at the Sorbonne that French secondary schools had purely and simply copied the Jesuit schools' methods. So, for three centuries, the French elite were molded on the dogmatic principle. Napoleon wanted "state Jesuits"[4] in his lycées. The Third Republic adopted the principles of Loyola and Bonaparte. "It is the state's duty," said Louis-Adolphe Thiers, who considered himself a liberal, "to mint the young in its image."[5] Jules Ferry believed that the object of public education was to transform its pupils into docile instruments of the republican state. Thus the lay spirit proceeds from the same nature as the clerical spirit for which it sees itself as a substitute. It is not pluralist, but unitary; it uses the old techniques to its own profit.

The Deification of Abstract Knowledge

Students are empty bottles the teacher must fill through a funnel. This was Anatole France's joking description of the student-teacher relationship. The teacher is the one who has everything to give and nothing to receive, the student the one who has everything to receive and nothing to give. It is the student, not the teacher, who must submit himself to the other's pace. If he fails to do this, the system rejects him. It is designed for elite youngsters whom it cultivates like plants in a greenhouse; it is harsh with less gifted children, who make up the majority.

Knowledge justifies the teacher's superiority, and the more abstract the knowledge, the purer the justification. The hierarchical structure of French education is based on degrees of abstraction: the further removed instruction is from reality, the higher its prestige. The less efficiently it prepares students for life, the nobler it is in the eyes of teachers, parents and the students themselves. Until recently, the hierarchy was dominated by the dead languages. "Modern" knowledge was the cast-off of classical knowledge, technical information was "modern's" cast-off. The only institutions that attempted to escape the Jesuit model at the end of the nineteenth century, the only ones that tried to make education simpler and more concrete, to devise an education fit for the masses and not the elite, were the *écoles primaires supérieures* (junior high schools) and they were finally absorbed by the system. Even today, technical training is struggling to win its patent of nobility by being as abstract as possible. The classifications of professional aptitude certificates are not based on the needs of the trades for which they are given, although these are forcefully expressed, but on the requirements of a Cartesian system.

Is Latin disappearing from the classroom? The system quickly rearranges its hierarchy around another sacred language: mathematics. But this must first be made even more abstract than before; it must be rid of old-fashioned arithmetic, the only element of it that most of us will be called on to use later on. In short, it must be made useless to everyone except a quintessentialized elite. So-called modern mathematics, then, is the reincarnation of the eternal Latin theme.

The schools, of course, are exploding, as are families and the Church. But teachers were trained in the didactic method: imperative pronouncements, deductive demonstration, dogmatic uniformity, reference to printed sources. Because such teaching is not designed as a response to students' curiosity, it is sustained by its authority, both intellectual and moral.

Hence it breeds a lasting inferiority complex in children from which only aggressiveness can free them. How can awareness of their personal dignity take shape in the minds of poor students—especially most of those who come from culturally underprivileged backgrounds—in this humiliating system that crushes them with its constant reminders of their ignorance and incapacity? It is illusory, then, to suppose that affirmation of the democratic spirit will automatically follow the quantitative democratization of education.

On the Playing Fields of Eton

We French can scarcely imagine that any other sort of education could be possible and yet effective. Only the shock of experience can teach us this. My shock came during a stay at Eton. What struck me first was the youngsters' self-discipline. They elected their own prefects and captains to exercise authority for a stated period. Responsible for the younger pupils, the elders helped them in their games, their sports, in preparing for exams; when necessary, the senior boys punished their juniors.

The system tries to develop a sense of community. Competition, which was lively, was among groups, not individuals. Classes were divided into four teams of roughly equal physical and intellectual strength. Rivalry was fierce for the greatest number of points, whether in mathematics or rugby, for leisure activities were part of the training.

But, you say, French schools are no longer as you describe them—and please God they might have remained as they were! Barracks they may have been, but wasn't that better than today's chaotic schools? And it is true that authoritarian teaching is now no more than a hollow, sapless trunk.

Gone is the austere discipline of the Napoleonic lycées, gone the authority of censors and study prefects. The students, who were always able to evade authority by ruse, now escape it through rowdiness, which is rarer in the Anglo-Saxon schools but more and more frequent in France. An American university I helped to research this situation in 1967 saw in it a characteristic of French schooling reflected in the citizens' attitude toward the state.[6] But the problem was minor then. In 1975 the university team returned. Most of the classrooms it revisited displayed constant tumult—the youngsters played games, talked louder than the teacher. The teachers were astounded at the visitors' surprise; they thought all the trouble had come from America. The Americans found it was not easy to dissuade them of this idea. French education has remained hierarchical but powerless, drained of its substance, decomposed.

The extension to age sixteen of mandatory school attendance has surely contributed (and this was an unexpected effect) to a rapid growth of juvenile delinquency since the late 1960s. Youngsters who could and would have dropped out at fourteen are stuck in school, and they think of this as a personal ordeal. One hundred fifty-six days of ill-tolerated constraint, 209 days of unorganized free time: the temptation to break loose into teenage gangs and contribute to the growing crime rate is very strong.[7] Making shift and sabotage are learned in the schools, and they are never forgotten.

The French school system cannot remain eternally in an equivocal position. The events of May 1968 did not change education's basic orientation; on the whole, the contradictions arising from the hierarchical system remain unresolved. The system has not been liberalized, the schools have not been reinvigorated by autonomy or responsibility or competition or internal discipline. Dogmatic schooling and the principle of hierarchical organization are united by a single logical system. An education based on confidence and competitive autonomy also has its system, which is diametrically opposed to the first. But one cannot be substituted for the other merely by decree.

The Keeper of the Keys

All the other hierarchical organizations are caught in the same storm, beginning with the Church. "Is God French?" a foreign observer wonders.[8] "Catholic and French forever," says the canticle. What is important here is not whether the French have kept their faith; almost always unwittingly, often despite their announced convictions, they remain Catholic by training and culture. This is why what happens in the Church closely concerns them, even if they affect indifference.

At every moment of religious practice, the Catholic is a tributary of clerical authority. Without priests there is no confession, no communion, no religious service; to live his religion, a believer is more or less obliged to take the hierarchical path. A child adopts the unconscious habit of believing that his salvation can only be guaranteed by the Church. Even if, as is more and more frequently happening, he stops practicing his religion when he reaches his teens, he will be marked throughout his life by the idea that other people hold the keys to hell and heaven.

Patriarchal Business

Head of firm equals head of family—a typically French equation. The mark left on France by its families, schools and religion is visible on its economy. In agriculture, industry and trade, the family structure has always predominated—and it still does.

I knew an ironworker whose business prospered in the mid-1930s. When legislation required that he grant his workmen social insurance, and then paid vacations, he refused. "If I give the workers these rights," he said, "how can I command them afterward?" He preferred to fire them all and run his shop with members of his family. Forty years later, the shop was as small as ever. Another firm, which was no bigger in the 1930s but had gone along with the new regulations, now employs about one hundred people.

This family structure strikes foreigners.[9] They see in it an essential cause of the Malthusianism that has always marked our economy. Our patrimonial obsession puts family interests before those of the business; more than one employer refuses to market shares in his company for fear that exclusive family control might be lost. They reduce their risks along with their profits, instead of increasing profits by spreading the risks. Firms sacrifice expansion to remain within the family circle.

In the past, family firms fought the joint-stock companies, corporations, department stores; today, they are battling group farming, supermarkets and shopping centers. When these new firms finally make their way, complicity links them to the archaic enterprises. In the interests of peace and to protect their acquired privileges, the big outlets consolidate the little men.

Even the big companies have reproduced the patriarchal model. "Management by divine right," as it jokingly calls itself, refuses to share its power. And the nationalized firms are no less conformist (an official report recommending the democratization of business even specified that this should not apply to companies owned wholly or in part by the government). The divine right is symbolized by a company president appointed by the government and embodying the authority of the state.[10]

Still rare are those French who have the initiative Voltaire nicely called "the spirit of mastery," asserting that the art of governing consists in "impressing on people the independence in which strength lies." Liberty and pluralism have become dogma in France, but they have never constituted realistic organizational principles in public, economic or social life. As long as they fail to do so, how can we hope to escape the Roman heritage of hierarchical order?

Caesar and the Turtle

France for long advanced like the *testudo,* the Roman Legions' turtle. Each legionnaire bent over and held his shield over his head and body. Every man's shield touched his neighbor's. Thus sheltered, the soldiers advanced slowly and the enemy's arrows and javelins bounced off the shell. If they attacked a rampart, they climbed one atop the other, converting the turtle into a pyramidal cover to allow the soldiers highest up to hoist themselves over the wall. The men on the bottom had to remain absolutely still; the slightest movement would send those above them hurtling down. The Latin societies have infinitely reproduced this finesse of Roman military organization in their civil lives.

Societies do not live by order alone, however. They must have a soul. This is where Caesar comes in as father, priest, teacher, employer. At the top of the hierarchy is the charismatic chief. Sovereign, he gives meaning to the automatisms below him. He is the paternal chief, both human and sacred, sure of himself and sure of redirecting the stream of history, whatever that history might be.

General Jean de Lattre de Tassigny, upon leaving his command in Germany in December 1950 to go to Indochina, was aglow with faith and joy, never doubting he would accomplish miracles. As indeed he would, reversing an unpromising situation in only a few weeks. "King Jean's" feeling was that of Richelieu before La Rochelle, of Louis XIV basking in the sun of his twenty years of age, of Bonaparte after his *coup d'état,* Clemenceau and Pétain in 1917, de Gaulle at the microphone in 1940 and in Paris in 1958: authority in crisis, the authority of a chief who imposes his will by force of character and faith in his star.

The lives of Roman-style societies are sometimes heroic, often dramatic. How are they to move from this high-tension current, this epic poetry, to the diffuse currents and confused prose of individual initiative? In a society where institutions are collapsing, will men's "spirit of mastery" be strong enough to spare them further need of masters?

CHAPTER 31

Resistance to Innovation

Immobility

All of society's cells mirror the images of an immutable order. This order became manifest in the seventeenth century as a subtle expression of the Counter-Reformation. It absorbed grammar along with Claude Favre de Vaugelas, poetry with François de Malherbe, drama with Corneille, philosophy with Descartes, theology with Bossuet, French vocabulary with the French Academy, politics with Richelieu and Louis XIV. And who can deny its grandeur? It is the order of France's landscapes, its wisdom, its officials and functionaries, of the comptroller of weights and measures, that playwright Jean Giraudoux would celebrate in our century.

French gardens symbolize this immobile world: they are measured, mathematically precise, hostile to nature's improvisations. A French garden devours time and money, for should the gardener's vigilance ever relax, it presents a picture of desolation. Ideally, trees become figures, paths reply to buildings, reason is imposed on nature. The art of designing immutable gardens, born in Italy, had to reach its peak of expression in France. These are the gardens of a hierarchized society—compartmentalized, military, artisanal and rural—the refined gardens of a closed world.

An English garden merely tries to arrange nature to fulfill it, to humanize it without browbeating it. It is so near to being a wilderness that it seems not to need gardeners. This is the garden of a society respectful of natural law and its artful exploitation, of confidence in spontaneity and growth. It is no accident that Cuvier was French and Darwin English: immobility flowers as naturally on one side of the Channel as change does on the other.

I have described the shock I felt in the 1950s when, my ears still buzzing with the explosive activity of West German and American cities, I found France's provincial cities buried in routine as though in a layer of dust. I was struck by how closely Provins conformed to the portrait Balzac drew of it 120 years earlier in *Pierrette*. "Don't try to change things," people told me. "They've always been this way and they won't budge."

They did budge, however, in Provins as everywhere else in France. They budged more in twenty years than they had in the hundred years before that.

It was as though the country had been swept forward, and it is still stunned. France still has trouble adapting to change, is still slow to react. Changing sets is easier than changing actors.

The Weight of the Past

We have largely remained a peasant people. Not only because the proportion of farmers has remained higher in France than in any other advanced country (15 percent in 1968, versus 2 percent in Britain, 3 percent in the United States and 3 percent in Belgium and the Netherlands), but deep in our instincts and our reflexes. It is not impossible that Vichy was, at least in 1940–41, the most popular regime France had known in a long time—it responded to the nation's deepest aspirations. Instead of the cities' agitation, it celebrated the rural virtues, a return to the land or the crafts. Conservative France had never been so reassured as it was by this powerful plunge into the past.

Rural life is an apprenticeship in patience. You can't make wheat ripen by yanking at its ears. Like it or not, you have to wait for the seasons to do their work. It takes a Briton or an American to think that time is money and to seek to mint it. In our Latin, peasant, bureaucratic eyes, time counts for little. Yet the rhythm of our epoch demands quick decisions, the uprooting of old habits.

Few countries feel so tied to their pasts as France; there are few in which a veterans' ministry has functioned for so long, or where the past so largely explains the present. I know a small city where the World War I armistice was celebrated every November 11 by a procession all across the city that began with placement of a wreath at the memorial for the Franco-Prussian War dead. In 1971, city officials decided—a century after the end of a war of which no survivors, no contemporaries remained—that this ritual could be eliminated. A delegation of war veterans expressed its surprised indignation.

When the chief of state receives a foreign sovereign, caricaturists depict him as the Sun King. Leftists still see themselves as members of the Paris Commune. When the miners strike, it's as though we were turning the pages of Zola's *Germinal*. Farmers blocking roads feel they are the heirs to the *jacqueries*. Even our ideologies are bequests accepted after considerable delay. Today's Marxists are the great-grandsons of the late nineteenth century's Rousseauists and, perhaps, the great-grandparents of late-twenty-first-century Gaullists. In the eternal quarrel between the old-timers and the moderns, it is usually the ancients who show up best.

The Temptation of Immobility

Since we live in an immutable world, anything we undertake must aspire to perfection. Progress exists; it does not aim for change, but for the completion of existing models. "Immobility," said the cartoonist Caran d'Ache, "is a soldier's finest movement."

Beginning with Richelieu, the rules of order, elegance and measure have applied to French technical and artistic production. The king's navy was built in the shipyards at Toulon. There Pierre Puget was the reigning spirit, designing for an army of painters and sculptors. Even Colbert was dismayed when he compared the French ships, with their burden of decorations, to the English ships, more sober, but faster, more murderous, more numerous. He urged that the decorative bagatelles be sacrificed to efficiency and quantity. The ship decorators complained to Louis XIV, whose grandeur required the maintenance of his fleet's artistic renown. Puget won the argument. Nothing was whittled from the splendor of the Sun King's vessels except the control of the seas, which they lost. For two centuries, there was no change in the mechanisms of French shotguns. But we ornamented them with a constantly increasing luxury of damascened steel and ivory inlays on the stocks. The British arms manufacturers concerned themselves vulgarly with making shotguns that killed, and with making them accessible to a steadily growing clientele; this is how they conquered the European market.[1]

Our attitudes have not changed much since then. The tidal-power plant on the Rance, given a few improvements, would be profitable if ten more like it were built. There won't be a second one. The solar oven at Montlouis is worth a visit, but it is still the only one of its kind. We endlessly perfect prototypes that never go into production. People come from everywhere to admire them, but no one imitates them. Instead of using available technology to devise things that will fill the immediate needs for a relatively short time, we aim for masterpieces that will defy time. And time has passed.

In their immutable world, the French are naturally Malthusians. They find it difficult to believe in the benefits of growth. They are moved to limit the number of their children so as to raise them more easily, the number of medical students and professors so as to avoid creating "cut-price" practitioners, the number of Paris taxi drivers so as to "avoid creating unemployment in their ranks." We have trouble accepting an expanding universe; we do not believe it can constantly create its own vital energy. Thus we deny ourselves the ability to reduce inequality by long-term contract. To a Latin, any agreement based on future expansion is null. These vicious circles create the conditions for their own perpetuation.[2]

Democracy accentuates and maintains these traits in our national character. Doesn't it reflect the popular will? It would be political suicide for leaders to force change on voters who reject it in all but words. Politicians are almost always victims of their initiatives, almost never of their immobility. A mayor or deputy who sees to it, if only because of his own inertia, that no new industry upsets his district's socio-professional make-up has a good chance of being reelected for life. The same people vote for him. They are used to him and to the small favors he does for them and they are gradually converted into clients. Should he rack his brain to create new jobs, to change things, he risks being thrown out of office.

What powers in France have ever called for industrialization? A higher birth rate? A cut in the number of farmers, artisans, small businesses? Priority for ultramodern industries over those of the past? There are no pressure groups for the future. How can a democratic state be blamed for conservatism if the people from whom it receives its mandate are so conservative?

Convulsions

One of France's paradoxes resides in the contrast between the immobility that prompts the country to resist innovation and the brusque mobility that propels it from one extreme to the other. "A people," wrote de Tocqueville, "so unalterable in its principal instincts that it can still be recognized in the portraits done of it two or three thousand years ago, and at the same time so mobile in its daily thinking and in its tastes that it is finally a spectacle unexpected even to itself, often as surprised as foreigners are at the sight of what it has just done."[3]

For however our nation may execrate change, it has a habit of rebellion. Authority is blamed for its reforms and its conservatism by a people that is by turns hostile to novelty and furious that nothing has changed. Is this contradictory? In the long run immobility proves insupportable. Social explosions in centralized, authoritarian countries are like fire damp blasts in a mine. Inflammatory gas accumulates slowly in the underground galleries of power; the merest spark can ignite it. Freud called this the "turning of the repressed."

The Fascination of a Jolt

"We're going to use our trailer trucks to block traffic," announce the truck drivers. "Maybe then they'll get going on that by-pass." "Until we shake them up," says a union official, "they won't remove regional wage differentials." "We'll keep our children home from school," pupils' parents declare, "and then we'll get the funds to build a new high school."

Shaking things up is a way of attracting the attention of officials who are too remote, too deaf to a demand. Since it is a way—almost the only way—of communicating, every Frenchman is a potential disturber of the peace. Social violence has lost the blind, almost desperate, brutality it had under the monarchy. It has, in a way, been incorporated into ordinary public life. Practically all of labor's gains in wages, paid vacations, fringe benefits, work week and productivity norms were wrested from management or the state (in its capacity of employer) after a major conflict. Why shouldn't workingmen be tempted to join unions that rely on conflict rather than joining forces? Why shouldn't they be encouraged to make threats? Revolt is gaining ground almost everywhere and almost nothing is won without it.

In the short term, shock fulfills an indispensable function: so many channels are blocked that upheaval alone can clear them. After the social crisis of 1936, after the liberation of France in August 1944, after the collapse of the Fourth Republic in May 1958, after the uprising in May 1968, constitutional and social changes long perceived as both necessary and "impossible" were accomplished in a matter of months. Some societies are irrigated by a whole network of canals. France achieves this only by building enormous dams, which it then blows up.

In normal times, formalism and anonymity are encouraged by predominantly impersonal rules. Strong personalities, uncomfortable with this sort of mediocrity, are shunted aside. In periods of upheaval, however, the need for strong leadership is greater than the hostility strong leaders generally inspire. "Saviors" take advantage of popular anxiety; crises give rise to crisis leaders.

The Furia Francese

In a society that facilitates autonomy, the individual must keep hold of himself well enough to forestall society's having to do it for him. It is not by chance that the words expressing responsible conduct are borrowed from English: self-control, self-government, self-service. An individual must maintain constant vigilance over his own actions. Psychiatrists would call his conduct obsessional.

In our collective conduct, on the other hand, they would find elements of hysteria. After long periods of apathy, we rush into action, in war or peace, with that frenzied passion made proverbial by the *furia francese,* eagerly burning what once we worshipped. Marshal Ney swore to bring the emperor Napoleon back in an iron cage and then offered him his regiment for the reconquest of Paris. Our sincerity is inconstant, but total.*

This, in fact, is why the convulsions of French society (with the exception of 1789) are rarely as serious as they are imagined to be abroad. We replace real aggression with verbal aggression. We also prefer the absolute novelty of a revolutionary rupture to the continuing innovation of reform. Our need to change everything sometimes reaches a point of delirium—we decree the abolition of the standard calendar and proclaim Year I of a new era. "Let's make a clean sweep of the past," people sing. Even reasonable men succumb to this dizziness. "Everything is possible," they assert. Alas! Not everything is possible.

* "My lord the duke of Savoie," said Saint-Simon, "finds himself in the same camp at the end of a war as at the beginning only when he has changed camps an even number of times."

The Conservative Revolutionaries

The German writer Friedrich Sieburg once described us as "one of the great cultivated peoples of the earth, opposing the technical perfection of its existence; what strength of resistance."[4]

The French have tended to organize themselves not only as though nothing ought to change but so that nothing *could* change. And their crises have often derived from a rejection of change. This was a "conservative" impulse in part; but, more subtly, it was also "revolutionary."

In every country, people shy at some of the constraints of progress. In the polycentric countries, this reluctance is overcome: conservatives cannot blame anyone for a change dictated by the times. Change envelopes them— it is a challenge they accept. This sort of pragmatism is distasteful to the monocentric mind: since the state can do everything, it must stop the sun or make the earth turn faster. Let it order change, at once and for everyone. Since this is impossible, the system is abstractly criticized (for its lack of perfection) while concrete changes are refused.

Unrest

From time to time the French press takes to talking about "moroseness" (de Gaulle used to call it "moodiness"). This is what we know as unrest or uneasiness. Like crisis, of which it is an early sign, it is almost always aroused by a change that is felt to be both inevitable and intolerable.

The unrest in the army in the 1960s? Military resistance to changes wrought by decolonization and nuclear weaponry. Farm unrest? Growers' resistance to new cultivation methods, new structures and outlets. Unrest among business managers arose from sharp changes in their situation and in techniques of corporate management. And so on. There was unrest in the Paris police department in 1945 because the minister of the interior wanted to introduce radio cars.

The proliferation of novelties weaves a thick tissue of melancholy around mulish minds. In an age when products, methods, even ideas are becoming obsolete at increasingly greater speeds, this perpetual movement dooms us to perpetual uneasiness. Finally we decide to join the movement and use in adapting to it the energy we had earlier preferred to expend in thwarting it. De Gaulle asked the French to "marry their time." Faced with our time, we feel like confirmed bachelors.

Deep down, we are afraid to let ourselves be swept up by the world current of competition that is overturning ideas and techniques. Is such anxiety just a specific case of our lack of self-confidence? Accepting comparison with others means calling our own conduct into question, our own way of thinking, the dogmas we have learned, and so running the risk of appearing to be inferior. Burrowing into the familiar protects us from the unfamiliar. Competition is a novelty that is being forced on us.

Hypocritical Neophobia

Now, in the late twentieth century, however, such "neophobia" is no longer paraded; it is hidden. A subtle amalgam is formed of fear and the desire for change. We do not like to confess that we are hostile to novelty. We prefer to say that we insist on it. But the occupations that are caught up in the movement despite themselves secretly hope for some divine surprise to save them from it.

No strike was ever organized to claim concrete reforms, yet many have been called to block them. For an adopted reform is never the one that was wanted, or ever comes at the right time. So it is rejected in the name of an ideal reform that will never be made.

It is in this mental landscape that reformists' efforts are often worn down, sometimes lost—for any reform disturbs something or somebody. To seek unanimity is to invite immobility or, at best, equivocation. But trying to impose reform on minds that refuse it is to run into a blockade. We oppose it with the inertia of an eiderdown quilt. Momentum wanes, delays grow longer, dossiers stray, new obstacles spring up. Between a lucid speech and the conquest of the goals it proposes there is a vast distance—that of attitudes—on which open the limitless possibilities of unconscious sabotage.

If, in spite of everything, reforms do become fact, they are frequently and subtly undermined by those they seem to threaten, and arranged so as not to inconvenience the resistants. The letter of reform is respected the better to change its spirit.

In a corporativist, centralized country, reform cannot come from within. All groups tend to persevere in their own identities—prison guards must not be expected to reform the guarding of prisons. Nor can it come from above: few reforms can be imposed by a government suspected of political motivation and more willingly opposed than supported, or by a chief of state who had better avoid eroding his prestige as an arbiter. And it cannot come from below, where anger simply hardens people's positions.

The only effective method for reform is the lateral method, through the organization of a spirit of emulation, of example, in which the pressure of facts is felt. This sidesteps obstacles, creates a favorable atmosphere and shows the movement on the march. We do not know how to oppose a change that is not imposed on us; it imposes itself on us, like the weather. Reformers who do not use this method will, it is to be feared, be destined, like Penelope, to reweave by day what they unravel at night.

CHAPTER 32

Submissiveness

Docility is like a vice: one cannot break the habit.
                                        —Jean Guitton[1]

A medal struck at the royal mint shows the young Louis XIV reviewing an elite corps. All the soldiers have an arm and a leg raised in an irreproachably harmonious movement.[2] It's a perfect symbol of a hierarchical order in which the group derives its perfection from the individual's effacement. So many freedoms curbed, so much initiative canceled, so that the hierarchical order might triumph! Yes, the ideal state would be one in which the people contributed through their docility to the exercise of authority, as a theater audience, captivated by the play's illusion, supports and stimulates the actors by its shudders, its laughter and its applause.

Captivation Through Submission

Men have a soul, a conscience, which the state covets as an offering. The Protestant philosopher Pierre Bayle expressed most neatly what the Church expects of a Christian: "His understanding must be captivated through submission to the faith."[3] The spirit is spellbound by God's truths. "Lord," cried St. Augustine, "it is when I am most obedient to your will that I feel most free." From the beginning, Rome knew that the principle of obedience could not be safeguarded without rules or unity.

The picture should not be painted unduly dark. Obedience, as Bayle noted, "captivates." It brings security and peace. Man is an uneasy animal, and submission spares him uneasiness. La Fontaine, in one of his fables, contrasted the sleek dog wearing a collar to the wolf that was lean but free. But suppose the dog felt that it needed its collar; it is lost without the master to whom the collar binds it. It loves even its fear of him.

Once a certain degree of habit is reached, one moves uneasily into dependence, fearing the risks and responsibilities of independence. When England freed the slaves in Barbados in 1838, two hundred blacks murdered one Glenelg, their former master, because he refused to keep them in bondage. Freedom was too heavy to bear.

A Dependent People

"Calves!" This disillusioned opinion of the French, sometimes pronounced by de Gaulle, more often attributed to him, was as intriguing as it was shocking. One felt that in his private vocabulary, these calves were not young bulls but future oxen.

History offers more than one example of a vigorous people easily unnerved and seemingly emasculated. The citizens of republican Rome were ready to give their lives for a state for which they were responsible—*res publica*. The same people, bastardized by the bureaucratic centralization of imperial Rome, could not summon the energy to govern themselves or even to defend themselves. Barbarians were recruited for the legions and the legion chiefs for emperors. No wonder people subjected to pervasive authority let themselves be carried by it.

Objects of History

"Me? I don't know anything about politics." No phrase could be more expressive of our civic indifference, proffered sometimes out of prudence, at other times as a proud claim to innocence. Our lack of interest in public life does not prevent us, a moment later, from complaining that the state is not being led to our liking and that those who are playing our politics for us are schemers or fools.

Need we look any further for the reason why the French, weakened by their old habit of turning to the state for everything, have collapsed under every blow of fate history has dealt them? The sole exceptions being when inspired leaders tap the springs of collective will with a call sounded in an almost forgotten language.

In the vast body of literature that foreign observers have devoted to us, our passiveness is often noted. "How faithful the French people remains to its own nature, which consists of passively accepting history," wrote Curzio Malaparte. "France only narrowly avoided Hitler as its destiny."[4] On his lecture tours, the playwright Sacha Guitry liked to tell of an incident that occurred in 1940, just after the fall of Paris. Hitler had come to survey his conquest. Early one morning, leaning over the Tuileries parapet, he was gazing at the Seine when a fisherman walked by on the quay below with his rod over his shoulder. The man glanced indifferently at the group of German officers and recognized the Führer among them. He went his way, simply murmuring: "Well! There he is!" Then he sat down at the water's edge a little further along and cast his line into the river. Guitry always brought applause from the audience when he praised this stout fellow. "There is the real French people!" he said. "There's a good Frenchman! There's a true patriot!" The fisherman's attitude, Guitry's panegyric and the audience's enthusiasm are all equally characteristic of the French.

Anyone who has tried to lead a city or a village knows how few people take part in public life. It's always the same ones who volunteer. The others act like idlers gawking at a truck that has scattered its load all over the street: not one will lend a hand to straighten things up.

The strange image of the French as idlers is probably only the consequence of a long historical malformation. "Every carpenter to his last." "I'm no nurse." "I'm not paid for that." Society has designated the civil defense people and the hospital staffs to take care of accident victims, the police to protect women from assault, the elected authorities to handle public affairs. Individuals do not want to deal with such things; they feel they should not. Let *them* make out as they can. Responsibility is thus permanently shrugged off.

Self-Justifying Mistrust

The more untrustworthy we consider people, the more they become so. Whether it is justified or not at first, the presumption of incompetence becomes legitimate in the long run. Can anyone drive a car safely who has never done anything but push a cart along a rail?

Whose vision of a people's culture is more innovative, that of a Malraux or that of a municipal councillor who wants to force a musical comedy on his cultural center? Who is more dynamic, an Economic Planning Commission or a routine-bound artisan? It must be conceded that it is the tentacular state, the Parisian planners, the abhorred technocrats who most often show their concern for the distant future. If France were suddenly to give free rein to local initiative, all we would hear spouting at first would be the local boosters. Centralized authority has succeeded in making itself irreplaceable by forcing us to choose between it and an infinite series of petty village wars.

This is to suppose that everyone has his particular level of competence, assigned to him once and for all by divine decree. But experience has surely shown us that new responsibilities often transform people. A man is carried along by his function. Why deprive ourselves of this prodigious spring of character?

Our society is subtly inhibitive. It places everyone on a ladder, each rung of which is assigned in advance until its occupant retires. Any hierarchical organization is inhibitive. Has anyone ever seen individual initiative in a Communist Party? It is the leftist fringe groups that have renewed the forms of political opposition; their spontaneous protest has been incomparably more effective in promoting change than that of the big revolutionary party. A powerful hierarchical party secretes order as a bee does honey.

This whole system, all these mental habits, keep the French people in a state of immaturity—a gifted adolescent, brilliant, often charming, but not quite ripe even as an adult. His childhood has left him passive, though he is moved by occasional whims. His enthusiasms are as quickly extinguished as they are inflamed; he is dreamy, posturing, inconstant. He plays, but quickly tires of his games.

The game he likes best is "Liberty." He even thinks he invented it. He is convinced that he wrote the Declaration of the Rights of Man and of the citizen, forgetting that he read it first in a Declaration of Independence that Benjamin Franklin trailed through Paris, and even in the old Compact proclaimed by the English Puritans in 1620. Charles Maurras quite rightly said that freedom remained "a noble stranger" in France. But the French do not know this. They speak the language of liberty, while their reflexes are those of authority, an authority they revere and fear at the same time like a family god.

In the long run, thought itself is inhibited by having no function but to compensate for the reign of the hierarchical order. For human initiative is like a battery: it is charged by use.

CHAPTER 33

Insubordination

Because authority is remote and inexplicable, because it evades dialogue and excludes any attitude but obedience, another attitude arises: that of rebellion.

A *Liberating Explosion*

Our daily lives are conditioned by the interplay between submission and insubordination. While taking my car out of an underground parking area, I was involved in an exemplary incident. Two workmen were repairing the garage door; one of them, on a ladder, was tightening bolts with tools passed to him by the other. I tooted my horn lightly to signal that I wanted to drive out. "You can wait until we're finished," the workmen told me belligerently. "How long will you be?" I asked. "At least an hour." I argued in vain. "The manager told us not to interrupt our work unless at least three cars were lined up."

A second car pulled up. The driver, a woman, hopped out, furious: "I don't pay for space in this parking area to let myself be caught in it like a rat in a trap!" "It's no use insulting us," the workmen retorted. I butted in: "The lady isn't insulting you." "Yes she is—she called us rats." I insisted on seeing the manager, but no: "He can't be disturbed." So the woman wielded the sole weapon remaining to us: commotion. She leaned on her horn. The noise was shattering. Passers-by clustered at the entrance.

Finally, a man arrived and ordered the workmen to let us through. They obeyed, in a rage. It was all over in a moment, as though by enchantment. A miniature social uprising, in which the two motorists played the role of citizens contesting authority, the workmen functioning as bureaucrats, the manager as the government. Government by remote control requires submissiveness, but it is at the mercy of revolution.

Protest Without Power

Protest and confrontation exist in every society. In ours, however, no channels have been laid out through which to express them. They are torrents forever digging their own courses, and must inevitably do damage. Opposition to holy authority is by nature blasphemous, profane. In the polycentric democracies, claims and tempers are vented on local authorities; moreover, there are a number of legal procedures open to the citizen by which he may contest or revoke authority.[1]

These are almost nonexistent in the monocentric democracies. Since the lamplighter is the sovereign's delegate, there is no way to protest inadequate lighting but to blame the sovereign. While waiting to take revenge at the ballot box for his many griefs, the citizen can only contest power illegally, in ways that are excessive and explosive.

The trouble is that there is no real contract between the citizenry and authority. The French mentality sees authority as illegitimate from the moment it loses its power to command obedience. Authority is not obeyed because it is legitimate; it is legitimate because it is obeyed. This is an all-or-nothing situation. It's like an old-time classroom: either there wasn't a fly stirring, or the air was full of flying inkwells.

The Weak Link

Insubordination does not diminish authority; it registers its absence or its ineptitude. It was our most indecisive king who was guillotined.

Rebellion only breaks down open doors. Masters and subjects constantly take each other's measure, like teachers and students. Authority's inhibitive power usually goes unchallenged. In some cases, the master needlessly makes his power felt out of sheer intoxication with it. The humiliation will be avenged, not on him, but on the demagogue who succeeds him.

This is also why it is so difficult to reduce authoritarian tension from the top. In a system that lives on authority, it is the most liberal citizens who pay for their iron-fisted leaders. And when the party is over, authority is back again, reinforced by its ordeal. The prisons were filled after the Bastille fell. Strong links replace the weak ones; the chain continues to bind.

The Anticlerical Break

A strong link did snap once, though, and the entire chain of authority was weakened. This was the break that unhooked the essential French soul from the Church. Religion has lost strength everywhere since the eighteenth century, but everywhere except in the strictly Catholic countries it has done so gradually. Religious influence remains strong in the Protestant countries, even in their governments. Many people in France's television audience were surprised to learn that America's astronauts praised God in their capsule, that the President of the United States takes his oath on the Bible and that the Congress observes moments of prayer.

In France, as in the other Latin countries, anticlericalism was aggressive because it was a channel of release. It played a major role in aggravating the French sickness. "No God, no master," cried the anarchists, being consistent with themselves. The master remained, firmly seated. Perhaps he even sought to turn anti-authoritarian pressure against the Church. If so, it was a dangerous tactic. Authority is easily sanctified when it is religious, less so if it succumbs to the temptation to oppose religion. Anticlericalism altered nothing in the patterns of authority, but it heightened the pressure against hierarchies. The balance between obedience and insubordination grew more precarious.

Associating in Order to Oppose

We are mistrustful. We seem able to join together only to oppose others, not to do something positive. The spirit of rebellion is systematized, as the spirit of authority was systematized over the centuries. This is why Marxism is so attractive in the Latin countries. The votes cast by communist voters, who so often feel like exiles in their own country, are protest votes, but they are also votes of sympathy. Our system today is rebellious as systems elsewhere are orderly. Tomorrow ours could become orderly. If so, it would be a strong temptation for Latins who have not yet recovered from their break with a divinely ordained order—Romans in search of a new Rome.

CHAPTER 34

Begging with a Snarl

We leave it to the state to care for our happiness—and reproach it for not making us happy enough. We beg from it what we are unwilling to obtain for ourselves—and snarl at it for not giving it to us, or not giving us enough of it, or fast enough. The novelist Maurice Druon once described us as having "a begging bowl in one hand, a Molotov cocktail in the other."

Since individual initiative is discouraged, since the organization of collective life is monopolized by the government, the French can hardly fail to expect authority also to settle their problems and iron out their troubles. This attitude of sponging off the state is merely the counterpart of the absence—or insufficiency—of intermediaries, of local democracy and individual initiative.

Every Man for Himself

Voters who come to see me in my Provins office often consult me about highly personal problems: "My son and I are losing touch. How can I catch up with him?" "My husband is philandering. What should I do?" If people will confide to an officeholder emotional problems that they alone can solve, one can imagine how they feel about more material issues. What individual officials cannot solve, the state will solve for them. A local official will turn to his prefect, deputies to the appropriate minister. Let him figure it out.

Since this collective mental attitude has been beaten into most local officials, they will act in the same way as their most resourceless constituents. When the state lifts its little finger, the mayor pulls back his hand. For decades, people have nattered about augmenting local authority, but it is the communities themselves that call loudly for subsidies which, when allotted, will curtail their freedom of decision. It is the communities that insist that the state build things for them and so rid local authorities of the nuisance, or nationalize a private secondary school and relieve them of having to bother about it.

This is why talk of fusing small communities with larger ones runs against the collective psychology. However tiny it is, a village resents being a hamlet in some larger township; the spirit of mistrust requires that each have an advocate of its very own.

"Nothing from the State?"

Everyone thinks he has a claim on the state, and many insist on trying to collect on the debt, however small it may be. They expend more energy on it than they would in finding a way to make a more substantial living on their own. "Make the state pay" is their dream, not in the form of such abstract values as security, independence or freedom, but in ringing, fully weighted personal advantages. Everyone aspires to a subsidy. Each is willing for everybody else to pay it.

Are the weak the only ones who become parasites on the state? Far from it—often it's the most solid citizens.

In May 1968, gasoline was rationed to a few liters per vehicle. A service station attendant noticed that a hustler at the wheel of a sports car had received a ration at a neighboring pump before moving on to his. The attendant began to bawl the driver out and then recognized him as Alain Geisner, one of the three young leaders of the revolution-on-the-march. Grabbing an iron bar, he began to beat on the car's hood. "Since you break up other people's cars," he shouted, "others have a right to break yours up." The great leader took off in a squeal of tires. Newsmen rushed to the scene to interview the first man to have routed the revolution.

In 1973, this exceptionally courageous man's garage was struck by a tornado; the repair shop collapsed, burying cars in the ruins. He asked my help. I contacted his trade association, which granted him a low-interest loan that would enable him to rebuild his business better than ever. The loan, combined with what he had collected on his insurance, closed the case as far as I was concerned. "And the state?" he asked. I explained that emergency government aid was being reserved for the needy in communities ravaged by the storm. He shook his head incredulously. He has renewed his plea several times since then: "There is really nothing to be gotten from the state?"

The Help That Paralyzes

Once people and their elected officials are trained to think like welfare cases, we should not be surprised if they are reluctant to undertake anything without help. Even in the eighteenth century the difference was felt between the French, who relied on the state, and the English, who relied on themselves. Again, Arthur Young is our witness. He was in Anjou and met the permanent secretary of the Angers Agricultural Society: "He commended greatly the plan of my travels, but thought it very extraordinary that neither government, nor the Academy of Sciences, nor the Academy of Agriculture, should at least be at the expence [sic] of my journey. This idea is purely French: they have no notion of private people going out of their way for the public good, without being paid by the public; nor could he well comprehend me, when I told him that everything is well done in England except what is done with public money."[1]

Much has been said about the Jews who leave the Soviet Union for Israel, drawn by freedom, the land of their ancestors, the call of the blood. But we hear less about those disappointed Jews who return to the Soviet Union. Yet these are the unusual cases. Why return, risking reprisal, to a country they had fled? Why choose freely against freedom?

In Israel, I interviewed some of these émigrés who were preparing to go back. Their answers were disconcerting. Taking initiative, scanning the want ads every morning, finding jobs and housing for themselves, coming face to face with themselves had proven distressing. After half a century of a regime that looks after everything, that surrounds and guides you and pays you from the cradle to the grave, how can you get used to working off the leash? When you've become a railroad car, how can you function without rails and a loco-motive?

CHAPTER 35

Hallowed Equality

The Grand Master of French Universities drew his watch from his waistcoat pocket and declared proudly to Napoleon III: "Sire, at this moment all the second-year students in all the lycées in France are attacking the same Latin text." It was a wholly French delectation.

"Where we are lucky is in the unitary state," de Gaulle told me in 1962. "It applies the same rules to everyone, it makes all particularisms and in-equalities disappear. Federated states have all the trouble in the world gov-erning themselves. Look at the United States and Germany. Everyone pulls in his own direction."

Even before 1968, as I have noted, de Gaulle had changed his mind about this and showed it. This took great courage, for the ideal of unity is at the bottom of our Roman mentality. Revolutionary messianism, in 1793 as in 1917, dreamed of internationalism: "Peoples, unite!" . . . "Workers of the world, unite!" . . . Does reality resist this? Is it still impossible for all men to submit to the same principles? Surely we could at least abolish the differ-ences within our own nation.

The Prestige of Uniformity

Yet the history of civilization teaches us that progress is based on differences. Monotony is death. Renewal springs from contrast. If nothing challenges our ideas, our intelligence dozes and so does our drive, our will to do things. An obsession with union impoverishes man; it eliminates the originality each can bring to the common effort.

Does unity emerge strengthened from this? We'll see. Doesn't a true sense of unity come from the acceptance of diversity, of tolerance? This was Erasmus' idea. It did not become a French idea. From Catholicism we have chiefly retained its affirmation of the universality—or catholicity—of correct doctrine. And the Revolution led us to reduce France to general and there-fore universal ideas. (The excellence of the French language is not enough for us; we must also proclaim its universality.) It was no longer France whose colors we bore beyond our frontiers, but the rights of man and of the citizen. France, the fatherland of ideals, could embrace all mankind in its citizenship.

While French universalism has caused us some vexation, it has also done wonders. The testimony of Gaston Monnerville, a black born in Madagascar during the French colonial period and later chairman of the French Council of State, reminds us of this, and we cannot fail to be moved by it: "At the communal school I heard tell of a country in Europe, nine thousand kilometers from the little place where I was born, of which, we were told, all free men thought with gratitude. . . ."[1]

French colonialism was powerfully assimilative. If the army, the local administration and a significant portion of the population could dream of integrating the Algerians into France, it was because they were answering the call of our unifying spirit. Everybody alike, from Dunkirk to Tamanrasset.

At the opposite extreme, Protestantism's particularist genius sometimes produces a contrasting delirium, that of segregation. In all good conscience, Danes affirm of the Eskimos in Greenland, Boers of the Bantustan Africans, Americans of the Indians that "these men are not like us. Our company harms them, so let them remain on their reservations, for their own good as well as ours."

The Egalitarian Obsession

Nothing is more irritating to the French conscience than to come up against personal diversity. We do everything we can to eliminate it. Environmental differences, we conclude, explain everything. If a young man is a murderer, it's because of his unhappy childhood. We forget that his brother, the product of a similar childhood, has not killed anybody.

So the myth remains intact. Men are the same, only circumstances make them different. Fatalism lays the blame on bad luck; in the revolutionary version, society is the villain. The notion that intellectual capacities might differ from person to person runs brutally counter to our profound sense of human unity. If man is a reasonable animal, then common sense must be the world's most equitably shared quality. Religion could hold men to be equal in the love of God; lay thinking requires them to be equal in themselves. Utopia follows from this. Rid of capitalist alienation, said Trotsky, "the average man will reach the level of Aristotle, Goethe, Marx."

The unitary obsession leads to an egalitarian obsession, the one as sterilizing as the other. Yet we cannot progress unless we seek to excel—or, if you wish, to equal; equality is an objective that implies inequality. There are creative inequalities. Egalitarian unitarism represses the instinct to excel, in which we have recognized history's greatest strength. It is all very well to see to it that everyone starts the race on an equal footing, but let's not eliminate the race by chaining all the runners together.

Unitarism Versus Unity; Egalitarianism Versus Equality

The centralist state's mythology naturally reinforces this unitary obsession as it does the refusal to recognize differences. It is expected to be a steamroller. The man who has less is robbed by him who has more, and it is the state's fault. Conversely, the state draws its most effective justification from its unwholesome interventionism, its permanent appeal to unitarism and egalitarianism.

The unitary state has developed its power without a consonant development of unity. Local and regional inequalities persist despite the state's continuous intervention. It has succeeded in stifling inequality, not in achieving uniformity. To assure greater equality, the Vichy government decided in 1940 to establish "zonal abatements": wages, officials' living allowances, family allocations were to be higher in the city than in the country, higher in the big cities than in the small ones to compensate for unequal living costs. Twenty-eight years later the system remained intact, although conditions had changed radically. The bureaucracy remained imperturbable. It took the dramatic Grenelle agreement (after the events of May 1968) to grant in a few moments what unions and members of Parliament had been repeatedly and vainly demanding for twenty years.

Centralism is based on the principle of equality through unity. But what if this endangers both unity and equality? Unity because this can truly exist only in respect for diversity; see how sorely tempted Brittany and Corsica still are by autonomy after centuries of administrative leveling. And equality because the centralized state, in principle responsible for making corrective adjustments, jams the self-regulatory mechanisms. It is striking that the spread of inequalities in estates and incomes is a little wider in France, the most centralized of the industrial nations, than in the others.[2] And those nations in which the spread is narrowest (Switzerland, Holland) are also the most decentralized. Thus, through its clumsy interference, centralism maintains greater inequality in France than elsewhere, and renders it more intolerable than elsewhere because in France it is supposed to abolish inequality.

If equality and unity have nevertheless progressed, it has been via machinery that owes nothing to centralization and everything to technical advances. What are the twentieth century's most spectacular phenomena? In all the advanced countries, ways of living and social conditions are increasingly similar. The middle class grows at the expense of the proletariat and the very rich. In an increasingly fluid society, obstructions are vanishing one after another. The relative decline in the cost of goods and services, the proliferation of audiovisual material, unifies societies much faster than the state has ever been able to do.

Logically, such progress should have curtailed the passion for egalitarianism. Instead, it has simply exacerbated it. The impulse is livelier and more widespread today than it was twenty years ago and certainly more than in the nineteenth century, when inequality was glaring and even glorious. The fact is that logic hasn't much to do with the way men feel and behave. Tocqueville had already remarked that an injustice that is tolerated when it is unrelieved becomes intolerable when it has begun to disappear.

Foreign observers have often noticed that the French are by nature envious and litigious. There was a time when these rabid litigants' complaints mainly concerned property boundaries and inheritances. But with the "massification" of modern life, pettifogging has taken on the proportions of class struggle that strips raw the increasingly insupportable sense of inequality.

There is far less inequality today than there was during the Belle Epoque or the period between the two world wars. But the inequalities that remain are far better known and therefore far more provocative. Television and magazine advertising project multiple images of luxurious living and implant them in the daily imagination—dreams of beautiful women and exotic vacations. The proliferation of goods has removed any limits on the desire for consumption. Before, a man had one pair of clogs and was satisfied; now he has three pairs of shoes and they are not enough if his neighbor has five. We can no longer tolerate differences. Even if the income spread is gradually narrowing, it is visible in every aspect of life. Inequality has receded and social enviousness has advanced.

Standard Ideas About Inequality

While this obsessive enviousness, then, proves that equality is increasing, it erases the awareness of that increase from our collective consciousness. We refuse to see it. The notion that the gap between minimum and maximum salaries in France is much wider than in the socialist countries is in our dictionary of clichés. In fact, although it is slightly wider than in the advanced, decentralized countries, it is a good deal narrower than in the communist countries with their powerful, centralized governments.

If we examine stated wages, we find that the ratio of the minimum wage for an unskilled laborer to the maximum salary, that of a minister, is on the order of 1 to 12 in France, before taxes. In the Soviet Union the ratio is 1 to 30. But the gap becomes incommensurable if we add in the perquisites available only to the privileged: dachas, official apartments, special stores, and so on.

There is no area in which the egalitarian passion is so vehemently expressed as in comparison of incomes. Statistics on inequality require delicate handling, but they are often handled indelicately. So we classify people by income levels without considering age levels, comparing the wage of an eighteen-year-old unskilled laborer with that of an engineer at the end of his career. The result is impressive but deceiving. If we compared wage inequalities for persons in the same age brackets, we would see that the spread for young people beginning their careers is slight (on the order of 1 to 3). Young French people today face their heaviest outlays—in setting up house, raising children—under conditions that are no longer, as they were until quite recently, notoriously unequal.

Equality of Opportunity

Until recently, too, our egalitarian masochism had spared one institution, the schools, thought by all French to be instruments of social advancement. In 1964, two young sociologists convinced the intelligentsia that, far from promoting equal opportunity, the schools in fact foster social conservatism, separating the "heirs" from the rest and exactly reproducing society as it was.

The success of this thesis was surprising. The sociologists based their conclusions on statistics covering the 1961–62 university year. They found that only 6 percent of the university population was made up of workingmen's sons, while the working class comprised 36 percent of the labor force. What they failed to realize, or to say, was that the figure had been only 1 percent in 1945 and 2.7 percent in 1958; moreover, the sociologists refused to foresee that the figure would rise to 13 percent in 1975—a proportional growth of 1,300 percent in thirty years and a numerical increase of 6,000 percent. Isn't the fact that the number of laborers' sons in universities was multiplied by over 60 in a generation one of the most solid reasons for optimism the times could have furnished? Besides, do we need statistics to establish what we can see for ourselves if we open our eyes? In the ten years following the end of World War II, a student at the Institut d'Etudes Politiques would have felt disgraced had he not worn a stiff collar and a black hat with turned-up brim and carried a black umbrella in a silk sheath. What was called for was not merely a bourgeois uniform but an haut bourgeois uniform. Today, you can't tell the president's from the gatekeeper's son among all those youngsters in their turtleneck sweaters and jeans. It may still be snobbery, but it is egalitarian snobbery.

The School of Despair

It is generally assumed that inequality has no other cause than money. This is the first simplification. The second is that we cannot imagine this "money" except as an immutable treasure, the only question being how to apportion it. If some have more, others have less. We always conceive of wealth as though we were old peasants in a finite world: I do not own my neighbor's field.

Since no one gladly relinquishes his share, we cannot imagine surmounting the inequality of incomes except through class warfare. The doctrines of expansion have not yet entered our minds. We are not used to the idea that increasing the share held by the underprivileged should be accomplished not at the expense of the most favored, but from the margin created by growth—in which process the privileged have an important role to play. The apostles of justice insist that "the wealthier society becomes, the greater the gap." The notion is false but popular, all the more so because it agrees with the tendency toward convulsive immobility.

Whether the question is one of equal revenues or equal opportunity, the egalitarian mentality finally destroys the very idea that economic expansion and progress in education can mobilize and move society. For our egalitarian absolutists, no one must be allowed to hope that forces of change are insensibly but powerfully at work; change must come from elsewhere, and it must come first. There is no salvation except in a revolution that assumes command of the state's highest levers of control.

All societies on the march toward equality risk reaching thresholds at which motivations are paralyzed. In 1957, on a visit to the University of Uppsala in Sweden, I was surprised to be told that it was difficult to give Swedish students reasons to work. Why consent to study hard if taxes level all incomes, if socialism planes down social prestige, if you can earn as much selling sausages on a street corner as you can teaching mathematics? And why strain on behalf of a company if salaries hardly reflect that effort and responsibility is accrued without corresponding increases in rewards?

The day may come in France, as it has in Britain, when the search for equality dries up the springs of prosperity propelling us toward greater equality. Our economy is not yet threatened by the ravages of inhibitive equality. But society itself is endangered.

CHAPTER 36

A Holiday from Reality

If there is one pleasure in which we like to indulge, it is certainly that of verbalizing. "In France," said the nineteenth-century writer Henri-Frédéric Amiel, "we always think that something said is something done." He could have extended this to all the Latin peoples: "When I do not talk, I do not think," and "When I speak, I act." We speak like sovereigns whose word alone determines good or evil, true or false, and can alter the course of things, as though action were a dream, to desire were to possess, and to fear were to demolish. We admire those who speak with the greatest assurance and brio. We don't expect them actually to do anything about what they are proposing. A well-turned phrase is enough.

Realization Is Secondary

In French, to be right is to "have reason," as one has a serve in tennis. We enjoy our temporary possession of it before disposing of it, since we juggle with ideas. In English, one says: "You are right." The truth is not a toy one may or may not own, or change as it suits or as the fashion prescribes; it is an attitude that entirely commits one.

Take a typical question from a collection of *Philosophy Dissertations for a Baccalaureate Degree:* "It has been said that 'it is not the result that counts, but the intention.' Analyze this opinion and demonstrate its value." Its value! There is nothing hidden about official doctrine. Nothing in our education accustoms us to consider reality as a touchstone or realization as a test. Rather, everything inclines us to consider reality as impure and realization as secondary. In case of failure, it's the facts that are wrong.

This intelligentsia of intention—wholly at ease in discourse, but clumsy and ill-suited to transforming discourse into action—is characteristic of the Latin countries. Its favorite activity is "posing the problem." The problem is posed, then dropped. The Briton and the American generally go about things the opposite way, seldom bothering to define a problem they do not intend to solve.

Few peoples have sowed as many ideas as we have; others have often reaped the harvest. We have regularly allowed ourselves to be despoiled of the fruits of our genius by others' ingenuity. The steam engine, the motorboat, the automobile, the airplane, nuclear energy, radio, television, laser beams and integrated circuits all derive from French discoveries. But it was the British, the Americans, the Germans and the Japanese who applied these discoveries and reaped the profits from them. We show immense skill in theory and equal weakness in practice.

But something is changing under the pressure of reality. New leaders are being trained by contact with business, and a sort of French counter-intelligentsia is being born of the very life that is slowly beginning to animate our economy. It is active and self-aware. The pity is that it has scarcely any links to the intellectual milieu, which views these young executives with a mixture of fear and contempt. Both groups could be enriched by their differences.

Since the eighteenth century, the history of France has been guided by theoretical debate. Suddenly, reality cracks under the pressure of ideas. The Revolution absolutely deserves its adjective "French": it was the work of intellectuals who had spent half a century preparing it and who were utterly unprepared for it when it happened. In his Swiss haven, Lenin lucidly worked out the scripts for seizing power. But the French philosophers, alight with abstract conceptions of liberty, justice and property, failed to pay the slightest attention to the concrete structures of authority and made no provision for changing them.

This lack of realism struck the positive mind of our irreplaceable witness Arthur Young. Passing through Limoges in 1787, he was welcomed by the Agricultural Society: "They meet, converse, offer premiums, and publish nonsense. This is not of much consequence, for the people, instead of reading their memoires, are not able to read at all. They can however *see:* and if a farm was established in that good cultivation which they ought to copy, something would be presented from which they *might* learn."[1]

Words and Things

An unrealistic intelligence replies to reality's challenge with classification. It reduces things to categories and norms. The more reality escapes us, the more we seek to enclose it in a law so as to make it reasonable and thus administrable. Our cultural characteristics are summed up in this editorial delirium. We delight in abstraction, legalism, Utopianism, preferring form to substance. Instead of direct contact, we like written orders that are not preceded by psychological preparation or followed by checks on performance.

In order to meet international competition, private companies have to use Anglo-American techniques and an imported vocabulary: "engineering" and "leasing," "management" and "public relations," "marketing" and "merchandising." No purpose is served in being indignant at this invasion of *franglais;* it only translates our mental weaknesses. We will remain awkward in *têtes-à-têtes* with others and with reality until we set ourselves to learn these techniques systematically. Anglo-Saxon man is trained from childhood for real life. The French will think abstractly as long as they are taught mechanical theory through formulas without ever having to install a piston or dismount a carburetor. They can declare with Cyrano de Bergerac (who was only paraphrasing Don Quixote): "No, no, it is far handsomer when it is useless."

Little Geography and Less History

That "the French know nothing about geography" is proverbial among foreigners. They are worse than ignorant, they are indifferent. For the French, the outside world doesn't exist. In Beziers, Arthur Young spoke to a "well-dressed" merchant: "He asked for the third or fourth time what country I was of. I told him I was a Chinese. How far off is that country?—I replied, two hundred leagues [800 kilometers]. *Deux cents lieus! Diable! c'est un grand chemin!*" Young gave other examples, and compared "this incredible ignorance . . . with the knowledge so universally disseminated in England."[2] Today the French are traveling more and more, but this is a recent development. At heart we remain ignorant. And the reality of which we are most ignorant is our own. For centuries, behind our mental walls, we cultivated a conviction of our superiority, interpreting our happiness and our unhappiness in our own way and at our own convenience. The adult people we are slowly becoming should be capable of standing reality. When we have acquired enough self-confidence to support our history, we will no longer need to tell ourselves tales.

From One Extreme to the Other

Once again we encounter our fragility—for lack of serious knowledge of other peoples with which to season our judgment of ourselves, we swing abruptly from euphoria to depression. We do not know the art of measured self-criticism, which is as far from self-satisfaction as it is from self-humiliation. This swinging between extremes discourages effort, which we feel is either superfluous or pointless.

We dislike conceding that progress has been made even when it is obvious. We live by old stereotypes without reflecting that they may be obsolete. For example: "The French don't read." We cite a hoary statistic (always the same one, dating from before the advent of pocket books) that only one French person in four reads more than four books a year. In 1974 I had a new survey taken.[3] It showed that the French have become readers: from 1964 to 1974, the proportion of those reading more than four books a year rose from one out of four to two out of three. This was a minor revolution, yet the survey that brought it to light is seldom mentioned.

Like drops of quicksilver, we slide from the most naive confidence in our collective genius to the blackest gloom. Since the end of World War II, it is the gloom that has predominated—at a time when the number of objective reasons for pessimism has actually shrunk. For we tend to deny the importance of truly important events and to magnify the unimportant ones. The consequences have sometimes been tragic. France has declared and lost wars because it lost its head. Too imaginative, not realistic enough, it begins them in a dream and ends them in a nightmare. In 1870, an impulse swept France into a confrontation with Germany that lasted for seventy-five years.

The French tend to think in real life as they think in dreams. They want ideas that will solve everything, that will flatten reality; they seek the ideal synthesis that can reconcile the contradictions and anomalies of real life.

As in dreams, amalgamation serves as synthesis. Our political universe abounds in half-truths gone wild. The spirit of logic abandons the field to the spirit of magic. Experts in political thinking sometimes act like that hero legend, Bayard, for whom a sword represented honor and a harquebus dishonor. The amalgam was fatal to him: he died of a harquebus ball, which saved his honor but left some doubt about his sense of reality.

Of all the fantasies that are supposed to preserve us from reality, one of the commonest our generous hearts and poor heads have invented is a poetic amalgam called "libertarian collectivism." It is an idealistic system that would impose a rigorously distributive justice on everyone, eliminate capitalist profit and property, and guarantee the citizens' total liberty by ridding them of governmental and managerial authority through worker management of enterprise. The dreamy spirit of French generosity cultivates the hope of reconciling the Revolutionary romanticism of 1848 and the Paris Commune with the efficiency required by an industrial society.

"Psychic Epidemics"

France is less stirred by problems than by misunderstandings. It is virtually impossible for the French to have a debate on capitalism, for example, that is not dominated by misunderstanding. For what is being pursued behind this bogeyman word is not really a system of capital appropriation but industrial society, of which we refuse the constraints while insisting on the benefits.

The French drift between submission to the state and hatred of the state, between the deified state and the desanctified state. They are at the mercy of a sudden gust of wind. Then follows the panic and collective madness.

At the root of these "psychic epidemics," as Freud called them, is surely the lack of direct responsibility, the lack of an anchorage in the realities of power, and a deep sense of the individual's impotence. From time to time an event, even a very minor one, can crystallize this mute anxiety, this lack of confidence in the system, this feeling that things are not going as they should.

Only the state can do something, but we have no hold on it. And if the state itself seems to be losing its grip, the vertigo grows stronger.

The French then feel at one with those who denounce authority. A vacuum forms around the state. Every time the miners, the mailmen or the farmers rebel against the state, public opinion is with them. But nothing can replace the state. After a few weeks of insurrection, we begin to fear the cold, letters don't reach us, we are sick of barricaded roads. Punch has thoroughly pounded Judy on their little stage. The children have dreamed their dream. And when they leave the theater, the traffic cop is always there to help them cross the street.

Our Wars of Religion

O Dieu! si vous avez la France sous vos ailes,
Ne souffrez pas, Seigneur, ces luttes éternelles,
Ces trônes qu'on élève et qu'on brise en courant,
Ces tristes libertés qu'on donne et qu'on reprend,
Ces flux et ces reflux de l'onde contre l'onde,
Cette guerre, toujours plus sombre et plus pro-
*   fonde,*
Des partis au pouvoir, du pouvoir aux partis,
L'aversion des grands qui ronge les petits,
Et toutes ces rumeurs, ces chocs, ces cris sans
*   nombre,*
Ces systèmes affreux échafaudés dans l'ombre,
Qui font que le tumulte et la haine et le bruit
Emplissent les discours . . . °

—Victor Hugo (1835)[1]

We do not like ourselves. We call for unanimity of thought and we thrash
about in a nightmare of endless quarrels. Many heads must fall if only one is
to be seen. Our political life is poisoned by our Manichaean insistence that
everything be all black or all white. People in politics sometimes admit this.
One of them, for example, organized a club to combat "the tendency to radi-
calize all debate." Another denounced the "civil wars" waged over every
subject in our teaching system. The list changes as interests shift, for these ridiculous wars are born, live and die as suddenly as storms. How can we
change the climate?

We can scarcely even understand that true unity prospers in diversity.
Switzerland, for example, is united *because* the cantons are sovereign, *be-*
cause the Grisons are governed differently from the Valaisans, the Genevois

---

° O God, if you have France under your wing, do not tolerate, Lord, these eternal struggles,
these thrones we raise, then tear down as we rush past, these sad liberties given and then re-
scinded, this ebb and flow of wave against wave, this war that grows grimmer and more profound, of parties in power that clutch power to themselves, the gnawing aversion in which
the great hold the humble, and all these rumors and clashes and countless cries, these frightful systems secretly devised, that fill all our debate with tumult, hatred and noise. . . .

from the Vaudois. In Switzerland, centuries of grass roots democracy has killed off the noxious growth of social aggressiveness.

In our permanently fallow democracy, aggressiveness grows wild as weeds.

Civil Wars by a Warrior People

Of all the countries in Europe, France is the one that has most often fought the others, the one for which the number of years of war, compared to the years of peace, is by far the greatest.

Cato attributed two dominant passions to the Gauls: "To be brave in war and to speak skillfully."[2] And Strabo said: "The Gallic race is obsessed with war; it is irritable and quick to come to blows."[3] The centralized state, itself a product of war, has cultivated our bellicose tendencies. Although fratricidal struggle was an evil endemic to the states of the Old World, none were so racked by it as France.

This propensity for civil war is the culmination of our aggressiveness. Montesquieu noted that the history of France was "full of civil wars without revolutions." Had he lived in our time, he would have said "with" rather than "without."

Rioting was a national sport well before 1789. From the Albigensian Crusade to the Bread Riots of 1775 and the countless uprisings in Paris and the provinces, the history of France is one long civil war full of assassinations, police sweeps and senselessness. The most atrocious of our civil wars—the nation still bears their scars—were the Wars of Religion. France was by far the slowest among the states of Christendom to choose its camp. The division, which quickly became armed conflict, raged here for nearly a century and recurred repeatedly throughout the period of the monarchy. The Revolution gave it a new form in the conflict of Church and state.

To understand the traces left by this period on our modern souls, we must call to mind how savage these struggles were and remember that the people clamored for them with all their strength. On Corpus Christi Day in 1535, amid great popular rejoicing, François I led a procession through Paris and personally lighted twenty-five pyres, raised like wayside altars, on which twenty-five Protestants were burned. Father Mariana, a fanatical Jesuit and so above suspicion of useless tenderheartedness, described the 1572 St. Bartholomew's Day massacre this way: "Some were massacred by order of the king, many more by the people. Everywhere there was wounding and killing, usually of innocents, as happens when the people have risen up."[4]

Henri IV had to bring pressure to bear on the magistrates of the Paris Parliament before they would register the Edict of Nantes because, as good interpreters of the public will, they wanted no part of it. He spoke like a man alone: "Distinction must no longer be made between Catholics and Huguenots, they must all be good French. . . . It is impossible to convert the Hugue-nots by force. I do not wish to shed the blood of my lambs, but to gather them together with the gentleness and goodness of a king and not the violence of a tyrant."[5]

This king was assassinated like a tyrant. The revocation of his Edict of Nantes nearly a century later expressed an almost unanimous public wish. In-tolerance had become consubstantial with France. It would later flourish in a thousand different forms.

As recently as the 1960s, it was remembered in scattered valleys of the Dauphiné, the Queyras and the Cevennes, where neighboring farm commu-nities of Catholics and Protestants lay forgotten by history. The two sects never joined on a single electoral ticket; they called themselves the "whites" and the "reds," the "right" and "left." They patronized different stores. They never greeted each other in the street or on a country road. They refused to play together at billiards or at love. Each clan had its God and its sanctuary. Sometimes it was the church that was burned, sometimes the temple, in re-venge for some outrage, some humiliation. These French were not savages; they simply remained consistent longer than the rest.

Daily Aggressiveness

Along with its record for foreign wars and civil wars, France holds another record: for daily, interiorized aggressiveness. It is in France that the number of highway deaths in proportion to the population is highest. The real reasons are apparently psychological—the unleashing of a desire for power arising from the need to assert the independence of one's decisions, an assertion given scant outlet in daily life. And our lack of civic spirit impels us to pass others on the road, to refuse others the right of way, to keep crossing the cen-ter line. In short, to outbursts of aggressiveness. This is sustained, too, by al-cohol—a new record and a new taboo.[6]

Would the French need to find release at the wheel or the bar if they could relax in rites of release such as other societies organize? There are fes-tivals in the calendar of all the Roman countries: carnivals, ferias, corridas in the Latin nations of Europe and America, Flemish fairs, the Rosenmontag in Catholic Germany. Surely an explosion of collective madness is a necessary compensation in societies burdened by the constraints of overly rigid struc-tures. Rome's Caesars considered festivals indispensable to their exercise of power. The *saturnalia*, when slaves became their masters' equals, were ex-tended to seven days by Domitian.

Only the countries that cultivate individual liberty can dispense with ritual fiestas. They are needed where authority's hold is strong. Perhaps it is a remnant of the Cathar or Jansenist spirit that has prevented the French from organizing them. But what it consciously rejects works unconsciously on it.

"He who would be an angel becomes a devil." For lack of fiestas, the people find their own ways to discharge their aggression in such flights from reality as revolutionary explosions, strike festivals, bloody Sundays, brawls between drivers, and drink.

Ours is an angry individualism—we grow drunk on conflict. France was long the promised land for duelists. It remains so in its bursts of temper, its verbal violence, its sonorous threats that come to nothing. In more refined circles, the shafts are lighter but deadlier; virtuosity in the art is more prized than good sense or competence. The "wittiest people on earth" has become more often disagreeable than droll. We seem to be trying to live up to Jean Cocteau's definition: "A Frenchman is an ill-tempered Italian."

Conflict as Dialogue

French aggressiveness has made economic life a new battlefield. In France we cultivate a special form of labor conflict. It combines the contrary characteristics such disputes have in the authoritarian countries and the liberal democracies. In the former, strikes are forbidden; if one does happen to break out, it becomes explosive. In the liberal democracies, strikes are legal and—at least today—rarely lead to violence.

In France, as in Italy, strikes are both spasmodic, as in the countries that forbid them, and as frequent as (or more frequent than) they are in any liberal democracy. Yet the fact that they are part of ordinary life does not relieve them of any of their violence. Social dialogue is usually reduced to them and it resembles a dialogue of Homeric heroes. For in the countries with a Roman tradition, social progress, like democracy, is born of violence. It is a bloody conquest wrested from an immutable order. Because workers are not treated as real partners, they are always moved to take by main force that which is elsewhere granted as a right. They convince themselves that without class warfare and violence they can never defend their interests. They do not want to know that those countries where labor's living standards are highest, such as Switzerland, West Germany, Holland and Sweden, are precisely the ones in which strikes have almost completely vanished from union arsenals and the class struggle has been discarded from labor ideology.

In France, each side shuts itself into this absurd logic. Employers have reason to mistrust the unions, which have reason to mistrust employers. And on it goes.

The Labor Ghetto

To gauge the depth of this breach, we must bear in mind the conditions in which class warfare arose in France and its tenacious if subconscious symbolism to working-class minds. The proletariat came into being in the nineteenth century as something entirely new, exceptional. Its poverty was terrible, yet this was scarcely perceived. Balzac did not even try to sketch it in at a time when Dickens was describing it with a bitter pen.

In the dynamic countries, however, a kind of solidarity soon grew up between employers and employees in big industry; it was the farmers, traditionalists and protectionists but dwindling in number, who appeared as society's marginal figures. In the static countries, on the other hand, it was industrial labor that was shoved off into the margin. The solidarity that developed was among small businessmen, artisans and farmers, outdoing each other in celebration of the values of a France that rejected systematic industrialization.

The consequence was that in France more than elsewhere, the industrial proletariat "camped at the city gates." Labor's world was one of empty lots and scabrous walls, of monotonous workers' suburbs and interminable travels to and from the job, of abject lassitude and vague anxiety, of juvenile delinquence and the smoke from factory chimneys. The denizens of this world fed on the feeling of being cut off from the normal world.

Their bitterness survived its causes. Nor have its causes all disappeared. The idea of class warfare is deeply rooted in the mentality of many industrial workers. They cannot believe that the "managerial class"—"the government and the bosses, it's all the same"—might bargain in good faith. They are convinced that the big guy will roll the little guy every time. The ideology is not confined to the labor ghetto; many office workers have adopted it. One French wage earner in three is convinced that the well-being of the other two is his own misfortune and that his own happiness can be won only to the others' detriment.

The Social Quarrel

Marxism lent its theory to the working class, and the working class gave Marxism its weight of frustration and blood. This made Marxism the intellectual dominant of the Latin left, born ideologically in a period when economic growth, slow to the point of imperceptibility, caused no appreciable change in the way national wealth was distributed. It was also a period when class was like race, a condition in which individuals were permanently encapsulated. Economic growth and social mobility have closed that period. The social quarrel cannot be a formula for the twentieth century. But our mentality is still imbued with nineteenth-century reflexes.

The atomic bomb has made the disproportion between the stakes of aggression and its dangers unacceptable. Why can't the same awareness unite our social partners? Class conflict in the nineteenth century was a rudimentary weapon in a rudimentary economy; it can only damage an advanced economy, which is as complex as clockwork. Why shouldn't the French, who have become international pacifists, become domestic pacifists as well?

The Franco-French War

One of the most tragic pages of the Franco-French war was written in the 1940s. In hindsight, our traditional Manichaeanism leads us to think that the good French, almost to a man, were on one side and the bad French, the few who strayed, on the other. The reality was less simple.

That the vast majority of French followed Marshal Philippe Pétain between 1940 and 1942 is difficult to prove because two thirds of the country was occupied, and freedom of expression, even in the unoccupied south, was nonexistent. We can only judge by what has been said since the war. We prefer to keep this buried. But honesty should compel us, after so long a time, to bring it to light, without hate and without fear. Like so many others, I witnessed, in Montpellier in March 1941, the enthusiasm Pétain inspired.* As a lycée student, I had been recruited as a monitor. The war memorial, a review of troops and war veterans, a visit to the university escorted by professors in their togas; we were hard-pressed to hold back the frantic crowd. People howled: *"Vive Pétain!"* at the tops of their lungs. Deeply moved women muttered: "I saw him!" None of which prevented them that evening from listening to de Gaulle through the radio jamming.

An Improbable "Third Way"

Every period of history bears traces of the sediment of new divisions. The gulf between the right and the left in France today seems unbridgeable. Sometimes it separates one group from another, as, for example, the reputedly rightist army and the supposedly leftist intellectuals. Or it can run between localities in a given region, in lines that have remained constant over the centuries. The only thing the opponents have in common is the simplistic virulence with which they excommunicate each other. Even a minor issue can revive the old divisions.

General de Gaulle liked to talk of a "third way"—a provocative phrase in a country gripped by dualism. He refused to link French policy to Washington, as the right pressed him to do, or to Moscow, as the strongest party on the left would have wished. He refused to bow to the financiers on the Stock Exchange, as the right did, or to the collectivism espoused by the left. He selected what he considered reasonable in the rightists' values and what was generous in those of the left, and denounced their antagonism as madness.

But his policy was too contrary to the evil genius of the French. The left refused to see itself in de Gaulle and gave him a reputation as a rightist. The men on the right opposed him vigorously, considering him "more dangerous than the left." He did succeed in wresting an appreciable number of French

*I had come to see Generalissimo Francisco Franco, who was returning from a meeting with Mussolini and took the occasion to make an official visit to the city.

from the Manichaean demon. But his exorcistic power gradually waned. After his departure, the political world relapsed slowly into the mental attitudes inherited from the Wars of Religion.

Once again we see the French synthesis threatened with disintegration. Part of the nation would impose its will, even its truths, on another. But since the adversary is never annihilated, imposed truths carry the germ of fresh struggle. For they revive our dogmatic mentality, which tolerates no contradiction, simply transforming discord, which could nourish dialogue, into conflict. It even eats away at our sense of national identity, without which no sick society can rediscover the route to a consensus.

V

THE LESSONS
OF FAILURE

In France, the loveliest churches never have more than one tower and the finest châteaux never have more than one wing, which clearly shows our nation's character, for we undertake everything, finish nothing and destroy with ardor rather than build with perseverance.

—Marquise de Créquy[1]

CHAPTER 38

Serendipity

In the strange land of Serendip—described in Horace Walpole's version of the fairy tale of *The Three Princes of Serendip*—everything happens in reverse. You accidentally find what you were not looking for; you never find what you *are* looking for. You make a mistake and it works to your advantage. You want to harm someone and you make his fortune. Learning from experience, you try doing things in reverse—and the results are even more unexpected.

Walpole called the phenomenon "serendipity."[1] It has always been important in history. Columbus went looking for China and discovered America. We are often Columbuses in politics, although we rarely discover America.

Violence creates a twisted kind of serendipity. The blockade of Cuba and the Bay of Pigs made Fidel Castro a communist despite himself—or so, at least, he told me. The blockade was later lifted, but Castro is still a communist.

With or without violence, France has often seemed to me like a kingdom of Serendip where surprises abound. Its leaders resemble billiards players playing on a bumpy table that makes the balls take odd bounces. The shrewder their calculations, the more widely they miss their mark. The player trusting to luck makes out better.

Other nations' political heroes have been brilliantly successful: Pitt, Disraeli, Churchill; Washington, Roosevelt; Bismarck and Cavour; Lenin and Mao. All these great men were great because they succeeded. In France, it's rather the other way around.

Who are the heroes of history we cherish in our imaginations today? Vercingetorix, chained to Caesar's chariot. St. Louis, who died on an unsuccessful crusade. Joan of Arc, who swore to throw the English out of France and instead was thrown into an English prison, abandoned by the king she vowed to place upon his throne. Louis XIV, who wanted "magnificence" for France and died in a kingdom reduced to poverty. Napoleon, who sought to starve out the British and was deported by them to an obscure island. Let's not even mention our republican heroes, almost all of them failures. We may even love them more for their failures than for their successes.

Serendipity is the daily bread of our history. It has affected all the regimes France has had until now, each of which achieved the opposite of what it was trying to do. Monarchy by divine right? The king's sacred nature was abolished forever in a ritual murder. The Revolution? The anarchy it created culminated in dictatorship. Napoleon? He thought of himself as the guardian of the Revolution and his excesses reestablished the monarchy. Louis-Philippe sought to reconcile royalty with the republican tricolor and succeeded in coalescing against him the legitimist whites, the republican blues and the red of the socialists. The socialist revolution of 1848 brought the party of order to power and, finally, an authoritarian Second Empire.

Napoleon III's foreign policy was a masterpiece of serendipity. It helped in the birth of new nations. But these new nations (not just the German, but the Italian as well) wound up as France's enemies. The republicans in September 1870 set off a monarchist reaction. The monarchists of 1871 founded the republic. They thought it was merely temporary; it is still with us.

Serendipity marked the Fourth Republic from birth to death. Those who brought it to life in 1946 saw it as wholly different from the Third, and made it identical to its predecessor. The ultras of May 13, 1958, supported the only man capable of pushing through the policy they had taken up arms to oppose: the emancipation of Algeria.

The Fifth Republic has not escaped serendipity either. Founded to rally all of France, it fostered polarization. In seeking to restore the state's authority, it heightened the bureaucratic process mining the state from within.

Skidding Out of Control

Why is France like a kingdom of Serendip? Because those responsible for it often seem to be driving a speeding car across ice, when the slightest maneuver, a twitch of the wheel or a touch on the brake, can cause the accident it was meant to avoid.

What gives the polycentric societies their coherence is their flexibility. A despotic society is compressed and, for that very reason, coherent. In it, impulses are transmitted undeviatingly along a channel laid out by those in command. In the polycentric states, a multitude of groups and individuals act autonomously and the compensating interplay of these actions is, in the long run, self-regulating. In one case, the state is obeyed; it eliminates serendipity. In the other, the state seeks as little as possible to be obeyed, intervening in a limited sphere to promote the regulation of independent movements; serendipity tends to eliminate itself.

French society is heterogeneous, neither truly despotic nor truly liberal. It has the monocentric structures of despotic regimes without benefitting from their ability to impose order. It observes the rules of a liberal regime without having its polycentric structures. The combination of these two logically incompatible systems causes unforeseeable jolts. It is not the French who are ungovernable. It is the French system of authority that is incapable of governing them, because in it generalized irresponsibility coincides with an allergy to leadership.

The Few Who Escape

France's society resembles the world of nations—being composed of juxtaposed and often hostile blocs. The state plays a diplomatic role. It deals with jealous powers that are called parties, trade unions, professional groups, bureaucracy, press. The game exists in other democracies, but in France it brings unforeseeable results, for negotiation and compromise are not acceptable as such. The French do not have a contractual spirit. Their aggressiveness transforms confrontation into conflict. We seek less to succeed for ourselves than to promote our partner's failure. No wonder that, in the final analysis, the percentage of failures is high.

Add to this the uncertainties arising from a national character exacerbated by bureaucratic tutelage—our all-or-nothing vertigo, the love of abstraction that hardens our stances, the emotional impulses multiplied by false ideas. A people with such disconcerting reactions is naturally stalked by unpredictable fate. "Who can anticipate the French mind, the strange leaps and zigzags of its instability?" asked Chateaubriand. "Who can understand how its execrations and its enthusiasms, its curses and its blessings are transmuted without apparent reason?"[2]

While the leaders thrown up by crises failed, leaving a wake of glory behind them, another type of leader succeeded: wily men who protected their flanks from attack better than the others, pursuing their ends with prudent tenacity, turning failure to advantage by outdoing it in unpredictability. Louis XI and Henri IV were such men; so were Mazarin and Talleyrand. To them, the art of politics consisted of seizing events instead of submitting to them. Their genius understood how narrow a margin for maneuver they had. Instead of floating with events, as so many others do, or, like some, trying to swim against them, they were patient enough to watch, observe, to await their chance, and, at last, to change the course of things.

To escape the Serendip effect, the society of mistrust must be cautiously infiltrated. Brutality will not convert it into a society of confidence. It is not through violent shocks, but by insidious, patiently repeated acts, that change will be wrought, by the example of well-chosen experiments, by "capillarity," persuasion and a public debate free at last from insistence on outmoded slogans. By apprenticeship and the creation of appropriate institutions. By irony and slow sapping. A thousand moles digging. . . .

CHAPTER 39

De Gaulle Enmeshed

Throughout our inquiry into society and the French mentality, we have pointed a finger with obsessive regularity at the inadequate distribution of responsibility in France. Why wasn't something done about this sooner?

Many reformers over the past three centuries, with the best of intentions, have prescribed the remedy and begun to administer it. All their efforts were turned against them. Why?

Because hierarchical centralization was very early on protected, so to speak, by a barrage of reflexes. And this barrage was interiorized. The exalted state grew by absorbing its opposition. History repeats itself with disheartening monotony. It is pointless to retrace these repetitions, which would only make us feel that without a mental revolution we will never get out of the trap.

De Gaulle did not succeed in interrupting the long series of failures. After curing France's visible sickness—its state sickness, the rot at the top—he felt that he had to deal with its social structures, especially the one that forms its skeleton: the bureaucracy.

He went about it in two stages. First, from 1963 on, he tried to deconcentrate the state's administrative framework, in other words, to entrust to local-level functionaries matters hitherto handled by those in Paris. Then, in 1968 and 1969, he attempted what no one had tried to do before, except perhaps at the end of the monarchy and the beginning of the Revolution: to decentralize, to effect a massive transfer of the state's powers to elective authority.

His second attempt grew out of the failure of the first. And it in turn failed, leading to his departure.

Post-Operative Reeducation

In 1963, having settled the Algerian business and crowned the Fifth Republic's institutional system with the popular election of the president, de Gaulle sought a way to improve the workings of the enormous machinery of state. Departing from his customary approach, he went about it cautiously, leaving most of the work to his prime minister, Pompidou, who was not a brusque man. The general sensed that public opinion, concentrated until then on the tragic developments of a few big national problems, remained unaware of such issues. But he was not displeased to act without stirring it up; after so many shattering conflicts, the prudent method was worth trying.

Although he neither sought out nor provoked his adversary, he nevertheless met him in the most tenacious of all forms—that of deeply rooted attitudes, confirmed habits, unconscious resistance. De Gaulle was soon enmeshed. He knew better than anyone that France is centralized, too much so. He also knew that centralization was not a recent phenomenon, and part of him accepted it as a French historical necessity. Wasn't it enough simply to eliminate its excesses? What de Gaulle sought, then, was not to relieve the state of its attributes, but to transfer them from remote functionaries to those who were closer to the problems.

His method was high-handed. Choice had no place in it. After the 1962 election, when the Parliament and the country's political establishment opposed him, the general was not feeling altogether tender toward any of the powers standing between him and the people or any authority distinct from his own.

The idea was to make the prefects the real bosses of the bureaucracy. As the repository of governmental authority, a delegate of the state in permanent contact with elective authority, the prefect was surely the person best placed to give the administration a human face. He could evaluate situations, allot the proper weight to things and men, bring the bureaucracy out of its hermetic world.

In 1964, the new system was set in motion. Instead of being responsible directly to its central administration, each local public service branch was placed under prefectoral authority. Naturally, the prefect could not see everything or decide on everything. But it was up to him to decide how much; he retained the option of intervening in any question, which gave him considerable power to influence events.

Simultaneously, each minister was asked to route decisions on a great many matters to his provincial offices. Every local technical director—of agriculture, equipment, health and welfare, and so on—became, in a way, the minister in his department, and the prefect was virtually a departmental prime minister. In turn, the regional prefects would coordinate the work of the departmental prefects. The Paris logjam would be broken.

The plan seemed unstoppable. It was—but only on paper.

What's Bred in the Bone . . .

Nearly ten years later, I had occasion to examine the results. What I learned appalled me. Not only had the goals of deconcentration not been reached, but the changes were the opposite of what had been sought. Paris had found the way to recover its power. While efforts were being made toward deconcentration, the ministers were multiplying the number of their actions requiring centralized decisions. Naturally, a minister wants to mark his passage by a new idea. This took the form, locally, of "experiments," "contracts" and "pilot projects"; the importance attached to each idea was measured by the control Paris maintained over its application.

Do we even have to look for prejudice? In itself, the hierarchical system contains all the means it needs to annul deconcentration. A prefect knows that any challenge to his decisions will go to Paris. Whether it is a letter from a member of Parliament or a newspaper report of a local protest, the appeal will land on the minister's desk. Deconcentration thus stimulated, rather than abolished, the traditional reflex.

In the dismal final analysis, deconcentration depersonalizes decision and dissolves authority. Since it is out of the question for the bureaucracy to exclude itself from the circuit of authority, it can only lengthen the circuit by superimposing itself on departmental and regional bureaucracies. Decision is shredded. Where, before deconcentration, a centralized decision required the attention of seven different services, all in Paris, a "deconcentrated" decision will bring fourteen into play in several cities: twice as many people, which means four times as many comings and goings. Thus, for the construction of an ordinary secondary school, twenty-four administrative relays through fourteen services are needed. And for building a university medical center, fifty services, one hundred operations—and ten years to follow through on this wild-goose chase.

There are so many decisionmakers that there end up being none. The very notion of responsibility disappears. Each service simply brings its own special contribution to an anonymous process. There are no longer any visible peaks on the peneplain of decision. A new power reigns: the paymaster-general, symbol of antidecision but haughty guardian of the circuitry. He sees to it that this enormous waste of the state's authority, of personal talent and public money, is properly carried out according to the rules.

CHAPTER 40

The Unfinished Symphony

Saturday, May 19, 1968: General de Gaulle, returning from a trip to Romania, led the few ministers awaiting him into the Orly VIP lounge. "So," he said, "the strikes are spreading, the public companies are being occupied, the crap has hit the fan!" His tone was heavy with reproach. During the five days he was away, what had his government done with France? He thrust out his chin: "We'll settle this the way we've always settled the big issues, by a direct appeal to the people's confidence."

His meaning was clear—a referendum. The idea had germinated in Romania on the basis of the news reaching there from Paris. The general did not yet know exactly what form the question of confidence would take, but he was determined to pose it.

The Right Word Rings Wrong

The road had opened up that would drive him, eleven months later, from office and back to retirement in Colombey-les-Deux-Eglises. It was a road littered with contradictions. De Gaulle usually incubated his decisions slowly in his own mind, announcing them at the opportune moment and carrying them out in a rush. This time he had made up his mind hastily, revealed his decision almost immediately, then hesitated to put it into effect. And he, who had always asked the French to make simple choices, was to lose their confidence over a complicated proposal, a bureaucratic translation of a mysterious idea: participation. If everything about this business was disconcerting, it was because, for the first time, the French were being called upon to go to the bottom of things, to look squarely at themselves. And we do not like to do that.

The outcome was evident at the start. On the evening of May 24, 1968, de Gaulle explained his analysis to the French and announced his project. Massed around Paris's Gare de Lyon, tens of thousands of students, their ears glued to transistor radios, punctuated the speech with derisive laughter. When it ended, a student waved his handkerchief. At once ten, then a hundred, then all of them imitated him, chanting: "*A-dieu de Gaulle, a-dieu de Gaulle, adieu. . . .*" That night, when the Stock Exchange was set ablaze, was the most violent of all. The demonstrators felt as though they had wings, since the general's wings seemed broken. "I bet wrong," he was heard to say.

It was authority and the state that was in question. And for the first time de Gaulle had replied with "society." It was so unlike him that people thought he was no longer himself. That evening there was a kind of reversal of roles. The "wild men" had gone beyond challenging society; the challenge was to authority itself. And de Gaulle abandoned the terrain of power, where he was at ease and where they had come looking for him, to meet them on the field of social evil—where they no longer stood.

De Gaulle had never diagnosed the ills of our society so deeply. And never, probably, was a speech of his so ill received. By May 30, Pompidou, reflecting the general feeling, finally persuaded him to substitute legislative elections for the referendum. To de Gaulle, this was merely postponing the problem. The elections restored to him the means of power, but only a referendum would say what purpose that power would serve.

Remodeling France

On January 9, 1969, the general spoke to me as though the referendum had already been won. There was no doubt in his mind that the "yes" vote would carry the day overwhelmingly. The need to restructure French society was as pressing as it had been in mid-May. And what could be closer to the secret wish of the French than to give them a greater say in their own affairs?

In March, however, doubt arose. Along with many others, I tried to dissuade him from his stubborn insistence on the referendum. An about-face was impossible, but couldn't we at least break the problem down, narrow the issues to be voted on? Why not simply consult the people on a few clear principles of obvious value that would bind the Parliament, and, after the necessary debate, be given practical legislative form?

"That would be too much to hope for," the general told me. "If we do as you say, the deputies will start niggling. The senators will put pressure on them. Everyone will come to an understanding about creating obstacles. We'll be bogged down in the swamp."

"You have a parliamentary majority of a size never before seen in the history of the republic," I said. "It will vote your laws even though the French might not. [The voters] find them extremely complicated and think that this is what deputies are elected to do."

"It's a question," the general said flatly, "of transforming people's mores and their thinking. It's not enough to decree change from atop Olympus. A popular current is needed for this reform to become a reality. All the French must be deputies for a day."

"Deputies for a day"—never had I heard such confidence in the people's wisdom. But, in fact, could the people decide on a matter toward which the resistance of habit and attitudes was so strong, one they had scarcely even thought about?

In the end, of course, the referendum failed. Asked to vote for regionalization and the reform of the Senate, abstruse issues hardly identified with the general himself and complicated by a variety of local feelings, the public backed away.

The Root of the Evil

The mind must come to grips here with a formidable contradiction. De Gaulle had won such improbable bets as the redressment of a France crushed in 1940; he won it a place at the victors' table, transforming the tragedy of decolonization into a new asset for France. And yet he failed on so banal a project as regionalization and Senate reform.

Behind the banality was something fundamental, the beginning of a vast change. But the French saw only the banality because they refused to see what was fundamental. An attempt was being made through the referendum to gain their consent to a change they didn't want.

De Gaulle's achievements had conformed to the great nation-in-danger tradition. But in 1969, the nation was not in danger; it was suffering only from its three-centuries-old sickness. Can a people's nature be altered in a single spasm? De Gaulle applied crisis methods to a chronic ailment. What was more, he could only apply them in legists' language. The nature of the French entrapped him.

The general had never attempted so radical a reform, since it touched the root of the evil; until then, he had treated only the symptoms. The participation he wanted to institute in the state, in the bureaucracy, in business, in the universities, was less a matter of laws than of manners. A disappointing gap opened up between the need he felt—powerful and vague—and the laws—cramped and precise—he had to propose. He wanted to establish more brotherly relations between more independent men, to replace anonymous hierarchies by individual and group responsibility. But the only existence his grandiose vision achieved was in the unreadable pages of the *Official Journal*.

Yet General de Gaulle's final recommendation will remain. The priority of priorities is to remodel France so as to liberate the energies of the French. Grandeur in the eyes of history and of foreign powers will come as a premium when France has achieved a new internal balance.

There is a personal postscript to these events. After the 1973 legislative elections, Pompidou offered me the Ministry of Justice. The thinking I had been doing for some time about the organization of French society made me wish for another mission. I suggested to the president that we create a Reform

Ministry to reshape the entire system of governmental command. Typically, he hesitated, but finally agreed to give me carte blanche in proposing any changes I considered desirable at the municipal, cantonal and departmental levels. As for the regions, he insisted that I confine myself to applying existing laws, which in his opinion already went too far. And instead of calling it the Reform Ministry, it would be called the Ministry of Administrative Reforms.

Pompidou had long opposed giving any sort of autonomy to the regions of France. I could see the logic in his arguments—that regionalization would simply favor the growth of regional metropolises over middle-sized cities and rural areas, and that only three or four regions in the country had any real existence; the others were artificial. The departments, on the other hand, had the sanction of long history and usage, and people were accustomed to being identified with them.

Pompidou's reform plan was thus much less ambitious, and could be put into effect simultaneously all over the country. It did not make the regions territorial collectives, as de Gaulle had wished, but mere public establishments with low budgets. It was up to me to follow this lead. So most of my attention was paid to reforms at another level, trying to convert the old departments and municipalities into modern settings for new responsibilities.

For eleven months, I kept Pompidou informed of my work and my conclusions. He kept close track of them, in spite of the fact that disease was undermining him, but it was clear that what I was doing worried him. He seemed dominated by a fear of releasing uncontrollable forces if he allowed a challenge to the nation's historical equilibrium.

Yet everything I had heard around the country confirmed my belief that regionalization was indispensable if it created contact points through which departmental officials could learn to squelch their rivalries. By necessity we were forced to move cautiously, and this we proposed to do not by removing or sapping the powers of those valuable individuals the commune mayors, but by offering them the opportunity to shift, to a higher level, certain functions of corporate management for which they were simply not prepared. Gradually, we suggested, a functioning district (composed of ten to thirty small localities, perhaps, or a single section of an urban conglomeration) would become the basic organizational unit. On that basis, departmental assemblies could be regenerated; and so on up the governmental ladder.

Naturally, this upheaval had first to be given a full-scale trial in a few departments in carefully selected regions. I outlined our ideas to Pompidou. Once again, he hesitated. "What you are hoping to do," he said, rubbing his eye with his thumb as if to chase away an obsessive idea, "is enormous. Even if you went about it cautiously and gradually, you would reopen all our power structures to question. I have to think about it."

I understood his hesitation. Both his nature and his function demanded it.

Such an enterprise had to mobilize the total energies of the state and, of course, its chief. I waited . . .

A few days later, at the close of a cabinet meeting, Prime Minister Pierre Messmer announced to a surprised cabinet that his government was resigning. My ministry was to be abolished; I would be given another portfolio. At the next cabinet meeting Pompidou, passing round the table, paused to speak to me. "You know," he told me, "your reforms—they will be for my second term." It occurred to me fleetingly that there was an edge of black humor in the comment: I had seldom seen him look so ill. He returned to me. "Don't be unhappy," he said. "Keep thinking about those problems. It's an enormous business. A long, hard business. We can't launch it at the end of a term."[1]

If Pompidou's second term had been something other for him than a distraction in his fight against death, what would he have done with these ideas? Would decentralization have been a part of his program? I believe that it would have. Following de Gaulle, and living as he did with the conviction of France's destiny, he had learned that consolidating France necessarily meant remodeling it.

CONCLUSION

OUTLINE OF A THERAPY

Where there's a will there's a way.
—William of Orange

CHAPTER 41

On Method

Justice in itself is the balance of antinomies, that is, the reduction to equilibrium of opposing forces. Through it, each of us feels himself as simultaneously a person and society, individual and family, citizen and people, man and humanity.

—Proudhon[1]

Is the French sickness incurable? To answer no already commits us to outlining the principles of a therapy. But no detailed prescription will be offered here—merely some ideas on the method and, as examples, a few paths along which we can venture. The purpose of this book was not to establish a "program" or present a "manifesto," but to reflect and to stimulate reflection, and perhaps, by arousing debate, to help nourish the programs and manifestos that others will later work out.

Becoming Conscious of the Sickness

What if the cure were, first of all, a matter of reflection? Suppose it required lucid and positive humility? To know that we are sick, to diagnose the illness and refuse to believe it inevitable—this is the core of therapy.

France would recover through collective psychotherapy, and all psychotherapy is first of all a truth cure. To cure a neurosis, recognition of its real origin is almost always necessary and often sufficient. Let's not look for the sickness anywhere but in ourselves.

It will not be exorcised by punishing a scapegoat. It does not have a single cause, does not emanate from a single ideology, nor does it affect a single class or social category. Besides, scapegoats know how to defend themselves in French society and, after all, they are right: either everyone is guilty or no one is. Which does not make the task any easier.

To complicate things still further, even if the diagnosis is apposite, if it is synthetic, it is rejected *because* of its relevance. It is striking, in fact, to see how deaf people are to the most luminous analyses. Some of these suffer from the defect of coming from the state. Here, too, we encounter an obstacle: the state, in France, is not an acceptable teacher. We mistrust a state that lives on mistrust. We suspect it, in its impersonal phase, of obeying a monstrously cold logic that is not the citizens' logic; when it is personalized, we think it is serving politicians' ambitions. It has so much power, people fear, that if it ever began shaking things up, it would disturb the balance by which the individual has at least managed to survive if not to blossom. French society is like a china shop. A bull-state suddenly determined to "make order" or create something new is a fearsome prospect.

Who can we believe, then? Who but the intellectuals—professors, journalists, but also men of action, respecters of action and even more of truth. Our people have always placed great trust in them, probably because they know that even when such men commit themselves, they commit *only* themselves. But what an effort French thinking must make—in its vocabulary, its ideas, its axioms—to escape the weight of the past. When will it stop mulling over the nineteenth century, living on the stock of dreams and ideas of a great but bygone century like an elderly Don Juan maundering on about his conquests? When will it free itself from that epoch's dogmatism, from its intellectual terrorism?

In truth, the words live on but their meaning is lost. What sense is left to such expressions as "left," "right," "bourgeois," "proletariat," "capitalism," or "socialism?" None that is universally accepted. Honesty dictates that we eliminate them from current usage, and especially from the language of the intellectuals, who should be rigorous in their use of words. "Most occasions of confusion," proclaimed Montaigne, "are grammatical." And Confucius, twenty-two centuries before him, declared that "to avoid war, one must begin by defining the meanings of words." Those whose profession it is to function in the world as it is often have the impressions that they are no longer communicating at all with the world as it is said to be. Isn't it up to the intellectuals to reestablish communication, to invent words for our time or, even better, to return to the simple words of all ages?

This requires a certain perspective, and is probably more difficult than it has ever been. How can we resist today's head-spinning haste? Fashionableness is king to those eager to obey it. If our society wants someday to reinvent its values and find the words to fit them, intellectuals will have to begin by forgetting the hurly-burly of relevance, of modishness, and to revive instead their sense of timelessness. The psychotherapy of the French must begin with that of their intellectual elite. If it rejects this, what hope is there that the great mass of French people may someday know themselves better and so be cured?

An End to Dreaming

If this intellectual and moral reform is to succeed, intellectuals will have to abandon the old and beloved paths of Utopianism and systems, those old passions that are in league with ideologies and so, sometimes, with violence and tyranny. In 1849, speaking to his judges, Dostoevsky described one particular Utopian program as "a peaceful system that seduces the soul by its harmonious structure, charms the heart and contains no point of hate." But, like lightning in a blue sky, he concluded: "Incontestably, this system is noxious because it is a system." Reality must remain the judge of our ideas. It is the great educator.

The New Opportunities

France can climb back up the slope of its own history. In fact, it has already begun to do so. Since Richelieu, its experience of free trade has been limited to two occasions, at the ends of the reigns of Louis XVI and Napoleon III, for brief periods cut short by tragedy. But it no longer lives by its internal clock,[2] hostile to disturbing innovations, mistrustful of what foreigners could bring, hermetically convinced of the superiority of its own culture, its own way of living. France has changed its clock. It has discovered the tonic wind blowing from abroad, the confrontation of economies and a lust for action.

The European challenge, as we have seen, was decisive. France jumped with both feet (and maybe with its eyes shut) into an unfamiliar world where the economic frontiers between France and its neighbors faded to the vanishing point. This was an act of faith, the first France had been energetic enough to make since the Second Empire.

In so doing, the nation committed itself to making up its tremendous lag. There was nothing impossible about this, as fifteen years of success have very well shown. Between 1868 and 1968, after all, Japan made up for five centuries in one. France has only a century to make up; a generation of effort ought to do it. There is nothing immutable about national rankings, however slowly they may change. At the beginning of the twentieth century, Sweden was a poor agricultural country; at the century's end, its standard of living is a match for any nation's. France has been advancing at a satisfactory pace since 1954, an exceptional one between 1960 and 1974. This is not an adequate goal for a nation, but it is a necessary preamble.

The Advantages of Backwardness

A long-standing backwardness can be an asset.

In manpower: While France is poor in manpower over the long term, its excess farm labor still constitutes a sizable reserve for growing industry to tap. On condition that it does not let the problem regulate itself, badly, by an exodus of young farm workers toward the underproductive sectors of retail trade and office jobs.

In space: France is rich in space. The country can, if it goes about it in the right way, design an industrial garden that will reconcile modernism and power with our sense of beauty and measure.

In speed: Our lag enables us to skip a technological generation. We can immediately use methods slowly developed elsewhere, benefitting from the most sophisticated equipment.

Starting later than the others also enables us to avoid repeating their mistakes. Until now we have been rather uncritical imitators; if we had avoided repeating the skyscrapers, the huge cities, the polluting concentration of people and industry, we would have sowed less abundantly the seed of American-style violence. But it is not too late for us to start playing our top cards.

Even our errors can be turned to advantage. Millions of French have changed their localities, trades, homes, working hours, and social environment. Too often they have done so painfully, without preparation. But the dismal period of workyards and quagmires does not last forever. Beyond these individual dramas dawns a collective opportunity. We have seen how human migration, from seventeenth-century Holland to nineteenth-century America, shattering old routines, fostered progress. In the past twenty years there has been a vast internal migration in France that can spur its renewal.

A revivified economy is beginning to create new conditions, new men. Not much more is needed for us to catch the contagion of confidence. Nor would it take much for mistrust to triumph. In France today, progressive energy and the drag of routine are just about in balance.

The Advantages of Durability

Our institutions can make the difference. The French now have a state capable of choosing its directions and its timing. A state solid enough to draw its force from democracy without becoming mired in it, durable enough to overcome three centuries of stubborn inertia. Having recovered its own dignity, our state can render the citizen his dignity and renew the meaning of a civic sense. It should be able to absorb and surmount the divisions of the French through the person of an elected arbiter. It is a state that can properly use the time that peace—and this is another asset—can give us.

The Asset of Friendship

France is playing the game on a global scale; the image others reflect of us, their attitudes toward us, will count heavily in how we picture ourselves and how ambitious we are. And since the 1960s, changes in the world, far from diminishing our opportunities, have actually reinforced them.

Our policy of independence—granted to our colonies and regained from the Americans and the Germans—has endowed France with considerable credit. No one fears its hegemony as they fear that of the superpowers, the United States and Russia. France can exert an influence out of proportion to its physical size. The heart of the nebula of public and secret friendships lies in the community of French-speaking nations. Even if French has ceased to be the world's diplomatic and juridical language, it is still the second language of the elite. At the United Nations the French-speaking countries form a bloc of some thirty countries, fewer than the English-speaking nations but more than are in the communist bloc.

Among the areas in which the French can still exert their influence, Europe is still the first. But Europe is a symbol for us of the competitiveness on which we have embarked, and so it should remain. Europe should resist the temptation to become integrated the way chestnuts are integrated in a chestnut purée. It is made up of countries that are too old for this; to neglect their national identities implies a mortal risk. It will wax rich only by respecting their differences. Europe should do nothing to restrain emulation, but it should not create a homogeneous power bloc. Let us renounce the temptation to transfer our problems to this welded Europe, to abandon our ambitions to it. An organized Europe can regulate competition and promote solidarity. But each European nation should find the springs of its achievement in itself. A united Europe protects us from protectionism and obliges us to open ourselves to the world.

A Beginning of Consensus

The French should take stock of their assets. They should understand that their national heritage now gives them a certain number of advantages that are worth defending fiercely. Things are changing without our realizing it. The socialists seem slowly to be escaping their Utopian ideology, be it supranationalist or pacifist. The communists affirm that they have given up the notion of a dictatorship of the proletariat in favor of political pluralism; they claim to support our nuclear deterrent and deny that they wish to do away with our political institutions. We can begin to dream of the day when nothing will distinguish them from the Social Democrats. Many people doubt their sincerity. But this revision of policy, even if it is tactical, is unprecedented; even our sense of the death of dogma is becoming common to all of us. The conditions for a conversion to reality seem gradually to be falling into place—one similar to that achieved by the West German Socialists in Bad Godesberg in 1959, when they opted to abandon the Marxist myths in favor of a free enterprise society and a "capitalist" economy.

For the first time, surely, since the Revolution, the French are slowly circumscribing the essential elements of a consensus. They prefer not to talk about it, out of modesty or fear of spoiling things. They are even compensating for it by pushing their political dualism to extremes. The tension is rising, and relationships between individuals and social groupings are degenerating. But living standards, consumption, fashions and social classes are all coming closer together. The French are becoming more contemporary with each other than they have ever been before. Curiously, the memory of de Gaulle, who was a symbol of division during his lifetime, is more and more frequently invoked now, as though he posthumously represents these national rediscoveries.

Of all our country's strokes of luck, this burgeoning consensus, still so timid, so threatened, is the most surprising, the most precious, the least understood—and the least exploited.

The Keys to Reform

How can we play our new luck—and win?

We are gripped by a sense of urgency, the mother of so many errors. We anticipate a day when our administrative, social and economic systems will blow up. We sense that they must be changed before we are buried under the debris. But how can we do this if they rock whenever we touch them?

The Need for a Goal

Motivational psychology has rediscovered an old truth: For a life to have meaning, it must have a goal, one that each of us can set for himself. One man burning with a sacred flame is worth ten who don't care what they do. Above all, his life is worth living.

What is true of people's lives also applies to nations. They need a pole by which to find their bearings. A common goal creates a harmony beyond social fragmentation. Through it, failures are digested and their lessons taught. And every success becomes a confirmation that renews a people's energy.

Look at Israel, or China: how many sacrifices they have consented to because they know they have a task to accomplish. And, in truth, their accomplishments are extraordinary—in one case the birth, in the other the rebirth, of a nation. Even our neighbor, Germany, has surpassed itself in its determination to prove that it can be an example of a prosperous and peaceful democracy.

France has neither to be born nor to justify itself. After three centuries of holding ourselves up as examples, we are a little bored with ourselves. More important, a centralizing and uniformist system has muffled our motivations. Our society has established norms instead of moving ahead. The job, therefore, is more awkward for us than for others. But our case is far from desperate. We grow skeptical only when we fail to find mobilizing themes. Let us try to sketch in some of these. They all revolve around a single idea—responsibility. It is this that gives them their coherence, their vibrancy.

Being Exemplary

Once again, France can become collectively responsible by accomplishing its strange vocation: to be exemplary. It is a French peculiarity to want to share with others its victories over itself. Such messianism has often shown itself in a brutal light; one cannot successfully make others happy despite themselves. But it is not without grandeur when it bears witness for mankind. "There are countries that are never so great as when they are trying to be great for everyone else: the France of the Crusades and the Revolution."[3] The time has come for a new humanism in which France can play a pioneering role.

If France has something to say to the world, it can do so henceforth without ambiguity. The end of the twentieth century and the start of the twenty-first will be a time of difficult coexistence for countries in sharply differing states of advancement in a shrunken world. That world is waiting for French engineers, scientists, technicians, doctors, teachers, administrators, traders, businessmen—yet France's young people fear unemployment!

National Ecumenism

World peace through national independence: France is probably the sole nation capable today of becoming the apostle of such a crusade. Neither the United States nor the Soviet Union nor the dozens of countries following docilely in their wake can signal its beginning. Not even China, which is too openly hostile to its northern neighbor.

This doctrine can be called "national ecumenism":—there can be no durable international order if any nation is another's satellite. Each must be the master of its destiny and the inventor of the ways it must follow, while being granted an absolute right to its own identity and culture, its independence and responsibility.

A mystique of supranationality grew up after World War II and still resists these ideas. Yet history shows that "integration"—a modern and subtle form of what used to be called "empire"—does not have the virtues ascribed to it. Except for the United States, a country with immense resources, the pilot countries in the development race are small nations that settle their own problems and find their equilibrium within themselves. To recognize and proclaim such a path as open to all nations—this can be a goal for France.

A Global Plan

But the French must first regain their self-confidence, must accept themselves as citizens, producers and members of a society. Which means that they must eliminate from their public, economic and social life the thick band of rules and reflexes that muffles their dynamism and keeps them from realizing themselves.

To become aware of the sickness, assess our chances and refashion our intellectual arsenal are all necessary moves toward mental recovery. But, France being what it is, it is once more the task of authority to mobilize this recharged energy and guide the transformation. Here again, questions of method are decisive. A global plan is needed. We have had enough of patching, of helter-skelter measures and piddling policy. When an entire structure is feeble, it must be repaired as a whole. A society as aged and as vulnerable as ours must be reinforced everywhere at once or it will give way at just the point that was neglected. It's like an old inner tube: a bubble squeezed in one place will pop out in another.

This is also psychologically necessary. Reform must cross the threshold beyond which public interest and support are aroused, otherwise it will be lost in the labyrinth of technological laws that only the technocrats understand. In transforming France, a vast plan is needed in which each particular reform can be seen as one element in the overall design. Then one reform supports another; and each measure, even a minor one, is made important by a process of convergence. When an army feels that even its skirmishes with the enemy are part of the battle plan, it attacks with greater spirit.

Gradual Transitions

If a plan is to be coherent, it must include a calculation of the time needed to implement it, thus making time an ally. Each state moves only a little beyond the last, without overly disturbing those people who would cling to the past. But the whole future can be read in each small advance, and this sustains its dynamic.

Psychology requires special skills. Pierre Mendès-France attacked the home distillers of liquor head-on. His fall, of course, was not caused—though it was accelerated—by their powerful pressure group in Parliament. Six years later, a wilier Michel Debré attacked the privilege but not the privileged; the distillers were allowed to keep their sacrosanct rights, but the privilege would die with them. He did not suppress the right, but he prevented its perpetuation. Opposition faded. The topic, until then a hardy perennial, disappeared from public meetings. There is no rushing things if you want to educate people.

Innovative Experiment

Care in planning, calculation of the time involved and respect for what already exists are all combined in the experimental method. The project should be global; reform can only be gradual. Instituting reforms requires both an overall view and the knack of partial application through innovative alterations, carefully developed with a view to their later generalization. Testing prototypes and then extending them. Done this way, the measure is practically self-extending. When an experiment succeeds, it elicits imitation.

Experience forms teams used to innovation. "The world will be saved by a few people," André Gide liked to say. Everything done in China since 1949 has been accomplished by a few hundred men whose characters were forged in the ordeal of the "Soviet Republic of Shensi" and the "spirit of Yenan."

"What gave the Wehrmacht its initial efficiency," the German general Hans Speidel once explained, "was that the Treaty of Versailles only authorized a small professional army of 100,000 men for Germany. This gave us an army of cadres, an instrument that worked like a clock; later, we were able to augment its size without its losing its discipline and its character. If we had had an army of conscripts, we would have been drowned in a magma."

Throughout our society, still semi-archaic in spots, a web of responsibility must gradually be woven. The difficulty is to create and reinforce this without destroying the links of the traditional networks—which are named family, Church, administration, justice, army. If, in order to change our society, we were suddenly to take an ax to these institutions, the current crisis of doubt and uncertainty might end in total—perhaps irremediable—decomposition.

CHAPTER 42

A Few Trails

Sleepers, awake!—Chorale by Johann Sebastian Bach

The reader who has properly understood this book will not expect it to end with a presentation of miracle reforms that can stabilize our progress and our democracy all at once. The essential elements lie in our characters and, especially, in our collective subconscious; measures and laws alone cannot change the course of things. History has worked its spells on the excellent intentions of three centuries of reformers.

I am tempted to let the ideas in this book make their way into its readers' minds, leaving it to each of them to think of possible applications. It might nevertheless be useful to suggest, as examples, a few ways in which those ideas could be implemented. No one should expect to find a finished structure here—nothing more than a few building materials.

Let us think first about the cornerstones.

Spread Public Responsibilities

It is the machinery of power that commands a society's destiny. The cure for our visible sickness, our state sickness, must be extended into the area of the French bureaucracy; that is where the hidden sickness is.

The first national task—first in urgency and first in importance—is to shore up our public institutions. "Confusion": the word summarizes the major defects we have recognized in those institutions. Confusion in the roles played by the state's principal players: the president, the cabinet, the Parliament, the bureaucracy. Confusion of levels, with national and local authority inextricably enmeshed; confusion of missions and mandates.

Separation of Powers

To escape this general confusion, we must reinvent the separation of powers, or, more precisely, we must make the vertical separation of powers called for in the Constitution more effective and reinforce it by a horizontal separation of levels, which the Constitution does not even mention. For executive authority has proliferated to such a point that isolating it is not enough; levels must be made distinctive and separate within that very authority, or the separation of powers becomes ineffective.

Let us fix the principles on which the architecture of these balanced institutions should be based. And there is no need to think of them in terms of a clean sweep; it will be enough to remodel the edifice history has bequeathed us.

A President for Unity

The president should protect his function as arbiter and recourse. The less he governs, the more he can preside. If he is careful not to behave as either the head of government or the head of a parliamentary majority, he can assure unity. If he is not committed by day-to-day political activity, he can speak for continuity.

Voters in presidential elections should not be called on to choose a government majority, but to designate the best man to preserve the nation's unity, the one most competent to rise above the half-truths we feed ourselves and to unite us in a higher truth.

Less Is More

The less a government administers, the more it can govern. It should not in any case be the universal and unique administrator. The state's inalienable responsibilities are already heavy enough.

The state should remain the master in foreign relations, defense, internal and external security, in economic and budgetary policy, taxes, the definition of and respect for people's rights, in the big items of national equipment, telecommunications, national development policy, in the big nationalized corporations and research priorities. For the rest—that is, for the great mass of public equipment and services—the bureaucracy should be made responsible to elected authority, the opposite of the situation today.

A Parliamentary Monitor

The Parliament should not be confused with the executive. Once, this tendency destroyed the executive by condemning it to periodic eclipses. Today, it is the Parliament that is destroyed by condemnation to permanent eclipse. The proper path is neither through government by the Assembly nor in a government assembly, but through respect for the distance between them.

"We Are the Administration"

More is needed than mere monitoring to democratize the civil service. This is the heart of the transformation which, fulfilling the mission of the Fifth Republic, should efface three centuries of errors. We have seen that our blocked mentalities derive from a hierarchical and centralized conception of the administration of men and things. Redressment is conditional on the adoption of a decentralized and democratic conception. To Louis XIV's "I am the state," relayed by his vast progeny—the bureaucrats who function as though by divine right—the French should be able to reply tomorrow: "We are the administration."

It is in this area that our realistic imagination will have the most to do, and in which the remodeling of our institutions will disrupt countless habits. But reform of our national structures will fail if we do not learn the lessons taught by social psychology, by history and by recent developments. A few simple ideas can be illuminating, but they will not change the outline I proposed to Pompidou in 1974.

De-bureaucratizing Without De-administering

Clearly, all this constitutes a kind of peaceful revolution.

First and foremost, a revolution in the civil service. For the state's responsibilities cannot be turned over to locally elected authorities without giving them both the human and financial means to deal with them—the functionaries as well as the functions.

This involves a thorough change in the bureaucracy's way of doing things. Instead of today's great, monolithic fiefs, independent and introverted, we would witness the appearance of a more aerated bureaucracy. It would be more alive because its methods could usefully vary from one territorial subdivision to another; there would be room for fecund variety. It would be more homogeneous because compartmentalization would be eliminated on the local administrative level; inter-service circulation would be easier and more spirited. And it would be more open because the people's needs and aspirations would exert more effective pressure on public servants under the direct authority of elected local officials. The change would humanize the bureaucracy, shortening the circuits between problem and decision, question and answer, infraction and punishment, merit and promotion. Men would know each other.

But we must be careful here: cracking the framework does not mean smashing the bureaucracy. The tragedy of centralization is that it made of the bureaucracy an intolerable evil when in fact it should be a necessary asset. There is no question of suggesting a system from which civil servants would disappear, but one in which they would cease to stifle themselves and us under their own weight.

Authority in Crisis

By thus disseminating public power through assignment of the major responsibility for local administration to responsible elected officials, through subjection of the central bureaucracy to serious parliamentary supervision and restoring of the government's political responsibility, we would finally restore his proper role to the chief of state. This role is to speak for France to the rest of the world, to the French and to history, and to see to the proper working of the country's redefined and better distributed public powers.

And, I would add, he would be ready at all times to exercise authority in times of crisis. We are unfamiliar with the distinction between normal authority and crisis authority, and for good reason. Our over-administration, our hierarchical centralism derive from an unconsciously but stubbornly maintained confusion between extraordinary circumstances, in which authority should be unified and flow unhampered from the head to the limbs, and ordinary life, in which this command system is not at all necessary and becomes debilitating. Our state is always governed as though normality were simply a mild form of crisis.

Accepting the Economy

By prompting us to dream of a "third way," de Gaulle did not steer our imagination into a dead end, but he certainly demanded a great deal of it. If the path of unity split under the feet of Erasmus, in the panicky youth of the sixteenth century, shall we be able to rediscover it in the evening of the twentieth?

The third way need not be invented from scratch. It is simply the refound unity of human progress. In a sense, we are already advancing along a third way. For the French phenomenon is not the free, enterprising road of pure capitalism; it falls short of a market economy, because it constantly turns market economy rules through protectionism, compartmentalization, guilds, informal cartels and bureaucratic intervention. Nor is it the rigid, "Roman" road of socialism, because it lacks socialism's inflexible rationality.

So far, however, this third way is an inverted image of the proper way, combining the disadvantages of capitalism and socialism. We must seek one that marries their advantages. Social humanism and a free enterprise market economy are compatible only if each absolutely respects the other; to marry them is to marry their differences. There is no better foundation for a dynamic economy than that formed by free enterprise and the rules of the market. There is no other principle of harmonious social existence except that of society's self-control. By keeping these two principles in mind, we can go a long way. Let's plant a few markers along the route.

Participation in Enterprise

Enterprise, for example, has had a bad press. The symbol of despised capitalism, a screen for mysterious powers, constantly accused of "exploiting the workers," governing monarchically and obscurely, the ineluctable daily setting for lives of subjugation—it has everything against it.

Yet it is no sooner threatened than everyone finds he is a partisan of enterprise: "We shall not shut down"—as, at Verdun, they said the enemy "shall not pass." And should an employer fail or the bankers be overly prudent, the reflex is to establish worker management. Worker management is useful only to make a transition, to call for a new boss, new capital, and wait for them to arrive.

I have more belief in the authenticity of such reactions than in the authenticity of the ideologies from which enterprise suffers. Only, we do everything we can to kill off our enterprises and then we appear inconsolable. It would be healthier to love them while they are still alive.

Participation should help here. But this is just where we spy the limit and the ambiguity of institutional reforms. What is worker management without a spirit of responsibility? Or worker participation in management when the reflexes of both sides are conditioned by the habit of confrontation? Participation will remain an empty idea as long as it is unwanted. As soon as it is wanted, when labor stops thinking of it as a weapon against enterprise and management stops using it as a fireship against the unions, it will become institutionalized. For, apart from the financial interest in a firm's success, so unfairly disparaged, and aside from keeping employees informed of management policy, which is much talked about but not always observed, nothing at all has been done to further what can properly be called participation.

Of course, it can be talked around and maneuvered around. But participation has a simple, concrete meaning: "to participate" means neither to take nor to share, but to be part of and take part in. Here again, the most effective method in promoting participation is to perform successful experiments and let them snowball.

Fostering the acceptance of the principle of enterprise is all the more important in that it conditions another, equally essential, objective: to make the French understand that a modern country's prosperity and progress depend on the relative weight of one and only one sector in the economy—industry. And that an economy must therefore be organized around this priority. Why, with its human, intellectual and natural resources, its luxury of space, shouldn't France have an industrial plant that is at least the equal of West Germany's? Before this can happen, however, the state and the French must reverse their attitudes. Since the time of Colbert we have believed in bureaucratic surveillance and control of industry. But an industrial market economy can only develop through initiative, innovation and competition.

Protecting Competition

Industrial vitality will blossom with a revival of competition. To profit fully from a market economy, there has to be a market. Since our bureaucracy does not believe in the virtues of the marketplace, it superintends it badly. It prefers to fix prices, quotas and plant locations rather than see to the rigorous play of competition. The result is that we sacrifice the efficiency of the market to the inefficiency of bureaucratic direction. The state allows the machinery of liberalism to deteriorate, permitting the establishment of monopolies and cartels because it thinks it can situate itself better in a simplified economic world. Yet a few simple policing measures would correct these vices, which we have identified with capitalism although they are in fact a perversion of a market economy.

Industry on a Human Scale

If we can properly combine a profound human aspiration with modern technological possibilities, we can organize industry on a human scale. We should be able to offer rural residents jobs in industry only a few kilometers from their homes by building plants all over the country, close to the human reservoirs our countryside still contains. Industry is no longer subject to the restraints once imposed by the problem of transporting energy. This eliminates the technical necessity for industrial concentration, which in turn led to the threeway deracination of those caught in the rural exodus: from their work (accustomed through the generations to working on the land or in the crafts, they are suddenly forced to live lost in great, anonymous cities and work within the narrow focus of an assembly line); from their homes (used to living in farmhouses, they are suddenly projected into dormitory cities without gardens or farmyards, without space); and from their land (uprooted from the landscapes and horizons of their youth, they feel their exodus as an expatriation). Diffused industrialization would cushion the shock of their inevitable occupational deracination by eliminating the other two factors.

A Responsible Society

We need supple institutions for efficiency, and an economy on a human scale to give us roots. And we also need a society that is tranquil, and therefore enterprising. France's society is terribly tense, but the tension is largely artificial.

A series of surveys since 1945 has shown that 80 percent of the French would prefer to live in private homes, versus only 20 percent who prefer apartments. Yet for years the housing we have built has been 80 percent apartments and 20 percent private homes. We also know that the French would like to find work in their native departments; instead, they have been exiled to frustrating cities. The technocrats who have presided over this great shift did not do so inadvertently; they were convinced this was what "modernity" demanded. They have succeeded only in making modernity traumatic. We obviously need another urban policy: to withdraw real command in the cities from the bureaucracy and restore it to the people who live in them.

Children and Confidence

We have seen that for the French quickly to become—and remain—a child-bearing people is a matter of national life and death. Three centuries of relative decadence, from the middle of the seventeenth century to the mid-twentieth, coincided with France's steady demographic decline; two decades of rapid recovery and progress coincided with a rising birth rate. When we have reached the density of some 300 people per square kilometer, as the Germans, the English, the Dutch and the Belgians have, we can allow ourselves to ease up. But not as long as our population density remains below 100 on the richest, most varied, best-endowed soil in Europe. France is much more vulnerable than its neighbors and competitors to the demographic consequences of a "permissive society," a fact it prefers to ignore. To talk about demography is unfashionable; it could cost the speaker his popularity.

Yet it is hard to doubt its importance. Progress toward justice is impossible without economic growth, and there is no durable economic growth without demographic growth, without an adequate population density or an adequate supply of young people. The population of France is still three times less dense than it should be. Nature abhors a vacuum. In a world without frontiers, the coexistence of high- and low-pressure demographic areas causes storms. Violent osmosis of other peoples would amount to an invasion of the sort that is now all too familiar. Even if the process were to be peaceful, it would still amount to an invasion—by immigrants who, despite our ridiculous claims to nonracism, would ultimately pose insoluble problems of assimilation.

The time is in sight when many grade schools will have to be replaced with homes for the aged. Sweden, the world's most advanced country in welfare terms, has had to raise the retirement age to seventy because of the drop in its birth rate. Lowering the retiring age now in France would only mean raising it again a few years hence because of a lack of children. If our birth rate were to drop still further, our social equilibrium would collapse and the size of pensions would shrink dramatically, while production would lose the internal market that justifies its existence. In short, we would be doomed to poverty and obscurity.

A vigorous pro-birth policy has already been delayed too long. It presupposes a collective, long-range effort so that no economic mishap can stifle this call to the future. Let us note merely a few of the effective measures at which we have balked: increased family and housing allotments, tax benefits for large families, maternity pensions. Three years of paid leave for each birth—at least beginning with the third child—would certainly be an effective measure. In Czechoslovakia, where the birth rate had fallen dangerously, this measure, adopted in 1974, caused a spectacular reversal of the trend within one year.

Make Education Realistic

In our society, knowledge is more vital than bread. Education should constantly help us to overcome the dislocations created by a constantly changing world. Instead, we have managed to make education an enormous machine that is almost as useless as it is costly, a burden instead of a tool.

To change this, we can base ourselves on a continuous training that must necessarily be realistic. We waste vast sums on small gadgets today while the Education Ministry's enormous potential remains closed in on itself. Continuous training can only be brought to life through the marriage of the schools and labor. This will be a forced marriage that will upset the schools as well as labor—which is why the bride has been left waiting at the church.

We must see to it that primary-school education is rooted in reality instead of fertilizing a lack of realism, as we do now. Students and teachers must be summoned to the establishment of an intellectual, spiritual and moral New Deal.

The collapse of prohibitions and taboos, the decline of religion, parental and teacher laxity, have all aroused in our young people the eternal anxiety of excessive permissiveness. "Everything is permitted," said Ivan Karamazov in despair. Both the young and their teachers are waiting to be shown the economic and social realities of which almost all of them are ignorant. We must find a third way between repressive and permissive instruction: a pedagogy of confidence and responsibility. This need not exclude subtle pressure, an insistence on effort. A happy school life is not one that satisfies a youngster's immediate desires. A burgeoning personality is only toughened by having demands made upon it, so that it becomes the source from which energy and love of effort flow. If we cannot have a plenitude of young people at once, at least let us see to it that those we do bear have the desire and the capacity to accept the modern world.

A Project for Responsibility

How can society be humanized so as to extirpate its fear of the modern world? How can it be given the mental and moral means to overcome that fear? It is not enough merely to cure our society of its rejection of modernity. Throughout this book we have recognized the signs of social division enclosing each of us in his own little world. We are divided less into classes than into castes, ideologies, fiefs. Suspicious, anxious and unfriendly, our society exudes aggressiveness and intolerance, which creates more division. Of this, too, we must deliver it.

"A plethora of performers": this could be the definition of the polycentric society the French must build. A multiplication of the number of authorities managing public affairs under the people's control, of the number of entrepreneurs (the initiators and innovators) in the economy. And a multiplication of the number of persons and groups capable of shifting for themselves in our society.

Mental Revolution

Because it lacks confidence, because it is not at peace with itself, our society dreams of radical transmutations. Largely ignorant of social chemistry, it longs for a miraculous alchemy, for the Faust who will transmute its base metal into pure gold.

It is this ill-defined hope, sadly adapted to a sick social body, that still gives revolution its chance. In France, what we call revolution is a prolonged spasm of collective life that can alter a few lines of force, change the men in power, enrich the popular vocabulary and stock of imagery, but which finally leaves the country more tense, more centralized, more divided and more dissatisfied with itself.

The only revolutions that count are those of the mind. It's a mental revolution that the French need and that this book proposes, one that could spare us a great many upheavals. A mental revolution can be gradual, free of the shock waves that always roll back on us from unpredictable angles and with unforeseeable violence. The progress of a mental revolution is measured by each successive person who becomes convinced of the revolutionary ideal, each one whose mentality changes. The advance is imperceptible, almost secret. It is not fed by hope, as exterior revolutions are; it nourishes hope, because everyone can wage it within himself.

The revolution we propose is in accordance with the realities of our modern society. It bears solely on the archaic mentality we have preserved amid these realities: competition, instead of the security to which we are attached; mobility and innovation, instead of our present immutability. Reality is a thing of relativity and compromise; yet we persevere in the search for absolutes and dogma. It leads to a fluid society, without closed castes or imposed uniformity, whereas we maintain our class reflexes while dreaming of a classless society. Reality conjugates responsible powers and freedoms; but in our minds power remains monolithic and freedom unbounded.

One fact locks our political democracy into civil war reflexes: year in and year out, at least one French voter in five votes for the Communist Party, giving rise to an obsessive anticommunist reaction. Moreover, the massive presence of a party with revolutionary traditions, geared down by solid transmission belts, blocks the establishment of any peaceful and regular system of political alternation.

There is a glimmer—a very faint glimmer—of hope here, however. Since the Communist Party's alliance with the socialists, cracks have appeared in the bastion. The possibility of accession to power through the parliamentary process has forced communist orthodoxy to become more flexible. The party, saturated though it is in Romanism, has begun its *aggiornamento* without collapsing from within. Surprises are still possible. It's a race against time. If power were acquired quickly, it would happen *before* the party had really changed, and a new revolutionary process would be set in motion—a new crisis of the "French sickness." If power is slow in coming, the party may crack, with an old guard clinging to legitimist Marxism while the rest move to democratic socialism.

A second small break must reinforce the first: socialism, freed of its restrictive shadow, must rid itself in turn of Marxist dogma, following in the path taken by West German Social Democracy. France would then be ripe for social progress through economic progress, instead of dreaming of social progress despite the reality of economic defeat.

Curbing Union One-upmanship

The disappearance or softening of communism would eliminate the most effective factor in the radicalization of our social system: trade-union one-upmanship. I am talking about one-upmanship, not politicization, which is merely a consequence of the unions' habit of continually raising their bids. To say that politicization is unacceptable is mere talk. Tackling the real problem would mean attacking the rivalry among labor organizations, the fragmentation of union representation, and the monopolization of that representation by the very people responsible for its fragmentation.

We have to invent a system that embodies our pluralist heritage while putting an end to the unions' bidding fever. This is where real democracy lies. Why not build an authentically representative labor structure in which the unions would play roles like those the parties play in the political system? The unions would "contribute to expression through suffrage," as the Constitution says, but they would not replace it. The government does not negotiate with the parties, it goes before the Parliament; in the cities there is only one municipal council, even if it is made up of candidates from several tickets. Similarly, negotiation of wages and working conditions should be conducted and concluded in each company, not with the unions themselves, but with the wage earners' elected representatives, after the various unions have proposed their candidates and exposed their platforms in what amount to election campaigns.

This reform would bring trade unionism out of the feudal age and into the age of democracy. Diversity of positions would probably persist, but it would be restrained by the need to represent the rank and file together, to form representational majorities. Greater responsibility would accordingly increase the social movement's real power. But it is responsibility that is the most frightening.

Progress Through Justice

I do not pretend that these changes in themselves would instill a spirit of unity in our society or root out its spirit of mistrust. They are simply two heavy bolts to be slipped. For our society to become one of mutual consent, it must also become a society in which justice functions.

Another "vast program"? I will touch on this only to issue a double warning. The first is to those who believe that the machinery of progress is hitched to that of justice. Now, expansion is necessary, though certainly not sufficient, to reinforce the feeling that France is a community in which fraternity and equality are progressing. To give the lie to the 1968 slogan that "You don't fall in love with a growth rate," growth must stop being a power ploy and become a path to justice.

The second warning is to those who like to attach the adjective "social" to the noun "justice." For the sense of justice and injustice is personal, not collective. Society will not be made more just by leveling. Everyone has the right to *his* justice—that which recognizes his rights and, most of all, rewards his efforts.

To excise inequality could sterilize society. On the other hand, pinching out the remaining pockets of poverty and limiting excessive privilege are objectives that can be circumscribed and measured, and that would allow us to eliminate situations of personal injustice.

True social justice is achieved through responsibility, through reward for work and for personal, family or collective effort.

Espousing Reality

This whole book has demonstrated that the mind models reality. It deformed reality when, in the sixteenth century, it fed on dogmatism and authoritarian reason. It did so again when, in the nineteenth century, reality came to us from abroad in the forms of the industrial and democratic revolutions.

A third battle in the campaign has now begun. Since the 1950s, the reality of an open, vital creative economy and society has gained ground in France. And we sense that despite their extraordinary resistance, our mental structures are now finally cracking, disintegrating, giving way. It would be tragic if, by a kind of backlash, everything else were to disintegrate with them. Society is deteriorating because modern reality has sapped the foundations of the old authority. Which would sweep it away sooner: an ideology of illusion that would stifle life to protect our mentality, or a change of our collective mind that would give us a chance for life, equipping us to live in our world and our century? "There is no need to burn the house down to roast a pig," says the proverb.

It is time that the two Frances, so often and so artificially arrayed against each other, overcame their resentments. The history of the Queyras shows that this is not impossible. As we have seen, hate between Protestants and Catholics had persisted in the remote valleys of the Hautes-Alpes from the sixteenth century to around 1960. Yet they achieved their mental revolution. It was around 1960 that the priest and the parson in Vars discovered that they both wanted to end this infernal round. The occasion was the construction of a new place of worship. Catholics and Protestants could not rebuild both church and temple. So they joined to build a common edifice. There you can see an old statue of the Virgin in gilt wood; it was the parson who asked the priest to put it there. Today, people of the different religions speak to each other, and their children can intermarry.

France was long a sclerotic society. Today, it is a threatened society.

To grow, we must believe, but in what? My answer is: in ourselves, in our ability to act on our own, to take initiatives and assume responsibilities, to become reliable. If we do not recover our self-confidence, by what right can we ask the state to trust us? Where can the circuit of confidence, broken for three centuries, be reconnected if not in ourselves?

Perhaps it will be thought strange that, given the somber portrait of France and the French drawn in these pages, I should conclude on this hopeful note. But, however deeply we have been fashioned by the system of mistrust, the system of confidence can still undo the wrappings of mistrust and render us equal to the best of our people—agile, mordant and tenacious. When the French are presented with a challenge and given the responsibility for meeting it, they succeed as well as or better than anyone else. We must trust in confidence once and for all, and make it the organizing principle of society.

Is there still time? We have refused to pay the price in the past, submitting to our misfortunes. If we continue to let our opportunities elude us, they will turn on us disastrously. The result will not necessarily be the Apocalypse; it may simply be the disgust and bitterness of a childless old age. But it could be the Apocalypse. When a collective structure no longer inspires faith, it cannot escape collapse. Let us hope that the sheer imagining of disaster will be enough to wake us now.

APPENDIX I

The "Prosperity Index"

The per capita gross national product for 1973 (the last year before the world economic and monetary crisis) and 1976, in dollars, for the twenty-six most prosperous industrialized countries.* Of the first twenty countries, sixteen are "sociologically Protestant"; three are Catholic (bordering Protestant areas: Belgium, France, Austria); and one is a communist country with a Protestant culture (East Germany).

Countries (in 1976 order)	1976 Population (in millions)	1976 Per Capita GNP	1973 Population (in millions)	1973 Per Capita GNP	1973 Rank by GNP
1. Switzerland	6,410	8,880	6,430	7,060	1
2. Sweden	8,220	8,670	8,140	6,360	2
3. United States	215,120	7,890	210,400	6,230	3
4. Canada	23,180	7,510	22,130	5,580	6
5. Denmark	5,070	7,450	5,020	5,870	4
6. Norway	4,030	7,420	3,960	5,190	8
7. West Germany	62,000	7,380	61,970	5,690	5
8. Belgium	9,830	6,700	9,740	4,990	10
9. France	52,920	6,550	52,130	4,810	12
10. Luxembourg	361	6,460	350	5,460	7
11. The Netherlands	13,770	6,200	13,440	4,670	13
12. Iceland	226	6,100	210	5,030	9
13. Australia	13,660	6,100	13,130	4,650	14
14. South Africa**	4,420	5,910	4,370	4,940	11
15. Finland	4,730	5,620	4,670	4,120	15
16. Austria	7,520	5,330	7,530	3,900	17
17. Japan	112,770	4,910	108,350	3,800	18
18. New Zealand	3,090	4,250	2,960	3,980	16
19. East Germany	16,790	4,220	16,980	3,210	20
20. United Kingdom	56,070	4,020	55,930	3,270	19
21. Israel	3,560	3,920	3,250	3,080	21

* This criterion eliminates such countries as Saudi Arabia and Libya, where oil resources mask the countries' underdevelopment.
** The figures for South Africa apply only to the white population (17% of the total). The estimate of average revenue per white resident is based on estimates of the apportionment of national revenues between the black and white communities.
Source: 1976 World Bank Atlas.

Appendix I

Countries (in 1976 order)	1976 Population (in millions)	1976 Per Capita GNP	1973 Population (in millions)	1973 Per Capita GNP	1973 Rank by GNP
22. Czechoslovakia	14,920	3,840	14,570	2,980	22
23. Italy	56,190	3,050	54,910	2,520	23
24. Spain	35,700	2,920	34,740	2,170	24
25. Poland	34,340	2,860	33,360	2,160	25
26. Soviet Union	256,670	2,760	249,750	2,110	26

APPENDIX II

The "Nobel Index"[1]

This index was established by comparing the number of Nobel prizewinners in the experimental sciences (physics, chemistry, medicine and biology), but not in literature, mathematics or the peace prize, per million residents (determined by averaging the 1901–60 populations).

The Nobel prizes awarded in the sciences between 1961 and 1976 show a remarkable consistency with these figures. Of the first twelve countries, nine are "sociologically Judeo-Protestant," three are Catholic (note that Austria's high rating is explained by the presence there until around 1933 of a large Jewish scientific community).

Country	Number of Nobel Prizewinners in the Sciences	Population 1901–60 (in millions)	Nobel Index (prizewinners per million residents)
1. Switzerland	11	4.2	2.62
2. Denmark	5	3.5	1.43
3. Austria	8	6.7	1.19
4. The Netherlands	9	7.8	1.19
5. Sweden	7	6.2	1.13
6. United Kingdom	41	44.7	.91
7. Germany	45	63.8	.71
8. United States	52	125.4	.41
9. France	17	42.6	.40
10. Finland	1	3.5	.29
11. Belgium	2	7.8	.26
12. Hungary	2	8.6	.23
13. Portugal	1	17.1	.14
14. Italy	4	40.8	.10
15. Argentina	1	133.4	.08
16. Czechoslovakia	1	14.7	.07
17. Spain	1	24.1	.04
18. Soviet Union	7	156.1	.03
19. Japan	1	69.2	.01
20. India	1	350.0	.002

Source: Léo Moulin, "La Nationalité des prix Nobel des sciences de 1901 à 1960," in Les Cahiers internationaux de sociologie, 1961, vol. XXXI, pp. 145–63.

Notes

Title Page

Poèmes, ballades, complaintes, rondeaux.
Ed. Louis-Michaud, 1909, p. 68–9.*

Epigraphs

1. *Quatrain,* in the *Poésies diverses* of
his collected *Oeuvres,* XIII, Garnier, 1970,
p. 152.
2. Harangue to the Paris Parliament to
persuade it, against its will, to register the
Edict of Nantes.
3. "The Rat and the Elephant," *Fables,*
VIII, 15.
4. Written in 1859 and reprinted in
Questions contemporaines in 1868.
5. *Dans les champs du pouvoir,* 1913.
The first sentence dates from May 18,
1913 (p. 82), the second from May 24 (p.
115).
6. In *La liberté, pour quoi faire?*
7. Political release by the Count of
Paris, June 26, 1954, entitled *Le Mal
français.*
8. Statement to the author on September 10, 1962. Cf. Chapter 5, p. 51.

Introduction

1. *Regards sur le monde actuel,* 1945, p.
39.
2. Cf. Jean Chardonnet, *Géographie industrielle,* 1962.
3. The German ethnologist Kurt Unkel
had taken the native name of Nimuendaju
after a stay with the Jai tribe of central
Brazil. Claude Lévi-Strauss uses this example in a suggestive analysis of the relativity of civilizations, *Race et histoire,* p. 54.
Cf. *Tristes Tropiques,* pp. 284 and 485.
4. *The Seven Pillars of Wisdom,* London, 1963, p. 355.

PART I
Chapter 2

1. *Dans les champs du pouvoir, op. cit.,*
p. 82.
2. Address on June 18, 1940.
3. Notably Marshal Albert Kesselring
(*Kesselring: A Soldier's Record* [New York,
1954]); Field Marshal Basil Henry Liddell
Hart (*The German Generals Talk* [New
York, 1948], esp. pp. 556–7; *History of the
Second World War* [London 1970, New
York 1971]); Jean Truelle, chief engineer
in charge of armaments ("La Production
aéronautique français jusqu'en mai–juin
40," a very important article published in
a special issue of *Revue d'Histoire de la
Seconde Guerre mondiale,* No. 73, 1969);
and many others. See especially *La Campagne de France* (Col. Fox and Squadron
Leader d'Ornano, "La Percée des Ardennes," pp. 77–119; Lt.-Col. Le Goaster,
"L'Action des forces aériennes," pp.
135–49; and Maj. A. Wauquier, "Les
Forces cuirassées dans la bataille—l'emploi des chars français," pp. 150–62), 1953.
Also J. Cuny and R. Danel, *L'Aviation de
chasse française 1918–1940* (notably pp.
179ff. and 190–92); Eddy Bauer, "Opinion
sur la bataille aérienne de mai–juin 1940,"

---

* Where no place of publication is given, the work was published in Paris.

All English renditions in the text are by the translator except for those from works published in English.

in *Revue des forces aériennes,* No. 119, October 1956 (pp. 696–700); John McHaight, "Les Négotiations pour la fourniture d'avions américains," in *Revue des forces aériennes,* No. 198, December 1963; John McHaight, "Des achats d'avions américains par la France," in *Revue d'histoire de la Seconde Guerre mondiale,* April 1965, pp. 1ff; Camille Blot, "Les Opérations aériennes britanniques durant la Campagne de France," in *Revue des forces aériennes françaises,* December 1954, p. 953.

4. I was particularly impressed by the statements of Chéry and Alias. Cf. Gen. Max Gelée, "La Percée des Ardennes vue d'en haut," in *Icare,* No. 57, 1971; Col. Henri Alias, "Le II/33 avait vu les Allemands percer sur la Meuse," *ibid.;* and Gen. René Chambe, *Histoire de l'aviation.*

5. This strict definition includes only those who took a personal and deliberate position of resistance to the enemy (escapees, enlistees in the FFL, the FFI or the France Combattante network, those who avoided forced draft and forced labor). It excludes the involuntary victims, who often suffered even more severely (hostages, those taken in round-ups, unresisting deportees, forced-labor conscripts).

Chapter 3

1. Of course, we are talking about Corsica in 1948. In the past thirty years it has changed more than it did during the three preceding centuries. But its evolution has been both too slow and too fast: too slow to enable Corsica completely to overcome its backwardness, too fast for its people's mentality to keep up with the changes.

Chapter 4

1. This exception applies only in the cases stipulated by the Constitution; for example, in questions of economics, currency, customs, foreign economic and financial relations, postal service and railways.

2. The number of refugees between 1945 and 1962 (including Germans ex-pelled from territory beyond the Oder-Neisse line) is estimated at 14 million; that of fugitives, properly speaking, at 3 to 4 million.

3. *La planification soviétique,* 1945.

4. Alfred Sauvy.

5. Statement by Franciszek Szlachcic, member of the Popu Central Committee's politbureau. Cf. G. Mond, "Les intellectuels des années soixante-dix en Pologne," in the *Revue de l'Est* (C.N.R.S.), No. 3, 1974; S. Kisielewski, *Der Spiegel,* March 8, 1976, pp. 118–19. Szlachcic's ideas were confirmed by the changes made in the Constitution in 1976, which were protested in writing by the Catholic Church and 40,000 Poles.

Chapter 5

1. Pierre Mendès-France in *L'Express,* July 5, 1957.

2. Curzio Malaparte, *Journal d'un étranger à Paris,* 1967, p. 93. These lines are dated November 1948.

3. Speech broadcast June 8, 1962.

Chapter 7

1. In four governments under General de Gaulle: Information (April–September 1962), Repatriates (September–December 1962), Information (December 1962–January 1966), Scientific Research and Atomic and Space Questions (January 1966–April 1967), Education (April 1967–May 1969); in two governments under President Pompidou: Administrative Reforms and the Economic Plan (March 1973–February 1974), Cultural Affairs and Environment (March–May 1974); and under President Giscard d'Estaing: Justice (1978–81).

2. Within a matter of months, France-Inter's rating rose from 9 percent to 39 percent. The channel quickly acquired and kept the habit of trying to beat out its peripheral rivals. France-Musique, on the other hand, free of competition and immune from the problem of ratings, tends to fall back into cliquishness. The time devoted to classical music dwindles and that given over to prattle increases; France-

Musique becomes France-Chatter. It is
less and less addressed to music-lovers,
for whom it was conceived, and more
and more to the musicologists who live
off it.

3. The initial plan—decentralization—
is still far from fulfilled, however. I believe
the stations should have been federated
and made responsible by turns for daily
programs of national interest. Our Jacobin-
ism is so strong that the third, so-called regional station almost exclusively airs programs produced in Paris, by Parisians and
for Parisians.

4. In Cayenne for the Americas, in
Numea for Southeast Asia and the Pacific,
in Djibouti for Africa and the Middle East.

Chapter 8

1. The plan was then to manufacture
H-bombs ten years later, in 1976, if the
principle of thermonuclear fusion was discovered before 1968, which was far from
being the case.

2. Pollution derives chiefly from the
tons of pulverized water swelling the radioactive cloud. When the device explodes
high enough, the fireball fails to reach the
seas; it climbs rapidly and the cloud, much
less radioactive, is more easily dispersed.

3. The most powerful blasts, detonated
from balloons in 1966, gave better results
as far as pollution was concerned than the
most optimistic theoretical models had allowed us to hope.

4. In 1966–67, our computers were
about as powerful as those used by the
Americans for their first thermonuclear
tests.

5. The situation was all the more serious in that, aside from any question of
prestige, a grave threat was posed to our
atomic arsenal: an enemy using the neu-
tron bombs could have neutralized ordinary A-bombs. Our deterrent force would
not then have deterred very much. So the
stakes were crucial. Either we entered the
thermonuclear sanctuary, or our arsenal,
for which we had made heavy sacrifices,
would prove a wet firecracker.

6. Plutonium turned out to be as usable
as enriched uranium. Pierrelatte wasn't a
loss, however. In 1967, its output was used
in the fuel for our first nuclear submarine
engine. Enriched uranium also allows for
greater flexibility in weapons design. In
addition, the construction of Pierrelatte
enabled the AEC teams and their partners
to master a number of techniques of which
they had been totally ignorant and from
which the industrial fallout has been remarkable.

PART II
Chapter 10

1. Jules Michelet, *Notre France, sa
géographie, son histoire* (written around
1833 and published in 1886), 1932, pp.
289–92. The provinces have not been uniformly weakened; such ports as Marseille,
Bordeaux and Rouen and their hinterlands
are prosperous.

2. September 2, 1661. *Lettres* III, pp.
379–85.

3. Letter from Fénelon to Louis XIV
published by Renouard in 1825 (and dated
1694 by him). It should be noted that the
letter was written during a particularly disastrous agricultural crisis.

4. In demography, military capacity,
diplomatic influence, cultural and artistic
vigor. But poverty was already widespread. Cf. Y. M. Bercé, *Histoire des Croquants*, Geneva, 1974, 2 vols.

5. See especially Henri Hauser, *Pensée
et action économique du Cardinal de Richelieu.* Michel Antoine, in his thesis *Le
Conseil du Roi sous le règne de Louis XV*
(Geneva, 1970), shows how the sterilizing
nature of Colbertism only grew worse
later and how the Louis XIV–style administrative monarchy was crowned during
the Revolution.

6. To avoid bankruptcy, some paid dividends out of capital while the English and
Dutch companies were paying 20 percent
a year to their shareholders. The Dutch
East India Company paid dividends of 25
percent or more from 1633 to 1642, and

averaged 20 percent from 1623 to 1712. Cf. Charles Wolsey Cole, *Colbert*, Columbia, 1939.

7. Cited by E. Pognon, *Histoire du peuple français*, p. 297.

8. Only now are Colbert's creatures being discovered—the Frémonts, Pocquelins, Pussorts, etc. Some are known to have ended up in prison. Cf. P. Goubert, *Familles marchandes sous l'Ancien Régime: Les Danse et les Motte de Bauvais*, pp. 117–18.

9. From the 1620s to the 1720s, a severe depression gripped Europe. This cannot be blamed on Colbert. But the Dutch, and then the English, the Swiss and the Swedes, largely escaped its effects through their merchant economies, which created many secondary and tertiary jobs. See P. Deyon, *Le Mercantilisme*, 1963, pp. 79–80. Goubert himself (*Louis XIV et vingt millions de Français*) admits that to some extent Colbertism is an effect rather than a cause.

10. It is true that, in this as in other areas, the gap narrowed considerably between 1850 and 1870, under the Second Empire, the most luxurious of all periods and the most ill-famed. See J. Marczewski, "Le Produit physique de l'économie française de 1789 à 1913 (comparaison avec la Grande-Brétagne)," *Cahiers de l'ISEA*, July 1965, p. lxxviii.

11. In 1806, 97 percent of Britain's iron was manufactured with coke, versus 20 percent in France. Cf. Monique Pinson, "La Sidérurgie française," *Cahiers de l'ISEA*, February 1956, pp. 15–16.

12. Marczewski, "Le Produit physique . . . ," *op. cit.*, p. XLV.

13. J. Marczewski, "Y a-t-il eu un 'take-off' en France?" *Cahiers de l'ISEA*, 1961; Angus Maddison, *Economic Growth in the West*, London, 1964, p. 225.

14. The United States, Canada, Denmark, Sweden, West Germany, Belgium, Switzerland, Norway, Holland, the United Kingdom, Italy and Spain. The INSEE's 1966 retrospective *Yearbook*, p. 561, charts the building-industry production

index as 109 in 1913, 133 in 1929, 96 in 1936, 109 in 1937 and 100 in 1938. The French index is relatively favorable between 1922 and 1930, but this is an artificial effect of the franc's drop in value. It was compensated by a serious recession from 1931 to 1938 that was much milder in the neighboring countries.

15. See Harry D. White, *French International Accounts, 1881–1913*, Cambridge, Mass., 1933; Rondo E. Cameron, *France and the Economic Development of Europe, 1800–1914*, Princeton, N.J., 1961; Jesse R. Pitts, "The Bourgeois Family and French Economic Retardation," an unpublished thesis for Harvard University, 1937; Charles P, Kindleberger, *In Search of France*, Cambridge, Mass., 1963; and Malinvaud, *La Croissance française*, 1974.

Chapter 11

1. Around 1965, a corner was turned by French research, thanks chiefly to the studies made at Alfred Sauvy's instigation by the National Institute of Demographic Studies (INED). A clearer view began to emerge of the obscure correlations between demographic fluctuations and economic and social balance (Cf. Goubert, *Les Fondements démographiques*, in *Historie économique et sociale de la France*, 1970, vol. II, p. 11). Since then, too, work in regional history, through research in provincial archives, has been done to correct, verify or moderate early attempts at partial syntheses like those of Jean Meuvret. Notable in this work have been Dean Godechot and his team for the Midi-Pyrenees, Emmanuel Le Roy Ladurie for the Languedoc, René Bechrel for the Basse-Provence, Abel Poitrineau for the Basse-Auvergne, Pierre Goubert for the Beauvaisis, Pierre Deyon for Amiens and Picardy. Systematic study of parish records is only now providing precise data on population movements. See also Jean Meuvret, *Les Crises de subsistance et la démographie de la France de l'Ancien Régime*, 1946, p. 642. Study by the INED in a special edition of *Population*, October 1975.

2. Louis Henry in a collection directed by Glass and Everley, 1965.

3. J. Beaujeu Garnier, *La Population française*, 1969.

4. Antoine de Montchrestien, playwright (*L'Ecossaise*, Rouen, 1601) and economist (*Traité de l'économie politique*, 1615). Cf. A. Vène, *Montchrétien et le socialisme économique*, 1923.

5. Cf. Marczewski, *Cahiers de l'ISEA* (AE series, No. 4). Figures modified by A. Wrighley, *Societé et Population*, 1969, p. 78.

6. *Ibid.*

7. A. Soboul, *La France à la veille de la Revolution, Economie et Société*, 1966, vol. I, p. 88.

8. Fliche and Martin, *Histoire de l'Eglise*, vol. XXI, 1952, pp. 114–18.

9. Of this number, some 3 million emigrated to the United States.

10. Montyon (under the pseudonym of Moheau), *Recherches et considérations sur les populations de la France*, Paris, 1778.

11. Cf. Meuvret, *loc. cit.*

12. Cf. Pierre Goubert, *Le Régime démographique français au temps de Louis XIV* in *Histoire économique et sociale . . .* , vol. II (1660–1789).

13. Letter from Fénelon to Louis XIV dated 1694 by Renouard and published by him in 1825.

14. Paris, and especially Bordeaux, Rouen, Lyon, Marseille and Nantes. See the works of Jean Meyers and Paul Dutel.

15. Jean Cawiage (*Trois Villages de l'Ile-de-France au XVIIIe Siècle*, INED, *Cahier* No. 40) proved by a study of the parish registers of three villages in the Vexin that couples in the eighteenth century systematically stopped procreating after the second or, at most, the third child.

16. The Harrod-Domar model (compound interest based on increased savings) reveals this slowing down of economic growth when demographic growth is accelerated.

17. In 1880, France still trailed only China, India and Russia. With 36 million inhabitants, it still led greater Germany, which was not yet a state (35 million), Japan (33 million), Great Britain (25 million), Italy (24 million) and the United States (23 million). In 1979, it ranked thirteenth after China, India, the Soviet Union, the United States, Indonesia, Japan, Brazil, Pakistan, West Germany, Nigeria, Great Britain and Italy.

Chapter 12

1. M. Dollinger and P. Jeannin have shown that this is an exceptional case; these cities prospered at the end of the Middle Ages and declined thereafter.

2. Roland Rousnier, *XVIe Siècle*, 1967, p. 371.

3. Pope Alexander VI's arbitration (May 1493) was altered, it is true, by the Treaty of Tordesillas (June 7, 1494).

4. The "gold" was mainly silver, extracted after 1545 from the Potosí mines in what is now Bolivia, which was then part of the Spanish viceroyalty of Peru. The American historian E. J. Hamilton (*American Treasure and the Price Revolution in Spain, 1501–1690*, Cambridge, Mass., 1934) calculated that between 1503 and 1600 (discounting fraud, which is impossible to calculate), 7,440 tons of silver and 154 tons of gold arrived in Seville from the Americas, making that city the "lungs of Europe" (cf. Pierre Chaunu, *Seville*, a monumental work in 12 volumes).

5. *Ibid.*

6. Semer, *Monarchie espagnole*, vol. II, p. 50.

7. As almost always in history, signs of this change can be found in the preceding period. Spanish expansion already concealed a germ that would multiply later on; territorial and religious ambition won out over commercial motives. The Castilian spirit, formed by the Reconquest and the Middle Ages, eliminated all who were not of "pure blood" (Jews, Moslems), thus ostracizing the population's most dynamic elements, and took badly to the new capitalistic phenomena. A little earlier and

more profoundly than in France, absolutist delirium and dreams of power weakened the Spanish society.

8. Buicciardini, cited by W. Sombart, *Le Bourgeois*, p. 132.

9. Semer, *Monarchie espagnole*, vol. II, p. 50.

10. Sombart, *Le Bourgeois*, pp. 132–3.

11. Hamilton, *American Treasure, op. cit.*

12. Léo Moulin, *l'Aventure européene*, p. 127.

13. *Encyclopaedia Universalis*, 1975 edition.

14. The climatic handicap can be invoked only for the equatorial band (occupied chiefly by the Amazonian jungle). The subtropical climate in Mexico and Brazil resembles that of the southern United States. And the climate of the states along La Plata and the Andean republics is similar to that in the northern temperate zones.

15. R. de Roover, *The Rise and Decline of the Medici Bank (1394–1494)*, Cambridge, Mass., 1969.

16. Letter from Leonardo da Vinci, cited in Jean Delumeau, *Civilisation de la Renaissance*, p. 176.

17. Pitrim A. Sorokin, *Society, Culture and Personality*, New York, 1947, pp. 540ff.

18. *Cambridge History of Poland*, 2 vols., Cambridge, 1950–51.

19. S. Kieniewicz, *Histoire de la Pologne*, 1971.

Chapter 13

1. Cf. Jean Chardonnet, *Les Grandes Puissances*, p. 239.

2. Cf. J.-A. Desourd and C. Gérard, *Histoire économique des XIXe et XXe siècles*, 1963, vol. II, pp. 390–91.

3. André Philip, *Histoire des faits économiques et sociaux*, p. 44.

4. The Catholic cantons (which opposed the Protestant cantons in 1848 in the Sonderbund war) are noticeably less advanced. They are rural, traditionalist regions. The Protestant cantons, on the

other hand, operate on a trade economy and are dominated by a "liberal" bourgeoisie.

5. See Appendix I, p. 307.

Chapter 14

1. Some similar remarks can be made about the United States and the Netherlands, but Calvinist predominance there was so great from the beginning that the Catholic communities in these two countries show few of the characteristics typical of Counter-Reformation societies.

2. Martin Offenbacher, *Nonfession und Soziale Schichtung; eine Studie über die wirtschaftliche Lage der Katholiken und Protestanten in Baden*, Fribourg, 1900.

3. Paul Seippel, *La Critique des deux Frances*, 1906, p. 28.

4. *Ibid.*

5. W. C. Scoville, *The Persecution of Huguenots and French Economic Development, 1630–1720*, University of California, 1960.

6. H. Lüthy, *La Banque protestante*, vol. I, pp. 15ff.

7. Jean-Marie Domenach, "Urgence au Québec," *Esprit*, July–August 1969.

8. Sigmund Diamond, "Le Canada français au XVIIe siècle, une société préfabriquée," *Les Annales*, March–April 1961, pp. 317–54.

Chapter 15

1. Followed, in order, by New Zealand, Italy, Spain, Ireland, Greece, Portugal and Turkey.

2. See Andrew Shonfield, *Modern Capitalism*, New York, 1966. A 1976 survey showed that 68 percent of the British consider the nationalized industries less efficient than private firms (compared to 55 percent in 1969). The proportion of those favoring further nationalization declined from 32 percent to 20 percent. The poll was conducted by Market and Opinion Research International and published in the *Financial Times* (London) July 30, 1976.

3. "Antagonismes dans l'Industrie Bri-

tannique et leurs origines," based on a report by the Institute for the Study of Conflict and published in *Le Monde moderne*, March 1974, p. 14.

4. In 1975–76, union leaders and the Labor government agreed to limit wage increases, which reduced labor's living standards but halved Britain's inflation rate in one year.

5. The Jones Commission, which studied the brain drain exhaustively, revealed that a third of every year's graduating classes of engineers, scientists and advanced technicians leaves the country to live abroad. See *Le Progrès scientifique*, March–April 1974, No. 169, p. 17. Note that the brain drain slowed in the 1970s, probably because of the recession in the United States.

6. It should enable Britain to supply all its own energy needs in time and to become invulnerable to pressure from the young nations in control of the world's oil wealth. Its resources may run out within ten years, but those ten years can give the country the second wind it evidently needs—unless it falls asleep on its bed of black gold, as Spain did on its gold and silver in the seventeenth century.

Chapter 16

1. M. Missenard, *A la recherche de l'homme*, 1954, pp. 198–211.

2. See especially *Le Racisme*, published by UNESCO in 1960.

3. See Karl Marx, *Le Capital*, Pléiade edition, esp. pp. 613ff., pp. 1177ff.; Friedrich Engels, *La Guerre des paysans*, a French translation, 1952, esp. pp. 203ff. and pp. 213ff.; Oscar A. Marti, *Economic Causes of the Reformation in England*, London, 1928; Corr. Barbagallo, *Età moderna*, Turin, 1958; and M. M. Smirin, *Die Volksreformation des Thomas Müntzer*, Berlin, 1956.

4. See, for example, R. de Roover, *The Medici Bank*, New York, 1943; Y. Renouard, *Les Hommes d'affaires italiens du Moyen Age*, 1949; A. Sapori, *Le Marchand italien au Moyen Age*, 1952; and Jean De-

lumeau, *Naissance et affirmation de la Réforme*, 1965, pp. 259–78. I believe Delumeau was the first to provide a basic refutation of Marx's theory of the capitalistic origins of Protestantism.

5. Excellent bibliographies of the Weber quarrel have been compiled by Bernard Bieler, H. Lüthy, H. R. Trevor-Roper and Philippe Besnard.

6. Italy must be excepted—see Amintore Fanfani, *Cattolicesimo e protestantesimo nella formazione storica del capitalismo*, Milan, 1934.

7. Max Weber, *L'Ethique protestante et l'esprit du capitalisme*, French trans. 1904, p. 242.

8. *Ibid.*, p. 234.

9. *L'Epargne forcée ascétique, ibid.*, p. 237.

10. E. de Girard, *Histoire de l'économie sociale jusqu'à la fin du XVIe siècle*, 1900, p. 48.

11. Erasmus and Hütten were hesitant. See P. Besnard, *L'Essor de la philosophie politique au XVIe siècle*, 1939.

12. E. Fischoff, *The Protestant Ethic and the Spirit of Capitalism*, Social Research, vol. II, 1944, pp. 54–77.

13. H. R. Trevor-Roper, *Religion, the Reformation and Social Change*, London, 1967.

14. H. Lüthy, *Banque protestante*.

15. When Hesiod in *The Works and Days* and Virgil in the *Georgics* exalted work on the land, they appeared as nonconformists. In some Greek cities, residents forfeited their citizenship if they worked in trade or a craft. To the Romans, *otium* (indolence or leisure) was a value in itself. See J.-M. André, *L' "Otium" dans la vie morale et intellectuelle romaine*, 1966.

16. Matthew, 29.

17. St. Paul, *Second Epistle to the Thessalonians*, 3:10.

18. Renouard, *Les Hommes d'affaires . . . , op. cit.*, pp. 124–31.

19. See Marcel Bataillon, *Erasme et l'Espagne*, 1937; M. Renaudet, *Erasme et l'Italie*, Geneva, 1954; Margaret and Mann, *Erasme et les débuts de la Réforme*

française, 1934; and J.-C. Margolin, *Erasme par lui-même,* 1965.

20. P.-J. Lecler, *Histoire de la tolérance au siècle de la Réforme,* 1955.

21. Cf. H. R. Trevor-Roper, *Religion, the Reformation and Social Change,* London, 1967; *De la Réforme aux Lumières,* French trans. 1972, p. 23.

22. I ask pardon of my teacher, Alphonse Dupront, despite all my admiration for his work, for not subscribing to his analysis of the "Catholic Reform" and persisting in sharing that of Henri Hauser. Cf. Hauser, *La Prépondérance espagnole (1559–1660);* H. Sée and A. Rébillon, *Le XVIe siècle,* pp. 218–19 and 24–25.

23. Bataillon, *Erasme, op. cit.,* p. 493.

24. H. Lapeyre, *Les Monarchies européennes du XVIe siècle* in *Les relations internationales,* 1967, pp. 85–6.

25. H. R. Trevor-Roper, *Religion, the Reformation and Social Change, op. cit.,* pp. 50–67.

26. In 1631, these émigrés constituted the most heavily taxed third of the Dutch citizenry. The Dutch West India Company was almost entirely controlled by Walloons. Nearly all the leading Dutch traders in the seventeenth century—the De Geers, the Momma brothers, Spiering, the Marcelises, Moeufft—came from the south, which was sacked by the duke of Alba and remained Catholic or returned to Catholicism. See Jean de Witt, *Mémoires* (probably written around 1660, but published in The Hague in 1709, long after the author's death), pp. 259, 267.

27. For example, progress in psychoanalysis and high-energy physics in the United States dates from the arrival there of numbers of Viennese psychoanalysts of the Freudian school and physicists of the Einstein school who were fleeing Naziism. See Barbour, *Capitalism, op. cit.*

Chapter 17

1. *Journal et Mémoires du marquis d'Argenson,* vol. I, p. 43n., Rathery edition. John Law (1671–1729) was a Scottish banker and financier who in 1716–20 tried

unsuccessfully to pull France out of its financial difficulties.

2. Luke, 2:1–3.

3. J. de Lasteyrie, *Histoire de la liberté politique en France.*

4. Argenson, *Considérations sur le gouvernement de la France,* p. 146.

5. For expressions of rebellion against the state, see the manifestos of the marquis de Miremont (1689) and the duc de Schomberg (1692). Cf. Bercé, *Croquants, op. cit.*

Chapter 18

1. H. de Balzac, *Ressources de Quinola,* I, 1 (1842).

2. With a difference, naturally: today's "underdevelopment" is worse because our biological balance (demography-resources) no longer functions. For convergent reasons (medicine, especially antibiotics; transportation; food scarcity rather than famine) population growth is no longer regularly restricted by hecatombs.

3. D. C. McClelland, "That Urge to Achieve," in *Think,* November–December 1966.

4. D. C. McClelland, J. W. Atkinson, R. A. Clark and E. L. Lowell, *The Achievement Motive,* New York, 1953; D. C. McClelland, *The Achieving Society,* Princeton, N.J., 1961.

5. F. Perroux, *La Pensée économique de Joseph Schumpeter,* Geneva, 1965, p. 93.

6. B. C. Rosen and R. C. d'Andrade, *The Psychosocial Origin of Achievement Motivation, Sociometry,* 1959, pp. 185–215.

7. Moulin, *op. cit.,* p. 146.

8. N. M. Bradburn, *The Managerial Role in Turkey,* Cambridge, Mass., 1960.

9. Edward F. Denison, *The Sources of Economic Growth in the United States and the Alternatives Before the United States,* New York, 1962.

10. N. M. Bradburn and D. E. Berlew, "The Need for Achievement and English Industrial Growth," in *Economic Development and Cultural Change,* October 1961.

11. Racine, *Port-Royal,* I.

12. Diderot, *Encyclopédie*, article headed *Novateur*.

13. Not until the Restoration did the potato spread over French farms, and "French fried" potatoes did not appear in France until the time of Louis-Philippe. Cf. Roland Mousnier, *Progrès scientifique et technique au XVIIIe siècle*, 1958.

14. *Ibid.*, p. 442.

15. Cf. also Sorokin, *Society . . . , op. cit.*, pp. 540ff.

16. Léo Moulin, "La Nationalité des prix Nobel des sciences de 1901 à 1960," in *Les Cahiers internationaux de sociologie*, 1961, XXXI, pp. 145–63.

Chapter 19

1. P. François-Xavier de Charlevoix (1682–1761), *Journal d'un voyage fait dans l'Amérique septentrionale*, Paris, 1744, vol. V, pp. 117–18.

2. Jean de Witt, *Mémoires, op. cit.*, pp. 46–7.

3. To be precise, what brings it into third place (behind the United States and the Soviet Union) is its gross national product. It is true that Japan's per capita GNP is well behind those of the western European countries, including Latin Europe. But it has closed up considerably on the lead group formed by the Western Christian countries. Herman Kahn has predicted that by the year 2000, the Japanese will have the world's highest living standard.

4. André Philip, *Analyse de l'industrialisation japonaise*, p. 188.

5. Maurice Crouzet, *Le XXe siècle*, p. 47.

6. *Le Monde*, June 15, 1972; Nicolas Vichney: "Le Japon, de la technique à la science."

7. F. Bluche, *La Vie quotidienne de la Noblesse au XVIIIe siècle*, 1973, p. 22.

8. *Ibid.* In *La France à la veille de la Révolution*, p. 63, Soboul gives the figure of 350,000 people, or 70,000 families.

9. In 1756, Abbé Coyer wrote a plea in favor of the *Noblesse commerçante:* "Has not commerce become the soul of political interests and of the balance of power . . . the basis of kings' grandeur and peoples' happiness?"

10. H. Lüthy, *La Banque protestante en France*, 1959, vol. I, pp. 13–14.

11. Fréville, *op cit.*

12. A. Bieler, *La Pensée économique et sociale de Calvin*, Geneva, 1961.

Chapter 20

1. Luke, 10:39–42.

2. The English historical review *Past and Present* presented very conclusive proof between 1960 and 1976 of the superior cultural level in Britain and the United Provinces in the seventeenth century compared to that of the Catholic countries.

PART III

Chapter 21

1. Arthur Young, *Travels During the Years 1787, 1788, 1789 (in the) Kingdom of France*, Bury St. Edmunds, 1792, p. 148. The phrase is given in French by Young.

Chapter 22

1. Henri IV's appeal to the Parliament of Paris for registration of the Edict of Nantes.

2. The proportion of ministerial appointments from the ranks of the top bureaucracy has risen steadily since General de Gaulle's withdrawal: 46.6 percent in the Chaban-Delmas administration, up to 68.9 percent under Pierre Messmer, 69.7 percent in the Chirac government and 69.4 percent under Raymond Barre. Graduates of the ENA, the Ecole Normale and the Polytechnique form the strongest battalion, according to the Bérard-Quélin *Bulletin quotidien* for August 31, 1976.

Chapter 23

1. *Correspondance littéraire, philosophique et critique du baron de Grimm avec un souverain d'Allemagne, depuis 1753 jusqu'en 1769*, Paris, 1813, p. 146.

2. Frédéric Le Play, *La réforme sociale en France*, 1864.

3. Marquis d'Argenson, *Mémoires*.

Chapter 24

1. Article on "Centralization" in the *Grand Dictionnaire Universel du XIXe siècle*, vol. III, 1867, pp. 723–8.

Chapter 25

1. Letter on March 9, 1965, from the Association of Clay-Mine Owners of the Provins Basin and Villenauxe-la-Grande to Gilbert Grandval, Minister of Labor.

2. Article L. 332 of the Social Security Code.

3. Article L. 334 of the Social Security Code.

4. Letter from Grandval dated August 23, 1965.

5. *Ibid.*

6. Draft of resolution, December 12, 1947.

7. Leaflet, November 1966.

Chapter 26

1. Gaston Roupnel, *Histoire et Destin*, 1943.

Chapter 27

1. "Centralisation," *loc. cit.*

2. Argenson, *Mémoires*, Janet edition, p. 140.

3. Report entitled *Paris et sa région demain:* 22 percent in 1974, according to the Hudson Institute in October 1974.

4. André Siegfried, *Géographie humoristique de Paris*, 1957.

5. Boisguilbert, *Le Détail de la France*, p. 325.

Chapter 28

1. Proudhon, *Oeuvres complètes*, Cahier 21, "Capacité politique des classes ouvrières," Marcel Rivière, 1924.

2. Anne Robert-Jacques Turgot, *Mémoire au roi sur les municipalités*, 1775.

3. Jules Simon, cited in the *Grand Dict.*

Univ. du XIXe Siècle, *loc. cit.* There are 2 million persons in the public service, 500,000 on the payrolls of the nationalized companies, 1.5 million retired government employees drawing state pensions.

PART IV

1. Written in 1859, published in *Questions contemporaines*, 1868.

Chapter 30

1. Robert Desnos, *Chantefleurs, Chantefables*, cited by P. Bourdieu and J.-C. Passeron in *La Reproduction*, p. 9.

2. Although Baudelaire worked out these *correspondances*, it was the French Symbolists, followed by the German Romantics, who made a recurrent theme of them.

3. It was not until 1945 that General de Gaulle imposed a voting right on France that had existed in the United States since 1868 (when women were granted the vote in Wyoming). The measure had been vetoed in France during the Third Republic by an anticlerical Senate that feared women would vote "under the priests' influence."

4. The saying is Hippolyte Taine's, but Napoleon expounded the theory before the Council of State early in 1806.

5. Statement to the Falloux Act Commission in 1849, cited by La Gorce, *Histoire de la IIe République*, p. 280.

6. William R. Shonfeld, "A Study of Secondary Schools in France," unpublished doctoral thesis, Princeton, N.J., 1970.

7. In 1970, the Academy of Moral and Political Sciences conducted a study (on which it based a report) on these unexpected consequences of longer mandatory schooling. A 1976 study of violence confirmed its findings.

8. *Dieu est-il français?* is the title given to a French translation of Friedrich Sieburg's *Gott in Frankreich?* (Berlin, 1929).

9. In *The Bourgeois Family and French Economic Retardation*, *op. cit.*, Jesse Pitts blamed the family business tradition for

France's economic backwardness. French historians have criticized the thesis, but I think it is by and large correct, even if some of its data need revising.

10. Another American researcher, historian David S. Landes ("Observations on France: Economy, Society and Polity," in *World Politics*, April 1957), pointed out how family businesses—and even corporations and nationalized firms, which have adopted the family model—have contributed to the creation of monopolies in France and to a market organization that eliminates effort. For they suppress competitiveness by suppressing competition.

Chapter 31

1. Cf. Nef, *Civilisation industrielle, op. cit.*

2. The existence of such vicious circles was highlighted by sociologists like Robert K. Merton and Alvin Gouldner, *Patterns of Industrial Bureaucracy* (Glencoe, Ill., 1969), and Michel Crozier, *Le Phénomène bureaucratique.*

3. Alexis de Tocqueville, *L'Ancien Régime et la Révolution*, p. 208.

4. Sieburg, *Dieu . . . , op. cit.*, p. 244

Chapter 32

1. *Césarine ou le soupçon*, 1971, p. 95.

2. Cf. Michel Foucault, *Surveiller et punir.*

3. Bayle, article entitled "Pauliniens" (note F) in the *Dictionnaire historique et critique.*

4. Malaparte, *Journal, op. cit.*, 1947.

Chapter 33

1. In the United States, for example, Congress or the judiciary, with press support, can sanction abuses of power through procedures that are rapid even if they are exceptions, from the recall of a sheriff to the impeachment of a President. In France, only one such process exists apart from elections: a motion of censure. For we have seen how seriously the bureaucracy takes the administrative courts.

Chapter 34

1. Young, *Travels, op. cit.*, p. 92.

Chapter 35

1. Gaston Monnerville, *Témoignage*, 1975.

2. According to an OECD report in August 1976. The report unfairly exaggerates some indications of inequality.

Chapter 36

1. Young, *Travels, op. cit.*, pp. 15–16.

2. *Ibid.*, p. 37.

3. Published by the Ministry of Cultural Affairs and of the Environment in April 1974.

Chapter 37

1. *Les Chants du Crépuscule*, August 30, 1835.

2. In *Rem militarem et arguto loqui.* Cited in Louis Chevalier's fine book, *Histoire anachronique des Français*, Paris, 1975, p. 70.

3. *Ibid.*, p. 71.

4. Y. M. Bercé counted 450 to 500 riots in Aquitaine alone between 1590 and 1715.

5. Henri IV's 1599 discourse to the Paris Parliament.

6. France is the world's leading producer of wine and alcohol, but also their biggest importer, according to a statement of Health Minister Mme. Simone Veil during a press conference on May 7, 1975. Four million men and women in France are alcoholics; 85 percent of all fatal road accidents, 15 percent of work accidents and 17 percent of all murders are blamed on alcohol. Nearly 50 percent of the country's hospital beds are filled with patients suffering from ailments of alcoholic origin. The problem costs the Social Security administration 10 billion heavy francs a year. Mme. Veil's 85 percent figure for highway casualties is higher than that given by other sources, even if the calculation is restricted to fatal accidents. According to the High Committee for Research and In-

formation on Alcoholism, 40 percent of the overall automobile accident total is due to alcoholism.

PART V

1. *Mémoires*, vol. IV, p. 100.

Chapter 38

1. The American sociologist Robert K. Merton (*Social Theory and Social Structure*, Glencoe, Ill., 1957) applies the notion of serendipity to scientific research to show the influence of unexpected and aberrant factors.

2. Chateaubriand, *Mémoires d'outre-tombe*, Pléiade edition, vol. II, p. 874.

Chapter 40

1. A letter of assignment was to confirm Pompidou's wish that I continue the work on an unofficial basis. Dated March 28, 1974, it reached me on the day of Pompidou's death. We continued our work officially for three months and unofficially after that, until publication of a synthesis by the French Documentary Office. A report by the Development Commission on local responsibility hewed closely to our ideas and the commission realized some of our suggestions. For once, Sisyphus' rock did not roll all the way down the hill again.

CONCLUSION

Chapter 41

1. Proudhon, letter to Langlois on December 30, 1861, *Corr.*, vol. II, p. 308, in the Lacrois edition.

2. Herbert Lüthy, *À l'heure de son clocher (essai sur la France)*, 1955.

3. André Malraux in the Paris Palais des Sports on December 15, 1965, reported in issue No. 2 of *Espoir*.

Index

[Topics cited in the index refer to France unless otherwise specified]

A Note About the Author

Alain Peyrefitte has had an extraordinarily varied political and diplomatic career—member of the French Parliament, mayor of Provins (a medium-sized city near Paris), envoy to the European Assembly, and head of eight French ministries, including the Ministry of Justice under Giscard d'Estaing. He is the author of several books, and a member of the Académie Française.